EVOLUTION AND MORALITY

NOMOS

LII

NOMOS

Harvard University Press

I   *Authority* 1958, reissued in 1982 by Greenwood Press

The Liberal Arts Press

II   *Community* 1959
III   *Responsibility* 1960

Atherton Press

IV   *Liberty* 1962
V   *The Public Interest* 1962
VI   *Justice* 1963, reissued in 1974
VII   *Rational Decision* 1964
VIII   *Revolution* 1966
IX   *Equality* 1967
X   *Representation* 1968
XI   *Voluntary Associations* 1969
XII   *Political and Legal Obligation* 1970
XIII   *Privacy* 1971

Aldine-Atherton Press

XIV   *Coercion* 1972

Lieber-Atherton Press

XV   *The Limits of Law* 1974
XVI   *Participation in Politics* 1975

New York University Press

XVII   *Human Nature in Politics* 1977
XVIII *Due Process* 1977
XIX   *Anarchism* 1978
XX   *Constitutionalism* 1979
XXI   *Compromise in Ethics, Law, and Politics* 1979
XXII   *Property* 1980
XXIII *Human Rights* 1981
XXIV *Ethics, Economics, and the Law* 1982
XXVI *Marxism* 1983
XXVII *Criminal Justice* 1985

XXVIII	*Justification* 1985
XXIX	*Authority Revisited* 1987
XXX	*Religion, Morality, and the Law* 1988
XXXI	*Markets and Justice* 1989
XXXII	*Majorities and Minorities* 1990
XXXIII	*Compensatory Justice* 1991
XXXIV	*Virtue* 1992
XXXV	*Democratic Community* 1993
XXXVI	*The Rule of Law* 1994
XXXVII	*Theory and Practice* 1995
XXXVIII	*Political Order* 1996
XXXIX	*Ethnicity and Group Rights* 1997
XL	*Integrity and Conscience* 1998
XLI	*Global Justice* 1999
XLII	*Designing Democratic Institutions* 2000
XLIII	*Moral and Political Education* 2001
XLIV	*Child, Family, and State* 2002
XLV	*Secession and Self-Determination* 2003
XLVI	*Political Exclusion and Domination* 2004
XLVII	*Humanitarian Intervention* 2005
XLVIII	*Toleration and Its Limits* 2008
XLIX	*Moral Universalism and Pluralism* 2008
L	*Getting to the Rule of Law* 2011
LI	*Transitional Justice* 2012
LII	*Evolution and Morality* 2012

NOMOS LII
Yearbook of the American Society for Political and Legal Philosophy

EVOLUTION AND MORALITY

Edited by

James E. Fleming and Sanford Levinson

NEW YORK UNIVERSITY PRESS • *New York and London*

NEW YORK UNIVERSITY PRESS
New York and London
www.nyupress.org

References to Internet websites (URLs) were accurate at the time of writing.
Neither the author nor New York University Press is responsible for URLs
that may have expired or changed since the manuscript was prepared.

Library of Congress Cataloging-in-Publication Data
Evolution and morality / edited by James E. Fleming and Sanford Levinson.
p.   cm. — (Nomos ; 52)
"This volume . . . emerged from papers and commentaries given at the
annual meeting of the American Society for Political and Legal Philosophy
(ASPLP) in Boston on August 28–29, 2008"—Preface.
Includes bibliographical references and index.
ISBN 978-0-8147-7122-8 (cloth : alk. paper) — ISBN 978-0-8147-3782-8 (ebook)
ISBN 978-0-8147-3843-6 (ebook)
1. Biopolitics. 2. Political ethics. 3. Science and law.   I. Fleming, James E.
II. Levinson, Sanford, 1941–
JA80.E85   2012
172—dc23   2012010673

New York University Press books are printed on acid-free paper,
and their binding materials are chosen for strength and durability.
We strive to use environmentally responsible suppliers and materials
to the greatest extent possible in publishing our books.

Manufactured in the United States of America

10 9 8 7 6 5 4 3 2 1

CONTENTS

Preface   ix
JAMES E. FLEMING AND SANFORD LEVINSON

Contributors   xi

PART I. NATURALISTIC ETHICS

1. Naturalistic Ethics without Fallacies   3
   PHILIP KITCHER

2. The Two Faces of Morality: How Evolutionary Theory
   Can Both Vindicate *and* Debunk Morality (with a
   Special Nod to the Growing Importance of Law)   31
   ROBIN BRADLEY KAR

3. Missing Heritability: Hidden Environment in
   Genetic Studies of Human Behavior   100
   JONATHAN BECKWITH AND COREY A. MORRIS-SINGER

PART II. LAW AND BEHAVIORAL MORALITY

4. Law and Behavioral Morality   115
   NITA A. FARAHANY

5. Rethinking *Un*reasonableness: A Comment on
   Nita Farahany's "Law and Behavioral Morality"   166
   AMANDA C. PUSTILNIK

6. A Case Study in Neuroscience and Responsibility   194
   WALTER SINNOTT-ARMSTRONG

7. Science Fiction: Some Unexamined Assumptions of
   Nita Farahany's "Law and Behavioral Morality"   212
   JENNIFER L. CULBERT

PART III. BIOPOLITICAL SCIENCE

8. Biopolitical Science   221
   LARRY ARNHART

9. Comment on Larry Arnhart, "Biopolitical Science"   266
   DANIEL LORD SMAIL

10. Arnhart's Explanatory Pluralism   277
    RICHARD A. RICHARDS

PART IV. NATURE, CONSERVATISM,
AND PROGRESSIVISM

11. Against Nature   293
    ELIZABETH F. EMENS

12. Nature, Culture, and Social Engineering:
    Reflections on Evolution and Equality   347
    LINDA C. MCCLAIN

    Index   393

PREFACE

This volume of NOMOS—the fifty-second in the series—emerged from papers and commentaries given at the annual meeting of the American Society for Political and Legal Philosophy (ASPLP) in Boston on August 28–29, 2008, held in conjunction with the annual meeting of the American Political Science Association. Our topic, "Evolution and Morality," was selected by the Society's membership.

The conference consisted of three panels, corresponding to the first three parts of this volume: (1) "Naturalistic Ethics"; (2) "Law and Behavioral Morality"; and (3) "Biopolitical Science." The volume includes revised versions of the principal papers delivered at that conference by Philip Kitcher, Nita A. Farahany, and Larry Arnhart. It also includes essays that developed out of the original commentaries on those papers by Jonathan Beckwith and Corey A. Morris-Singer, Robin Bradley Kar, Walter Sinnott-Armstrong, Jennifer L. Culbert, Daniel Lord Smail, and Richard A. Richards, as well as an additional commentary by Amanda C. Pustilnik. For the published volume, we added a fourth part on a topic that lies near the surface in many analyses of evolution, morality, and sociobiology—nature, conservatism, and progressivism—and included essays by Elizabeth F. Emens and Linda C. McClain. We are grateful to all of these authors for the thoughtfulness of their contributions.

Thanks are also due to the editors and production team at New York University Press and particularly to Ilene Kalish, Despina Papazoglou Gimbel, Aiden Amos, and Alexia Traganas. On our own behalf and on behalf of the Society, we wish to express deep gratitude for the Press's ongoing support for the series and the tradition of interdisciplinary scholarship that it represents.

Finally, thanks to our assistants. Joel Parker of University of Texas, as managing editor, ably assisted Levinson in organizing the conference. Courtney Gesualdi, Eric Lee, Natalie Logan, Emily Strauss, and Christine Renworth, Fleming's excellent research assistants at Boston University, and Danielle Amber Papa, his highly capable and extraordinarily efficient and resourceful secretary, provided critical assistance during the editorial and production phases of the volume.

JAMES E. FLEMING
Boston, May 2011

SANFORD LEVINSON
Austin, Texas, May 2011

CONTRIBUTORS

LARRY ARNHART
Presidential Research Professor of Political Science,
Northern Illinois University

JONATHAN BECKWITH
Professor of Microbiology, Harvard Medical School

JENNIFER L. CULBERT
Associate Professor of Political Science, Johns Hopkins University

ELIZABETH F. EMENS
Professor of Law, Columbia Law School

NITA A. FARAHANY
Associate Professor of Law and Philosophy, Vanderbilt University
Law School

JAMES E. FLEMING
Professor of Law and The Honorable Frank R. Kenison Distinguished
Scholar in Law, Boston University School of Law

ROBIN BRADLEY KAR
Professor of Law and Philosophy, Thomas Mengler Faculty Scholar,
University of Illinois College of Law

PHILIP KITCHER
John Dewey Professor of Philosophy, Columbia University

SANFORD LEVINSON
W. St. John Gorwood and W. St. John Gorwood, Jr., Centennial Chair
in Law and Professor of Government, University of Texas at Austin

LINDA C. MCCLAIN
Professor of Law and Paul M. Siskind Research Scholar,
Boston University School of Law

COREY A. MORRIS-SINGER
Harvard Medical School

AMANDA C. PUSTILNIK
Assistant Professor of Law, University of Maryland School of Law

RICHARD A. RICHARDS
Associate Professor of Philosophy, University of Alabama

WALTER SINNOTT-ARMSTRONG
Chauncey Stillman Professor of Practical Ethics in the Department of
Philosophy and the Kenan Institute for Ethics, Duke University

DANIEL LORD SMAIL
Professor of History, Harvard University

PART I

NATURALISTIC ETHICS

1

NATURALISTIC ETHICS
WITHOUT FALLACIES

PHILIP KITCHER

History, if viewed as more than a repository of anecdote and chronology, might reform the image of ethics by which we are possessed.[1]

1.

Naturalism about ethics is a notoriously problematic position, possibly the worst of all, except for its available rivals. Naturalists, when they are not viewed as being so crude as to be beneath notice, are typically charged with committing well-known fallacies. I shall outline a version of naturalism that will, I hope, escape the familiar accusations, and also challenge philosophical disdain.

"Naturalism" means many things to many people, and it will be well to begin by explaining what I do *not* have in mind. Some writers have understood naturalism as a claim about the omnicompetence of their favorite science and have concluded that ethical statements are derivable from the principles of that science—evolutionary biology or neuroscience, say.[2] These ventures *do* fall foul of familiar fallacies and are problematic in many respects.[3] More philosophically nuanced are approaches that suppose that fundamental ethical properties (like goodness) can be characterized in straightforwardly natural terms (say as "pleasure and the absence of pain") or that maintain that, although these properties cannot be so characterized, they can nonetheless be apprehended by familiar human faculties.[4] The former option is the historical source of many versions of the charges that naturalism invariably commits a fallacy. The latter, as we shall see, evades the accusations, but at the cost of engendering epistemological and metaphysical mysteries.

What, then, can naturalism consist in, if it diverges from the most well-known incarnations of the view? My answer begins from the concern just voiced about sophisticated contemporary programs, often advertised under the label "Moral Realism" (or related titles: "Projectivism," "Quasi-realism," "Noncognitivism," and the like). Fundamental to naturalism is the desire not to multiply mysteries—not beyond necessity but not *at all*. Naturalists are determined that (in Nelson Goodman's witty inversion of Hamlet) no more things should be dreamed of in their philosophies than there are in heaven and earth. This does not entail that the inventory of things they accept is restricted to the list of entities countenanced by current science. Any sophisticated naturalist should recognize that our scientific findings are provisional and incomplete, that, just as our forebears have split the atom, discerned quarks within "fundamental" particles, and now tantalize us with strings and branes, so our descendants may *warrantedly* introduce denizens of nature beyond our current imagination. The important point is that they will have *evidence* for doing so.

The naturalism I champion—*pragmatic naturalism*, to give it a name—is not narrowly scientistic. There are many rigorous forms of inquiry, practiced in academic institutions and other research centers that specialize in disciplines ranging from anthropology and art history to zoology. Naturalistic philosophy should begin from the picture of the world collectively provided by these diverse investigations, and, where it extends that picture, it should do so in ways that accord with the methods and standards of current inquiry or with methods that would convince current investigators that they improved on the contemporary versions. Pragmatic naturalism allows philosophers to advance new ideas and even to expand ontology, but they have to live up to the standards our most rigorous investigations set for themselves. *There are to be no spooks.* That means that invocations of the Forms, or of Natural Law, or of Processes of Pure Practical Reason, or even of Moral Properties accessible to ordinary human faculties all have to be shown to accord with standards of reliable inquiry—or they have to go.

To provide a more positive face for pragmatic naturalism, it is useful to consider one of the great naturalists and inspirations for

contemporary naturalism. Darwin outlined a program for connecting the ethical practices of our species with the behavior of
our closest evolutionary relatives,[5] and many brilliant scholars
since have endeavored to work out that program.[6] In my judgment, however, they have been inspired by the wrong aspect of
Darwin's work. A central achievement of the *Origin*[7] was its strategy
for explaining facets of the *contemporary* organic world in terms of
the *history* of life. Pragmatic naturalism proposes that we adopt the
same strategy in the case of ethics.

Dewey pioneered the way. In his part of the textbook he co-
authored with James Tufts, he writes:

> *Moral conceptions and processes grow naturally out of the very conditions
> of human life.* (1) Desire belongs to the intrinsic nature of man; we
> cannot conceive a human being who does not have wants, needs,
> nor one to whom fulfillment of desire does not afford satisfaction.
> . . . (2) Men live naturally and inevitably in society; in companion-
> ship and competition; in relations of cooperation and subordina-
> tion. These relations are expressed in demands, claims, expecta-
> tions. (3) Human beings approve and disapprove, sympathize and
> resent, as naturally and inevitably as they seek for the objects they
> want, and as they impose claims and respond to them.[8]

Combining Dewey's guiding idea with Darwin's methodological
insight (understand contemporary phenomena in terms of the
processes that have given rise to them), we can approach ethics by
investigating how it has grown—or might have grown: the distinction is important—out of the primitive conditions of pre-ethical
animals. *How did we get from there to here?*

Pragmatic naturalism conceives of ethics as a *project*, something
in which human beings have been involved for most of our history as a species. It is not complete but, rather, something that has
grown in various forms, something contemporary people have to
decide how to continue. To arrive at a clear, nonspooky view of
what we have been up to, we can do no better than to try to identify the route that has led from the pre-ethical condition of our ancestors to our complex contemporary ethical practices. As I shall
suggest, we can be relatively confident about the starting point and
even about some of the transitions that have occurred, but there
will be places at which the evidence is insufficient to discriminate

among various possible scenarios. That is unworrying, provided there is *some* naturalistically approved way of understanding all the necessary steps. Pragmatic naturalism seeks a replacement for the *fictitious* histories: those in which ethical truth is conveyed on large pieces of granite, or in which a brilliantly innovative thinker discerns the Moral Law Within, or in which ordinary people ordinarily perceive some New Moral Fact.

As we shall see, parts of the evolution of ethical practice are accessible, and these supply the basis for a warranted naturalistic meta-ethical stance. By taking the history of ethical practice seriously, pragmatic naturalism also puts pressure on rival philosophical accounts—they, too, need some historical narrative that will fit with their nebulous claims. Dewey concluded his own precis of ethics by making the issue of ethical change central.

> Special phenomena of morals change from time to time with change of social conditions and the level of culture. The facts of desiring, purpose, social demand and law, sympathetic approval and hostile disapproval are constant. We cannot imagine them disappearing as long as human nature remains human nature, and lives in association with others. The fundamental conceptions of morals are, therefore, neither arbitrary nor artificial. They are not imposed upon human nature from without but develop out of its own operations and needs. Particular aspects of morals are transient; they are often, in their actual manifestation, defective and perverted. But the framework of moral conceptions is as permanent as human life itself.[9]

Unfortunately, Dewey never fully articulated the approach to ethics toward which he gestures here. Pragmatic naturalism attempts to make good on his promissory notes. The following sections fill in some details, but they are inevitably an abbreviation of a far longer treatment.[10]

2.

Once upon a time, our human—or hominid—ancestors were not yet engaged in the ethical project. On the basis of investigations of the sites where they left traces of their presence, archeologists and anthropologists can construct a picture of how they lived. The population was divided into small bands, each containing between

30 and 150 members, and these bands were mixed by age and sex. Essentially, human social life resembled that of contemporary chimpanzees and bonobos in these respects.

For animals to live together in this way, a capacity for psychological altruism is required. Because the concept of altruism has fascinated researchers working in different disciplines, a number of variant notions have been proposed, and it is well to be clear and explicit. *Biological altruism* is a technical concept of great importance in evolutionary studies: a *biological altruist* is an organism that acts to augment the reproductive success of another organism at reproductive cost to itself. *Psychological altruists*, by contrast, are animals with a particular type of structure in their psychological lives: when they come to believe that their actions will have consequences for other animals, they adjust their preferences to align those preferences more closely with those they attribute to the others, and they do so without expectation that their subsequent actions will promote the wishes they previously had. Finally, *behavioral altruists* are animals who act like psychological altruists: they look as though they are aligning their wishes with those of their beneficiaries, although their reasons for doing so may result from a desire to promote their prior ends (they may be thoroughly Machiavellian).[11]

Primatologists have strong evidence for supposing that our evolutionary cousins, the chimps and bonobos, are psychological altruists in this sense.[12] That provides some basis for supposing the trait was also shared by our hominid ancestors and has been transmitted to contemporary human beings. Further, an analysis of the preconditions for social life in small groups mixed by age and sex strongly supports the hypothesis that psychological altruism is a necessary condition for bands of this sort to endure.[13] Among Dewey's "conditions of human life" are a particular type of social structure and a *pre-ethical* psychological capacity that makes that social structure possible.

Psychological altruism is a complex, multidimensional notion. Altruists can give more or less weight to the wishes they attribute to their beneficiaries: they can, for example, make only a minimal gesture, or they can subordinate their prior wants to the preferences they take the others to have, or they can treat others' desires exactly as their own. They can respond to some individuals and not to others. For the individuals to whom they do respond, they can adjust their preferences in some contexts but not in others: you may be willing to share with someone but not to sacrifice your life for that person. They can be variously discerning of situations in which their planned actions have consequences for others and variously adept at fathoming the preferences of those others. Each of us has an *altruism profile*, identified by the intensities of the responses we make to others across a range of actual and possible contexts.

If this were all human beings had to work with in fashioning our social lives, then those lives would be very different than they are. Psychological altruism enables chimpanzees and bonobos to live together, but it does not permit them to cohabit *easily*. Observations of chimpanzee and bonobo troops, in the wild and in the seminatural habitats that allow for easier supervision (the Arnhem colony, the San Diego Wild Animal Park), makes it abundantly clear that social life is often on the verge of decomposition. Almost daily, tensions arise, and they have to be dealt with by elaborate mechanisms of peace-making.[14] The grooming huddles, so familiar even to casual observers, occupy a far larger portion of the day than is needed for any hygienic purpose—usually at least three hours and, at times of social unease, as many as six hours a day. The social fabric is frequently torn and needs careful mending. In consequence, the band sizes are limited, and many opportunities for cooperation are missed.

Once this was our situation, too. Our ancestors lived in small groups, breaking up and making up on a daily basis, and that style of social life *might* have persisted, as it has for the chimps and bonobos. Yet, the descendants of those ancestors, even by eight thousand years ago, had learned how to live in far larger communities (more than a thousand people lived together at Çatal Hüyük and at Jericho). By the time writing was invented, five thousand years before the present, they had elaborate systems of rules for conduct. Among the earliest texts we have are documents providing codicils to much larger bodies of law, signaling an activity of rule-giving that had plainly gone on for thousands (indeed, tens of thousands) of years.

We can recognize similar activities of rule-giving in those preliterate societies embedded in an environment most similar to that of our pre-ethical ancestors. Bands of hunter-gatherers have complex rules for defusing social tensions—in fact, for avoiding just the sorts of problems that threaten the stability of chimp-bonobo social life—rules they work out together in discussions among the adult members of the band around the campfire. Rule-giving and rule-following seem to go very deep into the human past.

Even this cursory presentation of some central points about that past should inspire an obvious hypothesis. *Human beings were able to transcend the predicament common to the societies of chimpanzees, bonobos, and our pre-ethical ancestors by acquiring a capacity to formulate and follow rules.* Psychological altruism—in its pre-ethical form—enabled us to live in a particular way. The limitations of our capacities for psychological altruism caused difficulties and restrictions for that way of life. The ethical project, centered on what I shall call normative guidance, liberated us.

My formulation slides in one theme that has not yet been explicitly developed: I have taken the troubles of chimp-bonobo-hominid social life to stem from the limitations of altruism. To understand that idea, recall my emphasis on the multidimensionality of altruism, specifically the possibility that the intensity of response may vary with context, even to the point of vanishing. Animals living together may respond to the wishes of others in situations of perceived threat: we all band together when the neighbors attack. They may also promote the preferences they attribute to others when the costs are relatively small: my foraging has gone well, and it would not hurt much to offer you a small part of the spoils. When resources are scarce, however, trouble can easily erupt. This is exactly what is observed among contemporary chimpanzees and bonobos, where apparent allies (even "friends") suddenly desert one another.

It is useful to introduce the concept of an *altruism failure*. Suppose two animals, *A* (altruist) and *B* (beneficiary), belong to the same social group. For a range of contexts, *A* forms preferences that are psychologically altruistic with respect to *B*. Now, in context *C*, *A* does not align preferences with those attributed to *B*. *A*'s behavior in *C* constitutes an altruism failure. Chimpanzee and bonobo social life are rife with altruism failures, and these are the causes of the long bouts of grooming and the restrictions on band size and cooperation.

Normative guidance replaces altruism failures with (at least) behavioral altruism. Being susceptible to normative guidance involves an ability to formulate a command to yourself and to act on that command. You are tempted to do something that would constitute an altruism failure, but the command overrides the wish that would have been expressed in your action: instead, you act in a way that looks, from the outside, as though you are accommodating the wishes of the beneficiary. Perhaps your commitment to the command has indeed turned you into a full-fledged psychological altruist. More probably, certainly in the earliest stages and with respect to many situations even in present human life, your motives do not arise from anything like sympathy with the individual you aid.

The roots of normative guidance likely lie in the ability of our ancestors to perceive regularities in actions and consequences, to observe that following particular desires led to trouble, trouble for themselves. Acquiring a disposition to inhibit conduct of that sort saved them distress. The ethical project would thus seem to have been born in fear, and thinkers with Kantian predilections will suppose that the earliest ventures in restraining behavior hardly count as *ethical.* That point may be conceded to them, even though those initial exercises in self-command are the stuff out of which *fully ethical* conduct is generated. For the early motive of avoiding trouble can be supplemented, articulated, and superseded by a variety of other dispositions: a sense of respect or awe, a desire for social approval, solidarity with the group, desire to live up to ideals that emerge in group discussions, and so forth. Human beings have developed a whole arsenal of techniques that encourage self-command. As with biological functions generally, it is well to have multiple backup systems, and, in consequence, we have a hodgepodge of devices to get the job done. There is no point at which the "ethical point of view" emerges, for the very simple reason that the whole idea of an "ethical point of view" is a philosophical myth. Instead, pragmatic naturalism substitutes the vision of a complex human psychology, with many ways of securing normative guidance. Some of them are very crude and primitive, such as fear of punishment; others, like a sense of well-being in harmonizing with one's fellows, are far more refined, probably available only at later stages of the ethical project. Yet, it is a good thing that we have all of them and that we retain even those that prompt devotees of "the ethical point of view" to sniff.

Study of small contemporary foraging societies, hunter-gatherer bands like the !Kung, shows the social embedding of normative guidance. The adult members gather, typically at the "cool hour," and work out the framework that governs their social lives. They do so together, on terms of relative equality—and their framework often introduces intricate strategies for preserving that equality.[15] There is good reason for proceeding as they do. In a harsh environment, one in which the contributions of each adult are important for the well-being, even the survival, of the whole group, no member's wishes can be overridden. Thus, there is pressure to arrive at a set of social arrangements that all can accept. Pragmatic naturalism supposes that normative guidance has been socially embedded in this way for tens of thousands of years and that it may well have emerged as human beings acquired full linguistic capacities—in other words, at least fifty thousand years before the present. If so, approximately 80 percent of the history of the ethical project has taken the form of discussions among members of small groups, all of whom were intimately familiar with one another.

Socially embedded normative guidance marks a turning point in human social evolution. From this point on, human behavior was profoundly shaped by cultural transmission and cultural competition. Different bands of our ancestors probably found different problems salient and, where their difficulties were shared, arrived at alternative solutions to them. The ethical codes they developed—consisting not only of austere rules but also of stories designed to highlight commendable and repugnant conduct, as well as methods of social inculcation—constituted "experiments of living" (in Mill's famous phrase). The more successful experiments were emulated by other groups as migrants from one band joined up with another, and some items endured as core elements of contemporary ethical practices. The transmission of ethical resources can readily be identified in documents from the ancient world, where rules and stories migrate from Mesopotamia and Egypt into later cultures of the Near East, cropping up, for example, in the detailed prescriptions of the Pentateuch.

No doubt, at the very beginning, the ethical framework was crude and simple. Given the most obvious types of altruism failures that plague chimpanzee and bonobo societies, we would expect commands enjoining sharing scarce resources and forbidding initiating violence. Is it possible that such simple beginnings could lead to anything as multifaceted as the ethical perspective recognizable 2,500 years ago, when the privileged citizens of the *polis* engaged in reflections on the quality of the good life? Yes. Although it is impossible to say with confidence how the more refined ethical practices *actually* emerged from the primitive origins, a "how-possibly" explanation, one compatible with the strictures of pragmatic naturalism, is available.[16] Pressures to extend the supply of basic resources could favor divisions of labor, the creation of roles, role obligations, rewards for specially demanding jobs, private property, more elaborate forms of altruism, conceptions of the importance of active contributions and of personal relationships, ideals of friendship and love. Under plausible pressures of cultural and natural selection, these elements of the sophisticated (upper-class?) Greek conception of ethical practice could have gradually evolved from the simple framework attributable to the foraging bands of the ethical pioneers. Plato is a footnote to the history of ethical practice.

3.

Suppose this story, or something very like it, is true.[17] What, if anything, does this reveal about the status of ethics?

Many people have worried that approaching ethics from an evolutionary point of view would undermine it. The worries are various. Could any practice of this sort have the authority over human conduct with which it has been credited? Does a naturalistic account play into the hands of those troublesome characters, real or imagined, who think they can simply opt out? We shall come to these questions later, but I want to start with something more basic. Can the ethical project, viewed in the way I have just outlined, provide any basis for talking of ethical truth, ethical knowledge, or ethical progress?

I purposely left the history of the ethical project with the practices of the ancient world and with the first efforts at offering theories of those practices. Yet, one could continue the study of ethical evolution from ancient times into the present. Indeed, it might appear possible to consider episodes from *recorded* history, to determine how ethical changes were actually effected, and to identify, on the basis of the findings, the factors to which the ethical innovators responded.

Exploring the history does reveal something important. Although they may not be common, there are episodes in our past we find it hard not to view as constituting ethical *progress*. Scrutinizing the transition from the acceptance of chattel slavery in the New World colonies to the abolition of the "peculiar institution," there is a pull to regard the change as asymmetrical: getting rid of slavery is progressive; reintroducing it is regressive. A similar tug is exerted by episodes dimly discernible in the more distant past. Four thousand years ago, the prevailing versions of the *lex talionis* demanded that, in cases of murder, the life of the "corresponding relative" should be taken: if X murders Y's daughter, then X's daughter is to be put to death (X and Y being "senior" males). A millennium later, those principles give way to the more familiar idea that the corresponding condition is to be inflicted on the perpetrator: murderous X is to die. That may not be the last word on the subject, but it plainly seems better than the principle it replaces.

For progressive changes in the distant past, the modification of the *lex talionis* or the even deeper expansion of tolerance to allow interaction with neighboring bands (something that plainly occurred in the Paleolithic), there is no hope of analyzing the conditions through which the change was effected. We know the *millennium* in which the revision of the *lex talionis* occurred but nothing about the century, the place, or the people who advocated for change. As you come closer to the present, the facts are more plentiful. Even here, however, it is very hard to endorse any conception of ethical *discovery*.

To see why, consider the abolition of chattel slavery. If there is an episode of discovery to be found, there must have been individual people whose attitudes changed; the character of the discovery can then be fathomed by analyzing the circumstances in which they were led to the change. Many abolitionists, of course, were persuaded by others, people who had already made the shift. So we might be especially concerned with the early opponents of slavery, the people who sparked the abolitionist movement.

Fortunately, one early abolitionist bequeathed to us a relatively extensive record of his own thoughts and feelings, explaining the circumstances in which he was led to feel uneasy about chattel slavery and articulating the ways in which he attempted to persuade those around him. John Woolman left a journal.[18]

According to his journal, Woolman felt squeamish when his employer requested him to draw up a contract for the sale of a female slave. Although he did as he was asked, he was subsequently unhappy with his own conduct. In the weeks and months that followed, he reflected further and discussed his doubts with Friends —Woolman was a Quaker. Out of these reflections and discussions came a determination to oppose slavery, an attitude that intensified through years of traveling, preaching, and writing on the issue.

Compare Woolman's change of mind with cases of discovery in other areas. Röntgen famously discovered X-rays by observing fluorescence on a screen; Mendel discovered genes ("factors," as he called them) by crossing and counting pea plants. In instances like these, we can understand the discovery by connecting the psychological changes in the discoverer to the phenomena discovered. *Nothing analogous is available in Woolman's case.* There is simply no plausible story to show how a previously unrecognized ethical "phenomenon" registered on John Woolman but not on the thousands of his contemporaries who daily performed actions similar to his.

This point can be elaborated by thinking more carefully about truth, in ethics and elsewhere. Scientific truth (and truth for everyday statements about familiar objects) is readily understood in terms of correspondence. "The screen fluoresces" is true just in case the entity referred to by "the screen" belongs to the set of things that fluoresce. Röntgen can see the entity referred to by "the screen," and his powers of observation suffice to allow him to assign it to the set of fluorescing things. Given his background beliefs—that fluorescence is produced by some sort of radiation, that the screen is protected from familiar kinds of radiation—he can reasonably conclude that some novel type of radiation has been emitted. If we attempt to offer a similar account of Woolman's discovery, we would start from the truth of "Slavery is wrong": that sentence is true just in case the practice of holding people as chattels belongs to the set of wrong things. In the crucial episode, Woolman recognizes that a woman is being transferred within the prevailing system of slavery. Somehow he has to detect that transfer as belonging to the set of wrong actions. How exactly does he do that? What psychological ability does he have that enables him to classify the transfer as he does? What psychological capacity is lacking in those around him, for whom the selling of slaves is unproblematic?

There are two strategies for developing a semantics for "wrong" that address these questions: the realist and the constructivist strategies. The realist strategy supposes there to be a set of wrong actions delineated independently of our stipulation and construction. The simplest versions invoke an independent property of wrongness. Perhaps this property might be characterized in terms of other properties someone like Woolman could detect: a very crude elaboration of that idea would view painfulness as constitutive of wrongness and enable Woolman to recognize the pain inflicted upon slaves. However refined, approaches that pursue this option face the insuperable difficulty of rendering it mysterious why Woolman's contemporaries, equally able to recognize the pain, fail to draw the conclusion he does. *If you invoke a capacity to detect, familiar enough to be shared by all, you cannot differentiate the discoverers from the unenlightened.* Or maybe the property could be "irreducible"—wrongness isn't inferred from everyday observable features of actions but recognized in some other way. How exactly? Here, the demands of pragmatic naturalism kick in with a vengeance. No historian would tolerate a narrative in which Woolman's conversion was explained by his "detection of the irreducible property of wrongness"!

Here is a better proposal. Woolman was a young man with a penchant for taking his own emotional temperature. In his description of the crucial episode, he reports that he felt "afflicted in his mind."[19] Perhaps his feelings, generated in response to the situation, can be seen as the means through which detection of wrongness proceeds. Say that wrongness simply is the disposition to generate particular types of reactive emotions. When an observer comes to experience the sorts of feelings in question, there will no longer be any mystery about the judgment of wrongness.

This apparently promising option only disguises the difficulty discerned earlier. People feel all sorts of emotional responses to the events they observe. Woolman's untroubled fellows, for example, react to the transfer (and similar occurrences) with different feelings, and he is aware of this. What convinces him that the specific reaction he experiences warrants a judgment that the transfer is wrong? The natural thought is that *some* emotional responses are the *right* ones—these emotions are the "moral sentiments," representing "the party of humanity in the breast"—rather than idiosyncratic deviations. *But the emotion is not accompanied by some reassuring voice whispering "I am a genuinely MORAL sentiment."* Quite reasonably, Woolman describes his situation with modest perplexity—he felt "afflicted in his mind." Only later, after thorough discussions with others, does he become sufficiently confident to insist on the wrongness of slavery. As his journal and his other writings reveal, it was important to him to work through the religious questions raised by the defenders of slaveholding, to relate his own emotions to the religious texts he saw as divinely inspired, to consider various ways of reading them—in short, to enter into a debate with alternative points of view represented in his society. Conversation is crucial.

At this point, it will be helpful to take up the second strategy for offering a semantics for "wrong." According to constructivists, "wrong" picks out a set of events determined by our constructive activity. One very simple version of constructivism supposes that, relative to a particular society, "wrong" refers to whatever events members of that society agree to call "wrong"—this version simply acquiesces in the judgment that the evolution of ethical practice is a succession of "mere changes" and thus fails to support the judgment of asymmetry in episodes of apparent progress. Constructivists typically impose more stringent demands, suggesting that "wrong" selects events that individuals who followed a particular procedure would thereby judge as wrong. So, for example, "wrong" applies to actions that fail the test of the Categorical Imperative (their maxim cannot be thought as a universal law without contradiction), or "wrong" delineates those actions that would be disapproved by a group of rational agents ideally cognizant in some respects and ideally ignorant in others.

Concede, for the sake of argument, that some constructivist procedure can be delineated clearly enough to allow us to understand its demands. Application of the constructivist account to the case at hand will remain problematic. The more obvious but less important difficulty is that there is no evidence that Woolman (or any other ethical innovator) ever arrived at a new insight by following any such procedure. If he pursued an approximation to the favored procedure, it is one so rough as to be useless. To substitute some vague requirement of universalizability for the rigorous test of the Categorical Imperative would be entirely inadequate to settle the live eighteenth-century debates about slavery, for these turned crucially on the legitimacy of certain exceptions to strict universality, and vague thoughts about universalizability are powerless to endorse those exceptions or to repudiate them.

More critical is a point that runs exactly parallel to the objection leveled against realists who see wrongness as grounded in dispositions to produce particular emotions. Any ethical innovator, however clearheaded about the use of some constructive procedure to discriminate the wrong from the right, will know that the ambient society differs in its classification of the focal case(s). Under these circumstances, there are ample grounds for wondering if the procedure pursued is an apt one and, if it is, whether it has been carried out correctly. Even if Woolman thought he had some touchstone for making ethical distinctions, he would have been entirely unreasonable to make a judgment on that basis. Modesty, the kind of modesty he actually exhibited, would have been more appropriate.

There are, I contend, no moments of sudden insight in the history of ethics. Since I also maintain that there is no useful notion of truth without some explanation of how truth (understood in the proposed way) is apprehended and that we who come later in the unfolding of the ethical project have no special ways of apprehending ethical truth that were unavailable to our predecessors, out of whose efforts what we take as ethical truth emerged, I conclude that appeals to ethical truths, sometimes discovered in human history, should be abandoned. If you take the historical record seriously, the thought that individual people have successively discovered ethical truths their forebears did not know has to go.

That leaves us with an apparent problem. Can we make any sense of the apparent progressiveness of some transitions in ethical practice?

4.

That problem has a solution. Instead of taking ethical truth as the prior concept, and conceiving progress as consisting in the discovery of truth, we can invert the relationship. Progress comes first (conceptually), and truth is what you generate when you make progress. Pragmatic naturalism sympathizes with James's thought that "truth happens to an idea."[20]

For the solution to work, we need an adequate account of ethical progress. Before I outline my preferred approach, it is worth noting briefly that the concept of progress is more fundamental to our practical decision making than the notion of ethical truth. When we reflect on the historical record, the first target of appraisal is the progressiveness of particular episodes. When we look into the future, considering alternative directions our ethical practice might take, we effectively ask which modification of our current perspective would be most progressive. Questions about ethical truth are afterthoughts.

During the past four decades, it has become increasingly unclear that the notion of progress as accumulation of truth is adequate for understanding the domain in which it would seem to be most successful—the growth of science.[21] For other areas of human practice, the notion is plainly unsatisfactory. Technological progress, for example, consists in fulfilling functions we did not previously know how to fulfill or fulfilling them more thoroughly or more efficiently. I propose to use the example of technological progress as a model. If you like, ethics is, in its origins at least, a social technology.

Consider an obvious example of technological progress. The technology of transportation arises against a background of problems: some places are inaccessible, others can be reached only through long and laborious journeys. So devices, mechanized vehicles, are introduced with the intended functions of giving access to previously unreachable locations and of enabling quicker travel to destinations hitherto accessible only with great effort. The example suggests a general approach to functions. Initially, there is a *problem background*. A device, introduced into the problem background, solves the problem—and doing so constitutes its *function*.

Approaching the concept of function in this way enables a unified treatment of those functions that arise from human intentions and biological functions.[22] In the latter context, the problem background is set by Darwin's "hostile forces": the pressures of survival and (fundamentally) reproduction. So, for example, the problem background generates a cascade of needs: to reproduce, to survive, to obtain energy, to make use of items available in the environment as sources of food. Facing the last of these problems, an animal may acquire a modified biochemistry that allows digestion of some common plant. A novel enzyme solves the problem of obtaining food and, in virtue of that fact, has the function of enabling digestion of the pertinent plants.

The biological examples introduce an important point. Something can have a function through solving a problem that arises for an organism, even though the organism is not aware of the source of the problem. Remarkably few animals have any consciousness of the challenges their digestive tracts are built to overcome. This point is important for understanding ethics as a social technology: *the ethical project plays that role even though those who participate in it, even those who originated it, could not conceptualize it in that way.* Human beings often face problems—or problem backgrounds —without being able to diagnose the source of the trouble. Avid runners consult their doctors when annoying pains interfere with their exercise. They want the problem traced to its source and resolved, but they are rarely in any position to identify that source for themselves.

So, too, with ethics. Our ancestors recognized the unpleasantness of living in societies subject to constant tensions and consequent risks of dissolution. The problem background for the origins of ethics—the social technology—was the prevalence of altruism failures. As I maintained in §2, the ethical project arises from the limitations of our psychological altruism. *The original function of ethics was to remedy the altruism failures that are the sources of social tension.* A *preliminary* account of ethical progress can now be given: ethical progress consists in increasingly thorough and efficient means of fulfilling the original function of remedying altruism failures.

As it stands, that account will not do, and, to see why, I return to the case of the technology of transport. Developing new ways of reaching hitherto inaccessible places (or of going more easily to older destinations) brings new problems in its train. Mechanized vehicles require all sorts of things: highways, air traffic control centers, systems of regulation, methods of enforcement, safety standards, insurance, and so forth. Attention to an original problem background generates a different problem background for future efforts. The original function (discharged by introducing mechanized vehicles) generates further functions, *derived* functions, and progress in transportation technology can be made by fulfilling either the original function or one or more of the derived functions. Progress in transport technology is to be understood not in terms of decreasing distance toward some ideal goal—there is no ideal system of transportation toward which we are converging—but as progress away from problematic situations: we make progress by solving problems, by introducing or refining devices that fulfill the pertinent functions.

It is not always easy or even possible to find ways of fulfilling all the functions, original and derived. When that happens, we face functional conflict. With respect to transportation technology, there is an evident tension between shortening journey time and promoting the safety of travel. I now want to explore the ways in which something similar arises in the ethical case.

The original function of ethics was the remedying of altruism failures. To that end, the ethical pioneers introduced primitive rules against initiating violence and requiring the sharing of scarce resources. Effectively, they endorsed the desires of band members to satisfy certain basic needs—for food, water, shelter, and safety. As a "how possibly" story sketched in §2 suggests, that endorsement probably created pressure to increase the supply of basic resources, leading to division of labor, introduction of special roles, differentiation of contributions, and a far more extensive set of aspirations. Solutions to the problems generated along this route produce a situation in which people are no longer contented with the satisfaction of their basic needs. As is evident from the reflective writings of the ancients, the conception of the good life embraces the prospect of contributing to the surrounding society through the most extensive development of one's talents. Retrospectively, we can applaud this unfolding of the ethical project, recognizing a derivative function for ethics in the proliferation of human possibilities.

Yet, that function is in tension with the original function of remedying altruism failures. The first ethical ventures were directed toward maintaining the equality of all band members, securing adequate shares of basic resources for all. As human possibilities proliferate, however, inequalities are inevitably introduced: the emphasis shifts from responding to the wishes of all to enabling the truly talented to flourish. *Functional conflict*, as I shall call it, complicates the account of ethical progress.

Ethical progress consists in fulfilling the functions of ethics, original and derived, more thoroughly and more efficiently. In the absence of functional conflict, enhanced fulfillment of one function does not interfere with fulfillment of others. When functions conflict, however, transitions in ethical practice might enhance some functions at cost to others. One approach to ethical progress incorporates a Pareto-style condition: progress occurs only if none of the functions is compromised. A more inclusive attitude allows for progress so long as *some* function is enhanced, no matter what losses are incurred with respect to others. I adopt neither of these polar positions. Instead, I suggest, the successive problem backgrounds provide a basis for deliberation as to how to assess the advantages of different packages of gains and losses. This means that the meta-ethical account of pragmatic naturalism is entangled with a normative stance. The final section of this essay briefly reflects on the problem posed by that entanglement and offers a sketch of an appropriate normative stance.

Even though the account of ethical progress is incomplete, it should be possible to see the lines along which it will be developed. In taking ethics to have original and derived functions, pragmatic naturalism elaborates the Deweyan idea that "moral conceptions and processes grow out of the very conditions of human life." Those conditions are constituted by our social predicament and by the limits of our capacities for psychological altruism. Altruism failure is a deep fact about human existence, and, in its origins, the ethical project is a response to that.

I conclude this section with two brief links to the discussion of §3. To the extent that John Woolman had a moving insight, it lay in the possibility of regarding the selling of human beings as a form of altruism failure. Woolman's modesty in putting forward that insight was, however, appropriate. It was entirely possible that a more adequate point of view, one that embodied a more diverse set of perspectives, would undercut the idea that failing to respond to the desires of slaves constituted altruism failure. *In the manner of the ethical pioneers, Woolman began a conversation.* Given the unfolding of the ethical project over tens of thousands years and the hierarchies and doctrines introduced in that unfolding, the original conditions of conversation were distorted. Some people (slaves, for example) were excluded, and there were appeals to ethical authority that could never have been registered around the Paleolithic campfire. Yet, for all that, a flawed conversation, one in which different perspectives held unequal power, culminated in the endorsement of the neglect of slave desires as an altruism failure. *Progress is achieved through the conversation.* Woolman's great achievement was to initiate it and to keep it alive.

Second, in light of the account of progress at which I have gestured, a notion of ethical truth can be reintroduced. Prescriptive statements have descriptive counterparts: corresponding to "Refrain from A!" is "A is wrong." Ethical truths are the descriptive counterparts of prescriptions that would be stable under progressive transitions. That is: S is true just in case S is the descriptive counterpart of a prescription P, introduced in a progressive transition, and satisfying the requirement that it would be maintained in an indefinite sequence of further progressive transitions. It is reasonable to suppose that there are some ethical truths. The most likely candidates are vague generalizations of the sort we all learned at our parents' knees: "It is right to tell the truth," "It is wrong to initiate violence." Like many valuable generalizations in the natural sciences, these are surely not exceptionless. Even if our successors make progress forever, they may still fail to classify all the pertinent difficult cases. Nevertheless, we have reason to suppose that the vague generalizations will endure.

To recognize some instances in which ethical statements have truth-values does not entail that the notion of truth is applicable across the board. Pragmatic naturalism recognizes the possibility of ethical pluralism. For there may be statements such that neither they nor their negations meet the conditions required for ethical truth. When that occurs, rival traditions whose ethical practices have embodied the alternatives may progress indefinitely without ever converging. Behind their different trajectories will lie an irresoluble functional conflict.

5.

At the beginning of §3, I listed some familiar doubts about the impact of the history of ethical practice outlined in §2. I postponed important worries about the authority of ethics to concentrate on the more recondite issues of ethical truth and ethical progress. Armed with the ideas introduced in §4, we can now address the familiar concerns.

If ethics is a social technology whose original function was to remedy altruism failures, if it has developed in the ways outlined in my historical narrative, generating derivative functions along the way, can we credit it with the dignity and authority ethical theorists have taken it to enjoy? The question needs disambiguation. In one obvious sense, ethics has authority over human beings because, in their deliberations and appraisals, they take its requirements seriously. Naturalists have little difficulty in explaining that psychological fact. Ethical traditions contain methods for socializing the young, and *successful* ethical traditions (the ones that win out in cultural competition) latch onto good strategies for instilling dispositions to attend to the prescriptions and principles they commend. People who are properly brought up in these traditions are impressed with the rules and stories because they have been well socialized, and there is a cultural-evolutionary account, available in principle, that explains how the clever techniques of socialization have emerged.

Precisely because one version of the question is so easily answered, it is surely not the interpretation that underlay the worry. *Felt* authority is not the same as *real* authority, and to account for the former is not to explain the latter. But what exactly is meant by "real authority"? Something like this, I think. Just as facts have real authority over belief, so, too, with ethics and conduct: if you fail to subordinate your beliefs to the facts (or, perhaps, the evidence), you have exhibited some important kind of shortcoming, and, similarly, if you fail to subordinate your conduct to a correct ethical maxim, you are guilty of a significant defect. Hence, the substantive objection is tacitly dependent on issues about ethical truth and justification—which is why we had to explore those issues to tackle it.

There are tricky questions about how to frame the authority

of facts over beliefs, since there are some truths it would not be valuable for people to believe and there are circumstances under which no shortcomings are involved in accepting what is acknowledged as an approximation to the truth. Analogous problems may beset formulations of the thought that ethical principles are authoritative over human conduct. So my strategy will be not to identify a refined version of the thought and then to show how pragmatic naturalism can meet whatever challenge it poses but rather to argue that *however* the critic chooses to present the importance of conformity to correct ethical maxims it is possible for pragmatic naturalists to offer an analogous thought and to defend it.

The strategy was already implicit in the decision in §4 to abandon a direct specification of ethical truth in favor of identifying ethical progress as the prior notion. Critics contend that, while naturalists can explain the felt authority of ethics, the *real* authority of ethics consists in the hold *true* ethical principles exert over ethical practices and the actions of individuals. People who stand in misguided ethical traditions may feel the authority of the principles those traditions deliver, but they are not acknowledging the real authority of ethics. Pragmatic naturalism glosses this thought by recognizing the difference between responding to the rules of the ethical practice you happen to acquire and responding to practices that would be progressive refinements of that practice. Wherever the critic diagnoses a shortcoming in the acquiescence in felt authority, pragmatic naturalism can identify a similar defect —the only difference is that the contrast will be characterized in the one case in terms of divergence from the true ethical system and in the other in terms of deviation from an ethical practice that would be progressive with respect to the code to which the subject gives allegiance. However the critic chooses to elaborate the thought, pragmatic naturalism can provide an equivalent formulation and defend it on equivalent grounds.

Abstract worries about the authority and dignity of ethics can be made more concrete by focusing on some of the troublesome characters who crop up in the history of philosophical discussion. One way to point to the supposed defects of naturalism would be to argue that naturalists have no adequate means of response to those individuals, real or imaginary, who question the authority of ethical maxims in their lives. In tackling this issue, it is important that the standards of adequacy not be inflated. No *words*, however philosophically luminous, can be expected to bring determined rebels to heel; sociopaths have to be handled by other means.[23] The serious challenge for pragmatic naturalism concerns its ability to deliver the kinds of diagnoses of the mistakes made by conscientious rejecters that other, nonnaturalistic approaches to ethics claim to be able to provide.

Start with an ancient troublemaker. Thrasymachus responds to Socrates's question about justice with the cynical proposal that justice expresses the power of the strong.[24] Pragmatic naturalism responds to his complaint by inviting him to explain his evidence for thinking as he does: where exactly in the ethical practice of his society does this imposition of power make itself manifest? To the extent that Thrasymachus can identify features of ethical practice that plausibly support his view, pragmatic naturalism can sympathize with his complaints, viewing these intrusions as distortions of the ethical project, failures to develop the social technology to fulfill its original function. Thrasymachus should be seen as an *ally* in the proper reform of a project that has become distorted through the disruption of its initial sensitivity to the needs of all.

Hume's "sensible knave" poses a more serious threat.[25] Unlike Thrasymachus, knave is not interested in offering any general account of ethical practice. He does not want to expose it as a sham —indeed, he is more than happy if those around him feel themselves bound by it—but simply wants his own conduct to be outside its commands. His aim is to satisfy some of his egoistic desires. What can be said to bring him into line?

Much depends on the sorts of desires knave wants to satisfy. There are several possibilities. Perhaps what knave wants is to meet his most basic needs, in a situation in which those around him are meeting those needs quite adequately. If that is so, knave should be treated like Thrasymachus, invited to join in a reform of the ethical project, so that it no longer tolerates the inequalities the ethical pioneers aimed to eradicate. Or maybe knave hopes to satisfy his most basic needs in a predicament in which his fellows are equally struggling. In that case, he is opting for a return to the world of the chimp-style hominid society from which the ethical project liberated our ancestors, and there is plenty of evidence we can advance in support of the thesis that living in that way is far worse than the forms of life the ethical project makes possible. Alternatively, knave may aim to realize goals beyond those of meeting basic needs. A knave of this sort can be reminded that these desires became possible only through the evolution of the ethical project. His basis for rejecting the authority of ethical practice thus rests on desires that already presuppose the ethical project.

Knave may not be perturbed by these suggestions. He replies that this is all past history. It is a happy fact that so many people have gone along with the ethical project so that he can now develop the selfish aspirations he does—although he suspects that he is not the first person to want to exploit the docile participation of others. Any "contradiction" between aiming to satisfy his desires and rejecting the practice that makes the desires possible can be shrugged off. Nothing stops him from kicking away the ladder after he has climbed up it. Nor (contra Hume) does he fear the gnawing of his conscience in the wee hours.

Knave cannot be silenced. If he is sincere in his responses, then he has escaped whatever techniques of socialization are associated with his society's ethical practice: one way of dealing with him would be to try to socialize him better; if it is too late for that, we may have to confine him or at least watch him carefully. Recall, however, that the task is not to bring the rebel to stunned silence but to diagnose an error—one the rebel himself may not acknowledge. To evaluate pragmatic naturalism's success with respect to that demand, it is worth recalling the ways in which nonnaturalistic approaches cope with the troublemakers. Kantians, for example, will tell knave that he is guilty of a contradiction in practical reason. Knave is likely to reply insouciantly, declaring his total lack of interest in consistency within what is labeled "practical reason." If the Kantian solution is adequate, so is pragmatic naturalism's more concrete complaint that knave is rejecting the ethical project while aspiring to ends that that project makes possible.

Consider a last character, one modeled on Nietzsche's persona (or intended reader?). Free spirit diverges from Thrasymachus and equally from knave. He has no interest in a general understanding of ethics to be appreciated by all or in securing a place for his particular divergence from the ethical project. Rather, his aim is to secure the liberation of the most outstanding forms of human life. The ethical project is viewed as constraining the most vital forms of human existence, those available to the splendid few. What is needed is a "revaluation of values."[26]

The challenge is ambiguous. On one version, free spirit can be seen as acknowledging the authority of the ethical project but arguing for its reform. If this represents the challenger's intention, the authority of ethics is acknowledged, even though the contemporary ethical code is regarded as distorting the project. Free spirits of this sort can be welcomed, and, provided we can reach agreement with them on issues of functional conflict, they can participate in a conversation directed at cleansing the ethical project of its accumulated, confining distortions; (as we shall briefly see in the final section, the search for resolution of functional conflict raises very difficult issues). On the other hand, if free spirit intends to resist the ethical project in its entirety, it is appropriate to ask him what form of human life he has in mind. Something is known about hominid and early human life outside the demands of normative guidance—for that was once the predicament of our ancestors and remains the situation of our evolutionary cousins. Is that the existence to which free spirit intends to return us? If so, there is overwhelming reason to think it is hardly conducive to the flourishing of the splendid people whom free spirit so frequently celebrates. Yet what other alternative is there? Until one has been provided, we have no reason to take the challenge at all seriously.

My replies to the troublemakers are blunt, but they disclose the lines along which more elaborate answers can be given.[27] All these responses develop, in different ways, an important theme. Dewey took "morals" to grow out of the fundamental conditions of human life, and pragmatic naturalism elaborates that idea: the ethical project is the articulation of the possibilities of human social life in response to its difficulties. To try to escape the claims of ethics is effectively to turn one's back on the project that has made us what we are.

6.

I close by attending to a difficulty that requires a radical shift in our thinking about ethics. If pragmatic naturalism is to be developed fully, it will need a normative stance, and to understand how to adopt any such stance demands that we abandon the thought of ethical expertise. Contrary to philosophical claims that ethical discoveries can be made by following particular procedures or religious assertions that particular principles are fundamental to ethics, the ethical project is something *people work out together.* There are no experts here.

How then do we—might we, should we—go on from where we are? To take the ethical project seriously as a social technology worked out in conversation among people limits the philosophical role to one of making proposals (and to say that is to make an initial proposal). Philosophy serves as a form of midwifery, bringing useful conversation into being. Although he did not think of himself in that way, this is what John Woolman did, and aspiring latter-day reformers can do no better than to emulate him.

Achieving a normative stance requires continuing the ethical project, and that (I propose) might begin by using the narrative of §2 to understand our current predicament. Our ancestors began the ethical project by attending to the strains in their social lives, and similar strains remain with us. Effectively, we live today in a vast society, one as large as the human population and its descendants, for our lives are thoroughly causally interconnected. Altruism failures are as pervasive for us as they were for the ethical pioneers. Yet, any conversation we might have is distorted by the size of the group and the intrusions of power and supposed authority that the evolution of the ethical project has bequeathed to us.

It can be shown, I claim, that a certain package of proposals is internally coherent. The first continues to assert the importance of the original function of ethics, the remedying of altruism failures. The second suggests that the conversation out of which a normative stance might well emerge should attend to the voices of all members of the pertinent group (for many issues, the human population), treat each of them as having equal weight, and eliminate identifiable errors of belief. This package of proposals is a first step at realizing Dewey's hope that, with an understanding of our practices of valuing, we might proceed to make more "intelligent" valuations.

The coherence of this package of proposals is important, for it is not clear that any similar coherence can be achieved if one subordinates the original function of ethics, as a sophisticated "free spirit" might suggest. An ethical project that ignored the problem of altruism failures would essentially revert to the pre-ethical state —the dismal condition of chimpanzees and bonobos. Hence, our choices in pursuing the ethical project seem to be limited to a spectrum of approaches, all of which emphasize the problem of remedying altruism failures. If that is correct, there are possibilities for resolving some major functional conflicts, for refining the account of ethical progress, for completing the defense of the authority of ethics, and for constraining the threat of rampant pluralism. To justify this optimism is a task for another occasion.[28]

NOTES

1. T. S. Kuhn, *The Structure of Scientific Revolutions* (Chicago: University of Chicago Press, 1962), 1 (slightly amended). Kuhn himself said: "History, if viewed as a repository for more than anecdote or chronology, could produce a decisive transformation in the image of science by which we are now possessed." Ibid.

2. E. O. Wilson, *On Human Nature* (Cambridge, MA: Harvard University Press, 1978); Michael Ruse and E. O. Wilson, "Moral Philosophy as Applied Science," *Philosophy* 61 (1986): 173–92; Sam Harris, *The Moral Landscape* (New York: Free Press, 2010).

3. Philip Kitcher, *Vaulting Ambition: Sociobiology and the Quest for Human Nature* (Cambridge, MA: MIT Press, 1985), chap. 11; Philip Kitcher, *In Mendel's Mirror: Philosophical Reflections on Biology* (New York: Oxford University Press, 2003), chap. 15.

4. Jeremy Bentham, *An Introduction to the Principles of Morals and Legislation* (New York: Oxford University Press, 1996); Peter Railton, *Facts, Values, and Norms* (Cambridge: Cambridge University Press, 2003).

5. Charles Darwin, *The Descent of Man* (London: John Murray, 1872).

6. Wilson, *On Human Nature*; Frans de Waal, *Primates and Philosophers* (Princeton: Princeton University Press, 2007).

7. Charles Darwin, *Origin of Species* (London: John Murray, 1859).

8. John Dewey and James Tufts, *Ethics*, 2d ed. (New York: Henry Holt, 1932), 343.

9. Ibid., 344.

10. Philip Kitcher, *The Ethical Project* (Cambridge, MA: Harvard University Press, 2011).

11. For a full-dress articulation of these notions, see Philip Kitcher, "Varieties of Altruism," *Economics and Philosophy* 26 (2010): 121–48; Kitcher, *The Ethical Project*.

12. Jane Goodall, *The Chimpanzees of Gombe* (Cambridge, MA: Harvard University Press, 1986); Frans de Waal, *Good Natured* (Cambridge, MA: Harvard University Press, 1996).

13. Kitcher, *The Ethical Project*, chap. 1.

14. Frans de Waal, *Peace-Making among Primates* (Cambridge, MA: Harvard University Press, 1989).

15. Richard Lee, *The !Kung San* (Cambridge: Cambridge University Press, 1979); B. M. Knauft, "Violence and Sociality in Human Evolution," *Current Anthropology* 32 (1991): 391–428.

16. Kitcher, *The Ethical Project*, chaps. 2 and 3.

17. And, if you are skeptical, please look at the developed account in Kitcher, *The Ethical Project*.

18. John Woolman, *Journal* (Philadelphia: Citadel Press, 1961).

19. Ibid., 14–15.

20. William James, *Writings 1902–1910* (New York: Library of America, 1987), 823.

21. Kuhn, *The Structure of Scientific Revolutions*.

22. Kitcher, *In Mendel's Mirror*, chap. 7.

23. Philippa Foot, *Natural Goodness* (Oxford: Oxford University Press, 2001).

24. Plato, *Republic* (G. M. A. Grube translation) (Indianapolis: Hackett, 1992), Book I.

25. David Hume, *Enquiry Concerning the Principles of Morals* (Indianapolis: Hackett, 1983).

26. Friedrich Nietzsche, *On the Genealogy of Morality* (Cambridge: Cambridge University Press, 2006).

27. For more extensive answers, see Kitcher, *The Ethical Project*, chap. 7.

28. Ibid., chaps. 8 and 9.

2

THE TWO FACES OF MORALITY: HOW EVOLUTIONARY THEORY CAN BOTH VINDICATE *AND* DEBUNK MORALITY (WITH A SPECIAL NOD TO THE GROWING IMPORTANCE OF LAW)

ROBIN BRADLEY KAR

Charles Darwin was the first to propose that there might be an evolutionary explanation of the moral sentiments[1]—which, on certain contemporary views, might plausibly include or even largely consist in an evolutionary explanation of our capacities for moral judgment as well. Although more than a century has passed since Darwin first made this proposal, we are far from settling on a complete and definitive account. Recent decades, however, have witnessed a sharp uptick in the amount of good work that is being done on the evolution of morality, and this work has become increasingly suggestive.[2] Progress is being made, and—given this recent progress and the likelihood that it will continue into the indefinite future—I want to use this essay to ask the following question: will the correct evolutionary explanation, if any, of our capacities for moral judgment ultimately vindicate them by revealing our perceptions of their objectivity and special practical

31

authority to be grounded in something suitably real, or is it more likely to debunk them by explaining away those very same perceptions? (A third possibility is that evolutionary theory will reveal our capacities for moral judgment to have two faces—one that inclines us to participate in a recognizable species of moral life and another that coopts our moral psychologies for more competitive and antisocial purposes.)

I will also be suggesting a specific answer to this question. I will argue, in particular, that there is a specific set of circumstances, which may plausibly hold for us, in which we would be entitled to conclude that our capacities for moral judgment have at least a partial vindication, in a perfectly respectable sense of the word.

More specifically, we would be entitled to understand ourselves as having the natural capacities to see (in a clear but metaphorical sense) and be appropriately motivated by certain moral facts but to see them only imperfectly and only through a lens that sometimes distorts our moral vision in certain systematic and identifiable ways. Just as our ordinary sense of sight allows us to apprehend various natural facts about the world but also subjects us to certain optical illusions, our natural sense of morality would—if these same circumstances were to hold true—allow us to apprehend various moral facts while subjecting us to certain forms of what I will call "moral illusion." In addition, while we would be entitled to understand our natural capacities for moral judgment as functioning in part to help us track and respond appropriately to certain moral facts, we would also have to acknowledge that these capacities have other nonmoral natural functions, which can serve various programs of domination and exclusion.

The conclusion that our capacities for moral judgment admit of a partial vindication would also entitle us to begin engaging in a specific, naturalized approach to moral epistemology, guided in part by contemporary evolutionary insights. Under the approach I have in mind, we would seek to identify various nonobvious epistemic norms that validly govern our capacities for moral judgment by studying and describing those psychological patterns that produce moral judgments that most reliably track the moral facts. At the same time, however, we would use our best evolutionary insights to help us distinguish between those psychological patterns that are more or less reliable in this sense. In this way, evolutionary insights might help us not only expand our moral vision but also identify and respond better to a host of natural moral illusions.

I will—in other words—be arguing for the third possibility. In the process, I will be developing a distinctive form of naturalistic moral realism, which bears some affinities to the prior work of people like Richard Boyd, David Brink, Michael Moore, Peter Railton, and Nicholas Sturgeon.[3] As a corollary, I will end with a counterintuitive suggestion. I will suggest that the law—at least in some modern (but growing sets of) circumstances—may have the independent authority to override some of our first-order moral reasoning, even in its correct and conscientious employment.

Before doing any of this, I should, however, make some brief terminological remarks about how I plan to use the terms "objectivity" and "special practical authority" in reference to our moral judgments. I will be focusing on a particular subset of our moral judgments, namely those pertaining to right and wrong and to the special sense of obligation that those terms commonly express. Most of us take ourselves to have various nonmoral reasons for action, which arise from or are grounded in our antecedent desires, inclinations, or interests. When we sincerely judge an action to be wrong, however, we usually consider that purported fact to give us a special, moral reason for action, which has a practical authority that is in some sense independent of our antecedent desires, inclinations, and interests. For the special class of judgments under consideration here, this independence can be understood in terms of four basic items: (1) generality of application (i.e., we commonly take these moral judgments to apply generally to persons, regardless of their antecedent desires, inclinations, and interests); (2) basic reason-giving force (i.e., we commonly take these moral judgments to give rise to reasons for action that have authority that is independent of a person's antecedent desires, inclinations, and interests); (3) supremacy (i.e., we commonly take moral reasons to have the special authority to override or exclude certain other reasons that arise from antecedent desires, inclinations, or interests);[4] and (4) standing to make demands (i.e., we commonly take these moral reasons to involve obligations to others in the sense that they give some other person or group the standing to demand compliance or to hold us accountable or responsible for noncompliance, independent of our antecedent desires, inclinations, and

interests).[5] By the "special practical authority" of our moral judgments, I mean to refer to these four elements of this particular
class of moral judgments.

   As many people have noted, the surface grammar of our talk
of right and wrong suggests that we are also ascribing real properties to actions with our moral judgments. We not only act as if
these judgments express facts (with the special practical authority described earlier) but we also embed these judgments in more
complex logical and syntactic structures and then combine them
in forms of moral reasoning that obey the standard rules of logic.
In doing so, we act as if these judgments were truth evaluable,
tracking a realm of facts that exist independent of our perception
of these facts. We also engage in moral argumentation in social
contexts, and, in these encounters, we take fundamental differences in moral opinion to reveal inconsistencies in judgment that
rationally require the revision of one or another person's views.
Our talk of right and wrong thus has many of the standard hall-
marks of objectivity, and, in what follows, I will mean to refer to
these particular features of this particular class of judgments when
I speak of the purported "objectivity" of our moral judgments. I
will also be using the terms "moral" and "morality" to refer only to
the narrow domain of morality highlighted here.

   So what would it mean for an evolutionary explanation to vindicate the purported objectivity and special practical authority of
this particular class of moral judgments? We know that evolutionary dynamics are inherently selfish and competitive, and a breezy
understanding of evolutionary theory might therefore lead one to
assume that the correct evolutionary explanation of our capacities
for moral judgment must be debunking. Whether this assumption
is true will, however, ultimately depend on whether evolutionary
discoveries can help us make sense of a realm of facts that are rec-
ognizably moral; that are epistemically accessible to us in a plausible and nonmysterious way; that are needed to explain the content
of our moral judgments (rather than the other way around);[6] and
that can and should motivate us appropriately (i.e., with the special practical authority under discussion) by means of moral judgments that track these moral facts. This last description will need
to be spelled out in a number of ways, and I will engage in some
of that needed refinement later. Still, unless evolutionary theory

can contribute to the discovery of a realm of facts that meets this initial, first-blush description, there is a legitimate worry that evolutionary explanations of our capacities for moral judgment will reveal these judgments to be mere projections of our evolved psychologies.

I would nevertheless recommend caution before jumping to any such conclusion. Much more attention needs to be paid to the question of what a vindicating evolutionary explanation of our capacities for moral judgment would even look like. Absent such an account, it is not altogether clear what a debunking claim means to deny. One of the main aims of this essay is, in fact, to address this issue more squarely and to develop a clearer way of distinguishing between evolutionary explanations that might usefully be deemed "vindicating" and those that might be considered "debunking," so as to give more concrete meaning to these questions of vindication.

1. Some Brief Notes about Timing

In a moment, I will be turning to the core issues of this essay, but first I want to address a threshold concern. I myself believe that we are in a good position to address the core issues of this essay, but some will undoubtedly wonder whether the inquiry is premature. Much of the recent work on the evolution of morality is still partly speculative, and this work has not always been produced by evolutionary biologists.

In "The Deep Structure of Law and Morality," for example, I argued (as a moral and legal philosopher) that the natural function of our sense of obligation is to allow us to resolve social-contract problems flexibly.[7] Given the current state of our knowledge, many of my arguments for this proposition nevertheless rested on overall plausibility considerations and on attempts to triangulate from the most current findings of a broad range of cognate fields. As a result, my proposal may ultimately find further empirical support as our knowledge progresses, but it may also find empirical refutation. (Several recent developments have tended to increase the plausibility of my initial proposal.)[8] Scientists who work in evolutionary biology have also cautioned scholars from other fields that, absent appropriate scientific training, it is all too easy to misinterpret the current state of our evolutionary knowledge and hence its relevance to any larger moral and social issues.[9] Perhaps facts like these should send moral and legal philosophers away from evolutionary thinking and back to more familiar terrain.

Not so fast! Caution is indeed warranted, but we need to be careful not to assume that the charge of speculation is necessarily a bad thing. To be sure, the ultimate findings of the natural sciences require strict empirical validation and cannot rest merely on speculation (including even on good speculation, which is well grounded in overall plausibility considerations and in a host of known facts). There is nevertheless an important stage at which speculation plays an important, an appropriate, and an often underappreciated role within the sciences themselves: namely at the stage of hypothesis formation. Hypothesis formation is critical to the development of our empirical knowledge, and good hypothesis formation often involves precisely the type of balancing of various overall plausibility considerations and triangulations from the findings of a wide body of cognate fields that can be seen in work like mine and Philip Kitcher's.[10] Hypotheses can, moreover, be assessed not only in terms of their empirical promise and plausibility but also in terms of their relevance to the questions that brought us to the natural sciences in the first place. Where, as here, we are concerned with the potential implications of evolutionary findings for meta-ethics (by which I mean to include the study of the meaning, status, justifiability, and hence epistemology of our moral judgments), moral philosophers will have their own cautionary tale to tell. They will worry that, absent appropriate training in philosophical ethics and meta-ethics, it is all too easy to misinterpret the normative or meta-ethical significance of various natural facts. To develop the kinds of empirical hypotheses that are most likely to bear directly on central questions in meta-ethics would therefore seem to require the input of people who are both philosophically trained and knowledgeable about the most recent deliverances of the natural sciences.

We can therefore all agree that caution is appropriate. But caution, in this particular case, would seem to require a particular division of intellectual labor, with robust input from moral philosophers and meta-ethicists when we are trying to identify the classes of evolutionary hypotheses that might bear on various questions in meta-ethics and robust input from evolutionary biologists when we are trying to decide which of these hypotheses is most likely to be true. In what follows, I will proceed in just this spirit of inter-disciplinary cooperation. As a moral and legal philosopher, I will sometimes take certain liberties by asking the reader to assume that certain evolutionary explanations of phenomena are correct in order to clarify what the philosophical consequences of those assumptions might be. At the same time, the liberties I will be taking are not unconstrained. With some minor exceptions (which I will mark and use only for heuristic purposes), my aim will be to stick with explanations that have a high degree of plausibility, given the current state of our knowledge. Hence, many of the central explanations offered here should also capture an important part of the truth.

In any event, there is a second reason why it would be unwise to allow charges of speculation to prevent philosophers and social scientists from engaging in explicit and thoughtful evolutionary theorizing. Evolutionary theory is part of our larger web of knowledge; hence, implicit assumptions of evolutionary plausibility can sometimes affect our assessments of the plausibility of various psychological and behavioral proposals in other fields. Evolutionary theory is, for example, famously premised on dynamics like those of survival of the fittest, and this fact has led many to assume that it must support a fairly global vision of "nature red in tooth and claw"—to use Alfred Tennyson's memorable phrase.[11] Evolutionary theory also employs patterns of explanation that operate by means of specifying the consequences of certain traits for reproductive success. A breezy recognition of facts like these might therefore seem to make it implausible that evolutionary dynamics would produce anything other than instrumental forms of motivation that are largely centered in self-interested desires and inclinations.[12] In my view, implicit assumptions like these have done much to support the perceived plausibility of the so-called rational-actor model of human action as a general description of human action and motivation in the social sciences and law. Although this model has been subjected to a range of criticisms in recent decades, it is still the default model in many fields, and many of its harshest critics still assume that human motivation must be fundamentally instrumental in nature. The claim that we might have a distinctively moral and noninstrumental form of motivation, which operates by means of a sense that certain rules have intrinsic authority, is therefore treated with suspicion in many quarters, as somehow (and somehow obviously) naturalistically implausible.

Examples like this suggest that it may be very hard to avoid the effects of evolutionary speculation altogether within the larger web of our beliefs. Evolutionary theory is such a prominent theory that judgments of evolutionary plausibility can sometimes play a powerful role in shaping many of our other beliefs and research programs. Rather than trying to avoid evolutionary speculation altogether, philosophers and social scientists would therefore do better to try to replace those instances of loose and breezy evolutionary speculation that are relevant to their fields with more rigorous and explicit evolutionary thought.

With regard to human motivation, for example, we know that natural selection has favored the production of social dominance hierarchies in many social animals, including our closest primate kin.[13] These patterns of behavior plausibly involve perceptions of authority that are distinct from the attitudes that go into purely goal-oriented behavior (and which we share with many nonsocial animals). Because we are ourselves social creatures and because there is a deep history of social dominance hierarchies within the larger primate line, it is certainly possible that our moral psychologies would operate by getting us to perceive certain rules as having authority (rather than by giving us new desires for distinctive outcomes). So what explains the fact that many social scientists assume, to the contrary, that the best explanation of any putatively moral behavior in humans must reference only purely instrumental concerns (such as concern for one's reputation or avoidance of sanctions or moral reprisal)?[14]

This assumption cannot—in my view—be realistically grounded in direct empirical observations of human action, because it is notoriously difficult to determine whether people who engage in putatively moral behavior are doing so because they think the actions are right (i.e., out of a perception of the intrinsic authority of a rule) or because of some more instrumental concern. When social scientists see only instrumental forms of motivation in putatively moral behavior, their observations therefore appear to be highly theory laden. My suggestion is that the background theories that have been doing much of the relevant work here have often included certain forms of implicit evolutionary speculation and certain implicit assumptions of evolutionary plausibility that may be poorly rooted in the facts.

If the effects of some speculation like this are ultimately unavoidable, then the best course of action will be to combat poor speculation with well-grounded empirical hypotheses. Rather than ignoring evolutionary theory altogether (but still suffering its implicit effects), we need to develop more explicit, more thoughtful, and more contemporary judgments about the relative evolutionary plausibility of various propositions relevant to ethics, metaethics, and the law.

2. The Two Faces of Ordinary Cognition

We are now ready to develop the central distinction of this essay, between what I will call "vindicating" and "debunking" evolutionary explanations. Let me begin by emphasizing that I will be using these terms to refer exclusively to explanations of various human capacities for judgment. It is therefore important to recognize that we make many different classes of judgments, including moral judgments, aesthetic judgments, epistemic judgments, and purely descriptive judgments about the world. What these different classes of judgments share is a purported objectivity: they purport to state facts that exist independent of our perception of the facts. Hence, one important aspect of a vindicating explanation should be that it helps us understand what the particular subject matter of a given class of judgments might be and how we might have epistemic access to the particular facts that make up this subject matter. More specifically, we should be able to understand how, given our ordinary human psychologies and capacities, the facts in question could reliably produce a class of judgments that track those facts. At the same time, different classes of judgment often differ with respect to the type of authority that we perceive them to have in our lives. For example, we perceive moral judgments to have a special form of authority over action; we perceive aesthetic judgments to have authority over certain sentiments and emotions; we perceive epistemic judgments to have authority over our patterns of reasoning and belief formation; and so on. Hence, a second important aspect of a vindicating explanation should be that it helps us see why the particular facts that form the subject matter of a given class of judgments are the right ones to have the special authority that we typically grant them in our lives.

Given these initial remarks, it should be clear that both vindicating and debunking evolutionary explanations will have to be tied to specific classes of judgments, such that questions of vindication will need to be asked class by class. We can nevertheless clarify the distinction itself by focusing on one such class of judgments. In this section, I focus on the class of purely descriptive judgments about the world (or what I will call "cognitive judgments"), because they present a case where the distinction is particularly easy to understand. Later sections will then extend the distinction to our moral judgments.

If we study the psychology of cognitive judgment formation from a purely naturalistic perspective, we begin to notice certain systematically describable patterns in our psychologies. For example, we notice that we are disposed to form certain cognitive judgments based on direct observation; to revise our cognitive judgments based on the perception of newly acquired evidence; apply the standard rules of logic to our cognitive judgments; to resolve perceived inconsistencies between them; to learn cognitive judgments from others; to share them with others; to engage in argumentation with others over what the right cognitive judgments are; and to form some cognitive judgments that we might call "theoretical" (rather than "observational"), because we use them to explain and predict the course of our experience of the world and hold them responsive to observational evidence but because they cannot, strictly speaking, be derived from logic and observation alone.[15] With regard to authority, we tend to believe that our cognitive judgments should be practically inert in the following sense: they should not have any independent practical authority in our lives and should instead motivate us to act only when combined with certain desires, purposes, or principles that we take to have practical authority and that render our cognitive judgments relevant to action. We do, on the other hand, take our cognitive judgments to have theoretical authority of a kind. As a first approximation, we might say the following: we take cognitive judgments to have equal authority over the cognitive beliefs of all persons, although that authority is only as strong as the reasons that one can cite in favor of the judgment (including facts about relative expertise and the credibility of the source). The authority of a cognitive judgment is therefore always in principle defeasible by countervailing reasons.

There are other systematically describable features of our psychology of cognition, and I have—no doubt—misdescribed some of these features or described them only imperfectly. My point here is just that we should in principle be able to come up with a complete and accurate naturalistic description of the psychological mechanisms that lead us to form cognitive judgments, along with the systematic ties that these mechanisms have to other parts of our lives (such as deliberation and action). Let us call this complete and accurate description the "psychology of cognition" and ask whether we can distinguish between evolutionary explanations of the psychology of cognition that might be usefully understood as "vindicating," as opposed to "debunking."

To begin, we need to consider how evolutionary explanations work more generally. In producing them, the evolutionary theorist typically focuses on some set of phenotypes (which are any observable characteristics or traits) in a population and asks whether the existence or variation of these traits can be explained in part by reference to any known evolutionary processes. The most familiar such process is natural selection (although there are others, such as genetic drift and genetic hitchhiking), and I will be focusing on explanations in terms of natural selection here. To say that natural selection has produced a given trait is just to say that one can explain its development and proliferation through an ancestral population by reference to the relative reproductive advantages that the trait gave its ancestral bearers.

Evolutionary explanations in terms of natural selection can produce further insights if we specify the precise causal consequences of a given trait that made it contribute to an organism's reproductive success in its relevant environment of evolutionary adaptation. Different versions of a trait will typically produce these consequences more or less reliably, so—assuming that we have correctly identified the precise class of effects of a trait that allowed it to contribute to its bearers' reproductive success—those versions that were better at producing those effects should have been favored by the processes of natural selection over those that were worse. Over time, natural selection thus should have favored the development of versions of the trait that appear better and better designed for this particular purpose. In these circumstances, evolutionary biologists will say that the trait is an "adaptation for" the production of these consequences—or, alternatively, that the "natural function" (or "natural purpose") of the trait is to produce these consequences. It should be clear from this discussion that all of this talk of "natural functions" can be replaced, without loss, by talk of traits, causal consequences, reproductive success, and the dynamics of natural selection. Hence, we can use this particular concept of a natural function with a clear conscience and without taking on any questionable metaphysical commitments.

To illustrate, we know that the human heart regularly pumped blood to the human body in our environment of evolutionary adaptation, and the fact that human hearts regularly achieved these effects is undoubtedly a large part of what conferred reproductive advantages on the ancestral bearers of human hearts. To say this is just to say that, all other things being equal, those of our ancestors with hearts that pumped blood well to their bodies tended to do better in terms of reproductive success than those with hearts that did so only poorly—and it would be hard to deny this proposition. These facts thus should entitle us to use the following shorthand and say that the human heart is an "adaptation for" pumping blood to the human body—or, alternatively, that the "natural function" (or at least a "natural function") of the heart is to pump blood to the human body. If we have correctly identified a natural function of a trait, then that identification should, moreover, help us understand various features of the trait itself. It will begin to make sense, for example, why the human heart has its normal musculature; why it is connected up to neural circuitry that allows it to maintain a rhythmic pulse; why it is connected up to our systems of arteries and veins, which carry blood back and forth from the human heart to the human body; and, more generally, why the human heart appears so well designed, in these and other ways, to pump blood to the human body. The capacity of a proposed natural function to help explain various aspects of a trait can, in fact, lend credibility to the proposal itself. In the case of the human heart, we should not have to do extensive fossil research or know very much at all about the specific features of our environment of evolutionary adaptation to conclude that an important natural function of the human heart is to pump blood to the human body. This proposition should be highly plausible on the basis of what we know about ourselves today, even though claims about natural functions are causal-historical claims.

Returning to the psychology of cognition, we can now introduce a paradigmatic example of what I will be calling a "vindicating" evolutionary explanation. Let us assume that part of the correct evolutionary explanation of our capacities for cognitive judgment is that they conduced to the reproductive success of their bearers, within their environment of evolutionary adaptation, by disposing them to form true beliefs about the world. As so far stated, this explanation makes reference to truth, and some may worry that this reference is problematic (especially insofar as it is meant to play a role in a purely naturalistic explanation) because it is unclear whether truth is itself a natural property. To avoid this problem, we should therefore view the earlier explanation as shorthand for the following, longer explanation: part of the correct evolutionary explanation of our capacities for cognitive judgment is that they conduced to the reproductive success of their bearers within their environment of evolutionary adaptation by disposing them to believe that p if and only if p, for a broad class of propositions p about the world that were relevant to human life and action. (In saying this, I do not mean to suggest that natural selection operates to produce perfect biconditional symmetries concerning the belief that p if and only if p. I just mean to suggest that the reproductive advantages of this particular trait can depend upon its capacity to approximate biconditional symmetries of this kind. It is this fact that will allow us to reference these biconditionals in the underlying evolutionary explanation rather than the more controversial concept of truth.)

When I use the word "truth" in what follows, I will therefore use it in a way that is replaceable, without loss, by a set of biconditionals like these. But I also want to refrain from being wordy, and so I will use shorthand. The assumptions under discussion would entitle us to say, in shorthand, that one natural function of our capacities for cognitive judgment is to dispose us to form true beliefs about the world.

Although we are primarily concerned here with the philosophical consequences of evolutionary explanations like these, rather than with their truth values, this particular proposal has a great deal of plausibility to it—at least as a rough statement of the facts. Indeed, it would be incredible if this proposed explanation were not at least a significant part of the correct evolutionary explanation of our capacities for cognitive judgment. Our ancestors would not have been able to survive very long at all without some capacity to form true beliefs about the world,[16] and we can see the types of problems that modern humans face when their cognitive capacities are impaired. The proposed explanation would also help us understand many of the ways that our psychology of cognition functions. For example, it would make sense that we are inclined to subject our cognitive judgments to the standard rules of logic, because the standard rules of logic are truth preserving; it would make sense that we deliberate on the assumption that our cognitive judgments are true, because their function would be to track the truth; it would make sense that we are inclined to give cognitive judgments authority over our cognitive beliefs, but only as much authority as the reasons that can be cited in their favor; and so on.

What I want to suggest now is that, if this were a correct evolutionary explanation of our capacities for cognitive judgment, then we could understand this explanation as being "vindicating" in an important and perfectly respectable sense of the word. The explanation would give us a nonobvious set of evolutionary reasons to think that we are (at least in part) psychologically constituted with some tendency to form the cognitive judgment that p if and only if p. When our capacities for cognitive judgment are working well and when we use them to form the cognitive judgment that p, we therefore have a nonobvious set of evolutionary reasons for thinking that p likely played a causal role in producing the cognitive judgment that p via a psychological mechanism that reliably tracks the truth. It is important to recognize that the mechanisms by which p may have had this causal effect can be very complex and can involve not only direct interactions between p and the person who has formed the cognitive judgment (as through a personal observation of p) but also the use of memory, induction, theory construction, reasoning, reliance on testimony, argumentation, trust in others, and the like. On the present assumptions, we should be able to understand the entire psychology of cognition as a mechanism that is designed (at least in part) for producing true beliefs, and we might therefore try to identify a number of nonobvious epistemic norms by describing the ways this psychology functions when it is functioning well. There is, moreover, more than one logically possible psychological mechanism that might have this natural function. Hence, if we refer to these different mechanisms as different possible species of cognition, then the epistemic norms relevant to the human species of cognition are likely to depend in part on certain species-typical features of our psychological and biological makeups. For present purposes, the more important point to recognize is the following: by producing a nonobvious set of evolutionary reasons for thinking that facts about the world reliably cause us to form cognitive judgments that track those facts, the explanation under consideration would vindicate our perception that these judgments are objective in the specific sense that they reliably respond to a reality that is independent of our perception of this reality. The explanation under discussion thus would do the first half of the work that one might expect of a vindicating explanation.

The second half of the work one might expect of a vindicating explanation is to help us understand why the particular class of facts that forms the subject matter of a given class of judgments ought to have the special authority that we typically grant them in our lives. The explanation under discussion here would certainly explain why we might be psychologically disposed to treat cognitive judgments as having theoretical but no practical authority: their natural function would be to dispose us to form true beliefs about the world, not to motivate us independently to action, and so it would make sense if we were psychologically constituted so as to grant them the specific type of authority that we do. At the same time, we should also acknowledge that—strictly speaking—the explanation in question would vindicate our capacities for cognitive judgment only on condition that two other propositions are true: first, that our cognitive judgments and cognitive beliefs ought to aim at the truth about the world, and, second, that our cognitive judgments qua cognitive judgments ought to lack all independent practical authority.

This conditionality of vindicating explanations on certain propositions about authority merits further discussion. I want to be very careful not to overclaim anything here about the power of a vindicating explanation. My aim is not to produce a form of explanation that will answer all possible doubts but rather to describe a specific type of explanation, which should have some plausible and recognizable vindicating force and which will ultimately prove useful as part of a larger naturalized approach to epistemology, for distinguishing between the levels of credit we should give to different employments of our capacities for cognitive judgment. By the end of this section, I hope to have established this usefulness, and, later, when I extend this analysis to moral judgments, I will be happy to ask whether we can vindicate our capacities for moral judgment in roughly the same way (i.e., in a way that exhibits roughly the same strengths and roughly the same limitations) that we can vindicate the capacities discussed in this section. Before moving on, let us discuss some of the most important limitations on vindicating explanations, as so far presented.

The first limitation, which we have already begun to discuss, relates to the fact that vindicating explanations are conditional on the truth of certain propositions about authority—and, in particular, about the authority that certain classes of judgments or facts ought to exert in our lives. This conditionality may not prove unduly problematic in the present case, because the propositions under discussion are not all that controversial. Still, it is important to recognize that this conditionality exists and to acknowledge the sense of inquiring into the plausibility of the relevant conditioning propositions.

In this particular case, neither of the conditioning propositions in question appears to express a straightforward cognitive judgment—at least if we define a cognitive judgment as any particular judgment about the world that is produced by the specific capacities we have been discussing. Questions about the credibility of these conditioning propositions will therefore need to be asked and answered in ways that are to some degree independent of the vindicating force of the evolutionary explanation under discussion. In examining these propositions for present purposes, our goal should also be to try to understand the types of considerations that might render them more or less plausible, rather than to settle these issues definitively. For example, beginning with the first proposition (viz., that our cognitive judgments and cognitive beliefs ought to aim at the truth about the world), I will confess to a strong and immediate sense of its obviousness. It is also a proposition that should survive critical reflection, and we might therefore try to understand it as a considered judgment about the appropriate aim of our cognitive judgments and beliefs. At the same time, it is probably best to acknowledge that the vindicating explanation under discussion cannot refute more extreme views about the appropriate aims of our cognitive beliefs and judgments. This may perhaps be a limitation of this particular vindicating explanation, but it is not necessarily a limitation of its vindicating force—if, as one might plausibly think, these more extreme views are likely to turn out false, meaningless, or just not that helpful for the production of knowledge.

On the other hand, the second proposition (viz., that our cognitive judgments qua cognitive judgments ought to lack independent practical authority) seems much less obviously true to me. We nevertheless might give it some foundation by engaging in general reflections on practical authority. Consider the fact that a practical authority can function as a practical authority only insofar as it is capable of providing us with practical guidance in the real world. To the extent that this guidance depends for its content on facts about the world, these facts must also be some specific facts or other. It might make sense, for example, to be guided by the practical principle that one ought to run if one is facing a threat to one's livelihood, but facts about the world will be incapable of providing us with any real practical guidance if the guidance just says to run whenever we encounter facts that are true. When we describe cognitive judgments qua cognitive judgments, we are describing them at just this high level of generality—as simply aiming at truth about the natural world. Hence, cognitive judgments qua cognitive judgments should have no independent practical authority and should instead motivate us to act only when combined with aims, desires, or practical principles that single out some specific class of facts as relevant to human action.

I recognize that the reader may or may not be convinced by

these last arguments. My point here is just that they reflect the types of considerations upon which the strength of a vindicating explanation can depend and thus tell us something important about the types of limitations inherent in vindicating explanations.

The second limitation relates to the fact that the vindicating explanation under consideration here is deeply circular.[17] We have begun, in effect, by crediting our intuitive capacities to form beliefs about the world, at least in our daily affairs. Over the course of many millennia, we have then employed these capacities to develop what we consider to be an expanding body of knowledge about the world, including, most recently, numerous advances in the modern sciences, such as evolutionary theory. We have also been able to confirm the basic postulates of evolutionary theory in numerous, powerful ways and in many distinctive and surprising contexts[18]—but always, it should be remembered, by employing our human capacities for cognitive judgment. Evolutionary theory has, in turn, allowed us to frame a novel set of naturalistic questions about the origins and evolutionary explanations of these capacities and to propose a particular causal-historical explanation of what made these capacities so reproductively advantageous to our ancestors. The explanation is itself highly plausible given everything we know about the world, and it would—if true—give us a new and nonobvious set of reasons to think that we are creatures with cognitive capacities that can be relied on to track facts about the natural world with some reliability. This explanation has thus been called "vindicating," but the capacities we have "vindicated" in this way are just those capacities that we used to develop and test evolutionary theory in the first place and to develop the broad forms of knowledge that render this particular evolutionary explanation plausible. Hence, it should be clear that this form of vindication is circular.

At the same time, however, this particular circle is so large and so contingent upon such a wide constellation of empirical findings that—absent certain incredible possibilities (such as the existence of a miraculously intelligent and inexplicably devious deity)—it is hard to imagine how our use of these capacities could have led to the development of both evolutionary theory and this particular evolutionary account of our capacities for cognitive judgment if these capacities had not been in some kind of working order all along. When inquiring into the credibility of our human capacities, we also have no choice but to use these capacities, and so it is hard to see how we could ever break out of this particular type of circularity. Rather than denying these facts, let us therefore stipulate that vindicating explanations can be circular but must be nontrivially so if they are to count as genuinely vindicating in our sense of the term.[19]

A third limitation of vindicating explanations is that their vindicating force sometimes becomes apparent only under certain descriptions. This potential problem arises from the fact that natural functions can sometimes be described in more than one way. Earlier, for example, I presented both a long and a shorthand way of describing the same proposed natural function of our capacities for cognitive judgment, and one might have also described their natural function in much more general terms (though much more unhelpfully) as that of simply conducing to the reproductive success of ancestral humans. Although this possibility of multiple descriptions is real, it is in no way limitless, because any specification of a natural function must be framed with the appropriate concepts and at an appropriate level of generality to function as part of a correct evolutionary explanation of the trait with which it is associated. Still, this possibility means that the correct evolutionary explanation of a particular capacity for judgment might in principle appear vindicating under some descriptions but not others. To address this problem, let us therefore stipulate that the correct evolutionary explanation of a capacity for judgment will be called "vindicating" either if it is vindicating on its face or if it shows the capacity in question to have a natural function that can be redescribed in a way that would render it vindicating on its face. We should also acknowledge that the vindicating force of an evolutionary explanation can sometimes remain opaque to us until we have hit on the right description.

A fourth and final limitation on vindicating explanations relates to their possible incompleteness. We need to recognize, in particular, that the existence of a vindicating explanation cannot logically foreclose the possibility of competing evolutionary explanations, either of the same trait or of some of its parts. Until now, I have sometimes been speaking more simply, as if our capacities for cognitive judgment might have only one natural function, but

—while this is certainly possible—natural selection often operates in much more complicated ways. Sometimes a single trait will have more than one natural function, in which case we should expect to see evidence of how natural selection has shaped the trait in more than one way. In addition, the forces of natural selection are in no way limited to treating all adaptations separately, and so adaptations can often deploy or redeploy certain parts of other adaptations but not the whole—in which case the web of interactions can obviously become incredibly complex. Then there is the possibility that many biological phenomena may have no natural function at all or may be susceptible only to certain nonselective classes of evolutionary explanation. Finally, one should remember that an explanation in terms of natural selection does nothing on its own to establish just how well a given trait is adapted to its natural function. We should always expect some imperfection, and it will always be an empirical question just how much imperfection is species typical.

So what should we say about facts like these? Insofar as we can discover a vindicating explanation of a particular class of judgments, I think we should still consider the explanation to have some vindicating force, for all of the reasons already discussed. It will nevertheless be an empirical question whether this explanation is the sole (or even predominant) explanation of the capacity in question, how well the capacity is adapted to this particular natural function, and what, if any, other evolutionary explanations are part of a fuller story. As we fill in the details of a fuller story, we should also be able to make better and better judgments as to when precisely we should credit the judgments we make when using a particular capacity for human judgment. Still, the fact that our current understanding can always be improved does not mean that we should reject our best current understanding. We should, instead, view it as a work in progress, which might always be improved by new or better evolutionary findings.

With these four qualifications in mind, we are now ready to ask whether there is a useful distinction to be drawn between these so-called vindicating explanations and what I will now introduce as an example of a "debunking" explanation. Consider the well-documented fact that, cross-culturally, men engage in increased rates of infanticide when they are parenting a child that does not look like their own.[20] This is an unfortunate fact and one that offends our moral sensibilities, but it is also one that has a highly plausible evolutionary explanation. Human parenting is an incredibly costly affair, in both material and biological terms, and a behavioral tendency of this kind would have plausibly conduced to the reproductive success of ancestral men by allowing them to better channel their costly parenting efforts toward children who were genetically related to them.

Although we do not know the precise proximate mechanisms that motivate this infanticidal behavior, assume—for purely heuristic purposes—that natural selection has produced this behavioral tendency by disposing men to form the cognitive belief that any children that they are parenting but who do not look like their own are not fully human. A belief like this would not directly motivate infanticide, but it would remove a belief that might ordinarily prevent a father from engaging in infanticide—thus plausibly creating the behavioral tendency in question. What we would then have is an adaptation that functions to promote the reproductive success of men by coopting their cognitive faculties in a specific set of circumstances and disposing them to believe that certain children are not fully human.

It should nevertheless be clear that this explanation lacks the properties of the earlier one, which rendered it vindicating. If we define p as the proposition that a particular child is not fully human and if a man were to form the cognitive judgment that p by employing the particular capacities under discussion here, then the present explanation would give us a nonobvious set of evolutionary reasons for thinking that—however intuitive the cognitive belief that p might appear to those who have formed it—no fact that p played any role in causing the belief that p, let alone through a psychological process that reliably tracks the truth. The explanation thus would undermine the purported objectivity of this class of beliefs and would establish the beliefs to be mere projections of our evolved psychologies (where by "projection" I mean a belief that is susceptible to a psychological explanation that reveals the existence of the belief to be significantly unrelated to its truth value). I will therefore call this sort of explanation "debunking," and I will also call an explanation "debunking" if it reveals that we are psychologically disposed so as to treat certain classes of judgments with an authority that we cannot accept upon considered reflection.

In considering whether it is useful to distinguish between these two types of explanations, despite the many limitations of vindicating explanations, we should notice that all four of these limitations apply in some form to debunking explanations, as well. As an initial matter, the distinction between a vindicating and a debunking explanation should always be made conditional on the same conditioning propositions—at least with respect to any given class of judgments—so as to ensure that the terms are drawing a common distinction. Strictly speaking, the explanation in question here is debunking only on condition that our cognitive judgments and cognitive beliefs ought to aim at truth about the natural world (which is one of the conditioning propositions upon which our earlier vindicating explanation depended). Indeed, absent this conditioning proposition, we would be unable to disclaim the objective purport of the cognitive judgment that p because the capacity in question does in fact dispose men to form cognitive judgments that track natural facts of a kind. The facts in question are facts about the genetic relatedness of a child rather than its humanity, however, and these are therefore the wrong facts to capture the purported objectivity of our cognitive beliefs—conditional, once again, on the assumption that our cognitive beliefs ought to track the truth.

Second, the debunking explanation under discussion here is circular, because its power to debunk in this single instance depends heavily on certain forms of evolutionary reasoning and other cognitive judgments and hence on some vindication of our capacities for cognitive judgment in their more general employment. The present explanation thus inherits all of the circularities of our earlier vindicating explanation of these capacities. But the circularity here, as before, is highly nontrivial.

Third, the potential for multiple descriptions is always a potential problem for debunking explanations, because the vindicating nature of an explanation can—as noted earlier—sometimes remain opaque to us under certain descriptions. Strictly speaking, we should therefore conclude that the explanation here is debunking only if we are convinced that it assigns a natural function to this particular psychological disposition that cannot be redescribed as vindicating. We can be very confident of that in the present case, however, because the explanation in question shows that p is not part of a reliable causal process that generates the cognitive judgment that p, and because a child's lack of humanity (which is perfectly correlated with the truth value of p) is only barely correlated with the child's genetic unrelatedness to any particular man.

And, fourth, just as in the case of vindicating explanations, the mere existence of a debunking explanation can do nothing to foreclose the logical possibility of other, competing evolutionary explanations of the same trait or some of its parts. These other explanations can be either vindicating or debunking, and, indeed, if we combine the two explanations discussed thus far in this section, we will see how multiple evolutionary explanations can sometimes come together to simultaneously vindicate and debunk a single capacity for judgment in different circumstances of employment.

Hence, the two explanations developed in this section—one "vindicating" and the other "debunking"—share a common set of features and limitations. If both were valid, it should nevertheless be clear that they would highlight an important difference between our cognitive capacities in different circumstances of employment. This difference would also give us clear but nonobvious reasons to credit the judgments produced in these different circumstances somewhat differently—reasons that would exist independent of all of the limitations inherent in the present distinction. At the end of the day, it is the usefulness of this distinction to identify credibility differences like these that warrants our use of the terms "vindicating" and "debunking" to name it.

3. THE TWO FACES OF MORAL COGNITION AND ACTION

Our real concern in this essay is with moral judgments. In this section, I will extend the distinction developed in the last section between vindicating and debunking evolutionary explanations from the context of our cognitive to our moral judgments.

Moral Judgments and the Resolution of Social-Contract Problems

Let me begin, as before, by presenting a hypothetical explanation of our capacities for moral judgment, which might arguably qualify as vindicating, and then explain why I think it should in fact qualify for that title. To do so, I need to briefly describe some of my prior work, which argues that the natural function of our sense of moral obligation is to allow us to resolve social-contract problems flexibly. Because I have developed these arguments in great depth elsewhere and because our purpose here is to consider only the meta-ethical consequences of different evolutionary accounts of morality on the assumption that they are true (rather than to establish their truth value), I will rehearse only the main steps of the arguments here. I want to present just enough to render the explanation plausible and, hence, worthy of the attention we will be giving it. Readers interested in a more detailed exposition should consult "The Deep Structure of Law and Morality."

To get the argument started, we need to make two assumptions. First, we need to assume that we have psychological capacities that allow us to detect natural facts about what is in our (nonmoral) objective interests (or personal welfare) and respond to these facts by acting in ways that will promote our personal welfare.[21] These capacities need not be perfect, but we need to assume, second, that they conduced to the reproductive success of our ancestors by virtue of helping our ancestors promote their respective (nonmoral) objective interests. To say this is just to say that these psychological capacities are adaptations for the promotion of our personal welfare—or, alternatively, that the natural function of these capacities is to dispose us to promote our own personal welfare.

These assumptions should be highly plausible, at least in some form. They can nevertheless be specified in numerous different ways, depending on how one defines a person's (nonmoral) objective interests (or personal welfare), and only one of these specifications is likely to be psychologically true of us. Our primary concern here is nevertheless with the concepts of right and wrong, and I do not want my arguments here to depend on any particular account of personal welfare. I have therefore crafted the arguments in this section to work for any account of personal welfare so long as the two assumptions mentioned hold true for it.

The concept of a person's nonmoral objective interests can now be used to define a standard of individual rationality, against which it makes sense to inquire whether organisms with capacities like these would face any recurrent and identifiable game-theoretic situations in their environment of evolutionary adaptation. A moment's reflection will show that these organisms would, in fact, face a specific set of game-theoretic problems that are by now well understood: namely n-person prisoners' dilemmas. They would face these situations any time they encountered what we commonly think of as a "social-contract problem"—that is, anytime each could do better (as assessed in terms of his or her personal welfare) by following a rule on condition that all (or a majority of) others were similarly motivated but each could do better still if all (or a majority of) others were so motivated while he or she was motivated to pursue only his or her own personal welfare.[22] Because we have stipulated that our capacities to promote our personal welfare are adaptations, the promotion of personal welfare will also correlate with the promotion of individual reproductive success. Hence, organisms that began from this starting point would do better in terms of reproductive success if they all had the capacities to resolve these social-contract problems than if none did. In the right circumstances, natural selection might therefore favor the production of shared capacities that functioned to motivate us by certain rules, which in fact resolve social-contract problems, independent of our sense of personal welfare.

Of course, the fact that natural selection could produce such adaptations does not mean that it will. The capacities needed to resolve these social-contract problems would undoubtedly be very complex and would need to include, at minimum, a shared sense of the content of certain rules that in fact resolve social-contract problems (as defined by the metric of personal welfare under consideration), along with effective motivations to act in conformity with these rules even when those actions would undermine our sense of personal welfare. To the extent that these motivations are conditioned on the motivations of others, these capacities would also need to include a mutually concordant system of expectations of one another's behavior (along with a mechanism to ensure that these expectations remain coordinated).[23] Still, natural selection regularly produces adaptations that can literally stymie the human imagination, and hence there is nothing about the sheer complexity of these capacities that should rule out the possibility of their existence.

The more relevant question is whether it is empirically plausible that our sense of moral obligation might have this particular natural function. Right from the start, one might think that there is a problem with this claim. Because social-contract problems have the underlying game-theoretic structure of an n-person prisoner's dilemma, any decisions to cooperate (i.e., to follow the rules of the social contract) will be "strictly dominated" by the selfish alternative (i.e., by the decision not to follow the rules)—to use the language of rational-choice theory. (To say that these decisions will be "strictly dominated" is to say that, regardless of what others do, each would do better in terms of his or her own personal welfare not to follow the rules.)[24] Because we have stipulated that the standard of personal welfare under discussion here correlates with reproductive success, this means that the capacities described thus far would also be "evolutionarily altruistic": they would regularly dispose us to act in ways that conduce to the reproductive benefits of some other organisms at some cost to our own.[25] Traits that are evolutionarily altruistic are, however, not evolutionarily stable: they are subject to subversion from within by other traits that are more evolutionarily selfish. These more selfish traits would give each of their bearers reproductive advantages relative to the evolutionary altruists in a population, even if all would do better if all were evolutionary altruists than if none were. As so far described, the psychological capacities to resolve social-contract problems under discussion here should therefore be evolutionarily unstable— which should count against the empirical plausibility of the present proposal.

Rather than viewing considerations like these to be disqualifying, however, one might notice that they can be used to derive a concrete set of empirical predictions that must accompany the present proposal and that might therefore be used to test the present proposal in a more direct and concrete manner. We now know enough about the evolution of altruism that we can articulate the general conditions under which capacities with seemingly evolutionarily altruistic properties can arise and remain evolutionarily stable in nature. If we call organisms with seemingly evolutionarily altruistic traits "cooperators" and those that lack these traits "noncooperators," then Bryan Skyrms has observed that positive correlation among cooperators is the general feature that allows all of the mechanisms that we currently understand to produce traits with seemingly evolutionarily altruistic properties.[26]

We can, however, go one step deeper than Skyrms by noticing the following. The *reason* that positive correlation captures something important in the evolutionary dynamics is that it helps to ensure that any benefits of the cooperative enterprises that are produced by evolutionarily altruistic traits flow primarily to other cooperators. A positive correlation is, in fact, sufficient to allow for the evolution of altruism only if the increased benefits that cooperators obtain from their cooperative effort due to the positive correlation are larger than both the costs involved with cooperating and the benefits, if any, that noncooperators also obtain from the cooperative enterprise. But this suggests that what is fundamental is not positive correlation itself but, rather, this relational property concerning the distributions of evolutionary costs and cooperative benefits among cooperators and noncooperators. Where this distribution is not guaranteed by kin-selective forces or by mechanisms external to the group, a basic evolutionary stability condition for these capacities is thus that the cooperators must share internal psychological mechanisms that function to identify and exclude noncooperators from the benefits of the cooperative enterprises, either by preventing sufficient cooperative benefits from flowing to noncooperators or by engaging in precommitted acts of punishment that make noncooperation sufficiently costly. A natural capacity to resolve social-contract problems could—in other words—remain evolutionarily stable if failures to cooperate were to trigger emotions or other powerful impulses that would function to identify and exclude noncooperators from the benefits of the social contract. And this means that the present proposal —which suggests that the natural function of our sense of obligation is to allow us to resolve social-contract problems flexibly— will ultimately gain in empirical plausibility to the degree that we can find evidence of second-order psychological phenomena like these bound up with our sense of moral obligation.

As I have discussed in more detail elsewhere, we do see just these sorts of second-order psychological mechanisms in phenomena like the moral reactive attitudes (such as resentment and impartial anger) that tend to accompany our sense of moral violation; in the cross-cultural reactions that anthropologists have documented to the breach of informal communal norms (which can include ridicule, ostracism, physical sanctioning, exile, and sometimes even group killings of norm violators); in the way the law responds to the breach of legal obligations; and even in the behavior of many other social creatures that appear to have solved the evolutionary problem of cooperation and that encounter relevant instances of species typical noncooperation.[27] Given that our natural sense of moral obligation also attaches us to rules that often require some self-sacrifice, that the rules in question often reflect plausible resolutions to social-contract problems, and that we take these rules to have a certain generality and overriding authority to them (which we take to operate independent of our sense of personal welfare), these facts should therefore give some real empirical plausibility to the claim that the natural function of our sense of moral obligation is to allow us to resolve social-contract problems of some kind.

In "The Deep Structure of Law and Morality," I also trace out a number of other empirical predictions that should flow from the claim that the natural function of our sense of moral obligation is to allow us to resolve social-contract problems flexibly. When combined with a number of other highly plausible propositions about us and our environment of evolutionary adaptation, we should predict that our sense of obligation would attach us to relatively simple rules; that we would tend to formulate these rules in agent-centered rather than agent-neutral terms; that the attitudes that get us to identify and exclude noncooperators would be sensitive to a range of standard excuses; and that these attitudes would be bound up with psychosocial mechanisms that function (sometimes unconsciously) to shift our views of the right, so as to better track the changing social-contract problems that we face, but only through processes that tend to preserve a sufficient modicum of both interpersonal coordination over the content of the right and intrapersonal commitment to that shared content.[28] I will not rehearse these arguments here, but I mention them in this context because we do see phenomena like these accompanying our sense of moral obligation.[29] In their more developed form, arguments like these can therefore lend additional empirical plausibility to the present proposal.

Let us therefore explore the possibility that the natural function of our sense of moral obligation is to allow us to resolve social-contract problems flexibly. Before asking whether we should understand this explanation as vindicating our associated capacities for moral judgment, I need to make a few more comments about the finer features of the moral psychology being proposed.

On the present view, our sense of moral obligation should be understood as composed of both a facially cognitive and a deeply motivational part, which come together to serve a single natural function. The facially cognitive part disposes us to form moral judgments that seem to assign a special property to certain actions, and the deeply motivational part disposes us to treat that special property as having a complex set of practical implications in our lives. We can see these practical implications when, for example, people take moral obligations to be intrinsically motivating or to have general applicability or overriding practical authority. We can also see these practical implications when people make demands of one another or hold one another accountable or responsible for various breaches of a moral code. Practical implications like these are, in fact, the very same ones that we typically associate with the special practical authority of morality. Hence, our sense of moral obligation should be understood as including a distinctive capacity for moral judgment, which plays a critical role in structuring a highly recognizable and patterned form of human moral life. To try to understand this aspect of our lives as just another manifestation of our instrumental rationality would be to miss something important. We not only would miss a distinctive set of social and psychological categories, which can do real and independent explanatory work, but also would fail to see the special ways in which our sense of moral obligation structures a distinctive form of human social life and interaction.

To highlight these last points, I have sometimes called the psychological attitudes that go into our sense of obligation "obligata" —which is a term that should both keep their relationship to our sense of obligation clear and remind people that they are best understood as complex bundles of belief and desire-like states, along with attitudes toward and expectations of other persons and a portfolio of familiar moral emotions, which come together to produce a highly coordinated form of human social life—much like the obligato accompaniments of a larger musical performance. I have argued that obligata breathe life into our moral and legal practices and that they are the attitudes we express when we use the special normative terminology that morality and law share. In my view, obligata are also one of the central attitudes that H. L. A. Hart was trying to point to when he spoke of the "internal point of view" —or the perspective we take up when we believe that morality or law give rise to genuine obligations.[30] (I say "one" of the central attitudes because Hart also used the term "internal point of view" to refer to the attitude we take up toward rules more generally when we take them to be authoritative.)[31] Quite understandably, Hart was, however, unable to describe the psychology of obligation in as much naturalistic detail as we should be able to now.

Moral Facts, Objectivity, and Epistemic Access

So much, then, for background. What I want to suggest now is that, if the explanation just introduced were in fact the correct evolutionary explanation of our sense of moral obligation, then this explanation would vindicate the objectivity of our capacities for moral judgment in roughly the same way that we were able to vindicate the objectivity of our capacities for cognitive judgment. To see this, let us begin by defining m as the natural property that an action has insofar as it conforms to a behavioral regularity that would conduce to the personal welfare of each person in a group if conformed to by all (or a majority) of the other members of a group but insofar as its personal performance would prove costly to each, absent the kinds of secondary psychological mechanisms that stabilize obligata. This is a very complicated natural property, and it might therefore seem implausible that we would have special capacities to apprehend it. If, however, when employing our capacities for moral judgment, we were to form the judgment that a particular action is morally required, then the present explanation would provide us with just the right kind of surprising and nonobvious evolutionary reasons to conclude that facts about the property m (and, in particular, about whether this action has the property m) likely played a causal role in producing this moral judgment via a psychological process that reliably tracks this particular class of natural facts. We could infer this for two reasons. First, the fact that our capacities for moral judgment tracked actions with the property m, within our environment of evolutionary adaptation, would be part of the correct evolutionary explanation for why those capacities arose and proliferated through our species in the first place—thus making the property m an indispensable part of the correct explanation for the judgments these capacities produce; second, the present explanation would establish that the natural function of these capacities is to continue to track the property m with some reliability. Hence, the present explanation would reveal that our capacities for moral judgment are objective in the sense that they respond to a class of natural facts that exist independently of our perception of the facts.

Of course, no such account of objective moral judgment would be complete without some explanation of how we might have epistemic access to this particular class of natural facts. In the present context, it is therefore especially important to recognize that the causal routes by which the property m might interact with our capacities for moral judgment can be incredibly complex and highly indirect. For example, we would appear to have some innate sense of the salience of certain moral rules, many of which (such as rules prohibiting deception, wanton violence, or the breaking of promises) plausibly reflect resolutions to very common social-contract problems that we faced throughout most of our hunter-gatherer pasts. The property m should be understood as interacting with our capacities for moral judgment not directly and in the moment in these cases but, rather, indirectly, by having played a causal role in shaping the psychological capacities that produce this sense of moral salience.

The wide range of moral views exhibited in the larger ethnographic record suggests that our moral views are, however, also highly susceptible to cultural influence, and we tend to learn our first comprehensive moral code from the community into which we are born (much as we learn our first language). If things have been working well all along, then this moral code should—on the present assumptions—already be well adapted to solving the more particular social-contract problems that this particular community has faced. But this raises the question of how our moral codes might evolve so as to keep track of the property m through changing circumstances.

One peculiarity of our moral psychologies that deserves special

mention, in this regard, is that we are apparently inclined to believe that our moral judgments, if true, are uniquely, universally,
and timelessly true—even though a look at the facts clearly shows
that different communities develop different moral codes and that
their moral codes often evolve over time (much as do their languages). This deeper fact of moral pluralism is perfectly consistent
with the present proposal because more than one moral code can
resolve social-contract problems and because we have been posit-
ing a flexible capacity to resolve social-contract problems, which
should tend to produce some variation among the moral codes
of different groups. Still, the problem of how we might adapt
our moral codes to changing circumstances is a potentially difficult one for the present view. The present view suggests that our
capacities to resolve social-contract problems are stabilized by
second-order psychological mechanisms that function to identify
and exclude noncooperators from the benefits of these cooperative enterprises and that these noncooperators are identified in
part by their breaches of a shared moral code. If the moral views of
the various members of a hunter-gatherer band were highly uncoordinated in ancestral circumstances, then their moral psychologies would have therefore tended to produce a particular kind of
friction and instability: each member of a highly uncoordinated
hunter-gatherer band would have perceived various actions of
the others to be in breach of his or her own personal moral views
and to react accordingly, while each of the other members of the
group would have perceived many of these very same reactions to
be unwarranted (because they would not have shared the same
moral views) and would have reacted to them in ways that would
tend to lead to escalating cycles of conflict and violence. In order
to adapt their moral codes in the right way, our ancestors would
have therefore needed a special set of psychosocial mechanisms
that allowed them to change their views so as to better track the
property m in a more coordinated fashion—that is, while still preserving both a sufficient modicum of interpersonal coordination
over the content of the moral code within each band, and a sufficient modicum of intrapersonal commitment by each member to
that shared content over time.

As I have discussed elsewhere (drawing heavily on Allan Gibbard's work), one plausible set of psychosocial processes that might

allow for just this type of flexibility are the processes of moral discussion and moral disagreement themselves.[32] In cases of moral
discussion and moral disagreement, we sometimes press claims
that appear to serve our personal interests, but we are also apparently unwilling to be pushed too far, and we seem to have some
sense of when various claimants are being unfair or overreaching. At least in the context of discussions with people whom we
perceive to be members of our primary moral community, we also
sometimes leave these interactions with more agreement than
when we began—even if that agreement cannot be derived from
any reasons we antecedently accepted.[33] These facts suggest that
moral disagreement (including fundamental moral disagreement)
may itself be serving a natural function by helping us adapt our
moral views in a coordinated fashion so that they will remain sensitive to the changing interests and problems of a community. Psychosocial mechanisms like these might have worked quite well in
the context of small hunter-gatherer bands, where persistent and
prolonged face-to-face discussion between all the members would
have been the norm and where continuity in lifestyle (as well as
the relatively simple social structure needed for cooperation in
small groups) may have made it relatively unimportant to be able
to rapidly shift the content of our moral views. If processes like
these do indeed serve these natural functions, then the property
m should be understood as causally interacting with our capacities for moral judgment through forms of moral discussion and
moral disagreement that naturally function to bring our changing
interests, experiences, and problems to bear on the content of our
moral codes in the right way.

We also develop our moral views by reflecting on them, by trying to harmonize them and resolve inconsistencies between them,
by arguing about the factual and moral assumptions upon which
they rest, by trying to articulate the deeper principles that animate
them, and in many other related ways. Our tendencies to develop
our moral views in these additional ways should make sense, on
the present assumptions, because all natural facts (including facts
about whether various actions have the property m) are subject to
logic and explanation. For similar reasons, the present proposal
would explain why we embed our moral judgments in more complex logical and syntactic structures and combine them in forms

of moral reasoning that obey the standard rules of logic. When we do these sorts of things, the property m might be understood as causally interacting with our faculties for moral judgment by, first, making itself known in more limited and piecemeal ways and then, second, allowing us to draw out the true implications of our limited knowledge.

Some of these last remarks are, of course, speculative, but my purpose here is just to illustrate some of the highly complex and indirect ways in which the property m might in principle causally interact with our capacities for moral judgment. As in the case of our cognitive capacities, we should be able to develop a more complete and accurate naturalistic description of the psychological processes through which we form moral judgments. Let us call this complete and accurate description the "psychology of moral cognition." The critical point to recognize, for present purposes, is that we do not need to know precisely how our psychology of moral cognition functions in order to conclude that, by whatever (conscious or unconscious) means it employs, it is likely to be tracking the property m with some reliability, even through changes in moral content. We could instead draw this conclusion directly from the fact (if it is indeed a fact) that the natural function of our sense of moral obligation is to allow us to resolve social-contract problems flexibly (where this proposition is taken to include reference to a subcapacity to form moral judgments that plays its more particular role by naturally tracking facts about the property m). We could then infer the truth of this functional attribution from the fact that it provides the best explanation of a broad range of features of our sense of moral obligation. (This is, in effect, what I was arguing earlier and, in much more detail, in my prior work. It is, moreover, precisely at this stage that evolutionary considerations can advance debates over the plausibility of naturalistic forms of moral realism, because evolutionary considerations can help solidify and broaden the explanatory credentials of the moral property that I am citing.) Hence, the present evolutionary explanation would allow us to understand our ordinary forms of moral reasoning and moral cognition as having some reliability at tracking this particular class of natural facts, and we could begin to study the systematic ways in which our psychology of moral cognition functions as part of a naturalized approach to moral epistemology.

The present account would also allow us to revive a highly contemporary version of an old-fashioned (and much discredited) view of how our moral capacities work. We could say, with a perfectly straight face, that we have a "special moral sense" or "a special faculty of moral perception," which disposes us to "see" (in a clear but metaphorical sense of the word) various moral facts in part by getting us to see certain actions in a special moral light. To the oft-repeated charge that this moral vision would be nothing more than a projection of our psychologies,[34] we could respond that the psychologies we are projecting are ones that reliably track a specific class of natural facts. Hence, this moral vision would be more than just projection and would have a form of objectivity to it that parallels that of ordinary cognition. To the familiar charge that knowledge of these natural facts would require implausible or mysterious epistemic capacities,[35] we could answer that we have just provided a plausible naturalistic account of how we might have capacities that are specially adapted to give us epistemic access to these facts. As it turns out, the present account would also allow us to account for moral progress in terms of epistemic convergence on moral truth—and thereby offer a more realist alternative to the account of moral progress developed by Kitcher in this volume.[36] (The present account would be a bit closer to the one developed by Peter Railton,[37] although it would cite a natural property that is picked out by a contractualist, rather than a utilitarian, standard of the right. Like Kitcher's account, the present account would also avoid naturalistic fallacies.) And, to the question of how facts like these might plausibly motivate us to action, we could say that the present account explains exactly why we should expect to be psychologically constituted so as to allow this particular class of facts to play a special (moral) regulatory role in our lives.

The present account therefore would do the first half of the work that one might expect of a vindicating explanation by showing the purported objectivity of our moral judgments to be grounded in something suitably real and epistemically accessible. It would also explain why we take moral facts to have the special practical authority that we do.

Examining the Conditioning Propositions

This brings us to the second half of what one might expect of a vindicating explanation in the present context, which is that it should give us some reason to believe that we are giving the right class of facts this special practical authority in our lives. Let us begin by acknowledging more explicitly that the property m is a natural property upon which a fundamentally contractualist account of the right supervenes.[38] If the present explanation of our capacities for moral judgment is right, then we humans are therefore disposed to give a particular class of natural facts, which is picked out by a fundamentally contractualist standard of the right, the special practical authority that we typically associate with moral facts. Hence, the evolutionary explanation under discussion will be genuinely vindicating only on condition that this contractualist standard picks out the right class of facts to be given this special practical authority.

That the present vindicating explanation is conditioned on certain further propositions about authority is—of course—nothing new. We saw the same type of conditionality when we examined the earlier vindicating explanation of our capacities for cognitive judgment. It nevertheless makes sense to pause, at this point, to ask whether this new conditionality is problematic in this new context. There is, moreover, at least one special ground for potential concern. This new conditioning proposition appears to commit us to a substantive (and controversial) position in normative ethics: namely to a specific version of contractualism. At first glance, the vindicating nature of the present explanation might therefore seem to depend upon the rejection of many other plausible moral theories, such as the entire family of utilitarian theories and certain other versions of contractualism.

Let me nevertheless mention three general sets of considerations, which should—in combination—justify our reliance on this particular contractualist standard for present purposes. Our present purposes—it should be remembered—are to develop and defend a plausible distinction between "vindicating" and "debunking" explanations of our human capacities for moral judgment, which can be used to distinguish the level of credit we should give to different employments of this capacity as part of a larger, naturalized approach to moral epistemology.

First, one of the most common methods that people use to try to justify various theoretical accounts of morality is to argue that we would adopt them when seeking to place our first-order moral judgments into what is commonly referred to as "narrow reflective equilibrium."[39] Sometimes, this goal is mentioned explicitly, but—even when it is not—it often describes the basic form of argumentation that is being employed. The goal of this sort of process is to articulate a theoretical account of morality that would render our first-order moral judgments maximally coherent. Although the term "contractualism" (like the term "utilitarianism") ultimately refers to a broad family of views, contractualist theories have—on the whole—tended to fare much better than direct, act utilitarian theories at rendering the broadest range of our first-order moral judgments coherent. The present explanation of our capacities for moral judgment would, in fact, predict just this sort of asymmetry. If the natural function of our sense of moral obligation were to allow us to resolve social-contract problems flexibly, then we should expect that, in the process of seeking to place our first-order moral judgments into narrow reflective equilibrium, we would be naturally led to a contractualist principle that supervenes on the property m. The present explanation would thus provide us with a nonobvious set of evolutionary reasons to think that the contractualist standard under discussion would coherently explain the broadest range of our first-order moral judgments and intuitions.

The process of seeking narrow reflective equilibrium is, of course, inherently circular, but it is not trivially so. To the extent that many substantive debates in normative ethics rely on this particular type of reasoning, they will, in any event, share this same kind of circularity. The present considerations should therefore rule out the plausibility of any successful challenges to the contractualist standard under discussion based on this common form of argumentation—assuming, as we have been, the validity of the present evolutionary explanation. There is, moreover, always a legitimate question as to why we ought to render our moral views coherent in the first place, and the present explanation would answer that question by revealing our capacities for moral judgment to be tracking facts about the natural world (as opposed to, for example, just expressing emotions). Hence, this first set of considerations should give us some initial confidence in our reliance on the present contractualist standard for present purposes.

Second, one might try to reflect more deeply on some of the general properties that any principle ought to have if it is to qualify as an appropriate standard for moral judgment. The goal, at this second stage, should be to articulate properties that are independent of our first-order moral judgments about right and wrong so as not to duplicate any part of the process of placing these judgments into narrow reflective equilibrium.

Let me mention three such properties, which should be relatively uncontroversial, in part because they will be stated in such highly general terms. In order for any theoretical principle that we might settle upon in the process of seeking narrow reflective equilibrium to qualify as a plausible moral principle, that principle should, at minimum, (1) reflect some adequate sensitivity to persons and their welfare, (2) display that sensitivity in a relevantly equal or impartial form, and (3) pick out rules of action that we can identify and respond to given our ordinary human capacities for judgment. The contractualist standard under discussion here has all three of these basic properties, and it is therefore a plausible theoretical account of morality. These facts should give the present explanation some additional vindicating force. We would —after all—be in a very different situation if the evolutionary explanation under discussion here were to reveal our capacities for moral judgment to be governed by a principle that is not even plausibly moral in the present sense.

But it should be equally clear that many different principles have these three basic properties. Not only do many different versions of contractualism have them, but many different versions of utilitarianism do, too. (Indeed, it is facts like these that help to explain why these two families of theories remain the most plausible contenders for theoretical accounts of the right.) The fact that general properties like these cannot be used to pick out a single moral principle as uniquely valid is certainly of interest, but it need not undermine our present project. We might instead just concede this fact and refer to the different capacities for judgment that would be governed by these different principles as different logically possible "species" of moral judgment. The present explanation would then reveal our human capacities for moral judgment to be a recogizable species of moral judgment, even if they are not the only logically possible one. We could then proceed to draw the distinction between "vindicating" and "debunking" explanations of our human capacities for moral judgment in a way that we acknowledge to be species typical.

By doing so, we would clarify that the vindicating force of the present explanation does not—strictly speaking—depend on the rejection of a range of competing theoretical accounts of morality. For example, the explanation would be just as deeply vindicating if we were to conclude that there is no genuine fact of the matter as to how to resolve some of these debates between utilitarian and contractualist theorists. Unless there are facts that go beyond both these general features of moral principles and the capacity of some principles to survive the process of achieving narrow reflective equilibrium, it is hard to see what these further facts might be. (In a moment, I will discuss one further set of facts that may be relevant to these debates—as well as to the process of reaching what is sometimes referred to as "wide reflective equilibrium"[40]—but argue that these other considerations do nothing to undermine our reliance on the contractualist standard under discussion in the present context.) Alternatively, even if there is a genuine fact of the matter and even if the contractualist standard under discussion here were to turn out to be false, we presumably would be entitled to understand our human capacities for moral judgment as a deficient species of moral judgment in virtue of the plausibility of the moral principle under consideration. Hence, it would still make sense to inquire into the circumstances in which our capacities for moral judgment are (or are not) a deficient species of moral judgment, and the vindicating force of the present explanation could be preserved in this way, in at least a deficient form.

Third, we should recognize that the explanation offered here would remove some of the deep philosophical concerns that have sometimes led people to favor utilitarian over contractualist accounts of the right—even when the resulting views have either led to highly counterintuitive results or represented philosophically unsatisfying formulations of the view. In "Contractualism and Utilitarianism," T. M. Scanlon has used the term "philosophical utilitarian" to refer to people who are drawn to normative utilitarianism (i.e., to some form of utilitarianism as an account of the right) by the following highly plausible set of philosophical concerns.[41] These are people who find it credible that there might be facts about what makes a person better or worse off; that we might have epistemic access to these facts; and that we might find these facts motivating, in something like the way we think moral facts ought to be. They also observe correctly that facts about human welfare are relevant to morality and play an important role in our moral reasoning. They are, therefore, willing to allow facts about human welfare to qualify as fundamental moral facts, but they find it much more difficult to understand how there could be any other class of fundamental moral facts that might be analogously objective, epistemically accessible, and intrinsically motivating. When trying to give a theoretical account of their moral judgments, these people therefore feel pressured to account for the right in terms of the production of human welfare. Considerations like these have led many people to adopt normative utilitarianism "in spite of the fact that the implications of act utilitarianism are wildly at variance with firmly held moral convictions, while rule utilitarianism, the most common alternative formulation, strikes most people as an unstable compromise."[42]

But the present vindicating explanation would supply just the missing, alternative account of fundamental moral facts needed to avoid this difficult choice. For reasons already discussed, facts about whether actions have the property m are clearly objective, and the present explanation would explain why these facts would be both epistemically accessible and intrinsically motivating to us. The present account would also explain why considerations of human welfare play a role in our moral reasoning: facts about human welfare are relevant to the contractualist standard under discussion, and so we might expect to be psychologically constituted so as to give these facts some weight in our moral reasoning. At the same time, however, facts about human welfare would not be relevant to moral judgment in quite the way the act utilitarian is picturing things. In order to contribute to fundamental moral facts, these facts about human welfare would need to be filtered through a contractualist standard that sometimes rejects the sacrifice of individuals for certain group purposes. Hence, the present account would explain equally well why we are not inclined to follow act utilitarian reasoning to some of its logical extremes. These facts suggest that—if the present vindicating explanation of our capacities for moral judgment were correct—then we should reject many of the deep philosophical concerns that might lead us to reject contractualism and should acknowledge that contractualism provides the best available theoretical account of human morality.

Together, these three sets of considerations thus strike me as powerful enough to render the explanation under discussion "vindicating" in a genuine—though admittedly limited—sense of the word. More specifically, the explanation would reveal our capacities for moral judgment to be governed by a principle that is (i) plausibly moral, that would (ii) render our first-order moral judgments maximally coherent, and that would (iii) supervene on a class of natural facts that are objective, epistemically accessible and intrinsically motivating. If our capacities for moral judgment were to lack any of these three features (and especially (i) or (iii)), then it also seems clear that we should credit the judgments produced by these capacities somewhat differently in our thinking. Hence, we can now define a "debunking" evolutionary explanation of our capacities for moral judgment as any explanation that reveals these capacities to lack one or more of these three features ((i)–(iii)), in at least some circumstances of employment.

Before turning to an example of this phenomenon, we should finally acknowledge that the entire preceding discussion has been assuming the more basic proposition that moral facts exist in the first place (i.e., in the specific sense that there are some facts or other that should be given the special practical authority of morality in our lives). Strictly speaking, this assumption should be considered another conditioning proposition about authority upon which the present vindicating explanation depends. Just as in the case of the vindicating explanation of our capacities for cognitive judgment, we may also have to acknowledge that the present vindicating explanation can do nothing on its own to refute certain forms of extreme moral skepticism.

There is, on the other hand, one very common route to moral skepticism, which proceeds from the same premises of the philosophical utilitarian and tries to distinguish the principles of instrumental rationality (which are to be credited, on this kind of view) from those of morality (which are not) on the ground that only the former can be understood as constituting a plausible, objective, and epistemically accessible practical subject matter. For reasons just discussed, the present vindicating explanation would remove this particular ground for distinction and should therefore provide an answer of sorts to this particular form of moral skepticism. With regard to more extreme forms of practical skepticism (which apply to both instrumental and moral reason), the present vindicating explanation may still lack an answer. But, once again, this fact may ultimately prove to be a limitation of this particular vindicating explanation and not of its vindicating force— if, as one might plausibly think, there are other grounds to reject these extreme forms of practical skepticism.[43] It is, finally, worth remembering that the vindicating explanation of our capacities for cognitive judgment from the preceding section made certain assumptions about the practical authority of our cognitive judgments qua cognitive judgments. Hence, extreme skeptical possibilities like these may not meaningfully distinguish the vindicating explanations of our moral from our cognitive judgments.

More important, however, we should now be able to see that the present vindicating explanation of our capacities for moral judgment exhibits many of the same strengths and many of the same limitations as the earlier vindicating explanation of our capacities for cognitive judgment. The limitations in both cases are real, but, in both cases, the distinction between a "vindicating" and a "debunking" explanation can also clarify a distinctive set of reasons to credit our capacities for human judgment somewhat differently in different circumstances of employment, depending on the type of explanation that is applicable. These credibility distinctions exist independent of the limitations under discussion, and the distinction developed here should therefore work perfectly well for present purposes. These arguments also show that our capacities for moral judgment need not stand on any weaker foundation than our capacities for cognitive judgment. The relative strength of these foundations should, instead, be viewed as raising a largely empirical question.

Debunking Morality's Competitive Nature

With these definitions in hand, let me now introduce a paradigmatic example of a debunking explanation of our capacities for moral judgment. Even if the natural function of our sense of moral obligation were to allow us to resolve social-contract problems flexibly and even if this fact were to vindicate our capacities for moral judgment in their general employment, this fact would do nothing to foreclose the logical possibility that these capacities might sometimes serve other natural functions, as well. What I want to consider now is a very simple but plausible scenario in which these capacities would serve one other natural function in a specific set of circumstances.

As noted earlier, part of the evolutionary stability conditions of obligata (and hence of our sense of moral obligation) is that they are bound up with certain second-order psychological mechanisms, which function to identify and exclude noncooperators from the benefits of our cooperative enterprises. In real life, these secondary mechanisms often operate by mobilizing powerful group sentiments against purported noncooperators. While these sentiments might ordinarily function to stabilize a form of cooperation that reflects a genuine species of moral life, there is nothing in principle to prevent natural selection from coopting these group sentiments for more competitive purposes.

In *Chimpanzee Politics,* Frans de Waal has, in fact, documented the numerous and complex ways that chimpanzees, which typically operate within clearly defined social dominance hierarchies, often form transient political alliances and engage in a wide range of other activities meant to alter the perceived relationships of various members of the group to the hierarchy.[44] In some cases, these activities can lead to the placement of a competitor (or even a former alpha) outside the dominance hierarchy altogether, in which case group sentiments can sometimes be mobilized to bully, dominate, exclude, or even kill the competitor. Given our close relationship to the chimps, it is more than plausible that evolutionary forces have selected for similar competitive impulses in us. Let us therefore assume, for a moment, that evolutionary forces have selected for adaptations in us that sometimes dispose us to manipulate the content of our moral codes (in either conscious or unconscious ways) so as to mobilize powerful group sentiments against competing members of our communities by making them out to be moral noncooperators. If so, then we, too, would be inclined to engage in a kind of chimpanzee politics with the content of our moral codes.

We can identify a number of factors that might help us identify if and when our capacities for moral judgment might plausibly be serving this more competitive natural function. Because our moral psychologies would not be functioning to resolve social-contract problems, many of the views generated by these particular mechanisms would presumably fail a contractualist test. Because our moral psychologies would be functioning not to track a coherent moral reality but rather to further various programs of social domination and exclusion, these same views might predictably be hard to render coherent with a broad range of our other moral views, and we might similarly expect to find ourselves resistant to revising these views when the relevant inconsistencies are pointed out. (We might instead just cling to the idea that some things are "just wrong.") For similar reasons, we might expect to see these judgments operate in a particularly robust way in certain group settings, where commitment to certain social alliances can be developed and displayed. And we might expect to see some evidence of these moral judgments functioning to dominate and exclude certain people from communities who might otherwise appear to have normal levels of moral motivation.

Do we see any examples of phenomena that might plausibly qualify for this sort of description? Consider the view that some people hold that homosexual sexual activity is "just wrong." There are many different versions of this view, but some people who hold it are apparently unwilling to revise it, even when it is revealed to be inconsistent with certain other moral principles that they cherish (such as principles of liberty or tolerance—or, if the view is religiously based, with certain principles of faithful biblical interpretation).[45] The behavior is also harmless to the nonmoral objective interests of others, and most people do not even care to engage in it. Hence, it is not really the kind of behavior that one would either need or want to give up in order to guarantee that all others would, too, and prohibitions against consensual homosexual sexual activity are not very good candidates for resolutions to social-contract problems. Moral judgments about homosexuality are also clearly used to mobilize powerful group sentiments of domination and exclusion. Curiously enough, it is, in fact, often easier to mobilize people's sentiments today around issues like homosexuality than around issues like promise keeping, even though promise keeping would appear to be much more critical to the foundations of moral society.[46] Many of the people who are excluded from communities by these particular moral judgments are, finally, clearly capable of ordinary levels of moral motivation. So, despite the many complexities of this issue, certain moral judgments about homosexuality may provide a good example of the phenomenon in question.[47] Other plausible examples include the broad range of facially moral (and related evaluative) judgments that sometimes play a central role in identity politics and in tribal and ethnic conflict, along with certain thick evaluative concepts (like that of being "weird"), which appear to focus primarily on certain salient but shifting and morally arbitrary differences between the majority in a group and some of its less lucky members. Racial epithets, finally, appear to be a very good example of the phenomenon.[48]

If, in fact, the correct evolutionary explanation of our tendency to form moral (and related evaluative) judgments like these is that these tendencies allow certain members of a group to form alliances and mobilize powerful group sentiments to dominate and exclude others, then this explanation would be debunking in the sense developed in this article. The explanation would provide us with a nonobvious set of evolutionary reasons to think that, if someone were to form a negative moral judgment about another while employing these particular capacities for moral judgment, no facts about the property m (or about any other plausible moral property) would have played a causal role in producing the relevant moral judgment, let alone via a psychological process that reliably tracks a plausible class of moral facts. The explanation would thus give us a nonobvious set of evolutionary reasons for thinking that our capacities for moral judgment are serving a competitive function, rather than inclining us to participate in a recognizable species of moral life. Regardless of how compelling these moral judgments might seem to those who have formed them, the present explanation would therefore reveal them to be mere projections of our competitive natures and to lack the kind of objectivity and special practical authority that our other moral judgments have. (For those who have been keeping track, the explanation would reveal that, in these particular circumstances of employment, our capacities for moral judgment would lack all three of the earlier properties (i)–(iii), which rendered the earlier explanation vindicating.)

Once again, all of the limitations of the earlier vindicating explanation of our capacities for moral judgment should apply, in some form, to the present debunking explanation. For example, both explanations depend (for their vindicating or debunking force, respectively) on the same conditioning propositions, and both are inherently (but nontrivially) circular. Still, if these two explanations were both correct, then they would highlight an important difference between the natural function of our capacities for moral judgment in these two different circumstances of employment. This difference would, moreover, seem to imply that we should credit the different classes of moral judgment produced in these different circumstances somewhat differently in our thinking—at least insofar as we are interested in the moral facts. It follows that credibility differences like these can in fact exist—and can be established with the present methods of argumentation—regardless of the limitations under discussion.

Stepping back for a moment, human morality may therefore have two faces. If we refer to the first part of morality (which is susceptible to evolutionary vindication) as its "Kantian" face, then we might refer to its other, more competitive part as its "Nietzschean" underside. Nietzsche—after all—famously charged that many aspects of our modern moral codes are the product of an epic power struggle that occurred sometime near the dawn of Western history and by which various early Christian groups that had been enslaved by the Romans were able to wrest power from their captors by engaging in a long-term systematic program to revalue the values of the classical world.[49] They did this—in Nietzsche's view—by mobilizing a powerful set of moral sentiments (which he called "ressentiment") against the entire classical way of living. Many of the new moral rules relating to sex and sexuality that were erected in this process would have been foreign to the classical mind, including prohibitions against homosexuality. And Nietzsche believed that many aspects of this new moral code have proven psychologically disastrous for us, because they have led us to live lives wracked with guilt and self-flagellation and have sometimes alienated us from the kinds of attachments needed to give us the will to live. Nietzsche's points about sex and sexuality were, of course, much broader than the one mentioned here, and Nietzsche was famously prone to hyperbolics. Still, it strikes me that the fate of many gay people in the Western world provides a perfectly sober and nonhyperbolic example of the problem that Nietzsche had in mind. We might, in fact, now restate Nietzsche's criticism of morality in our own terms as follows: Nietzsche believed that certain groups in the West have, in effect, been playing chimpanzee politics with our moral codes for some time now and have ended up playing a dangerous game, which has blown up in our face.

At the end of the day, philosophers like Nietzsche may have been a bit too critical of morality and may have missed its better, Kantian face. But philosophers like Kant may have been a bit too charitable and may have missed morality's other side, which is Janus faced. Both sides plausibly exist, and it is ultimately an empirical question which side predominates and when. Further evolutionary and psychological research should therefore help us sort this question out. But, as we pursue that research, the present distinction—between "vindicating" and "debunking" explanations of our capacities for moral judgment—should also clarify the questions that we need to be asking, so we can determine better when our moral psychologies might be serving these two highly opposed natural functions.

4. Moral Illusions and a Naturalized Approach to Moral Epistemology

At the beginning of this essay, I suggested that the views developed here would allow us to understand ourselves as naturally and systematically prone to certain "moral illusions"—which are analogues in the moral domain to the types of optical illusions that sometimes skew our sense of vision. I will now say that we are subject to "moral illusions" whenever we are systematically inclined to maintain false moral judgments (or false judgments about morality) by moral psychological tendencies that either are not susceptible to evolutionary vindication or are susceptible to evolutionary vindication but disserve their natural function in modern circumstances. So defined, moral illusions are more than just errors. They are persistent and species-typical tendencies toward error, which can be especially hard to identify and correct because we are subject to them collectively. Our human species of moral vision is, moreover, the basic lens through which we either bring moral facts sharply into focus or distort them, and so we cannot simply rely on this vision to determine which we are doing.

Given the present definition of moral illusions, the examples that ended the previous section (which construed certain classes of moral judgment as reflecting moral psychological tendencies that serve a competitive, rather than a cooperative, natural function) would be obvious candidates. At least in principle, however, moral illusions can also arise in relation to our perceptions of the status or the appropriate role of moral judgments in our lives, either standing alone or in relation to other systems of obligation, such as legal obligations. They might also arise in tendencies toward judgment that have more to do with practices of claim making (i.e., where we charge one another with having done wrong) than with judgments about the content of right and wrong. Because I have been suggesting that the views developed here might be used to guide a specific, naturalized approach to moral epistemology, which is tutored by our best contemporary evolutionary insights, I want to use this last section to discuss some of these broader potential classes of moral illusion. My goal will be to illustrate these broader potentials by describing several plausible candidates for moral illusions to which we would be subject if our capacities for moral judgment were susceptible to the evolutionary vindication developed in the preceding section. Some such assumption of evolutionary vindication must be made if we are to clarify these broader potentials, because the concept of a moral illusion has been defined in terms of the concept of a vindicating explanation. I will end with some suggestions about how we may need to view the relationship between legal and moral authority if we are to resist certain natural moral illusions, and, in particular, with a distinctive set of reasons to think that the law may sometimes have the independent authority to override morality—even in its correct and conscientious employment.

As a threshold matter, we should notice an important asymmetry: it would be wholly unsurprising if we were much more deeply and problematically prone to moral illusions, in modern circumstances, than to optical illusions. The evolutionary problem of vision goes very deep into our natural history, and its resolution has clearly been critical for the survival of our species. The basic problem that our sense of vision solves has, however, remained largely unchanged throughout most of the course of our natural history, and we might therefore expect that our sense of vision will be relatively well adapted to its natural function even in modern circumstances. When we look at the social problems that we face in the modern world, we will—by contrast—quickly see that current social circumstances mark a radical departure from the most common ones in our environment of evolutionary adaptation. We humans spent most of our natural history not in large-scale nation states with high population densities, laws, and political authorities but in relatively small and independent hunter-gatherer bands. The members of these separate bands typically remained in close, repeat contact with one another over the course of their lifetimes, and, although these bands also tended to have some contact with neighboring bands, this contact appears to have been quite limited. It follows that our natural sense of moral obligation evolved almost entirely in a setting where the predominant social-contract problems that we faced were with other members of a single hunter-gatherer band.

In this setting, there would have been a biological need for coordination over the content of our moral codes within each hunter-gatherer band, for reasons already explained (i.e., to avoid the problems of friction and instability that would have arisen from highly uncoordinated moral views). In the preceding section, I therefore proposed that face-to-face moral discussion and moral disagreement served this natural function in ancestral circumstances by allowing the members of various hunter-gatherer bands to adapt their moral views together so as to better track the property m in a coordinated fashion. But this particular coordinating mechanism would have required sustained opportunities for face-to-face contact among a relatively small and stable group of people, and the rise of agriculture, urbanization, and industrialization changed the basic character of our social relations by vastly increasing human population densities around the world. In these modern circumstances, the psychosocial mechanisms that once functioned to coordinate our moral views in small-group settings are—I would now like to submit—no longer capable, on their own, of producing consensus among these much larger groups of interacting people.

This proposal would provide an evolutionary explanation for why—as John Rawls has observed—our conscientious attempts to reason with one another about the right, under free political institutions, do not always lead to reasonable agreement, even over the long run (unlike our conscientious attempts to reason with one another in the natural sciences).[50] The present account would thus supplement Rawls's explanation of what he calls the "burdens of judgment," or the fact that persons who share a common form of human reason and similar powers of thought and judgment can nevertheless come to different moral conclusions through the correct (and conscientious) exercise of these powers in the ordinary course of political life.[51] Rawls is limited in the means by which he can explain the burdens of judgment,[52] even though he thinks that a public willingness to accept these burdens, along with the corresponding fact of what he calls "reasonable" pluralism (and what I will later call the "deep truth of moral pluralism"), is absolutely critical for the type of public culture needed to support a constitutional regime with free political institutions.[53] On the present view, the burdens of judgment arise not only because of the many ordinary difficulties in determining moral truth[54] but also because we are employing capacities for moral judgment that are naturally adapted to produce coordination only in the types of relatively small, stable, and independent group settings that characterized our long hunter-gatherer pasts. For reasons that I am about to explain, our transitions from hunter-gatherer forms of life and to more modern social conditions have therefore created the perfect conditions for our moral psychologies to begin disserving their natural moral function, in at least some circumstances, and to embroil us in a set of highly interrelated and pernicious forms of moral illusion. In what follows, I will end this essay by describing three plausible classes of this phenomenon.

The first plausible class of moral illusions involves our perceptions (which were mentioned in the previous section) that our moral judgments, if true, are uniquely, universally, and timelessly true. These perceptions appear to be very natural and very difficult for us to shake. Still, the vindicating explanation offered in the previous section of our capacities for moral judgment purported to vindicate only their claim to objectivity and special practical authority, not these further perceptions about their status. The explanation also accounted for the objectivity of our moral judgments in terms of a specific, natural property of actions (namely the property m), which our sense of moral obligation was said to track and which was said to help give moral judgments their truth values. At the same time, however, we noted that social-contract problems typically underdetermine their own solutions; that more than one moral code can pick out actions with the property m; and that the ethnographic record displays many different social groups with many different moral codes, all of which pick out some actions with this special property. Hence, the vindicating explanation under discussion would, if valid, suggest that our further perceptions about the uniqueness, universality, and timelessness of moral truth are—strictly speaking—false. Natural and seemingly inescapable but systematically false judgments like these would appear to be very good candidates for moral illusions.

Even if false, the perception that moral truth is universal may have worked well enough in the context of relatively small and independent hunter-gatherer bands, because universality would have served as a pretty good proxy for generality and because the moral code of any single hunter-gatherer band would have needed to include rules that applied generally to its members. The perception that moral truth is timeless might have also worked well enough so long as the members of these groups could in fact adapt their moral codes to new circumstances through the processes of face-to-face moral discussion and moral disagreement. And the perception that moral truth is unique might have served a valuable function by helping to secure coordination over the content of the moral codes in each hunter-gatherer band. (Note that an explanation of this perception in terms of the biological need for coordination would not vindicate the full objectivity of this perception, because it would explain it in terms of a pragmatic need rather than a natural fact that the perception tracks. The present explanation thus suggests that there is a dimension to perceived moral truth that is merely conventional—even if we are naturally unconscious of the fact. These conventional aspects to perceived moral truth might settle certain logical indeterminacies, but only relative to a group and only by reference to certain contingent

facts about the group's history of experience and moral discussion
and the psychology of its members. Hence, there would be no further fact of the matter that these conventional aspects of our perceptions of moral truth would be tracking, and it is for this reason
that I have been referring to the "deep truth of moral pluralism,"
rather than just to the "fact of reasonable pluralism"—as in Rawls's
formulation of the problem.)

Still, these same perceptions are much more problematic in
modern circumstances, because we must interact with many different people who are relative strangers and who may not share
our moral views. In these circumstances, these same perceptions
can incline us to attribute moral error to other members of our
communities when there is in fact none. They can also make it
especially difficult to see and then keep clearly in focus the full
burdens of judgment and the deep truth of moral pluralism. As
a result, we can easily misconstrue the political ideal of toleration
as requiring us to accept moral error (or perhaps "reasonable"
moral error), rather than the deep truth of moral pluralism—or,
relatedly, we can sometimes be inclined to misconstrue the commitment to tolerance as a form of moral laxity. Moral illusions like
these can be especially pernicious because, even if we recognize
them as illusions on an intellectual level, they do not seem to simply vanish from our perceptions. Much as in the case of optical
illusions, we must keep reminding ourselves of the facts if we hope
to correct for these natural deficiencies in our moral vision.

A second plausible class of moral illusions is related to this first
one but arises more directly in our practices of claim making and
in our psychological capacities to identify moral noncooperators.
I will be arguing that these capacities have made us insufficiently
sensitive to an increasingly important distinction: namely the distinction between people who breach a moral code because they
have insufficient moral motivation and those who breach it because they are motivated by a different moral code.

Remember that moral noncooperators have been defined as
persons who have insufficient moral motivation. For reasons discussed earlier, we also need psychological mechanisms to identify
and exclude these noncooperators from the benefits of our cooperative enterprises, because these mechanisms provide the evolutionary stability conditions for our species of moral life. Clearly,

however, we cannot literally see into one another's heads.[55] Hence, there is an evolutionary design problem as to how we might naturally make these identifications, and one way to answer this question is to offer a purely naturalistic description of the epistemic capacities that we employ for this purpose.

In "The Deep Structure of Law and Morality," I spend some time describing the ways in which we make just these identifications. We appear to rely very heavily on what are, in effect, two distinct classes of evidence. On the one hand, we are inclined to perceive facial instances of the breach of a moral code as evidence of insufficient moral motivation. For example, if one person were to cause another person to die by giving that person poison, we would be inclined to infer that the death was caused by insufficient moral motivation and, hence, by a relevant instance of wrongdoing. (I have taken and modified this example from Aristotle.)[56] There are, however, also a number of regular and predictable circumstances in which any of us, even if we were to have sufficient moral motivation, would act in ways that facially breach a moral code. These circumstances are none other than those of the standard excuses, where the facial breach of the moral code has been caused by something like a mistake of fact, a mistake of consequence (or accident), forces external to us that are beyond our control, duress, certain common and species typical lapses of self-control (like sleep or childhood), and the like. Clearly, it would undermine our cooperative enterprises altogether if we were to exclude all perfectly capable cooperators from our communities, and we are therefore naturally inclined to credit the standard excuses as undermining (or at least significantly mitigating) our prima facie attributions of wrongdoing—at least if we come to believe that the facial breach was caused by one of the standard excusing conditions. Evidence of a standard-excusing condition is thus correctly taken to undermine the validity of the standard inference from breach of a moral code to insufficient moral motivation.

Returning to the modified example from Aristotle, we might learn, for example, that the person who did the poisoning sincerely believed that she was administering medicine that was sorely needed to help the recipient recover from a seizure.[57] We would then conclude that the facial breach was caused by a mistake of fact (which is an excusing condition) and would be naturally inclined to think that the person who did the poisoning did not really mean or intend to do wrong. We would also be naturally inclined to withhold (or at least significantly mitigate) our attributions of blame, wrongdoing, and insufficient moral motivation.

In part for these reasons, Aristotle has suggested that we can use the standard excuses to identify what we typically mean when we say that an action was "voluntary" and is thus one for which one might be held responsible.[58] We take an action to be "voluntary," in his view, just insofar as it was performed without any of the standard excuses. Long ago, however, Aristotle also noticed a highly intriguing feature of our moral psychologies: we are apparently inclined to treat mistakes of fact or consequence as excusing conditions but not analogous mistakes of value or moral content.[59] There is a highly plausible evolutionary explanation for this asymmetry. In ancestral circumstances, all of the adult members of a hunter-gatherer band would have been thoroughly steeped in its traditions and would have been very familiar with the content of its moral code. The views of each band would have also been highly coordinated, and there would have been many fewer occasions for sustained daily interaction with people from other bands that had internalized different moral codes. Hence, it would not have been credible for us to have breached a moral code, in any of our ordinary social interactions, either because of a mistake in moral content or adherence to a different moral code. We are—accordingly—naturally insensitive to these possibilities.

But these same features of our moral epistemic capacities may now be inclining us toward an increasingly problematic form of moral illusion. To see the problem, consider a moral code that requires people to pray twice a day, once at sunrise and once again at sunset. In modern circumstances, people who have internalized this moral code (and whom I will call "praying folk") may encounter two very different types of people who breach this aspect of their moral code in their ordinary social interactions. On the one hand, they may encounter genuine sociopaths in their midst. These are people who are part of their primary moral community but who sometimes fail to pray because they suffer from a more general and problematic lack of moral motivation. On the other hand, these praying folk may encounter people who have ordinary levels of moral motivation but who do not pray because they have internalized a moral code that does not require them to do so. Given our natural moral epistemic capacities, both of these types of people could end up triggering perceptions of prima facie wrongdoing (and hence inferences of insufficient moral motivation) in the minds of praying folk, because both could end up not praying. Both would, moreover, be unable to cite any excusing condition that praying folk would be naturally inclined to accept—which fact is reflected in our tendency to think that there would have been nothing involuntary about either group's failure to pray. (Both classes of persons would have meant or intended not to pray.) Hence, there would be nothing, in the minds of these praying folk, to undermine the inference from breach of a moral code to insufficient moral motivation. But this means that we can be systematically inclined to attribute insufficient moral motivation to some people when there is in fact none and to view some people as morally corrupt when they are in fact morally ordinary. A systematic tendency to form false judgments like these should clearly qualify as a plausible candidate for a moral illusion.

This second class of moral illusions is especially pernicious in modern circumstances, because it can dispose large groups of perfectly morally competent people to misperceive one another and react to one another in ways that can lead to escalating cycles of moral conflict and violence. This phenomenon should be very familiar from the world historical record (and also, perhaps, from the tenor of modern political debates in the United States, which still seem to reflect a deeper history of moral conflict between the North and the South).[60] But there is also a much more intimate and personal aspect to the problem. This second class of moral illusions can blind us to much of the moral beauty in the world, which exists in other people's motives and actions. We can therefore see each other only through a distorted moral lens, which can prevent us from forming authentic interpersonal relationships based on the truth about who we are. When this happens, our lives are not only deficient in moral insight; they are worse lives. And the world can seem to be a much darker place than it really is.

The third and final class of potential moral illusions that I want to discuss relates to the special importance that we attach to morality and to the ways in which this perception can affect our views of the appropriate relationship between morality and other important systems of obligation, such as those of the law. Both morality and law purport to have the same kind of special practical authority, the basic features of which were described at the beginning of this essay, but we are often inclined to think of moral obligations as somehow more existentially real or more foundational. This perception can come out in a cluster of related views. For example, we can sometimes think that, in order for someone to believe that the law is giving rise to a genuine obligation, that person must believe that the law is giving rise to a moral obligation[61] or, relatedly, that in order for the law to give rise to a genuine obligation, we must be morally obligated to do what the law tells us to do. At other times, it is natural to think that moral obligations are intrinsically authoritative, whereas legal obligations are more conventional and hence incapable of intrinsic authority. It is a short step from here to the conclusion that the law must borrow its authority from morality in some way, either, for example, by directly reflecting moral content (with perhaps some limitations or differences rooted in pragmatic considerations, or in facts about reasonable pluralism); by having legal content that can be justified by substantive, first-order moral reasoning; by being interpreted in the most charitable moral light;[62] by helping us identify what ideal first-order moral reasoning would tell us to do better than our own moral reasoning can;[63] or in some other way. Another common thought is that the law should always be subject to moral criticism[64]—where moral criticism is viewed as providing us with a foundational standard that is itself beyond reproach. Not everyone holds all of these views, of course, but they are very common, and, indeed, they have often provided framework assumptions within which many of our modern jurisprudential debates take place. (Indeed, these views can also be understood as affecting our perceptions of the relative importance, or foundational status, of moral as opposed to legal philosophy. These perceptions would therefore help to explain why so much more philosophical attention has been paid to morality than to law and why the pursuit of moral philosophy is sometimes thought of as having logical priority.)

Because these assumptions are so basic and widespread, people who hold them do not always feel the need to justify them explicitly. We can nevertheless reconstruct a powerful set of considerations that tends to support this cluster of views. I begin with the proposition, just noted, that morality and law purport to have the same kind of special practical authority, which is the authority of genuine obligation. When someone sincerely believes that the law gives rise to an obligation, that person must therefore believe that it gives rise to all of the same practical implications that would arise from a moral obligation (i.e., that the law is genuinely reason-giving, that it has overriding authority and general applicability, and that it gives some person or group the standing to make demands or hold us accountable or responsible for violations). The most obvious and straightforward explanation of such a belief is that people who are taking the law to give rise to genuine obligations are construing the law to give rise to moral obligations, and it is, in fact, unclear what other type of explanation there might possibly be.[65] The special practical authority that morality and law purport to share is also overriding, and so it would seem impossible that morality and law could both literally and independently have this authority. When choosing which one is more foundational (and, hence, which one has the real claim to overriding authority), it is also natural to think of morality as more real, universal, and timeless and to think of law as more conventional. Hence, to believe that the law gives rise to a genuine obligation, one must believe that it gives rise to a moral obligation. I call this conclusion the thesis of "moral semantic foundationalism," because it analyzes the meaning of the term "genuine obligation" in our beliefs about legal obligations as synonymous with the term "moral obligation." From the thesis of moral semantic foundationalism, many of the other members of the cluster of views described earlier should quickly follow.

I understand the attraction of moral semantic foundationalism, but I want to end by suggesting that the view may be generated by a natural moral illusion. Before developing this suggestion, I should note that there is, however, at least one other legal philosopher who consistently rejected the thesis of moral semantic foundationalism. This is H. L. A. Hart, who believed instead that:

> [A]t least where the law is clearly settled and determinate, judges, in speaking of the subject's legal duty, may mean to speak in a technically confined way. They speak as judges, from within a legal institution which they are committed as judges to maintain, in order to draw attention to what by way of action is "owed" by the

subject, that is, may legally be demanded or exacted from him. Judges may combine with this, moral judgment and exhortation especially when they approve of the content of specific laws, but this is not a necessary implication of their statements of the subject's legal duty.[66]

Unfortunately, Hart also analyzed sincere statements of obligation as expressive of a particular psychological attitude (which he called the "internal point of view"),[67] and he never was able to develop a satisfying naturalistic way of distinguishing between the psychological attitudes that we express when we make sincere statements of legal obligation and those we express in our sincere statements of moral obligation.[68] Hence, very few contemporary legal philosophers have followed Hart in rejecting the thesis of moral semantic foundationalism, and, in fact, many prominent ones now claim not to understand how one could logically do so. For example, Scott Shapiro has suggested that:

> We can see that Hart's attempt to distinguish the legal from the moral is seriously flawed. For once we focus on the role that legal judgments and claims play in social life, it becomes hard to deny that they are constituted not only by normative concepts and terms, but by moral ones as well. . . . For if legal judgments are normative judgments, they must be moral judgments as well.[69]

One way to view the concluding remarks in this essay is thus to see them as offering a clear and precise way to render the distinction between judgments about moral and other genuine species of obligation and, hence, to revive a neglected aspect of Hart's views.

To understand the possibility I have in mind, let us remember that obligata (which are the attitudes that animate our sense of obligation on the present view) have been defined in purely functional terms (i.e., in terms of the natural function they serve in allowing us to resolve social-contract problems flexibly). From an evolutionary standpoint, there is, however, nothing about the processes of natural selection that would foreclose the logical possibility of our having more than one set of adaptations that serve this same natural function. Indeed, this happens with some frequency. Attitudes that are defined functionally can, moreover, be multiply instantiated. Hence, it is logically possible for us to have more than one natural sense of obligation, each of which functions in many identical ways, by appearing to us to have precisely the same set of practical implications.

Given this possibility, consider now a view that I will call "Legal Parallelism." Legal Parallellism asserts that law and morality have deep structural parallels owing to the fact that they engage psychological attitudes (viz., obligata) with the same natural function (namely to allow us to resolve social-contract problems flexibly) and not because they engage the same psychological attitudes (namely those that instantiate our sense of moral obligation more specifically). Morality and law nevertheless engage different classes of obligata, which are better or worse suited to different classes of social-contract problems. For reasons already explained, our sense of moral obligation is best adapted to allow us to resolve the most common and recurrent social-contract problems that we faced throughout our environment of evolutionary adaptation, which were with other members of a relatively small and independent group with whom we spent most of our lives. Our sense of legal obligation is, by contrast, better suited to allow us to resolve the types of social-contract problems that arise in much larger groups, with moral views that are uncoordinated. The reason for this is as follows: our sense of legal obligation is bound up with a shared social psychology that naturally inclines us to defer to a smaller group of officials to determine the content of what the law requires and that allows these officials to learn a shared and technical form of legal judgment and to engage in a specialized form of official interaction that tends to produce coordinated legal content. The law can therefore produce coordination over legal content in much larger groups of people, who cannot all engage in persistent and stable, face-to-face discussions with one another. This is the thesis of Legal Parallelism.

If the thesis of Legal Parallelism were true, then a number of important consequences would follow. First, we could account for the meanings of the special normative terminology that morality and law share as expressive of obligata and yet still offer a perfectly naturalistic distinction between the more particular classes or instantiations of this type of functional state that we are expressing when we make sincere statements about legal, as opposed to moral, obligation. We could thus render a precise naturalistic account of the distinction that Hart insisted upon for his entire career but that has been largely rejected in more contemporary discussions. We could also join him in rejecting the thesis of moral semantic foundationalism and thereby relieve much of the pressure toward the larger cluster of ideas that this thesis tends to support. Second, we could provide a straightforward evolutionary explanation for why we perceive the law to have the same special practical authority as morality without having to reduce that sense of authority to moral authority. Rather than assuming that our ordinary moral reasoning necessarily or automatically provides us with a credible and foundational standard for criticizing the law, we could also begin to explore the evolutionary vindicability of morality and law independently and in parallel. An independent evolutionary vindication of our capacities for legal judgment would establish that —in at least some circumstances of employment—our legal judgments have both the objectivity and the special practical authority that they purport to have. Hence, there would be no need for the law to borrow its authority from morality (in those same circumstances of employment).

There would still be the problem that both morality and law claim to have overriding authority, whereas both cannot have it at once. But, when we are trying to figure out which one really has it, it would be inappropriate—on the present view—to rely solely on our natural perceptions of the special importance of morality relative to law. If the thesis of Legal Parallelism were true, then we would perceive things this way because our sense of moral obligation was critical to resolving the most recurrent classes of social-contract problems that we faced during our environment of evolutionary adaptation, whereas our sense of legal obligation was rarely needed. Our sense of moral obligation would thus be the product of long-term selective pressures, which have left us with a very powerful and highly evolved perception of moral authority, whereas our sense of legal obligation would have come under heavy selective pressure only quite recently (i.e., after the rise of agriculture and the development of larger-scale civilizations). Hence, natural selection would have left us with only a relatively weak and unevolved perception of legal authority. (It is worth noting, in this regard, that, while the amount of time that has transpired since the rise of agriculture is relatively short in evolutionary time, we do have evidence of natural selection operating on humans since this transition, mainly in the form of the development of lactose tolerance and resistances to certain diseases—both of which are clear adaptations to an agricultural form of life with higher population densities.)[70] The historical record suggests that our transitions to large-scale societies with the rule of law have not always been smooth or easy, however, and our treatment of legal noncooperators and the practices of punishment that we have employed during these processes have often been incredibly harsh—as Nietzsche was wont to bring to our attention.[71] I therefore predict that we will learn, one day, that our sense of legal obligation has been one of the most intensive sites of selective pressure on humans since the rise of agriculture.

Rather than relying on our natural perceptions of the relative authority of morality and law, we therefore need to ask the following question: what classes of social-contract problems do we actually face today, and which systems of obligation are functioning well to resolve them? The correct answer to this question will undoubtedly leave a large place for morality in our modern lives. But, given the new and much larger classes of social-contract problems that we have been facing since the rise of agriculture and given the fact that our moral psychologies apparently incline us toward certain forms of moral illusion that have been creating some of our most pressing social problems and have been generating some of our most difficult obstacles to exhibiting a larger scale species of moral community, the correct answer will also almost certainly have another dimension: it will suggest that the law has the independent authority to override our correct and conscientious moral judgments in an increasingly broad set of circumstances.

I recognize, of course, that this final proposal may well seem counterintuitive (and perhaps even morally wrong or blasphemous, depending on the audience), but my suggestion is that these perceptions may well be the result of natural moral illusions. If so, then I also think that we can do better: we can learn to exhibit a more authentic form of moral relation to one another by resisting these natural moral illusions and by changing the glasses on our nose. Moral truth is something that every genuine religion endorses; hence, there should be room within every genuine religion to help combat these misperceptions. Moral truth is also endorsed by every secular moral person, and my hope is that this project might therefore give both secular and nonsecular groups common cause.

Given all of these facts, we clearly need to know whether the thesis of Legal Parallelism is true. I myself believe that it probably is, but I have not been able to present all of my reasons for this belief here, and it would go well beyond the scope of this essay to try. For present purposes, I will therefore conclude with the following observations. First, it is very important that we figure out the answer to this question, and, second, the question is itself an empirical one (just as it is an empirical question whether many of the other evolutionary explanations proposed in this article are valid). Hence, whether we are subject to the moral illusions described in this article and whether we should accept many of the philosophical consequences that I have been describing depends in part on facts that can be settled more definitively only through a more probing and directed line of evolutionary research. Facts like these present a perfect opportunity for heightened interdisciplinary cooperation among evolutionary theorists and moral and legal philosophers, and establish concrete ways in which all sides could profit from this critically important form of engagement.

NOTES

1. Charles Darwin, *The Descent of Man*, 2d ed. (London: John Murray, 1874), chap. 4.

2. See, e.g., *Moral Psychology*, Vol. 1: *The Evolution of Morality: Adaptations and Innateness*, ed. Walter Sinnott-Armstrong (Cambridge, MA: MIT Press, 2008); Richard Joyce, *The Evolution of Morality* (Cambridge, MA: MIT Press, 2006); Robin Bradley Kar, "The Deep Structure of Law and Morality," *Texas Law Review* 44 (2006): 877–942; Marc Hauser, *Moral Minds: How Nature Designed Our Universal Sense of Right and Wrong* (New York: Harper-Collins, 2006); G. Boniolo and G. De Anna, *Evolutionary Ethics and Contemporary Biology* (Cambridge: Cambridge University Press, 2006); Shaun Nichols, *Sentimental Rules: On the Natural Foundations of Moral Judgment* (Oxford: Oxford University Press, 2004); William Casebeer, *Natural Ethical Facts: Evolution, Connectionism, and Moral Cognition* (Cambridge, MA: MIT Press, 2003); Leonard Katz, ed., *The Evolutionary Origins of Morality: Cross-Disciplinary Perspectives* (Exeter, UK, and Bowling Green, OH: Imprint Academic, 2000); Christopher Boehm, *Hierarchy in the Forest: The Evolution*

of Egalitarian Behavior (Cambridge, MA: Harvard University Press, 1999); Elliot Sober and David Sloan Wilson, *Unto Others: The Evolution and Psychology of Unselfish Behavior* (Cambridge, MA: Harvard University Press, 1998); Bryan Skyrms, *The Evolution of the Social Contract* (Cambridge: Cambridge University Press, 1996); Frans de Waal, *Good Natured: The Origins of Right and Wrong in Humans and Other Animals* (Cambridge, MA: Harvard University Press, 1996); Matt Ridley, *The Origins of Virtue* (New York: Penquin, 1996); Allan Gibbard, *Wise Choices, Apt Feelings* (Cambridge, MA: Harvard University Press, 1990); Philip Kitcher, *Vaulting Ambition* (Cambridge, MA: MIT Press, 1985); Robert Axelrod, *The Evolution of Cooperation* (New York: Basic Books, 1984).

3. See, e.g., Richard Boyd, "How to Be a Moral Realist," in *Essays on Moral Realism*, ed. G. Sayre-McCord (Ithaca: Cornell University Press, 1988), 181–228; David O. Brink, *Moral Realism and the Foundations of Ethics* (Cambridge: Cambridge University Press, 1989); Michael S. Moore, "Moral Reality Revisited," *Michigan Law Review* 90 (1992): 8; Peter Railton, "Moral Realism," *Philosophical Review* 95 (1986): 163–207; Nicholas Sturgeon, "Moral Explanations," in *Morality, Reason, and Truth*, ed. David Copp and David Zimmerman (Totowa, NJ: Rowman and Allanheld, 1985), 49–78.

4. For a useful discussion of how these three elements are needed to give sense to the special practical authority of moral imperatives, insofar as they are considered to have "categorical" force, see David Brink, "Kantian Rationalism: Inescapability, Authority and Supremacy," in *Ethics and Practical Reason*, ed. Garett Cullity and Berys Gaut (New York: Oxford University Press, 1997), 255, 255–67, 280–87.

5. Stephen Darwall has recently emphasized these last dimensions of the practical authority of morality—at least in relation to those aspects of morality that I will be concerned with in this article. See generally Stephen Darwall, *The Second Person-Standpoint: Morality, Respect and Accountability* (Cambridge, MA: Harvard University Press, 2006).

6. This feature will distinguish the present view from some recent, so-called quasi-realist accounts of morality, which aim to account for all of the objectivist features of our moral judgments except this one. Quasi-realists assert that no natural facts are needed to explain the content of our moral judgments and that our moral psychologies (along with the content of our corresponding moral judgments) instead explain which natural facts constitute the supervenience basis of these judgments. See, e.g., Allan Gibbard, *Thinking How to Live* (Cambridge, MA: Harvard University Press, 2008), 251–67.

7. Kar, "The Deep Structure of Law and Morality," 877–942.

8. For a representative sample of important, recent work that is—in my view—broadly consistent with and supportive of central views developed

in my "Deep Structure of Law and Morality," see, e.g., John Mikhail, *Elements of Moral Cognition: Rawls' Linguistic Analogy and the Cognitive Science of Moral and Legal Judgment* (Cambridge: Cambridge University Press, 2011); Owen Jones and Robert Kurzban, "Intuitions of Punishment," *University of Chicago Law Review* 77 (2010): 1633; Elinor Ostrom, "Beyond Markets and States: Polycentric Governance of Complex Economic Systems," *American Economic Review* 100 (June 2010): 641–72 (Nobel Prize Lecture); John Mikhail, "Moral Grammar and Intuitive Jurisprudence: A Formal Model of Unconscious Moral and Legal Knowledge," in *Psychology of Learning and Motivation*, vol. 50: *Moral Judgment and Decision Making*, ed. D. M. Bartels, C. W. Bauman, L. J. Skitka, and D. L. Medin (San Diego, CA: Academic Press, 2009), 27–100; Fiery Cushman, "Distinguishing the Roles of Causal and Intentional Analyses in Moral Judgment," *Cognition* 108, no. 2 (2008): 353–80; Paul H. Robinson, Robert Kurzban, and Owen Jones, "The Origins of Shared Intuitions of Justice," *Vanderbilt Law Review* 60 (2007): 1633; John Mikhail, "Universal Moral Grammar: Theory, Evidence, and the Future," *Trends in Cognitive Sciences* 11, no. 4 (April 2007): 143–52; Alfred Mele and Fiery Cushman, "Intentional Action, Folk Judgments and Stories: Sorting Things Out," *Midwest Studies in Philosophy* 31, no.1 (2007): 184–201.

9. See, e.g., Jonathan Beckwith and Corey A. Morris-Singer, "Missing Heritability: Hidden Environment in Genetic Studies of Human Behavior," in this volume.

10. Philip Kitcher, "Naturalistic Ethics without Fallacies," in this volume.

11. Lord Alfred Tennyson, *In Memoriam A.H.H.* (1849), Canto 56.

12. Lynn Stout has also noted this tendency in *Cultivating Conscience* (Princeton: Princeton University Press, 2011), 67–68.

13. For a good discussion of the evidence for social dominance hierarchies and their biological value in animals, nonhuman primates, and humans, see Denise Cummins, "Dominance, Status, and Social Hierarchies," in *The Handbook of Evolutionary Psychology*, ed. D. M. Buss (Hoboken, NJ: Wiley, 2006), 676–97.

14. For an example of this common form of reasoning in a highly influential part of the secondary literature, consider the following claim by Eric Posner: "An explanation for nonlegal cooperation begins with the observation that people who defect suffer injury to their reputations. If a person develops a bad reputation, then people will not cooperate with him in the future. Since cooperation is valuable, if a person cares enough about the future he will not defect in the present." *Law and Social Norms* (Cambridge, MA: Harvard University Press, 2000), 15. Statements like this are very common in the economic literature on social norms and in the literature on behavioral economics.

15. This familiar proposition is derived from the work of Pierre Duhem and Willard Van Orman Quine. See Pierre Duhem, *The Aim and Structure of Physical Theory*, 2d ed., trans. P. W. Wiener (Princeton: Princeton University Press, 1954), originally published as *La théorie physique: Son objet et sa structure* (Paris: Marcel Riviera et Cie., 1914); W. V. O. Quine, "Two Dogmas of Empiricism," in *From a Logical Point of View*, 2d ed. (Cambridge, MA: Harvard University Press, 1951), 20–46; W. V .O. Quine, "Epistemology Naturalized," in *Ontological Relativity and Other Essays* (New York: Columbia University Press, 1969), 69–90.

16. Although this basic form of argument should be familiar, I have been personally helped in my thinking by Allan Gibbard's rendition of it, which he presents in the context of what he calls a "deep vindication" of our capacities for ordinary vision. See Gibbard, *Thinking How to Live*, 252–67. I am discussing cognition, rather than seeing, however, and Gibbard and I ultimately use this type of argumentation to support very different conclusions about the vindicability (or "deep vindicability," in his terms) of different regions of our practical judgments.

17. See ibid., 254–55.

18. For a recent synthesis of much of this existing evidence, see Richard Dawkins, *The Greatest Show on Earth: The Evidence for Evolution* (New York: Free Press, 2009).

19. Once again, Allan Gibbard has made a similar argument when discussing the relevance of this type of circularity to what he calls "deep vindications" in *Thinking How to Live*, 254–55.

20. See Margo Daly and Martin Wilson, *Homicide: Foundations of Human Behavior* (New York: Aldine Transaction, 1988), 80–94.

21. For one helpful account of how this might work, see Railton, "Moral Realism."

22. Strictly speaking, we should add the requirement that the costs of having these rule following capacities must also not be larger than the overall benefits in question—but I will assume that this requirement has been met in what follows.

23. See Kar, "The Deep Structure of Law and Morality," 894–941.

24. This is a well known feature of n-person prisoner's dilemmas. See generally Thomas Schelling, *Micromotives and Macrobehavior* (New York: Norton, 1978).

25. See Elliot Sober, "Did Evolution Make Us Psychological Egoists?," in *From A Biological Point of View: Essays in Evolutionary Philosophy* (New York: Cambridge University Press, 1994), 8 (defining evolutionary altruism).

26. Skyrms, *Evolution of the Social Contract*, 61.

27. Kar, "Deep Structure of Law and Morality," 914–17.

28. Ibid., 919–41, 894–901.

29. Ibid.

30. See H. L. A. Hart, *The Concept of Law*, 2d ed. (Oxford: Clarendon Press, 1994), 82–91.

31. Ibid., 88–89.

32. Kar, "The Deep Structure of Law and Morality," 934–41; Gibbard, *Wise Choices, Apt Feelings*, 64–80.

33. Jonathan Haidt has described psychological research that suggests that the process of expressing our moral intuitions to one another and trying to give reasons for them in social contexts "exert[s] a constant pressure toward agreement if the parties [are] friends and a constant pressure against agreement if the two parties dislike[] each other." Jonathan Haidt, "The Emotional Dog and Its Rational Tail: A Social Intuitionist Approach to Moral Judgment," *Psychology Review* 108 (2001): 814–34, 820.

34. See, e.g., Gilbert Harman, *The Nature of Morality* (New York: Oxford University Press, 1977); Gilbert Harman, "Ethics and Observation," in *Moral Realism*, ed. Geoffrey Sayre-McCord (Ithaca, NY: Cornell University Press, 1988), 119–24.

35. See, e.g., John Mackie, *Ethics: Inventing Right and Wrong* (New York: Penguin, 1977), 40–41.

36. Kitcher, "Naturalistic Ethics without Fallacies."

37. See Peter Railton, "Moral Realism," in Railton, *Facts, Values and Norms* (Cambridge: Cambridge University Press, 2003), 21–29.

38. I use the term "contractualism" to refer to that branch of social contract theory that aims to account for the right in terms of principles of conduct that are the object of a rational agreement among moral equals. See Stephen Darwall, Introduction to *Contractarianism/Contractualism*, ed. Stephen Darwall (Malden, MA: Blackwell, 2003), 1, 4. This basic idea can be further specified in a number of different ways. I also use the term "supervenience" in its most common philosophical sense. See generally R. M. Hare, *The Language of Morals* (Oxford: Oxford University Press, 1964). To say that a contractualist account of the right "supervenes" on a natural property, in this sense, is to say that two actions cannot differ in their rightness, under this contractualist standard, without their differing in having some specific natural property.

39. See John Rawls, "The Independence of Moral Theory," *Proceedings and Addresses of the American Philosophical Association* 47 (1974–75): 8; Norman Daniels, "Wide Reflective Equilibrium and Theory Acceptance in Ethics," *Journal of Philosophy* 76 (1979): 257–58.

40. Daniels, "Wide Reflective Equilibrium," 257–58.

41. T. M. Scanlon, "Contractualism and Utilitarianism," in *Utilitarianism and Beyond*, ed. Amartya Sen and Bernard Williams (Cambridge: Cambridge University Press, 1973), 103–28.

42. Ibid., 103.

43. See, e.g., Christine Korsgaard, "Skepticism about Practical Reason," *Journal of Philosophy* 83 (1986): 5–25.

44. See generally Frans de Waal, *Chimpanzee Politics: Power and Sex among Apes* (Baltimore: Johns Hopkins University Press, 2000).

45. The passages of the Bible that are often cited as condemning homosexuality are not unambiguous, and a number of people have suggested alternative interpretations. See, e.g., John E. Dwyer, *Those 7 References: A Study of 7 References to Homosexuality in the Bible* (Washington, DC: BookSurge, 2007); Robin Scroggs, *The New Testament and Homosexuality* (Minneapolis: Augsburg Fortress, 1982). The views I am concerned with are thus those that purport to be religiously based but would be resistant to considering evidence such as this and would maintain that the Bible unambiguously condemns homosexuality.

46. On the importance of promising to moral agency and moral society, see Seana Valentine Shiffrin, "On the Divergence of Contract and Promise," *Harvard Law Review* 120 (2007): 708, 714 ("Absent a culture of general mastery and appreciation of promissory norms and the moral habits and sensitivities that accompany them, I doubt that a large-scale, just social system could thrive and that its legal system could elicit general patterns of voluntary obedience. Further, I doubt that, absent a strong promissory culture, the individual relationships that give rise to and sustain moral agency and relationships of equality could flourish.").

47. I am deeply indebted to Robert Kurzban for bringing home to me the evolutionary oddity of moral judgments prohibiting consensual homosexual activity.

48. I am indebted to Richard Brooks for conversations that have helped me develop my thinking here, and I believe that the phenomenon I am discussing is closely related to some that he identifies in his work in progress on titling.

49. Friedrich Nietzsche develops these themes most explicitly in *On the Genealogy of Morals* (Oxford: Oxford University Press, 2009).

50. John Rawls, *Political Liberalism* (New York: Columbia University Press, 1993), 54–55.

51. Ibid., 55–56.

52. Ibid., 56–57.

53. Ibid., 54.

54. Ibid., 55.

55. Or at least we cannot without highly modern technologies, such as MRI equipment, and so could not throughout most of our natural history. But I would not want to suggest that MRI imaging would give us the right kind of information anyway.

56. Aristotle gives a number of examples of persons who might at first appear to have acted in a blameworthy manner but whose involuntariness can be established on other grounds, including: "One might mistake . . . some other kind of stone for a pumice stone; and one might strike something to save a man but kill him instead." Aristotle, *Nichomachean Ethics*, III: 2, in *Selected Works*, 3d ed., ed. Hippocrates G. Apostle and Lloyd P. Gerson (Grinnell, IA: Peripatetic Press, 1991), 463–64.

57. Ibid.

58. Aristotle says that actions "which are voluntary are praised and blamed, while those which are involuntary are pardoned and sometimes even pitied." Aristotle, *Nichomachean Ethics*, III: 1. He then suggests "that involuntary things are those which are done by force or through ignorance." Ibid. From this he reasons that "[s]ince that which is involuntary is done by force or through ignorance, the voluntary would seem to be that whose [moving] principle is the agent who knows the particulars on which the action depends." Ibid., III: 3.

59. See, e.g., Aristotle, *Nichomachean Ethics*, III: 2 ("[F]or ignorance in intention of what should be done is a cause not of what is involuntary but of evil; and [involuntariness] is not universal ignorance (for through universal ignorance men are blamed), but ignorance with respect to particulars in which action exists and with which action is concerned.")

60. For an insightful look into how some of the moral codes tend to differ between people in different regions of the United States, see Dov Cohen and Joseph Vandello, "Patterns of Individualism and Collectivism across the United States," *Journal of Personality and Social Psychology* 77, no. 2 (August 1999): 279–92.

61. Scott Shapiro says, for example, that "once we recognize the social role that legal concepts are typically made to play, it becomes hard to resist the conclusion that these concepts must be moral as well. For concepts such as AUTHORITY and OBLIGATION are characteristically employed in contexts where moral notions are uniquely apt." *Legality* (Cambridge, MA: Harvard University Press, 2011), 114.

62. For early versions of this view in Ronald Dworkin's work, see Ronald Dworkin, *Law's Empire* (Cambridge, MA: Harvard University Press, 1986), 87–113, 176–275.

63. One version of this view arises in Joseph Raz's "normal justification thesis," which states that the normal or primary way that the law can have the authority that it claims is by providing us with guides to what we should do better than our own first personal deliberation would. See, e.g., Joseph Raz, "Authority and Justification," in *The Authority of Law*, ed. Joseph Raz (New York: Oxford University Press, 1990), 115, 129.

64. Hart, for example, famously believed that one of the central ben-

efits of developing a purely descriptive account of law was that a clear understanding of this kind can be "an important preliminary to any useful moral criticism of law." Hart, *Concept of Law*, Postscript at 240.

65. I am indebted to Michael Moore for conversations that have helped me clarify this part of my thinking.

66. H. L. A. Hart, "Commands and Authoritative Legal Reasons," in *Essays on Bentham* (New York: Oxford University Press, 1982), 243, 253.

67. See, e.g., Kevin Toh, "Hart's Expressivism and His Benthamite Project," *Legal Theory* 11 (2005): 75–123.

68. For further discussion of this point, see Robin Bradley Kar, "Hart's Response to Exclusive Legal Positivism," *Georgetown Law Journal* 95 (2007): 393, 450–52.

69. Shapiro, *Legality*, 115. For a similar view, see Joseph Raz, "Hart on Moral Rights and Legal Duties," *Oxford Journal of Legal Studies* 4 (1984): 121, 130–31.

70. S. A. Tishkoff, et al., "Convergent Adaptation of Human Lactase Persistence in Africa and Europe," *Nature Genetics* 39 (2007): 31–40; P. C. Sabeti et al., "Positive Natural Selection in the Human Lineage," *Science* 312 (2006): 1614–20; D. P. Kwiatkowski, "How Malaria Has Affected the Human Genome and What Human Genetics Can Teach Us about Malaria," *American Journal of Human Genetics* 77 (2005): 171–92; T. Bersaglieri et al., "Genetic Signatures of Strong Recent Positive Selection at the Lactase Gene," *American Journal of Human Genetics* 74 (2004): 1111–20.

71. See Nietzsche, *On the Genealogy of Morals*, Book II.

3

MISSING HERITABILITY: HIDDEN ENVIRONMENT IN GENETIC STUDIES OF HUMAN BEHAVIOR

JONATHAN BECKWITH AND COREY A. MORRIS-SINGER

Philip Kitcher argues that the sciences of sociobiology and evolutionary psychology are severely limited in their utility for understanding human nature and contributing to the ethical project. He argues for a much broader set of approaches that would necessarily lessen the importance of biology in this effort.[1] Nevertheless, some biologists have made the strong case for the relevance of the biological sciences to this project. For instance, E. O. Wilson proposed in his 1975 catalytic book *Sociobiology* that "scientists and humanists should consider together the possibility that the time has come for ethics to be removed temporarily from the hands of the philosophers and biologicized."[2] Like Kitcher, we as geneticists worry that some in the social sciences and humanities, in order to enrich their analyses, are too eagerly grasping at claims emanating from certain research areas in genetics and biology. In our commentary, we focus, in particular, on a complementary area of biology—the search for biological explanations of variation in human behavior and aptitudes. For the most part, these explanations have been provided from the field of human behavioral genetics. We do not say that any relevant biology should be ignored but rather argue that this field has had a sorry history of failed and biased studies that continues to this day and that has tragically influenced social attitudes and policies. We urge a much more critical look at the science and its underlying assumptions, before it is used to support particular ethical, legal, and social policy proposals.

An examination of the history of the field of human behavioral genetics reveals a research area that has repeatedly been forced to reexamine its assumptions.[3] Perhaps this is not surprising; the social attitudes of the researcher on such topics as intelligence, criminality, and so on are difficult to eliminate from the approaches of the research itself. Scientists who were eminent in their own right, such as Sir Francis Galton (who coined the term "eugenics" in the nineteenth century), and Charles Davenport, along with other leading geneticists in the early twentieth century, extended their science well beyond what it could really tell them.[4] The consequent impact on social policy of the eugenics movement in the twentieth century was the sad outcome. But this overextension of the field of genetics and the attendant controversies have continued, most notably in the reports of strong genetic contributions to intelligence and antisocial behavior and in research on gender differences in aptitudes. It is this history that provides a warning that we should look at contemporary research quite closely to see if, in fact, the conclusions drawn are warranted and worthy of taking into consideration for social and ethical political interpretations.

Today, the two main efforts to correlate genetic variation with variations in human behavior are (1) the classical studies of genetically identical twins and (2) research to directly correlate human behavioral variation with alterations of specific sites on the human genome. These two classes of studies are tied together in that the claims for strong heritability of certain behavioral traits derived from twin studies have given confidence to genome researchers that their search for relevant genes will be successful. However, the assumptions underlying the twin studies have been repeatedly and seriously challenged, requiring a more tempered view of their conclusions. Furthermore, studies carried out since the human genome was completely sequenced in the year 2000 reveal a much greater complexity than expected in the relationship among genes, environment and human traits, including behavior. This development has led to talk in the scientific literature about "missing heritability"—the ostensible gap between the heritabilities for traits calculated by those doing twin studies and the actual contribution of genes detected by genome mapping.

1. TWIN STUDIES AND HERITABILITY

The almost universally misunderstood meaning of the scientific term "heritability" represents a starting point in judging how much we might learn from twin studies. Before actually delving into how heritability numbers are arrived at, we will focus on this word. To make this discussion less abstract, we will use scores on an IQ test, presumed by researchers to reflect intelligence, as an example of a trait that is often measured in twin studies.

The heritability of a trait is the amount (or percentage) of the *variance* of that trait in a particular population that can be attributed to genetic factors.[5] However, a heritability number (say 60 percent) for intelligence in a population says nothing about the degree to which the intelligence of an *individual* in that population is influenced by genes. It also says nothing about what the heritability of intelligence would be in a *different population*. Furthermore, since the variance of a trait is measured *in a particular environment* and *at a particular time*, the variance of the trait in that population could be dramatically different in a different environment and different time. In fact, a published study of twins, some of whom came from impoverished environments and some from well-off backgrounds, reports: "In the families of low SES [socioeconomic status], the heritability of IQ is around 10 percent while in families of high SES it is 78 percent."[6] This result strikingly illustrates how a trait such as IQ or any other behavioral trait may vary enormously in its heritability depending on the environment people inhabit. (In discussing problems with twin studies later in this essay, we will raise questions about the significance of high heritability numbers such as 78 percent for high-SES twins reported in this study.)

With all of these limitations to the application of heritability calculations, one might think that researchers in the field and the media would be particularly careful in presenting the results to the public. Unfortunately, despite the fact that twin studies yield information only about the particular population under study in a particular environment at a particular time, a very different impression is often communicated to the public. This miscommunication arises, in part, because the term *herit*ability shares the same root as in*herit*ed and is thus conflated with inheritance. For instance, a typical journalistic representation of studies that reports on an IQ and genetics study will use phrases such as "IQ is shown to be 60 percent heritable." These representations of the science, more often than not, lead to a description of the trait as being one that is relatively fixed and unchangeable. This conflation may be further exacerbated by statements of the researchers themselves or because of the way in which the media presents the results.

Thus, the misuse or misrepresentation of the word "heritability" and the limitations to its significance when applied to human studies have been controversial from the inception of such research. Leading population geneticists and others have criticized the use or misuse of this approach and its language ever since it began to be applied to human studies. Some examples follow:

> Apparently it does little good to warn against oversimplifying the idea of heritability. Perhaps this is a basic argument for coining a new word when an idea is to be presented precisely and in a way in which it cannot be misunderstood.[7]

> [Heritability] is one of those unfortunate short-cuts which have emerged from biometry for lack of a more thorough analysis of the data.[8]

> When a word [heritability] has both technical and folk meanings, it is the responsibility of the specialist to avoid promoting confusion by either using extremely cautious and precise language when using the term or . . . abandoning the term in favor of one without a widely understood folk meaning.[9]

> The problem with heritability is that it sounds like a property of the feature itself, when in fact it is merely a description of the population in which the trait appears.[10]

2. TWIN STUDIES AND ENVIRONMENT

It is also instructive to consider how the use of the term "heritability" came to be applied in genetics initially. Agricultural scientists were the first to calculate heritability coefficients. In their studies, they sought to understand the relationship between genes and environment in contributing to traits valuable for agricultural purposes. To do this, they varied the environment of their animal or plant research subjects and varied the genetics by using different genetically inbred strains. To apply this approach to humans, behavioral geneticists had to argue that they could also control the environment and the genetics of human research subjects. They pointed out that the genetics could be controlled by studying genetically identical twins. There are two major classes of studies utilizing identical twins. First, researchers have compared human behavioral traits in genetically identical twins who were raised by their biological parents with the traits of those who were raised by adoptive parents. In order to assess the strength of genetics versus environment in this case, it would be necessary that the environments of the adoptive families be different from those of the biological families. If that were the case, this class of experiment would crudely, at least, mimic agricultural experiments where, for instance, plants with the same genes were placed in different environments.

The second class of studies examines identical twins who have been raised by their biological parents but, in this case, compares them with nonidentical twins also raised by their biological parents. Fraternal twins share, on average, 50 percent of their genes, while identical twins share all of their genes. The difference of the degree to which the identical and fraternal twins show expression of a particular trait allows the calculation of heritability. It is argued that, since twins grow up together at the same time in the history of their family and the history of their culture, a pair of genetically identical twins (with 100 percent shared genes) can be considered to have grown up sharing the same environment to the same degree as do a pair of nonidentical twins (with 50 percent genetics shared). This would not be true of ordinary (nontwin) siblings born at different times in the history of their family. This Equal Environment Assumption (EEA) allows researchers to claim that the environment is effectively controlled.

To many observers, the simplification of concepts of environment in these studies is problematic, raises questions about the studies' conclusions, and thus limits the application of their conclusions to questions of social or moral import. (For a more detailed discussion of the issues that follow and of the meaning of heritability, we highly recommend either one of two similar impressively lucid essays by the philosopher Elliott Sober.)[11]

The failings in the treatment of environment can be attributed both to the simplifying of the complex nature of human social interactions and to the limitations in our knowledge of the environmental factors that contribute to behavioral traits. In studies comparing adopted identical twins with twins raised by their biological families, the nature of the adoption process itself can seriously interfere with this apparently well thought-out experiment. Twins who are adopted, either via adoption agencies or through the efforts of the biological parents themselves, are rarely placed in homes with environments very different from those of the biological parents. This criticism, which suggests that environment and genetic contributions to behaviors cannot be distinguished by these studies, was made most convincingly in the 1970s.[12] As a result, behavioral geneticists made an effort to directly assess the "environment" of adoptive homes. When studying the heritability of IQ, for example, they counted the number of books in the homes and noted other features that would indicate (or not) an intellectually rich environment.[13] While certainly the environmental features noted are ones that seem *potentially* relevant to IQ, simply counting the number of books and similar accoutrements does not give a direct sense of that environment. Paradoxically, although the question presumably being asked in such studies concerns the sources of higher IQ scores, the researchers are assuming that they already know the "trait-relevant" environmental factors for which to test.

Strong criticisms have also been raised of the Equal Environment Assumption, a central assumption of the twin studies that compare fraternal and identical twins raised in their biological families.[14] There are several reasons for suspecting that, in contrast to this assumption, the environments experienced by fraternal twins are different from those experienced by identical twins. First, the physical identity of identical twins can. influence similarly the behavior of identical twins which would not be the case for the less physically similar fraternal twins. How people respond to an individual's physical features, such as short stature, physical beauty, obesity, or skin color, can vary with cultural attitudes. These responses, which vary from positive to negative, can, in turn, influence the behavior of identical twins in ways that would not be the case for fraternal twins. In the face of these criticisms, behavioral genetic researchers have attempted to assess the validity of the EEA assumption. If the EEA for the trait under study is incorrect and identical twins indeed experience environments that are more similar than those experienced by fraternal twins, then the calculation of heritability coefficients in such studies would be artificially high, since different concordance of IQ scores in the two types of twins could be due to either genetic or environmental differences.

We have recently reviewed studies that attempt to test the EEA and concluded that they do not establish the validity of the EEA.[15] We point out how difficult a task it is to tease out the complex environmental effects that can occur in such studies. The studies published were done with small sample sizes with low statistical power, used problematic retrospective interviews with parents and children in evaluating the childhood environments, and made assumptions about what trait-relevant environmental differences to measure (see the earlier discussion). Furthermore, several of the studies contained evidence that the EEA had been violated.

3. How Heritability Reports Can Mask Environmental Influences

Beyond the potential confounding environmental influences characteristic of these types of twin studies, we want to point out a surprising way in which researchers can turn what some might consider an environmental factor into a genetic one and thus calculate "inflated" heritabilities. We have talked earlier about how identical features of twins can result in identical interactions with their parents and identical experiences with people in society at large. Such effects that may influence their behavior are thought of by many as a gene-environment interaction. Let us consider an extreme example. In the United States, people with genes that determine dark skin color are likely to meet prejudice to such an extent that their behavior, education, blood pressure, and so on are significantly influenced. It is true that the genes are responsible for causing the skin color, but it is our culture and prejudices at this time in history that cause discriminatory behavior and its impact. In this case, the genes and the environment are interacting, but, in another less prejudicial environment, this effect could disappear. However, behavioral geneticists often turn this argument around and include such gene-environment interactions as genetic components in calculating heritability. Twin researcher Thomas Bouchard, among others, has presented this rationale, stating: "Identical twins elicit, choose, seek and create environments very similar and, accordingly, the impact of these environments is considered a genetic influence." He and others appear to agree that the environment of identical twins may be more similar than that of fraternal twins but argue that this similarity is caused by the genes themselves.[16] Their argument may have some validity in a technical sense, but it hides from view the important impact of environmental context on heritability calculations, thus leaving to the reader a sense that the studies have shown the strong direct and immutable influence of genes on behavior.

4. A Shift in Human Behavioral Genetics

We have argued that the field of behavioral genetics, through much of its history, has treated environment in a simplistic manner in its efforts to define heritability of traits. This oversimplification was surely influenced by the success of methodological reductionism in other fields of science, particularly molecular biology, alongside which behavioral genetics developed in the twentieth century. Within the past ten years or so, however, there have been indications of a significant shift in the emphasis that behavioral geneticists have placed on the role of the environment. We have already mentioned the paper on the enormous shifts in heritability of IQ with changes in environment, which has challenged basic assumptions.[17] Elsewhere, one of the authors of this paper has pointed quite clearly to the difficulties confronting his field in defining trait-relevant environments that influence the development of specific behaviors or aptitudes.[18] Furthermore, the leading behavioral geneticist James Flynn has roiled the field with his studies of changes in average IQ of populations over the several-decade-long period from 1950 to 2000.[19] He sought to test the underlying assumption in the field that IQ scores, deemed to have a strong genetic component, remain fixed and do not change with time in a population. What he found was a steady increase in average IQ of populations over the years; in addition, he observed that the gap between black and white IQs in the United States had steadily narrowed. Flynn suggests that various cultural and educational changes are responsible for these increased IQ scores.

A very different class of behavioral genetic studies that indicate a shift in direction for this field has emerged. These studies take as their starting point gene-environment interactions. A requirement for such studies is that there be an already identified gene that, because of its function, is a candidate for being one that affects human behavior. Caspi et al. reported that people carrying a variant of a gene (MAOA) that should control serotonin levels in the brain were susceptible to exhibiting antisocial behavior.[20] However, that susceptibility was observed only with those individuals who carried the variant copy of the gene *and* who had been subjected to child abuse. The authors conclude that taking into account potential environmental factors on a behavior can actually help researchers to detect genetic contributions to that behavior. This gene-environment approach may reflect an interesting trend. Nevertheless, as an indication of the difficulty of coming up with meaningful results, subsequent attempts to replicate this study have yielded mixed results. The mixed results themselves may indicate complex environmental or genetic differences between the populations that were used in each study.[21]

One last example illustrates the problems in treating environment too lightly when seeking biological contributions to human behavior or aptitudes. In a 1980 study on math performance of boys and girls, researchers reported in *Science* magazine that eighth-grade boys outnumbered girls 13:1 at the highest levels of scores on the SAT math test. In their article, the authors of the report implied that scientists should pay more attention to biological differences in explaining the gap between boys and girls in math achievement.[22] Unfortunately for this proposal, the significance of the finding has almost disappeared in the thirty years since the study, as the boy/girl ratio of 13:1 among high achievers fell to 2.8:1 in 2005.[23] Furthermore, the percentage of women who obtained PhDs in mathematics increased from 6 percent of those receiving that degree in 1970 to 30 percent in 2003.[24] These changes occurred (obviously) without any genetic engineering or time for evolution. These dramatic changes may have been the result of the success of the women's movement since the 1970s in instituting numerous educational programs to enhance the interest and performance of girls in math.[25] While this example does not represent studies that used twins as their subject, it is relevant in that it shows the danger of treating environment in a simplistic way.

5. The Human Genome and Human Behavioral Genetics

With the initiation of the Human Genome Project in the late 1980s, hopes surged that scientists would be able to identify genes involved in the human behaviors and aptitudes studied by behavioral geneticists. These hopes were bolstered by the initial rapid identification of genes in which mutations were highly correlated with specific but rare diseases. For example, mutations were identified in a single gene that caused Huntington's chorea, in another gene that caused muscular dystrophy, and in another that caused Gaucher's disease. However, in recent years, it has become clear that for many common human diseases, single mutations in single genes do not provide a causative explanation. Many, perhaps most common human diseases are much more complex in terms of their genetic, genetic/environment-interaction, and environmental sources than was thought. This complexity is illustrated by recent investigations into genetic contributions to Crohn's disease. Using an approach called Genome Wide Association Studies (GWAS), researchers found thirty different genetic locations in human chromosomes where mutations made small contributions to Crohn's.[26] Further, from statistical analyses, they predicted that mutations at approximately one hundred such sites total will eventually be found to contribute to Crohn's disease. That is, perhaps mutations in one hundred genes, each mutation having a small effect, contribute to this disease.

It has been significantly more difficult to identify genetic variants associated with behavioral traits or mental illnesses such as schizophrenia. And no replicable finding has been made of a gene that correlates with IQ scores. Researchers in the field have concluded that many human trait variations may result from small effects of a large number of genes, interaction of those genes with the environment, or predominantly environmental factors.

6. MISSING HERITABILITY

In a recent article, researchers have used the powerful tool of GWAS to identify genes related to a wide variety of personality traits. However, they report: "No genetic variants that significantly contribute to personality traits were identified while our sample provides over 90 percent power to detect variants that explain only 1 percent of the trait variance. This indicates that common genetic variants of this size or greater do not contribute to personality trait variation."[27] The authors refer to the problem of "missing heritability" discussed in our Introduction and predict that "[n]ewer technologies . . . and novel statistical approaches combined with larger samples and meta-analyses" will overcome this problem. The appeal to newer genetic technology and larger sample sizes has become a common refrain in the search for gene-trait correlations; however, what is not commonly acknowledged is that these studies often reveal diminishingly small effects on the trait under study. Furthermore, nowhere do these authors mention the possibility that the heritability calculations may be biased by deficits in the consideration of environment in twin studies. Instead, we suggest that a major reason for the problem of finding proposed genes involved in human behavior may be a simple one. The researchers who have used the twin study approach with the goal of determining whether there are strong genetic influences on such traits as intelligence have simplified concepts of environment, minimizing its definition and its effects, to make their studies feasible. Alternatively, their methodology may obscure ways in which environmental influences of human behavior are hidden within their heritability estimates of genetic effects. The result is that they either overestimate the heritability for the traits they study or include environmental influences in their calculations of heritability. There may be no missing heritability, but there is certainly missing or hidden environment.

Rather than being at a time where sufficient information has now accumulated from behavioral genetic approaches to start employing them for an understanding of human social behavior, we are instead at the beginning of a new era of exploration that recognizes complexity. New approaches are being taken to incorporate environment in a more significant way than in the past as we try to understand the role of the environment in the development of human traits. To those who would like to use the approaches or some of the results of behavioral genetics, we cannot emphasize enough how important it is to look with a critical eye at the kinds of assumptions that underlie research in this field.

NOTES

1. Philip Kitcher, "Naturalistic Ethics without Fallacies," in this volume.

2. E. O. Wilson, *Sociobiology: The New Synthesis* (Cambridge, MA: Harvard University Press, 1975).

3. J. Beckwith, "Simplicity and Complexity: Is IQ Ready for Genetics?" *Current Psychology of Cognition* 18 (1999): 161–69.

4. D. Kevles, *In the Name of Eugenics: Genetics and the Uses of Human Heredity* (Berkeley: University of California Press, 1985).

5. D. S. Falconer, *Introduction to Quantitative Genetics*, 3d ed. (London: Longman Scientific and Technical, 1989).

6. E. Turkheimer et al., "Socioeconomic Status Modifies Heritability of IQ in Young Children," *Psychological Science* 14 (2003): 623–28.

7. A. E. Bell, "Heritability in Retrospect," *Journal of Heredity* 68 (1977): 297–300 (citing J. L. Lush from 1936).

8. R. A. Fisher, "Limits to Intensive Production in Animals," *Journal of Heredity* 4 (1951): 217–18.

9. S. F. Stoltenberg, "Coming to Terms with Heritability," *Genetica* 99 (1997): 89–96.

10. J. Marks, *What It Means to be 98 Percent Chimpanzee: Apes, People and Their Genes* (Berkeley: University of California Press, 2002).

11. E. Sober, "The Meaning of Genetic Causation," in *From Chance to Choice: Genetics and Justice*, ed. A. Buchanan, D. W. Brock, N. Daniels, and D. Wikler (Cambridge: Cambridge University Press, 2000), 347–70; E. Sober, "Separating Nature and Nurture," in *Genetics and Criminal Behavior*, ed. D. Wasserman and R. S. Wachbroit (Cambridge: Cambridge University Press, 2001), 47–78.

12. L. Kamin, *The Science and Politics of I.Q.* (Potomac, MD: Erlbaum Associates, 1974).

13. T. J. Bouchard Jr. et al., "Sources of Human Psychological Differences: The Minnesota Study of Twins Reared Apart," *Science* 250 (1990):

223–28; D. C. Rowe, *The Limits of Family Influence: Genes, Experience and Behavior* (New York: Guilford Press, 1994).

14. J. Joseph, "The Equal Environment Assumption of the Classical Twin Method: A Critical Analysis," *Journal of Mind and Behavior* 19 (1998): 325–58; J. R. Alford, C. L. Funk, and J. R. Hibbing, "Twin Studies, Molecular Genetics, Politics and Tolerance," *Perspectives on Politics* 6 (2008): 793–97; J. Beckwith and C. A. Morris, "Twin Studies of Political Behavior: Untenable Assumptions?" *Perspectives on Politics* 6 (2008): 785–91.

15. Beckwith and Morris, "Twin Studies of Political Behavior," 785–91.

16. Bouchard Jr. et al., "Sources of Human Psychological Differences," 223–28.

17. Turkheimer et al., "Socioeconomic Status Modifies Heritability of IQ in Young Children," 623–28.

18. E. Turkheimer, "Mobiles: A Gloomy View of Research into Complex Human Traits," in *Wrestling with Behavioral Genetics: Science, Ethics and Public Conversation*, ed. E. Parens, A. R. Chapman, and N. Press (Baltimore: Johns Hopkins University Press, 2006), 100–8.

19. J. R. Flynn, *What Is Intelligence?* (Cambridge: Cambridge University Press, 2007).

20. A. Caspi et al., "Role of Genotype in the Cycle of Violence in Maltreated Children," *Science* 297 (2002): 851–54.

21. J. Kim-Cohen et al., "MAOA, Maltreatment, and Gene-Environment Interaction Predicting Children's Mental Health: New Evidence and a Meta-analysis," *Molecular Psychiatry* 11 (2006): 903–13; C. Morris et al., "Deconstructing Violence," *Gene Watch* 20 (2007): 3–10.

22. C. Benbow and J. Stanley, "Sex Differences in Mathematical Ability: Fact or Artifact?" *Science* 210 (1980): 1262–64.

23. R. Monastersky, "Primed for Numbers," *Chronicle of Higher Education* 4 (2005): A1.

24. S. J. Ceci and W. M. Williams, "Sex Differences in Math-Intensive Fields," *Current Directions in Psychological Science* 19 (2010): 275–79.

25. J. Beckwith, "Gender and Math Performance: Does Biology Have Implications for Educational Policy?" *Journal of Education* 165 (1983): 158–74; Ceci and Williams, "Sex Differences in Math-Intensive Fields," 275–79.

26. J. C. Barrett et al., "Genome-wide Association Defines More Than 30 Distinct Susceptibility Loci for Crohn's Disease," *Nature Genetics* 40 (2008): 955–62.

27. K. J. Verweij et al., "A Genome-Wide Association Study of Cloninger's Temperament Scales: Implications for the Evolutionary Genetics of Personality," *Biological Psychology* 85 (2010): 306–17.

PART II

LAW AND
BEHAVIORAL
MORALITY

4

LAW AND BEHAVIORAL MORALITY

NITA A. FARAHANY

Behavioral morality is a new brand of moral philosophy with the central tenet that bad behavior attributable to a physical cause is either less blameworthy than intentional behavior or not at all morally blameworthy. As evolutionary biology, cognitive neuroscience, and moral philosophers meet on an inevitable collision course, a more alluring incarnation of behavioral morality has emerged. This movement turns to evolutionary science, genetics, and neuroscience to challenge the social institutions that regulate human behavior. The criminal justice system, as the first and most obvious of such institutions, has been the most vulnerable to its scrutinizing gaze.

Scientific studies that report on the physical correlates to criminal conduct appear regularly in the popular press, as does evidence about the physical correlates to feelings like rage, empathy, disgust, and joy—feelings to which moral sense could be attributed. With physical correlates to deviant behavior and moral sense in hand, behavioral moralists are armed. They can and do claim that those who act contrary to societal norms—but because of their evolutionary history, genetic foundation, or neurobiology—are less blameworthy than others who act similarly and therefore should be subject to lesser societal reproach. If deviant behavior, moral conduct, or even moral conscience is largely determined, the argument goes, what normative justification can society rely upon to assign criminal responsibility? What is the basis for societal stigmatization?

This chapter provides a new taxonomy to name, contextualize, and critique this new brand of moral philosophy that I identify as "behavioral morality," particularly as it relates to the criminal law. Part 1 traces the scientific advances in understanding human behavior from evolutionary science, genetics, and neurobiology, which motivate the moral claim. This part situates behavioral morality as a movement distinct from evolutionary biology and the law and demonstrates the points of divergence. Part 2 illustrates the tension between behavioral morality and existing normative accounts of criminal responsibility, which embrace human agency. It also discusses cases in which behavioral moralism has been introduced and the basis for their success or failure. Part 3 then seeks to reconcile behavioral moralism with the normative purposes behind criminal law and to potentially bring the movement within the fold of the broader law and evolutionary biology movement. To do so, this chapter offers an alternative approach for adherents of behavioral moralism to explore. It suggests that behavioral moralism may gain more traction by embracing the fundamental underpinnings of the criminal justice system, while still working to integrate scientific evidence. Because the concept of reasonableness underlies much of criminal responsibility doctrine, behavioral moralists could, for example, inform that concept with more scientifically robust data, rather than attempting to remove it entirely from the criminal law. Finally, Part 4 opens the debate on the question of stigmatization of individuals who have scientific accounts of their behavior. It proposes that what may be partially motivating the use of behavioral morality to attack criminal responsibility is a discontent with attaching criminal stigma when the internal proximate causes of a criminal behavior have been offered. And it concludes by offering a starting point to engage in that dialogue.

1. UNDERSTANDING BEHAVIORAL MORALITY

Behavioral morality is a form of moral reasoning. It focuses on the internal proximate causes[1] of deviant behavior to determine whether the actor is morally blameworthy for that conduct. If the causes of the behavior can be attributable to factors outside the conscious control of the individual, by engaging in the reasoning of behavioral morality (or being a "behavioral moralist"), one can find the actor less or not at all morally blameworthy. Behavioral morality generally goes one further step still, to conclude that, as science progresses to reveal the causes of human behavior, a criminal justice system based on retributivism will no longer align with moral intuitions about responsibility. Joshua Greene and Jonathan Cohen advance this view, arguing:

> In our view, neuroscience will challenge and ultimately reshape our intuitive sense(s) of justice. . . . Cognitive neuroscience, by identifying the specific mechanisms responsible for behaviour, will vividly illustrate what until now could only be appreciated through esoteric theorizing: that there is something fishy about our ordinary conceptions of human action and responsibility, and that, as a result, the legal principles we have devised to reflect these conceptions may be flawed. . . . [N]ew neuroscience . . . will undermine people's common sense, libertarian conception of free will and the retributivist thinking that depends on it, both of which have heretofore been shielded by the inaccessibility of sophisticated thinking about the mind and its neural basis.[2]

Greene and Cohen's approach reflects and guides a broader movement that stands in contrast to legal positivism, which holds that law need not draw from morality or moral intuitions for its legitimacy and that no conceptual barrier prevents the development of legal rules that hold all agents equally accountable for their actions.[3] Behavioral moralists argue that if a system deviates too far from the moral intuitions about human capacities, that system will and should face rejection by the people under its rule.[4] To make stark the claim, consider the position of a modern legal positivist like Joseph Raz, who offers an account of law that draws its authority from its source, rather than from morality. According to Raz, the law provides an independent requirement for action, apart from morality, and courts may recognize the law and its requirements entirely from social facts rather than moral insights.[5] Behavioral morality would reject this claim—and argue instead that a system of laws derives its legitimacy by tracking social mores and that mores require excusing individuals who can offer a causal explanation of their deviant conduct.

As the scientific revolution in human behavioral sciences expands, reasoning by behavioral morality has taken hold. As research in brain sciences and the human mind expands, evidence of behavioral moralism abounds. A discussion of some of the scientific contributions animating the philosophy follows.

Physical Correlates for Human Behavior

Evolutionary Causes

The study of the human brain and body has led evolutionary biologists and cognitive neuroscientists to the "unassailable fact" that human minds are the product of evolution.[6] This fact seems to naturally follow from embracing the nervous system as a product of evolution and human behavior as a "product of activities of the nervous system."[7] It follows that human behavior also arises from evolutionary forces. Likewise, unless one adopts a Cartesian dualist approach to the mind and the body,[8] the human mind must also be the product of evolution.

Evolution-based claims about criminality usually focus on explaining phenomena related to group-wide criminal behavior, rather than criminal behavior by any one individual. So, for example, it has been observed that criminal behavior varies by sex and by age.[9] Males commit the majority of crimes of violence against other males, and males with poor socioeconomic prospects commit the majority of homicides.[10] Moreover, criminal behavior decreases in an age-dependent manner, where males in their reproductive prime commit the highest proportion of crimes and then taper off in their criminal activity with increasing age.[11] Evolutionary accounts for such phenomena may attribute violent behavior by these males to intermale rivalry for reproductive success, particularly given that reproductive competition and success is generally more stable among women.[12]

Evolution-based accounts for particular kinds of criminal conduct have proliferated. Rape has become a particularly well characterized and also a hotly debated area in evolutionary theory. Male and female reproductive interests are not always aligned, and male sexual coercion appears much more frequently than female sexual coercion.[13] Evolutionary theorists note that rape victims are differentially likely to be females of reproductive age. The account does not, however, claim that a desire to reproduce drives heterosexual rape, which arises as an immediate motivation in only the rare instance. Instead, evolutionary theory attributes sexual stimulation as the primary motivator and the common explanatory factor across all human rapes.[14] The sexual passion of men, these theorists suggest, arose from evolutionary forces driving a desire for sexual access to many females of reproductive age.[15]

The murder of children, too, has been ascribed evolutionary roots. It seems nonsensical to murder one's offspring. Yet, humans follow a pattern observed often in other animals: male hostility toward offspring of their female partner from a previous mate.[16] Notably, the rate of homicide of a child under five rises dramatically in households where a stepfather parent is present.[17] Most mothers who kill their infant offspring are young and poor; evolutionary theorists suggest that this may be because her reproductive success overall may be hampered by raising that child.[18]

Evolutionary scientists also attempt to untangle phenomena such as differential treatment of family members and strangers in crimes such as homicide or theft. The relative paucity of kinship homicide, for example, is attributed to the fact that humans, as a species of animals, act to increase not only their own reproductive success but also that of their relatives.[19] This nepotistic concept of altruism turns on an evolutionary theory that individual fitness is diminished by violent conduct toward kin and is bolstered by empirical evidence that shows that murder among blood relatives is relatively rare across societies throughout time.[20] The explanatory power of evolutionary science goes beyond just individual crimes —it has been used to explain shared human intuitions about the grading of criminal offenses and relatively consistent perception of severity of crimes across cultures.[21]

Evolutionary biology has also been used to explain the motivations for certain types of criminal or antisocial behavior. Linda Mealey, for example, differentiates between "primary sociopaths," individuals of a certain genotype incapable of experiencing social emotions that generally motivate human behavior, who appear in any society in low frequency, and "secondary sociopaths," whose pathology arises from social and environmental conditions related to disadvantage in social competition.[22] Primary sociopaths are likely to exhibit persistent antisocial behavior over the course of their lifetime, while secondary sociopaths are likely to exhibit antisocial behavior in a context-specific fashion and generally decrease antisocial behavior with increasing age and greater socioeconomic prosperity.[23]

Evolutionary science, neuroscience and behavioral genetics overlap, just as theories about human behavior and criminal conduct do. For example, deep within the human brain lies the limbic system, sometimes referred to as the emotional brain.[24] This ancient and interconnected network of structures has changed very little anatomically or chemically over hundreds of thousands of years of human evolution.[25] In situations of extreme stress, the limbic system is capable of overwhelming the cerebral cortex and thereby overwhelming a person's interpretation, judgment, and restraint. In most instances, the limbic system is an asset, arousing fear when danger may be present and triggering flight to avoid advancing danger.[26] But damage to the limbic system can also cause specific and individual difference in behavior, leading to outbursts of rage and violence.[27]

While other relevant evolution-based arguments inform behavioral moralism, one final category of evolutionary theory requires discussion here—claims about an evolutionary basis for morality. Evolutionary theory of morality occurs in three popular forms: (1) evolution has hard-wired intuitive moral thinking into the brain; (2) moral decisions are innate and during development become attached to external stimuli;[28] and (3) evolution favors a predisposition toward easily assimilating morality.[29] These three forms are not mutually exclusive. Indeed, the advocates of these approaches do not necessarily argue that every moral decision involves only one mechanism. Nor does it necessarily follow that all actions with moral character are hardwired or predetermined by evolution or the physical brain. External stimuli, different sociocultural learning, and environmental changes may trigger varying moral responses by individuals. The innateness of morality has implications for behavioral morality. If moral thinking and moral conduct are innate, so, too, are deviations from such thinking and conduct. Such behavior is a mere biological vestige, behavioral moralists would argue, and therefore the criminal law lacks normative justification for punishing it.

Genetic Causes

Genetic predisposition evidence has provided a major foothold for behavioral moralism. Twin, family, and adoption studies, as well as the more recent quantitative trait loci and candidate gene studies, have vastly expanded our knowledge of the genetic and environmental correlates that contribute to human behavior.[30] Behavioral moralists have coalesced around studies in behavioral genetics of addiction, violence, and antisocial personality disorder. Indeed, such studies have *converted* many into behavioral moralists. Two recent studies have gained particular attention. Both studies have served as the scientific basis for expert testimony in recent criminal cases, usually on behalf of criminal defendants who seek to explain their criminal behavior and to argue either for a lack of capacity to premeditate a crime or for mitigation of punishment.[31]

In 2002, the research team led by Avshalom Caspi, based in New Zealand, published a seminal paper proposing a mechanism through which a person's genetic makeup and childhood experience might combine to increase the risk that that individual will become violent as an adult.[32] The team concluded that individuals with a particular allele of the monoamine oxidase A gene (*MAOA*), together with a history of serious childhood maltreatment, were more likely to manifest violent and antisocial behavior as adolescents and adults.[33] The 2002 study focused on a polymorphism in the promoter region of *MAOA*, which has either four repeats (causing high activity of the *MAOA* enzyme), or three repeats (causing low activity of the enzyme). The scientists characterized the incidence of childhood abuse for study subjects and generated a statistical correlation among the *MAOA* promoter-region polymorphism, incidence of childhood abuse, and expression of violence as adults. From this, they reported a statistically significant correlation between the 3-repeat polymorphism, childhood maltreatment, and violent antisocial behavior in adolescents and adults. They concluded that "[f]or adult violent conviction, maltreated males with the low-*MAOA* activity genotype were more likely than non-maltreated males with this genotype to be convicted of a violent crime by a significant odds ratio of 9.8."[34]

One year later, the Caspi-led team published a second groundbreaking study reporting another gene-environment interaction.[35] The second paper detailed a functional polymorphism discovered in the promoter region of the serotonin transporter gene *SLC6A4* (also referred to as SERT and 5-HTT). As with *MAOA*, the team focused on a polymorphism in the promoter region of *SLC6A4*, which appears as either a long or a short allele. The long allele is correlated with high activity of the serotonin transporter system, while the short allele is correlated with low activity of the serotonin transporter system.

The researchers sought to understand the genetic and environmental interaction between the serotonin promoter gene variants and stressful life events. Specifically, they examined the divergent responses to stressful life events, such as depression and suicidal thoughts versus resilience. On the basis of the statistical correlations they identified in the study, the scientists concluded that high activity of the serotonin promoter had a protective effect against stressful life events. By contrast, "[i]ndividuals with one or two copies of the short allele . . . exhibited more depressive symptoms, diagnosable depression, and suicidality in relation to stressful life events than individuals homozygous for the long allele."[36]

Other candidate genes for violence have been characterized and introduced into criminal cases. Testosterone and its androgenic and estrogenic metabolites have been implicated in some candidate gene studies for violence, in particular because of the increased prevalence of violence among males relative to females.[37] Adrenal steroids (including glucocorticoids, such as cortisol and corticosterone) and the pituitary hormone *ACTH* (adrenocorticotropic hormone) have also come increasingly under study because of early animal studies that demonstrated a link with animal aggression.[38]

Alcoholism and addiction have also piqued the interest of behavioral moralists, given the significant overlap between addiction and criminal conduct. At least ten major twin studies have been undertaken on the heritability of alcoholism. Behavioral geneticists claim that genetic differences account for 50 percent and 60 percent of the variation in risk for alcoholism seen in the population.[39] By contrast, fewer studies have been undertaken on illicit drug use, in part because of the obvious difficulty in finding test subjects. On the basis of the several twin and adoption studies to date, however, scientists believe that genetic factors also influence illicit drug abuse.[40] In reported twin studies of illicit drug use, the genetic contribution to differences in risk of drug addiction across the population ranges from 25 percent to 79 percent.[41]

Quantitative trait loci studies and candidate gene studies of addiction have also yielded promising linkages among particular genes, loci, and risk of addiction. Thus far, the most commonly studied candidate genes for alcoholism include *ALDH*, several alcohol dehydrogenase genes (ADH), and cytochrome P450 variants.[42] As with most behaviors studied by behavioral geneticists, the serotonin transporter promoter has been implicated by association between the short promoter variant and increased risk of alcoholism.[43] The Collaborative Study on the Genetics of Alcoholism, a prominent quantitative trait loci study, yielded results suggesting susceptibility to alcoholism on loci of chromosomes 1, 2, 4, 5, 7, and 15.[44] The Collaborative study analyzed linkage in 105 multigenerational families identified by centers in the United States. There was suggestive evidence of linkage on chromosomes 1 and 7, with protective locus on chromosome 4.

Finally, a number of behavioral genetics studies have focused on antisocial personality disorder and related diagnoses. These genes encoding for serotonin, dopamine, and the enzymes *MAOA* and *MAOB* have been linked to antisocial personality disorder (and have also been implicated in nearly every other behavior).[45] The role of serotonin in aggression and antisocial personality has been particularly well characterized.[46] The advances in serotonin research are evident by its introduction in countless criminal cases, some of which are detailed in Part 3. Despite the advances in this area, the mechanism underlying the relationship between serotonin and antisocial personality disorder remains unknown. Scientists have speculated that antisocial personality disorder may arise from differences in central nervous system concentration of serotonin (with both high and low serotonin levels implicated) or from polymorphisms in the promoter region of the gene encoding for serotonin. Despite these uncertainties, claims already have been made about specific serotonin variation and antisocial personality disorder, including polymorphisms in variants of the serotonin transporter.[47]

A dopamine metabolite (cerebrospinal fluid homovanillac acid) has been negatively correlated with human aggression and appears more frequently in recidivist criminal offenders than in first-time offenders.[48] Animal studies suggest that increased dopamine function is correlated with increased aggression, and human studies support this loose correlation, as well.[49] Another dopamine-related gene, the DRD2 gene, which is a receptor gene for dopamine, has also been correlated with antisocial personality disorder and related behaviors.[50]

Behavioral geneticists have even characterized the more generalized behavior called criminality. Large-scale twin and adoption studies of criminal behavior have been conducted in the United States, Sweden, Denmark, and Norway.[51] From these studies, behavioral geneticists conclude that there appears to be a genetic basis for certain kinds of criminal behavior, including property crimes such as theft or vandalism.[52] Adoption studies support a similar conclusion, identifying a greater correlation between a biological parent with a conviction and a child adopted away than between an adoptive parent with a conviction and the adoptee.[53] But these studies suggest that the risk extends only to property crimes but not to violent offenses, as a result of either the biological or the adoptive-parent criminal background.[54]

Neurobiological Causes

Neurobiology has captivated behavioral moralists more than any other scientific discipline. The reason for the more particularized attention paid to neurobiology rather than to genetics or evolutionary biology may be understood from the following perspective, offered by the oft-quoted bioethicist Henry T. Greely:

> I am more than my genes. The genes are an important part of me, but I can be certain that they are not my essence; they are not my soul. When we shift that notion to the neuroscience area, though, I am not so confident. Is my consciousness—is my brain—me? I am tempted to think it is.[55]

Likewise, neuroscientists and other scholars, when describing the interaction of the brain and the law, have said: "Modern empirical endeavors support the claim that the human PFC [prefrontal cortex] . . . is what makes us rational, intellectual, and moral entities."[56]

The idea, then, that the driving force behind an individual or the very conscious reality one experiences is located, dependent upon, and inextricably bound up with the brain underlies much of the theory of behavioral moralism. As a consequence, attempts to blame or to shift responsibility from a defendant as an agent of choice to the neurological underpinnings of criminal behavior have taken root.

Scientists echo the belief that the secret to the criminal mind lies within the brain. Adrian Raine, one of leading researchers in antisocial behavior, has said: "It's becoming increasing clear that we're never going to solve the problem of violent crime if we don't address the link between brain damage and criminal behavior."[57] To that end, Dr. Raine and a team of research scientists have conducted brain-scanning studies on violent offenders. In one such study, they used positron emission tomography (PET) to scan the brains of forty-one individuals who had committed acts of homicide but who had pleaded not guilty by reason of insanity and forty-one control subjects matched for mental disorders and for age and gender.[58] They found that those who had committed acts of homicide showed lower rates of glucose uptake in certain regions of the brain,[59] demonstrating weaker activity in the left hemisphere of the brain, and stronger relative activity in the right hemisphere of the brain.[60] They concluded that poor functioning in the limbic areas of the brain helps to explain why violent offenders are less likely to regulate their emotions and more likely to act on impulse.[61] Their research suggested a link between brain differences and criminal violence.[62]

The claims arising from neurobiology and the near-daily reports of neurological contributions to behavior are too vast to capture in this brief review. But a few examples illustrate the claim. Recent population-based studies of childhood lead exposure and the brain have found a correlation among lead exposure, brain damage, and criminal behavior.[63] The researchers compared blood-level histories of lead, gathered from before birth, to measurements of grey-matter volume in different regions of the brain.[64] They found dose-dependent decreases in the volumes of grey matter in particular areas of the brain, meaning that, when there are increased levels of lead in the blood, certain regions of the brain exhibited decreased volume.[65] In a second study, the researchers correlated early blood levels of lead with arrests and violent offenses, drugs offenses, theft or fraud, obstruction of justice, major motor vehicle offenses, and other disorderly conduct.[66] They found a statistically significant adjusted rate ratio for arrests for violent crimes and a high frequency of arrests, at 55 percent.[67] Lead exposure contributes only one part to the overall risk of offending, but it does suggest a link between neurological damage and impact upon executive functioning and impulse control.[68]

The association between pedophilia and brain abnormalities raises controversy, but researchers have found associations between brain lesions and sexual orientation toward children.[69] One study, for example, concluded that "bilateral temporal lobe disturbances involving the right more than the left result in hypersexuality."[70] This hypersexuality, the researcher argued, could explain a predisposition or orientation toward molesting children. Walter Sinnott-Armstrong introduces another such study on pedophilia in his response to this paper.[71] He introduces the case study of a forty-year-old man who was diagnosed with a right orbitofrontal tumor.[72] The man had an interest in pornography dating back to adolescence but denied any earlier interest in or attraction to children.[73] After his advances toward his prepubescent stepdaughter were discovered, he was legally removed from the home, found guilty of child molestation, and ordered either to undergo a twelve-step program for new-onset pedophilia or to go to jail.[74] Despite claiming that he strongly desired to complete the program, he made sexual advances toward the staff and other clients in the rehabilitation program and was expelled. The evening before his prison sentence began, he was referred to the hospital on complaint of headache, where his tumor was discovered.[75] The tumor was surgically removed, and, thereafter, he successfully completed the twelve-step program and was returned to his home.[76] When his sexual impulses returned, a later brain scan revealed that the tumor had returned.[77]

Neurological evidence invites questions about the extent to which legal conceptions of premeditation and planning comport with scientific ones. Premeditated or planned criminal activity is generally treated more harshly in law than unplanned or impulsive activity. A deterrent rationale generally motivates the distinction—if an action is premeditated or planned, it can be deterred. One might also argue that premeditated crimes are more blameworthy and deserving of greater retribution because they reveal a more malicious criminal mind. So, for example, the individual who purposely drives a car at another car will generally be held to higher level of criminal accountability than a driver who accidentally runs a car into another one.[78] As a result of this distinction, neurobiology studies in impulsiveness or premeditation have been introduced as relevant to these determinations in criminal law. Psychopathy, for instance, is associated with an increased risk of both instrumental and reactive aggression. Instrumental aggression is by definition intentional; the individual is engaged in antisocial behavioral to achieve planned goals.[79] Reactive aggression instead involves unplanned, enraged attacks, directed toward the source of the perceived threat or frustration.[80] Neurological studies of psychopathy reveal a correlation between these behaviors and dysfunction in particular areas of the brain—particularly the amygdala, the ventromedial prefrontal cortex, and the superior temporal cortex.[81] These results, in conjunction with evidence from other electrophysiological and hemodynamic studies in psychopathy, have led researchers to conclude that psychopathy may be associated with abnormalities in the paralimbic system.[82] And, where abnormality exists, behavioral moralists have likewise argued that such abnormalities suggest that psychophaths have diminished responsibility.[83]

Behavioral Morality versus Law and Evolutionary Biology

Behavioral morality might easily be confused with the broader and more established law and evolutionary biology movement, which draws from much of the same science. This law and evolutionary biology movement, largely characterized by its attempts to understand the evolutionary contributions to human behavior and institutions, has some common heritage with behavioral morality. In particular, adherents of both behavioral morality and of law and evolutionary biology seek to understand and incorporate a scientific perspective on human behavior and social institutions into law. But the overlap generally ends there. The law and evolutionary biology movement has a different approach to the scientific facts at issue and is not driven by a normative agenda. These differences distinguish behavioral moralism both substantively and theoretically.

Proximate versus Ultimate Causes
Perhaps the biggest difference between behavioral moralists and law and evolutionary biology theorists is their different focus

on proximate versus ultimate causes. A proximate cause is generally the event that is the closest or most immediately responsible cause for an observed result or outcome. Ultimate causes, by contrast, tend to be more distant causes but are considered the higher-level or broader theory driving the event or outcome. Law and evolutionary biology theorists tend to focus on ultimate causes and seek to understand what selective advantages favor a particular behavior and thereby predict its prevalence in a given species, in contrast to some other behavioral response.[84] Ultimate causes might be characterized as answering the *why*, while proximate causes might be characterized as answering the *how*.

Owen Jones, one of the leading scholars in law and evolutionary biology, illustrates ultimate versus proximate causes through a description of singing by the male robin. The ultimate causes of the male robin singing include its attempts to claim territory, advertise its health, and attract mates, each of which provides a selective advantage and helps to explain both the prevalence and the predisposition toward singing in robin populations.[85] By contrast, the proximate causes for a male robin's singing "include the hormonal changes triggered by the lengthening of successive days, the activation of particular motor neurons to the vocal apparatus, and each bird's individual experience of songs heard and songs practiced."[86] Ultimate causes, therefore, describe and predict the biological reasons behaviors came to be commonly observable,[87] the existence and distribution of such behaviors in a species, and the environmental conditions that are most likely to serve as biological proximate causes for those behaviors.[88]

Behavioral moralism could be characterized as relying on proximate causes in its reasoning. In studying the claims advanced by behavioral morality, we do not come to understand, for example, *why* a particular group of criminals or criminal defendants has an evolutionary, genetic, or neurological contribution to their behavior, only that they *do*, and as a result they are less morally blameworthy because the cause identified is outside the conscious control or choice of the individual. This focus on certain but not other proximate causes of behavior is in itself problematic, but ignoring the ultimate causes of behavior may defeat any normative power of the argument itself. Describing how a criminal act occurs may afford very little insight into why society should treat such action as less blameworthy than other behavior for which we do not have a full accounting of the proximate causes.

Naturalistic Fallacy

Unlike behavioral morality, the law and evolutionary biology movement does not claim that scientific facts give normative support for particular legal outcomes. Rather, it recognizes that there are empirical facts about the world and that there are value judgments about those facts. The conceptual move made in behavioral moralism—to draw value judgments from new facts about the world—has been otherwise called the naturalistic fallacy.[89] Law and evolutionary biology theorists avoid this fallacy.[90] Instead, they emphasize that right and wrong in the moral sense derive from humans pursuing their interests, not from the facts of nature.[91] Thus, law and evolutionary biology theorists[92] are more likely to be legal scholars who are deeply committed to exploring and reformulating legal policy based on the ultimate causes of behavior and less likely to be driven by a normative agenda.[93]

Law and evolutionary biology theorists generally do not accept that the proximate causes of human behavior necessarily excuse criminal conduct. Using normative analyses and biological fact, some, in fact, argue the contrary position. A common alternative theory is that law exists to address the shortcomings that arise from human nature. If humans were perfectly adapted to every environmental context, law might be superfluous.[94] In other words, law can function to curtail human behaviors that have negative social consequences, behaviors that, though they may have been adaptive in the Pleistocene era, have negative consequences in modern times.[95]

2. COMPETING APPROACHES TO CRIMINAL LAW

Behavioral Moralists' Account

Behavioral moralism takes a soft or a hard determinist approach to human behavior. The theory goes beyond arguing that conscious reality is located, dependent upon, and inextricably bound up with the evolutionary history, genetics, and neurolobiology of the individual. Behavioral moralism views these proximate causes as competing with preexisting notions of free choice or free will, particularly as that concept is understood and applied in criminal law. Once descriptive accounts of criminal behavior are found, the determinists' arguments are aroused. If the proximate cause is known, behavioral moralists demur, why say that the criminal action arises from human agency or control, rather than recognizing this behavior is a product of these causes?[96] In short, questions about criminal responsibility and blame come into focus as the causes of human behavior become increasingly more descriptive and specific. The studies discussed in Part 1 have been used in legal scholarship, in criminal cases, and in philosophical debates to justify this form of moral reasoning.

Behavioral morality seems to be coalescing around neuroscience and biology to disclaim moral responsibility on the basis of biological correlates to human behavior.[97] Behavioral moralists like Greene and Cohen predict a sea change in popular conceptions of morality: as neuroscience offers more and more compelling mechanistic accounts of behavior, societies will come to view wrongdoers as mere "victims of neuronal circumstances."[98]

Behavioral moralists call for criminal law to reconsider "the model of free will" it adopts, "in light of increasing support for deterministic influences."[99] They argue that the correlation among evolutionary, genetic, and neurological factors favors the doctrine of "biological determinism and disfavor[s] the doctrine of free will as related to the causation of criminal behavior."[100] By dispensing with notions of free will, proximate cause can lessen or negate responsibility for individuals with compelling theories of biological predisposition.[101] The scientific studies discussed in Part 1 lead behavioral moralists to claim that all criminals are not created equally with respect to their predisposition to and ability to refrain from criminal conduct. Instead, some individuals are predisposed to or predetermined to commit crimes through a confluence of evolutionary, genetic, neurobiological, and environmental factors. These individuals should be held to a different and lesser standard of criminal responsibility than those who have more "complete" control over their conduct. In short, "[if] a [criminal] offender demonstrates that a genetically [evolutionarily, or neurobiologically] caused chemical imbalance has significantly impaired his free will, he should not be held criminally responsible to the same extent as an offender without such impairment."[102] This form of moral reasoning has been introduced, with limited success, into the criminal justice system.

Challenges to Criminal Responsibility

The call by behavioral moralists to excuse criminal defendants based on the proximate causes of their behavior has largely failed in U.S. court cases. Yet, the theory has proven to have true staying power. It continues to gain supporters and the sympathy of some jurists, and even constitutional law doctrine has yielded in some areas to its claims. What this suggests is that, properly redirected, behavioral moralism could gain more traction. Indeed, while majority opinions in most cases express skepticism regarding the claims raised by behavioral moralists, over time, judges have granted greater leeway in admitting this evidence and have afforded it more weight. The review here explores some of the categories of claims that behavioral moralists have advanced in criminal law.

Agency

A finding of criminal liability requires finding a concurrence of a criminal act[103] attributable to the defendant,[104] with a guilty mind. Criminal law presumes that a defendant intended to engage in the specific act in question, absent specific evidence to the contrary.[105] This presumption is consistent with the more generalized approach in criminal law, which assumes that any particular defendant has the average mental capacities of an ordinary member of society. This presumption of agency may be challenged and successfully overcome if a defendant demonstrates that his bodily movements arose from natural phenomena or *external* forces. A claim of involuntariness based on internal factors is traditionally rejected, because criminal law generally rejects a dualistic view of behavior in favor of a system that recognizes the capacity of agency.

Behavioral morality claims about *action* focus on the involuntariness of conduct when it arises from evolutionary, genetic, or neurological causes. These claims arise relatively infrequently, in part because involuntariness as a defense is quite limited under criminal law statutes. *Ex Parte John Wayne Rice*[106] provides a useful illustration of the claim. The defendant claimed that he acted involuntarily in committing homicide because the act arose from his frontal-lobe brain damage. He introduced psychiatric testimony at trial to the effect that "a person with physical damage to the frontal brain lobes might respond with greater emotion than a normal person to any particular situation. . . . [S]uch an emotional response is not voluntary if it results from frontal lobe brain damage."[107] The court rejected this conception of involuntariness. As the majority explained, "there was no evidence that [the defendant] involuntarily pulled his gun and shot [the victim]. The testifying forensic psychiatrist opined that a person with frontal-lobe brain damage could have an impaired ability to control his *emotional* reaction to stimulus. But he had not evaluated the defendant about the specific *act* involved in the . . . shooting."[108] On the basis of this testimony, the court held that a neurological predisposition toward certain emotions does not displace the presumption that individuals generally are agents of their actions and that the defendant in this case was the agent of the shooting. While the defendant may have reacted with greater rage than an average person without frontal-lobe brain damage, he still acted voluntarily when shooting the victim.

The court's rationale underscores the concept of voluntariness and agency at play in the criminal law—attributions of agency focus on the act in question rather than on the more distant but still proximate causes of the act. If the defendant engages in an action, criminal law attributes to his agency that action, even if proximate causes of the action include his internal predispositions (including the neurological ones raised here). In short, criminal law presumes that when an individual physically engages in conduct, he does so intentionally.

Blameworthiness

The second part of liability, mental state, goes most directly to the criminal mind. Unsurprisingly, many challenges based on the proximate causes of a behavior have been introduced to challenge whether a defendant had the requisite *mens rea* or to undermine the notion of *mens rea* as currently understood in criminal law.

The modern conception of *mens rea* has historical roots in the common-law principle of wickedness of intention. Today, *mens rea* has a much simpler meaning: did the defendant have the necessary state of mind to engage in the specified criminal element (e.g. the act, under the circumstances) in question. To answer whether a criminal defendant willfully killed another person, the criminal law asks: did the defendant engage in the act that ended the person's life with purpose? In homicide by shooting, did the defendant mean to pull the trigger of the gun that he pointed at the other person? Was he aware that the person was, in fact, another human being? If so, then he will be found to have engaged in willful conduct, irrespective of his motive for doing so.

The distinction between motivation to act and intention to act presents serious problems for claims based on the biological causes. If intention is narrowed to mean only whether a defendant meant to engage in the act in question and does not ask how or why he engaged in that act, the biological precursors or predispositions of that act may have little relevance.

Equally problematic for these claims is the accepted inference of subjective intent based on objective manifestations of a defendant's mental state. To see this in practice, consider the case of *People v. Speights*,[109] where the defendant challenged on appeal the use of jury instructions that permitted inferences to be drawn from the circumstantial evidence to establish the mental state for second-degree homicide. To establish his mental state, the prosecution introduced evidence such as the defendant's statements to others after he had killed his girlfriend in an assault, the state of the apartment where the assault had taken place, and the condition of the victim's body and nature of her injuries.[110] The defendant used evolutionary and neurological biology to prove otherwise.[111] The defense expert testified that the defendant had ingested methamphetamine, a stimulant that excites electrical activity in the brain, increases heart rate, elevates mood, and arouses behavior.[112] He explained that violent behavior can arise as a complication of use, because of the interaction with the "limbic system of the brain, which 'controls the raw emotions of fear, flight, fight and fornication,' while it simultaneously 'bypasses the higher cortical center where we think about rules of conduct, right and wrong, compare previous behavior patterns and think about things.' "[113] The jury convicted the defendant of second-degree murder. The appellate court found no error or prejudice in allowing the jury to infer the defendant's mental state from the circumstantial evidence presented.[114]

The relationship among the limbic system, its evolutionary role, and various genetic and neurological deficits has proven popular in challenges to mental state. Earlier, in *State v. Payne*,[115] the defendant claimed he was incapable of forming the knowing mens rea required for second-degree murder because of deficits to his limbic system.[116] The defense introduced expert testimony about the "various inhibitory systems in the brain" that have evolved to protect humans from acting impulsively over "many millions of years."[117] An expert testified about the link between low serotonin level and explosive impulsive violence and about one's "biological capacity" for control.[118] Together with certain environmental stressors, the expert testified, individuals with low serotonin, like the defendant, were "virtually incapable of controlling their impulsive behavior."[119] The appellate court upheld the defendant's conviction, finding that the objective manifestations of the defendant's intent supported the jury's conviction.[120]

Such claims have enjoyed some limited success.[121] In *People v. Reinoso*,[122] the California Court of Appeals reversed a trial court motion denying the introduction of expert testimony in support of a behavioral morality claim. The defendant had argued that his frontal-lobe brain disorder and attention deficit hyperactivity disorder (ADHD) rendered him unable to project himself into future situations or to think about the consequences of his behavior. As a result, he could not think about "the possibility of getting into a car, drunk, and harming someone," so he did not act with the necessary mental state of recklessness required by the statute.[123] Essentially, he argued that his objective conduct should not inform his mental state because the outward action-internal intention norm did not describe his mental processes. Although the legislature had precluded the defense of diminished capacity (discussed later), the court found that this evidence could inform whether the defendant acted with the "conscious disregard" of the risk to human life that the statute required. The court did so carefully, however, noting that the questions and answers asked and given of the expert would have to be monitored. At the very least, however, expert testimony should have been permitted on whether the defendant suffered from a mental disease or defect, the effect of these conditions, and the types of behavior or mental processes that can be expected from people suffering from those conditions.[124] The jury would then be entitled to draw inferences from the defendant's conduct as to whether he suffered from the mental disease or processes and how other people who suffered the same would be expected to have acted under the circumstances. While this norm shifting is generally rejected in criminal law, it sometimes appears in the form of diminished capacity.

In a few jurisdictions, the evidentiary rule or defense known as diminished capacity complicates an otherwise objective *mens rea* analysis. Diminished capacity enables a criminal defendant to claim a partial excuse for having a "greater than normal difficulty in conforming to the law."[125] In states that recognize a diminished-capacity defense, for example, a defendant may argue that, as a result of his impulse control disorder, he could not form the requisite intent for first-degree homicide—premeditation.[126] Behavioral morality claims often arise under this evidentiary rule.

In *Ex parte Jennings*,[127] for example, the defendant, who shot a police officer three times in the back of the head in the course of a robbery of an adult bookstore, claimed on appeal that evidence should have been introduced during his capital trial that he did not deliberately shoot a police officer but did so because of damage to his frontal and temporal lobes and the debilitating effect of this damage upon his impulse control.[128] The court conceded that "[a] brain-damaged defendant with diminished impulse control is less likely to have acted deliberately than a person with normal self-control."[129] It nevertheless found that the objective indicia of the defendant's subjective intent to deliberately cause the police officer's death was sufficient to find no reasonable probability that a juror would have been swayed by this evidence.[130] The defendant in *People v. Ledesma*[131] appealed his murder conviction by also claiming that he did not premeditate the killing, arguing that "his extensive use of . . . PCP . . . combined with . . the effects of brain damage"[132] made his conduct a product of his brain, rather than his agency. The court sustained his conviction on appeal because it was reasonable to assume that a juror would reject the expert testimony as inconsistent with the objective indications of the defendant's subjective intent.[133] In other words, in both of these cases, the court took note of the outward or circumstantial manifestations of the defendants' mental states, which suggested planning and considered action. In both cases, the court used this objective evidence to infer mental state. And it concluded that the outward manifestations trumped any evidence of proximate cause for the defendants' conduct suggesting otherwise.[134] This approach of inferring mental state on the basis of what an average person in society would have intended if he were to exhibit the same behavior permeates criminal law. Put simply, courts use objective reasonableness to inform mental state.

Capacity

In many of these cases, the court struggled with whether the evidence introduced went to mental state or to the capacity to act as an agent of responsibility. Courts struggle with this question because objective reasonableness is a normative function of criminal law that has outer limits. Those entirely wanting of capacity are not assigned criminal responsibility when they are deemed lacking in agency of action. This outer boundary on responsibility ensures that criminal law does not stray too far from punishing those whom society believes morally blameworthy. By doing so, criminal law preserves its legitimacy as a social institution and makes more likely that the rules and proscriptions of the system will be obeyed.

In most jurisdictions, the outer boundary of responsibility allows a defendant to assert insanity as an affirmative defense to criminal liability. To succeed, the defendant ordinarily must prove that he suffered a mental disease or defect, lacked awareness of his actions, could not appreciate the nature and quality of his act, or lacked the ability to distinguish right from wrong. A successful insanity defense results in indefinite commitment to a mental institution, incarceration, or both, depending on the law of the governing jurisdiction. Genetic and neurological evidence has already been extensively introduced to establish or bolster a defendant's claim that he has a mental disease or defect and to address fears of malingering of mental conditions when defendants assert the insanity defense. In the majority of these cases, the insanity defense fails. More often than not, it fails because the defendant's conduct is again being judged by a norm, rather than on the merits of his subjective impairments. The test for legal insanity requires more than just that the defendant manifest a mental disease or defect;

most states require that, as a result of the impairment, the defendant not understand the wrongfulness of his conduct. When the objective evidence bespeaks otherwise, the defendant's insanity defense generally fails. Such was the case in *People v. Urdiales*,[135] where the defendant entered a plea of guilty but mentally ill but was convicted of first-degree murder and sentenced to death. To satisfy the statutory requirements of a legal insanity plea, the defense presented expert testimony and evidence, including MRI and SPECT scan data, to demonstrate that the defendant suffered from shrinkage of the brain, which could explain his criminal conduct. The court instead credited the state's expert, who rebutted the diagnosis of organic brain disease and testified that the defendant's actions at the time of the murder did not bespeak someone who suffered significant impairment of the central nervous system. Likewise, in *U.S. v. Eff*,[136] where the defendant attempted to prove legal insanity by introducing testimony that he suffered from Klinefelter's syndrome, a genetic condition that, from birth, negatively affects brain development.[137] The expert testified that individuals with Klinefelter's syndrome show deficits in "their ability to plan, their ability to anticipate and appreciate the consequences of their actions, and their ability to inhibit inappropriate behavior, resulting in 'childlike decisions' or 'magical thinking.' "[138] The court did not allow this evidence to go to the jury, because the evidence established only that Eff might have a diminished capacity to appreciate the nature and quality or wrongfulness of his actions, not that he was completely unable to appreciate such things, as was required under the statute.[139] These courts layered objectiveness over insanity to find that an objective perspective of the defendants' behavior put them within the action-intention norm, rather than lending support to treat them as nonagents to whom the norms should not apply.

This boundary of the insanity defense, or nonagency, would be better informed by a standard of objective reasonableness that tracks to actual average abilities in society. This approach is discussed in detail in Part 4. As criminal law currently recognizes, the boundaries of agency cannot be addressed by science alone —there is a normative question embedded in the issue, which is to whom the criminal law should apply. Physical capacities may help to inform societal response to that question.

Reconciling the Alternative Normative Account

Understanding the content of the criminal justice system requires an understanding of the modern and historical social context that made certain acts criminal.[140] What is criminal may be largely traceable to the legislature acting on behalf of the community.[141] Because many acts become criminal on the basis of legislative response to social outrage, criminal law punishes conduct that the community finds blameworthy or unacceptable. And yet criminal law prohibits both more and less than morally blameworthy behavior, and its legitimacy does not depend upon its perfect overlap with morally wrongful conduct. As both the legal positivist H. L. A. Hart and the realist Oliver Wendell Holmes, Jr., have noted—especially in the context of the criminal law, where social opprobrium is at its highest and the state exerts the greatest power in limiting liberty—one would expect to see greater overlap between unlawful and morally condemnable behavior. To preserve the legitimacy of the state in this liberty-limiting context, criminal law cannot stray too far from punishing *conduct* the community finds to be morally blameworthy. Otherwise, the system will be at odds with the moral intuitions of the community in which it operates. Nevertheless, criminal law can and does go beyond punishing conduct that society demands legislatures to circumscribe.

Behavioral moralists focus on a different notion of blameworthiness. They argue that the criminal law must be limited not only to conduct that society finds morally blameworthy but also to *criminals* who have a blameworthy cause for having engaged in prohibited conduct. Behavioral moralists like Greene and Cohen go further to argue that a deterministic account of *criminals*, like all other human actors, will inevitably reshape societal intuitions about justice such that moral opprobrium will be unjust and ultimately rejected in favor of a consequentialist approach. This approach treats individuals with a scientific account of their behavior as lacking any blameworthy cause for engaging in criminal conduct.

While criminal law gains its legitimacy in part by ensuring that the conduct it proscribes is that which society also finds blameworthy, the test for criminality is largely an external one, rather than the internal one that behavioral moralists would favor. Holmes aptly clarified:

It is not intended to deny that criminal liability . . . is founded on blameworthiness. . . . It is only intended to point out that, when we are dealing with that part of the law which aims more directly than any other at establishing standards of conduct, we should expect there more than elsewhere to find that the tests of liability are external.[142]

At the core of any system of criminal law are those crimes that comport with societal intuitions about wrongful behavior. Beyond that core, criminal law also circumscribes many other types of conduct. This includes regulatory offenses like driving through a stop sign when no one else is present. Such a system creates norms of conduct that all members of that community are required to meet or exceed. It does not excuse a failure to meet those norms on the basis of the internal physical proximate causes of such a failure except in limited circumstances. Those limited circumstances are categorical and bright-line rules around the normative concept of agency.

The criminalization of behavior and creation of external norms of general conduct by which all members of society will be judged secures a social advantage to society.[143] It creates aspirational goals for members of society to act in a manner that benefits the whole. Criminal responsibility serves those goals by allowing for individual accountability to society and penalizing the violation of social norms. As a concept of accountability, criminal responsibility also operates as a distinct, although perhaps necessary, precursor to criminal culpability, a concept of moral opprobrium and blame, discussed in Part 4. Criminal responsibility focuses on the legal liability of an individual for criminal conduct. Criminal culpability focuses on moral blameworthiness of an individual for criminal conduct and personal circumstances. Two individuals may have identical criminal responsibility and yet differ on their extent of culpability; the appropriate societal response to each should likewise differ.

This notion of criminal responsibility presumes that individuals have both the capacity for rationality and control over their actions when they engage in criminal conduct.[144] Behavioral moralists face a near insurmountable hurdle in overcoming this premise because none of their behavioral models provides an absolute or deterministic account of human behavior. Evolutionary, biological, or neurological accounts of human behavior may show that defendants are *more* impulsive than the average person, *less* likely to have premeditated their actions, or acted as a product of their brain, rather than their agency. The behavioral moralists believe that such evidence challenges the presumption of free choice and thereby the foundation of accountability in criminal law. But criminal law accepts that human behavior exists along a continuum —that many factors affect human choice—and yet these factors simply influence action choices by agents, who face responsibility for conduct and not circumstances.

The criminal justice system posits that human actors have the capacity to engage in or refrain from criminal conduct and creates societal standards of conduct and responsibility.[145] This model assumes a different notion of responsibility from medical or scientific models that reduce all human conduct, human disease, and natural phenomena to responsible causes and correlates to enable diagnosis and treatment.[146] Referencing the "proximate causes" of criminal conduct does not adequately rebut the normative presumption of accountability and agency in criminal law. The presumption of human choice enables a maximally efficient system of criminal law by allowing for human autonomy and responsibility.[147] Without presuming human choice, reifying and encouraging new social norms of behavior would be futile. Social systems such as the criminal law can persist only if individuals in some sense both can believe that they are responsible for their conduct[148] and can achieve or aspire to achieve the norms of conduct that have been set. If actors within the system believe themselves to be determined, fated to act in a particular way, whether as a mechanism of evolution or as a deviation in their brain, they have no incentive to attempt to comply with the requirements of the law. Indeed, some studies have found that the very language of determinism pushes people to act irresponsibility and to engage in socially disfavored behavior.[149] Thus, to shift responsibility to the many factors influencing human behavior, including every environmental factor or family historical interaction or even the environment within the womb, would enable every person to deflect blame or responsibility to a secondary source. Norms of behavior cannot have meaning within such a system except as artifacts of causal influences.

Deviations from norms of conduct would be blamed on failed causes instead of on failings by individuals. Social norm-enforcing institutions like the criminal law can persist only if humans are treated as responsible agents, capable of exercising control over their impulses, desires, and actions.[150]

Criminal law has a positive role in norm *setting*, aside from its role in norm enforcing. This positive role necessarily must be ahead of and disconnected from evolution. Norms are behaviors that are encouraged, aspired to, and set for future generations to meet, rather than ones that are evolved, set, and determined by past generations. Social institutions like the criminal law develop and stabilize by codifying into law an agreed-upon set of norms, which may begin with a shared set of embedded values. But the system need not and does not stop there, once it comes into existence. A social institution like the criminal law may create new norms of conduct—aspirational goals for members of society to meet.

Behavioral moralists reject the autonomous view of human choice and the aspirational nature of the criminal justice system, arguing instead that new explanatory causes of human behavior undermine the system.[151] So, as science discovers new contributions to human behavior, they argue that the criminal law must accordingly redefine its system of criminal responsibility.[152] Such claims subjugate the field of criminal law to science and presume that the foundation and objectives of the criminal justice system must be rooted in scientific explanations of human behavior.

Science and human agency can coexist. Despite the current direction of behavioral moralism, the theory could have a role in reshaping a fundamental component of criminal responsibility—the notion of reasonableness underlying it. As the rationales in the cases discussed earlier reveal, while agency permeates criminal law, the notion of agency is made by reference to an objective and societal conception of reasonableness—or the average expected capacities of the members of society. Rather than throwing out the baby with the bathwater by calling for a complete overhaul of theories of responsibility, behavioral moralists may gain greater traction by guiding the objective concept of reasonableness in criminal law.

3. RETHINKING REASONABLENESS

Criminal law expressly relies upon an objective notion of reasonableness. The norm of reasonableness is apparent throughout the cases discussed and is foundational in criminal law. Actions are presumed voluntary because the average person intends to act when he acts. Criminal defenses that enable the defendant to introduce his unique deficits turn on reasonableness by asking what an average person would have believed about the need to self-defend, whether he would have experienced duress or provocation under the circumstances. The minimum requirements of the criminal law are pegged to those with which the average member of the community can comply, while the maximum requirements of criminal law must comport with social intuitions of justice.

Behavioral morality reflects a basic discontent with the objective formulation of the reasonable-person standard in criminal law.[153] Behavioral moralists believe that the individual infirmities of the defendant should inform the extent to which he is held responsible under law. Such an individualized and subjective standard is unlikely to replace the norms-based standard of criminal law. Nevertheless, behavioral moralists could gain traction by instead arguing that reasonableness should be informed by emerging scientific evidence to reflect the actual average capacities of society.

Oliver Wendell Holmes, Jr., described the "reasonable person" as:

> an ideal being, represented by the jury when they are appealed to, and his conduct is an external or objective standard when applied to any given individual. That individual may be morally without stain, because he has less than ordinary intelligence or prudence. But he is required to have those qualities at his peril. If he has them, he will not, as a general rule, incur liability without blameworthiness.[154]

In Holmes's description, the individual attributes of the defendant relate only to the defendant's capacity to conform his conduct to the norm or average person and capacities in society. The reasonable-person standard embodies norms of behavior under the relevant circumstances against which the jury measures the defendant's conduct; it does not inquire into the "proximate causes" acting on a defendant's behavior. To the contrary, the person who deviates from societal norms may himself lack moral blameworthiness, but he will be held responsible nonetheless for transgressing rules of conduct. The Holmesian view also provides a tool by which a jury may set and codify societal norms of behavior.[155] Reasonableness in effect serves two functions. It both reflects the judgment of what humans will do under a given set of circumstances and serves as an aspirational tool "to foster, sustain, and articulate norms" of behavior in society.[156]

As I've discussed more fully elsewhere,[157] four interrelated reasons support the objective reasonable-person standard: creating standards of conduct, fostering equality and predictability in case outcomes, enabling administrative ease in case management, and preventing a paradox of responsibility where the least dangerous are held the most accountable. These four interrelated goals promote the more general purpose of the criminal law—to safeguard the welfare of society and foster law-abiding behavior. Thus, maintaining a notion of reasonableness by which to judge a defendant's conduct has normative value that may be difficult, if not impossible, to replicate in a system that judges each individual according to his unique capacities to obey the law. But how do we assess objective reasonableness?

The reasonable-person standard embodies the capacities of an average member of society—one who does not excel, can err in his choices and makes mistakes, suffers from fear and selfishness, and possesses other shortcomings.[158] But how do we presently decide how that average member of society will act under a given set of circumstances? Today, we ask the judge (in a bench trial) or the jury (in a jury trial) to inform this standard based on their beliefs about the capacities of the ordinary person. As one might expect, these actors inform that standard based on their own experiences and capacities. I propose that behavioral moralists would better focus their energies on this issue. While reasonableness does and must have a normative component that society will define, what better way to inform the definitional concept of reasonableness of average human capacities than through empirical testing?

Concepts such as "normal" and "average" are social constructs that have both normative and descriptive content. Yet, once a construct or definition is established—such as conforming one's conduct to the law—scientific evidence can inform the robustness of that definition. Testing the social constructs of average or reasonable is one that behavioral moralists could meaningfully inform, challenge, and transform.

Behavioral sciences cannot define average or normal. Yet, these disciplines can help to displace outmoded social constructs of average or reasonable with more robust ones that are informed by population-wide data. Population-wide studies of human genomes, human brains, evolutionary biology, and environmental contributions to human behavior can inform average and subaverage human features and behaviors. The Human Genome Project mapped the human genome, and studies since have linked genetic variations to behavioral variations in the population. Likewise, projects such as the Human Brainome Project seek to map the human brain and to associate neurological variations with behavioral variations across the population.[159] Population-wide evidence linking genetic, neurological, and environmental variations are under way (see some discussed earlier), and many such studies have yielded and continue to yield meaningful results. While neuroimaging studies are presently small-scale studies, efforts to assimilate the results and images generated across a large number of these studies into meta-studies will yield meaningful and comparative results. While society cannot presently predict whether an individual will suffer minor or major behavioral deficits by simply looking at a brain image, population-wide data linking neurological and behavioral differences may enable robust predictions of exactly that sort in the near future.[160]

Likewise, both past and future research linking environmental influences to variations in human behavior help inform which environmental influences are likely to have the greatest impact on human behavior. Some environmental and genetic influences are already well characterized. In behavioral genetics, for example, which employs population statistics as the major methodological tool of study, scientific studies have demonstrated linkages between certain polymorphisms in promoter regions of particular genes, which, when combined with particular environmental stressors, greatly increase the likelihood of a particular behavioral reaction.[161]

As neuroscience, behavioral genetics, and scientific studies of human behavior progress, these disciplines will become increasingly more relevant to societal constructs of average or normal behavior. The capacities and limitations of human behavior and the ability of individuals to conform their conduct to the confines of the criminal law could be more accurately described. Ideally, brain-environment (BxE), gene-environment (GxE), and brain-gene-environment (BxGxE) interactions will provide a better understanding of human behavior under a given set of circumstances. Then, rather than relying upon a fictional or arbitrary understanding of the average or objectively reasonable person in society or simply deferring to a judge or jury to decide these issues, we may start to actually know what we can expect from the ordinary person with average neurological, biological, and environmental endowments. Whether at a global level (through jury instructions and reformulation of the charge about average or reasonableness) or through the introduction of expert testimony at trial on the average capacities of an individual to have acted differently than the criminal defendant, population-wide data could inform what the reasonable person would likely do under the circumstances. And herein the behavioral moralists may have their best claim—once we have a better understanding of human behavior, why should we base the average or reasonable person solely on fictional predictions of human capacities? Why wouldn't we use scientific information about the average person, as empirically tested and validated by science? This information would inform the normative decisions that society will continue to have to make —where to draw lines for who will be held as nonagents. These normative choices will benefit from better evidence about human capacities under given sets of circumstances.[162]

Suppose, for example, that science is able to predict that all people with lesions of a certain size and shape in the frontal lobe who also have certain environmental triggers, such as childhood abuse, will commit robberies as adults. Society may decide that, given the distribution of normal human capacities, such persons cannot be held as agents under criminal law when they later rob as adults. Or, society might also decide that, because of the aspirational goals of the criminal law—to set other norms of human behavior—even those people will be held criminally accountable when they commit violent robberies but not when they commit nonviolent ones. This choice will depend in part on whether retributivist or consequentialist justifications are used. Under either approach, the definition of reasonableness employed would be better informed with such evidence.

By focusing on reasonableness more generally, behavioral moralists would integrate their views into the broader law and science fold. Law and evolutionary biology theorists, for example, recognize that "humans share a psychology that is the product of evolution"[163] and that this "psychology tends to reflect an adaptive logic."[164] This shared psychology creates, in aggregate, a distinct and fairly uniform "behavioral repertoire"[165] that the law may use to more fully understand and therefore govern behavioral proclivities in the aggregate. This evolutionary standing of the distinct and uniform behavioral repertoire could help to inform the development of a more robust reasonable-person standard. Law and evolutionary biology theorists may concur with such an approach, since they are quick to note that the legal conception of behaviors is rarely subject to rigorous scrutiny.[166] As a result, the law may fail in its inquiry into and understanding of species-wide behavior, thereby amplifying, "even if unintendedly, the importance of individual psyches over naturally selected behavioral predicates."[167] Rather than elevating the individual conception over the norm, evolutionary biology may have much to offer on the development of a more robust reasonable-person standard.

Criminal law will have to balance its goals—promoting social welfare, reifying and setting social norms—with preserving its legitimacy. If, indeed, 100 percent of individuals are unable to comply with a set norm in criminal law and science can inform this, criminal law will likely need to reformulate that norm. A scientifically robust standard of reasonableness, informed by the normative decision of where to draw the line as to who will be treated as an agent of criminal law, provides a more promising venue for behavioral moralists to realize their aspirations of incorporating genetics, evolution, and neuroscience into criminal law.

4. FOCUSING THE DEBATE ON CULPABILITY

A finding of criminal responsibility does not ultimately address the appropriate societal *response* to criminal accountability. Societal responses to responsibility could range from retributive ones, to preventive detention, rehabilitation, release, or no response at all. Many scholars and behavioral moralists have investigated the myriad of appropriate societal responses in light of introducing descriptive causal information about human behavior into criminal law. This chapter seeks to identify a unifying theme among the myriad of proposals that have been offered, and proposes that criminal stigma is the unnamed discomfort driving much of the debate.

Use of Neuroscience to Rebut Culpability

An individualized inquiry into the personal culpability of the defendant arises by matter of constitutional right in the context of death penalty cases. Thus, the majority of attempts by behavioral moralists to introduce neuroscience into criminal cases have been challenges to the imposition of the death penalty. The U.S. Supreme Court has interpreted the Eighth Amendment of the Constitution to require individualized assessments of blameworthiness for imposing the death penalty, which includes a defendant's constitutional right to introduce mitigating evidence on his behalf. Thus, defendants often challenge the imposition of a death sentence by arguing that the judge improperly excluded or the defense attorney failed to investigate developmental evidence, genetic-predisposition testimony, and neurological evidence. Because of the procedural requirements of death penalty cases on appeal, capital defendants must frame their argument as a claim of ineffective assistance of counsel for a failure by their trial counsel to introduce such evidence during the sentencing phase of their trial. Because defendants face substantial legal hurdles in demonstrating ineffective assistance of counsel ("IAC") during trial, in most instances, a defendant's IAC claim fails.[168]

In *Woodhall v. Commonwealth*,[169] for example, after being convicted of capital murder, kidnapping, and first-degree rape and being sentenced to death, the defendant moved to vacate, set aside, or correct his sentence, alleging that trial counsel was ineffective for failing to raise a genetic-defect defense and failing to pursue further neurological testing to substantiate other mental health defenses. The motion was denied, and defendant appealed. The court held that the decision not to investigate one of the plethora of mental health defenses must be professionally reasonable under the circumstances and that the reviewing court gives deference to trial counsel's decisions. But the reviewing court found that, even if the genetic and neurological evidence had been fleshed out and presented, the balance between aggravating and mitigating circumstances would unlikely have tipped away from death. Most cases proceed this way; the reviewing court balances the heinousness of the criminal offense against the defendant's claim of a neurological or biological contribution to his behavior and finds the mitigation of his culpability wanting.

The behavioral morality claim takes nearly the same form in rebutting culpability as when rebutting responsibility. In addressing culpability, the behavioral moralist acknowledges that the defendant will be held accountable for his crime but argues that he should be punished less severely than other defendants because of the causal contributions to his behavior. *Hoskins v. State*[170] is illustrative. In this case, the defendant appealed his conviction for rape and murder, as well as his capital sentence. On appeal, the Florida Supreme Court vacated his sentence and remanded for a PET scan and a subsequent evidentiary hearing to determine whether the PET scan showed an abnormality and, if so, whether the results would cause the expert witness to change his testimony. Following a new sentencing hearing, the defendant was again sentenced to death. The defendant again appealed, in part claiming that the trial court improperly rejected the mitigator that he was "under the influence of extreme mental or emotional disturbance."[171] On appeal, the court held that, although the defendant had demonstrated he suffered a hypofrontal-lobe abnormality and potential brain injury that can result in reduced impulse control, the defense expert found no connection between the brain abnormalities and the defendant's subsequent criminal actions. The expert testimony, together with the objective evidence demonstrating the defendant had planned the murder, substantiated the trial court's rejection of this mitigator.[172]

Despite Hoskins's failure to prevail, he nevertheless had intermediate successes by relying on neurological claims in challenging his sentence. In general, the behavioral morality claim has greater traction when framed in terms of culpability than when framed in terms of responsibility. This makes sense—our moral sense of opprobrium and our desire to punish is more likely to be reduced in some circumstances when we understand the causes of deviant behavior than when the conduct is just bewildering to us. But, until there is some meaningful way to give effect to the purposes of criminal law—general welfare as well as norm setting and enforcement—and this lessened sense of moral opprobrium is achieved, society has little venue for giving value to it. In the context of the death penalty, where the choice is death or life imprisonment, the choice is an easier one—jurors can realize feelings of mercy by voting for life imprisonment without sacrificing the general welfare of society. But, in other contexts, where the choice may be to free a responsible and dangerous defendant, but one for whom a juror feels less moral opprobrium, there is no way to realize this lessened sense of blame.

This decreased moral opprobrium helps to explain some of the outcomes in culpability-based cases. In *Crook v. State*,[173] for example, defendant Crook introduced expert witnesses during his sentencing hearing to assert that he suffered from frontal-lobe brain damage and impulse-control disorder arising from "his organic brain dysfunction rather than any character disorder."[174] The trial court sentenced Crook to death without considering the defense expert's testimony.[175] The Florida Supreme Court vacated Crook's death sentence and remanded the case to the trial court because "[c]learly, the existence of brain damage is a significant mitigating factor that trial courts should consider in deciding whether a death sentence is appropriate in a particular case."[176] On remand, the trial court again imposed the death penalty,[177] and Crook appealed the proportionality of his sentence in light of substantial evidence of the neurological and genetic basis for his behavior.[178] The Supreme Court of Florida again reversed, finding Crook's mental deficiencies were highly relevant to his degree of culpability, focusing on "the unrefuted testimony of the mental health experts that relate the rage and brutal conduct in this crime to the defendant's brain damage and mental deficiencies."[179]

Likewise, "proximate cause" evidence has proven powerful in the establishment of categorical exemptions to the death penalty under the Cruel and Unusual Punishments Clause of the Eighth Amendment. In *Roper v. Simmons*,[180] the U.S. Supreme Court held that juveniles under the age of eighteen are ineligible to be sentenced to death. In *Roper*, the Court cited to amicus briefs that introduced behavioral studies demonstrating that adolescent brains are not fully developed and observed that therefore juveniles are less likely than adults to make thoughtful and well-planned decisions. And, in *Atkins v. Virginia*,[181] the Court held that the mentally retarded are not sufficiently culpable to be sentenced to death, drawing again from the behavioral sciences to substantiate a finding of reduced culpability. Defendants regularly attempt to introduce scientific evidence to make analogous claims. And, most recently, in *Graham v. Florida*,[182] the Court made explicit its reliance on developing brain evidence by citing it as objective evidence in deciding that life without the possibility of parole is cruel and unusual punishment for juvenile offenders who have not committed a homicide-based crime.

Stigma: Naming the Issue

Despite the broad reach of the criminal justice system to *malum prohibitum* crimes, in general any criminal conviction begets an associated social stigma. In rare instances, such as misdemeanor offenses, because the criminal nature of the offense escapes notice by virtue of its label and attendant punishment, a small category of criminal offenders avoids stigmatization.

John Stanton-Ife proposes two concepts of stigma that provide a useful framework for criminal law: the psychological sense and the normative one.[183] The psychological sense pertains to that which is in fact stigmatized, and the normative pertains to that which ought to be.[184] Psychological stigma may therefore resound in the moral sense or evolutionary model of opprobrium discussed earlier. As a psychological notion, it dovetails with that which the community intuitively finds blameworthy.[185] The actualization of stigma can be viewed in society's reluctance to interact with one who has a criminal record or to treat that person with the same regard with which society treats those without a criminal record. This may, in fact, diverge from that which a normative sense may justify as truly deserving of stigma or blame.

Psychological stigmatization may result in understigmatization —that is, the moral sense that arises may fail to fully account for the effect of regulatory offenses on social welfare, for failure to meet aspirational norms, or for small effects that have significant aggregate harm, particularly when universally dismissed.[186] It may likewise result in overstigmatization, whereby the harmful impact of the criminal offense results in psychological stigmatization of the criminal, without considering the extent to which the individual could have avoided the harm in question.

This chapter proposes that the struggle of the behavioral moralists—and, indeed, much of their focus on issues of culpability—lies in whether descriptive causes of human behavior should relieve individuals of normative stigmatization. Greene and Cohen, for example, argue that neuroscience will inevitably lead to the adoption of a consequentialist model that eliminates the moral stigma and judgment that retributive justice implies.[187] And it seems evident that many behavioral moralists may in fact be motivated by the sense that individuals ought not be stigmatized if there is a physical cause for their behavior. Or, more aptly put, those individuals who fall outside the norm or range of average capacity to control their conduct ought to be held to a different level of social blame than those who can meet the capacities of the criminal law.

To open the dialogue on this issue, I offer the following provocations:

First, perhaps the psychological rather than normative sense is being aroused by descriptive causes of human behavior. It may be difficult to psychologically internalize the physical existence of both the body and the mind, such that when descriptive accounts of human behavior are provided, they are integrated into a singular view of human behavior that accepts that recognized physical causes are all part of an integrated human agent. Thus, psychologically, behavioral moralists may react against stigmatizing criminal conduct that can be causally described, but this may not normatively justify displacing stigma under these circumstances.

Second, the normative ought of stigmatization will likely dovetail with changing conceptions of reasonableness in criminal responsibility. The harm caused by an individual who can causally explain his behavior and the harm caused by one who cannot are exactly the same. The difference between these two actors is simply whether the individual in question should have been expected to conform to the norms established by society. If the person falls outside the norm, such that attributions of human agency are inappropriate, so, too, will attributions of criminal stigma. But, if not, even if one's psychological sense of stigma varies, the normative sense should not.

Finally, stigma and social norms must be considered in light of each other. If criminal law is intended to both enforce and create new norms of conduct, there may be a normative justification for stigmatizing individuals, even if the psychological sense of stigma turns one against it in the individual case. Norm creation itself has a normative purpose—to guide individuals in society to act in a manner deemed in the best interest of society. Stigmatizing individuals who fail to do so may serve as an effective tool for enforcing norms and creating new norms of conduct.

5. CONCLUSION

Behavioral moralists have made little headway in the criminal justice system. But they just might, with a redirected focus. While criminal law has a normative commitment to treating humans as autonomous agents, capable of making choices and being held responsible, it also relies upon a fictitious concept of reasonableness, one that is ripe for reexamination. The purpose, then, of this chapter is not only to name, situate, and describe the behavioral moralists' claim but also to redirect it to more productive ends. With a more robust understanding of human behavior, the concept of reasonableness could be informed by both a scientific understanding of human behavior and the normative purposes of the criminal law.

With a sound conception of criminal responsibility, one still must address the appropriate societal response to criminal conduct. And only time will tell which theory of punishment will have true staying power. But, while that debate may continue indefinitely, in the interim, the psychological and normative attachments to stigma must be addressed. This chapter invites a dialogue on whether and to what extent criminal stigma should attach if the behavioral moralist claim rings true—and scientists are able to provide more robust descriptions of human behavior. It proposes that, while the psychological sense of stigma may suggest otherwise, normative justifications may persist.

NOTES

Thanks to Walter Sinnott-Armstrong, James Fleming, John C. P. Goldberg, Dan Kahan, Sanford Levinson, Amanda Pustilnik, Nicholas Quinn Rosenkranz, Edward Rubin, Jeff Schall, Kevin Stack, and participants in the 2008 Annual Meeting of the American Society for Political and Legal Philosophy for their comments on earlier drafts. Alex Fenner and Brandon Wadell provided invaluable research assistance.

1. By "internal proximate causes," I mean those unique to the physical body of the individual, whether genetic, neurological, or otherwise. See Part 2 for a discussion of proximate versus ultimate causes.

2. Joshua Greene and Jonathan Cohen, "For the Law, Neuroscience Changes Nothing and Everything," *Philosophical Transactions of the Royal Society of London B* 359 (2004): 1775, 1775–76.

3. See, e.g., H. L. A. Hart, *Punishment and Responsibility* (Oxford: Oxford University Press, 1968), 226 ("The interesting differences between legal and moral responsibility arise from the differences in the particular criteria falling under these general heads. Thus a system of criminal law may make responsibility strict, or even absolute, not even exempting very young children or the grossly insane from punishment. . . . We may condemn such a legal system as barbarous or unjust, but there are no conceptual barriers to overcome in speaking of such a system as a legal system.").

4. See, e.g., Peter Singer, "Famine, Affluence and Morality," *Philosophy and Public Affairs* 1 (1972): 229, 237 (discussing Sidgwick's and Urmson's theories about the requirements that a moral code comport with capacities of ordinary people or it will suffer a breakdown of compliance); Greene and Cohen, "For the Law, Neuroscience Changes Nothing and Everything."

5. Robin B. Kar, "Hart's Response to Exclusive Legal Positivism," *Georgetown Law Journal* 95 (2007): 393, 414.

6. Cornelia Dean, "Science of the Soul? 'I Think, Therefore I Am' Is Losing Force," *New York Times*, June 26, 2007, F8.

7. Margaret Gruter, *Law and the Mind: Biological Origins of Human Behaviors* (New York: Sage, 1991), 53.

8. See, e.g., John Foster, *The Immaterial Self: A Defence of the Cartesian Dualist Conception of the Mind* (London and New York: Routledge, 1996).

9. Vernon L. Quinsey, "Evolutionary Theory of Criminal Behavior," *Legal and Criminological Psychology* 7 (2002): 1, 2.

10. Ibid.

11. Ibid.

12. Ibid.

13. Ibid., 4.

14. Randy Thornhill and Craig T. Palmer, *A Natural History of Rape: Biological Bases of Sexual Coercion* (Cambridge, MA: MIT Press, 2000).

15. Ibid.

16. "Why We Are as We Are," *Economist*, December 18, 2008.

17. Ibid.

18. Ibid.

19. Quinsey, "Evolutionary Theory of Criminal Behavior," 7–8.

20. Ibid.; Martin Daly and Margo Wilson, *Homicide* (New Brunswick, NJ: Aldine Transaction, 1988).

21. Paul H. Robinson, Robert Kurzban, and Owen D. Jones, "The Origins of Shared Intuitions of Justice," *Vanderbilt Law Review* 60 (2007): 1633; Quinsey, "Evolutionary Theory of Criminal Behavior," 7.

22. Linda Mealey, "The Sociobiology of Sociopathy: An Integrated Evolutionary Model," *Behavioral and Brain Science* 18 (1995): 523.

23. Ibid.

24. "Limbic System," UHS Neurobehavioral Systems, accessed January 28, 2009, http://www.ragebehavior.com/limbic.htm.

25. "The Fiction of the 'Reasonable Man,'" *Washington Post*, May 17, 1989, C3.

26. "Limbic System."

27. See e.g., "The Fiction of the 'Reasonable Man'" (discussing situations where brain damage to the limbic system could cause violent outbursts and rage disorder).

28. E.g., William D. Casebeer, "Moral Cognition and Its Neural Constituents," *Nature Neuroscience* 4 (2003): 841, 843 ("The moral emotions are crucial for effective moral cognition.").

29. See, e.g., Jonathan Haidt and Fredrick Bjorklund, "Social Intuitionists Answer Six Questions about Moral Psychology," in *Moral Psychology, Vol. 2: The Cognitive Science of Morality*, ed. W. Sinott-Armstrong (Cambridge, MA: MIT Press, 2007), 181, 201 ("At the mildest extreme is a general notion of preparedness, the claim that animals are prepared (by evolution) to learn some associations more easily than others. . . . At the other extreme is the idea of the massively modular mind, championed by evolutionary psychologists. . . . On this view the mind is like a Swiss army knife with many tools, each one an adaptation.").

30. Laura A. Baker, Serena Bezdijian, and Adrian Raine, "Behavioral Genetics: The Science of Antisocial Behavior," *Law and Contemporary Problems* 69 (2006): 7, 13.

31. See William Bernet et al., "Bad Nature, Bad Nurture, and Testimony Regarding MAOA and SLC6A4 Genotyping at Murder Trials," *Journal of Forensic Sciences* 52 (2007): 1362.

32. A version of this summary first appeared in Nita Farahany and William Bernet, "Behavioural Genetics in Criminal Cases: Past, Present and Future," *Genomics, Society and Policy* 2 (May 2006): 72. See also A. Caspi et al., "Role of Genotype in the Cycle of Violence in Maltreated Children," *Science* 297 (2002): 851–54.

33. A. Caspi et al., "Role of Genotype."

34. Ibid., 853.

35. A. Caspi et al., "Influence of Life Stress on Depression: Moderation by a Polymorphism in the 5-HTT Gene," *Science* 301 (2003): 386–89.

36. Ibid., 386.

37. Klaus A. Miczek et al., "An Overview of Biological Influences on Violence Behavior," in *Understanding and Preventing Violence, Vol. 2: Biobehavioral Differences*, ed. Albert J. Reiss et al. (Washington, DC: National Academies Press, 1994), 5.

38. Miczek et al., "An Overview of Biological Influences on Violence Behavior," 7.

39. Kenneth S. Kendler and Lindon J. Eaves, *Psychiatric Genetics* (Washington, DC: American Psychiatric Publishing, 2005), 176.

40. Ibid., 185.

41. Ibid.

42. Ibid., 177–78.

43. Ibid., 178.

44. Ibid.

45. Baker et al., "Behavioral Genetics," 34.

46. Ibid.

47. Ibid., 35.

48. See ibid., 36; Mitchell E. Berman et al., "Neurotransmitter Correlates of Human Aggression," in *Handbook of Antisocial Behavior*, ed. David M. Stoff et al. (New York: Wiley, 1997), 305; Rhona Limson et al., "Personality and Cerebrospinal Fluid Monoamine Metabolites in Alcoholics and Controls," *Archives of General Psychiatry* 48 (1991): 437, 439.

49. Baker et al., "Behavioral Genetics," 36.

50. Ibid., 37.

51. E.g., Remi J. Cadoret et al., "Genetic-Environmental Interaction in the Genesis of Aggressivity and Conduct Disorders," *Archives of General Psychiatry* 52 (1995): 916; Sören Sigvardsson et al., "Predisposition to Petty Criminality in Swedish Adoptees: III. Sex Differences in Validation of the Male Typology," *Archives of General Psychiatry* 39 (1982): 1248; Barry Hutchins and Sarnoff A. Mednick, "Registered Criminality in the Adoptive and Biological Parents of Registered Male Criminal Adoptees," in *Genetic Research in Psychiatry*, ed. Ronald R. Fieve et al. (Baltimore: John Hopkins Press, 1975), 105; S. Torgersen et al., "The Psychometric-Genetic Structure

of DSM-III-R Personality Disorder Criteria," *Journal of Personality Disorders* 7 (1993): 196.

52. Baker et al., "Behavioral Genetics," 18.

53. Ibid., 18–19.

54. Ibid.

55. *Neuroethics and ELSI: Some Comparisons and Considerations*, accessed December 15, 2008, http://perpich.com/neuroed/archive/139.pdf.

56. Dean Mobbs, Hakwan C. Lau, Owen D. Jones, and Christopher D. Frith, "Law, Responsibility and the Brain," *Public Library of Science (PLoS) Biology* 5 (2007): 693.

57. "Research Links Brain Damage and Violent Crime—USC Studies Point to Underlying Causes of Violent Crime in Young Offenders," *Science Daily*, September 13, 1997, http://www.sciencedaily.com/releases/1997/09/970913073401.htm.

58. Ibid.

59. Lower rates of glucose uptake were found in the prefrontal cortext, the corpus callosum, and the posterior parietal cortext. Study subjects who had committed homicide showed weaker activity in the amygdala and the hippocampus in the left hemisphere and stronger activity in the thalamus, amygdala, and hippocampus of the right hemisphere. Ibid.

60. Ibid.

61. Ibid.

62. Ibid.

63. David C. Bellinger, "Neurological and Behavioral Consequences of Childhood Lead Exposure," *Public Library of Science (PLoS) Medicine* 5 (2008): 690.

64. Ibid.

65. Ibid. Researchers found a dose-dependent volume correlation in the ventrolateral prefrontal cortex, the anterior cingulated cortext, the postcentral gyri, the inferior parietal lobule, and the cerebellum. Ibid.

66. Ibid.

67. Ibid.

68. Ibid.

69. See generally Mario F. Mendez et al., "Pedophilia and Temporal Lobe Disturbances," *Journal of Neuropyschiatry and Clinical Neurociences* 12 (2000): 71.

70. Ibid.

71. Walter Sinnott-Armstrong, "A Case Study in Neuroscience and Responsibility," in this volume, 196–98.

72. Jeffrey M. Burns and Russell H. Swerdlow, "Right Orbitofrontal Tumor with Pedophilia Symptom and Constructional Apraxia Sign," *Archives of Neurology* 60 (2003): 437.

73. Ibid.
74. Ibid.
75. Ibid.
76. Ibid., 438.
77. Ibid.
78. R. J. R. Blair, "The Cognitive Neuroscience of Psychopathy and Implications for Judgments of Responsibility," *Neuroethics* 1 (2008): 147, 153.
79. Ibid.
80. Ibid.
81. Ibid., 154.
82. Kent A. Kiehl et al., "Brain Potentials Implicate Temporal Lobe Abnormalities in Criminal Psychopaths," *Journal of Abnormal Psychiatry* 115 (2006): 443, 451.
83. Ibid.
84. See, e.g., Owen D. Jones and Timothy H. Goldsmith, "Law and Behavioral Biology," *Columbia Law Review* 105 (2005): 405, 455.
85. Ibid.
86. Owen D. Jones, "Evolutionary Analysis in Law: An Introduction and Application to Child Abuse," *North Carolina Law Review* 75 (1997): 1117, 1148.
87. Ibid.
88. E.g., Timothy H. Goldsmith and Owen D. Jones, "Evolutionary Biology and Behavior: A Brief Overview and Some Important Concepts," *Jurimetrics Journal* 39 (1999): 131, 135 ("To view human behavior in evolutionary terms is to hypothesize how natural selection might have biased the brain to attend to particular sensory signals or to weigh the importance of particular environmental circumstances. Such reasoning is therefore never in conflict with efforts to understand proximate causes, as often popularly supposed, because proximate and ultimate causes are complementary modes of explanation").
89. John Teehan, "On the Naturalistic Fallacy: A Conceptual Basis for Evolutionary Ethics," *Evolutionary Psychology* 2 (2004): 32, 36.
90. See, e.g., E. Donald Elliott, "Law and Biology: The New Synthesis?," *St. Louis University Law Journal* 41 (1997): 595, 617 ("[T]he notion that somehow law ought to codify these biological absolutes . . . is a position that others such as John Beckstrom have taken, but it is one which I specifically deny."); Jones and Goldsmith, "Law and Behavioral Biology," 492 ("[I]t is essential that behavioral biology not be thought to provide normative support for particular legal outcomes." "What is natural, therefore, is never good or bad in itself—except to the extent that it is interpreted against a normative background that originates from somewhere else."). See generally Bailey Kuklin, "Evolution, Politics, and Law,"

Valparaiso University Law Review 38 (2004): 1129 ("Modern sociobiologists typically acknowledge the chasm between fact and value and deny that they succumb to the naturalistic fallacy."). Nevertheless, critics note that the claim made by some proponents that the avoidance of needless human suffering suggests that "rules of law should be framed in harmony with rules that nature has built into the biology of our species, except where some clear ground of public policy dictates otherwise," itself is actually a normative prescription about what the law "ought" to be. Douglas A. Terry, "Don't Forget about Reciprocal Altruism: Critical Review of the Evolutionary Jurisprudence Movement," *Connecticut Law Review* 24 (2002): 477, 486. See, e.g., ibid., 487 ("While the proponent's attempts to downplay the normative implications of sociobiology is therefore understandable, the consequence of doing so is that evolutionary jurisprudence is unable to describe the role the law should play in society—one of the significant purposes of jurisprudence.").

91. Thornhill and Palmer, *A Natural History of Rape*, 5–6.

92. Erin Ann O'Hara, "How Neuroscience Might Advance the Law," in *Law and the Brain*, ed. Semir Zeki and Oliver Goodenough (New York: Oxford University Press, 2004).

93. Ibid.

94. Elliott, "Law and Biology," 606.

95. Ibid., 607.

96. This seems particularly true when those descriptive causes have neurological and environmental components. Placing a picture of the human brain before an arbiter of justice and saying, "See, *this* is what caused the criminal act," seems to help in the dissociation of the human agent from the criminal act in question. This is so, even though the physical brain belongs to the human agent in question, unless one adopts a dualistic view of human action that assumes a metaphysical brain acts on the physical body.

97. See, e.g., Marsha Farah, "Neuroethics: The Practical and the Philosophical," *Trends in Cognitive Science* 9 (2005): 34, 38 ("We naturally perceive [evidence of neurological dysfunction] as relevant to the defendant's responsibility for his behavior. . . . This puts us on a slippery slope, however, once we recognize that all behavior is 100 percent determined by brain function, which is in turn determined by the interplay of genes and experience."); Michael S. Gazzaniga, "The Law and Neuroscience," *Neuron* 60 (2008): 412, 413 (arguing that increasingly detailed descriptions of neurological activity tend to undercut retributivist theories of criminal punishment).

98. Greene and Cohen, "For the Law, Neuroscience Changes Nothing and Everything," 1781.

99. Maureen P. Coffey, "The Genetic Defense: Excuse or Explanation?," *William and Mary Law Review* 36 (1993): 353, 397.

100. Marcia Johnson, "Genetic Technology and Its Impact on Culpability for Criminal Actions," *Cleveland State Law Review* 46 (1998): 443, 455; Matthew Jones, "Note: Overcoming the Myth of Free Will in Criminal Law: The True Impact of the Genetic Revolution," *Duke Law Journal* 52 (2003): 1031, 1053 ("[W]ith the recent advancement in the field of genetics [] the free will foundation upon which the criminal justice system is based is in serious jeopardy. Justifications of punishment that rely on the individual culpability of the actor become difficult to justify when causal factors influence their behavior.")

101. Johnson, "Genetic Technology and Its Impact on Culpability for Criminal Actions," 470.

102. Amanda Evansburg, "'But Your Honor, It's in His Genes:' The Case for Genetic Impairments as Grounds for a Downward Departure under the Federal Sentencing Guidelines," *American Criminal Law Review* 38 (2001): 1565.

103. Douglas N. Husak, *Philosophy of Criminal Law* (Totowa, NJ: Rowman and Littlefield, 1987), 78.

104. Finbarr McAuley and J. Paul McCutcheon, *Criminal Liability: A Grammar* (Dublin: Round Hall Sweet and Maxwell, 2000), 121.

105. In other words, a "voluntary act" in criminal law names a concept different from a "voluntary act" in other disciplines. See Kevin Jon Heller, "Beyond the Reasonable Man? A Sympathetic but Critical Assessment of the Use of Subjective Standards of Reasonableness in Self-Defense and Provocation Cases," *American Journal of Criminal Law* 26 (1998): 1, 14; Jeffrie G. Murphy, "Involuntary Acts and Criminal Liability," *Ethics* 81 (1971): 332, 333 n.3. Criminal law provides that a criminal act may be attributed to the accused (and therefore "voluntary") by making two presuppositions: first, individuals have control over their behavior (legal free will), and second, a human agent causes the actions he performs by the exercise of his capacities and control. Thus, one can infer that a defendant chose to act from proof that he engaged in the prohibited act. Because criminal law allows this inference, the question whether the defendant engaged voluntarily in an act does not usually arise.

106. 415 S.E.2d 819 (S.C. Ct. App. 1991).

107. Ibid., 821.

108. Ibid., 821–22.

109. 2008 WL 2333083 (Cal. Ct. App. 2d. 2008).

110. Ibid., *5–*6.

111. Ibid.

112. Ibid.

113. Ibid.
114. Ibid.
115. *State v. Payne*, 2002 WL 31624813 (Tenn. Crim. App. 2002).
116. Ibid., *5–*6.
117. Ibid.
118. Ibid.
119. Ibid.
120. Ibid.
121. E.g., *In re Little*, 2008 WL 142832 (Cal. Ct. App. 2008) (finding ineffective assistance of counsel for failure to investigate defendant's post-traumatic stress disorder claim with brain damage, which may have affected the defendant's intent by impacting his perception and awareness of the circumstances of the crime).
122. 2007 WL 4126843 (Cal.App. 2 Dist. 2007).
123. Ibid., *1.
124. Ibid., *4.
125. *Clark v. Arizona*, 548 U.S. 735 (2006).
126. In the majority of jurisdictions that recognize this defense, evidence of diminished capacity can be used only to refute the specific intent element of the crime—thus, with general intent crimes, the doctrine is inapplicable.
127. 2008 WL 5049911 (Tex. Crim. App. 2008).
128. Ibid., *6.
129. Ibid.
130. Ibid.
131. *People v. Ledesma*, 140 P.3d 657, 722 (Cal. 2006).
132. Ibid., 659.
133. Ibid.; see also *State v. Daniels*, 2006 WL 3071329, 10 (Tenn.Crim. App. 2006) (Expert testified that fifteen-year-olds generally are not capable of exercising the same judgment as an older person because the central nervous system and specifically the frontal lobe of the brain are not fully developed at that age. The court held that whether there was premeditation is a question of fact for the jury and can be inferred from the circumstances surrounding the crime.); *State v. DeBow*, 2005 WL 3695784 (N.J.Super.A.D. 2006) (Defendant was convicted of murder after raising a diminished-capacity defense based in part on frontal-lobe dysfunction. The diminished-capacity defense was "that, because of [defendant's] borderline mental retardation and frontal-lobe dysfunction, he was unable to form the requisite intent to commit first-degree murder." The appellate court upheld his conviction, noting that such evidence did not bear on the defendant's capacity to make conscious and willing choices with full appreciation of the wrongness of his acts.).

134. *People v. Ledesma*, 659.

135. 871 N.E.2d 669 (Ill. 2007).

136. *U.S. v. Eff*, 524 F.3d 712, 715–16 (5th Cir. 2008).

137. Ibid.

138. Ibid.

139. Ibid., 718.

140. Steven I. Friedland, "The Criminal Law Implications of the Human Genome Project: Reimagining a Genetically Oriented Criminal Justice System," *Kentucky Law Journal* 86 (1997): 303, 328–29 (discussing social constructivist theory).

141. Ibid.

142. Oliver Wendell Holmes, Jr., *The Common Law* (1881; New York: Dover, 1991), 50.

143. See Henry M. Hart, Jr., "The Aims of the Criminal Law," *Law and Contemporary Problems* 23 (1958): 401, 414–19.

144. Herbert Fingarette, *The Meaning of Criminal Insanity* (Berkeley: University of California Press, 1972), 72–73.

145. Richard C. Boldt, "Construction of Responsibility in the Criminal Law," *University of Pennsylvania Law Review* 140 (1992): 2245, 2304–5.

146. Ibid., 2304.

147. Cf. *United States v. Moore*, 486 F.2d 1139, 1241 (D.C. Cir. 1973) (Wright, J., dissenting) ("[I]n determining responsibility for crime, the law assumes 'free will' and then recognizes known deviations 'where there is broad consensus that free will does not exist' with respect to the particular condition at issue.").

148. Seymour L. Halleck, M.D., "Responsibility and Excuse in Medicine and Law: A Utilitarian Perspective," *Law and Contemporary Problems* 49 (Summer 1986): 127.

149. See, e.g., two sources cited by Amanda Pustilnik, "Rethinking *Un*reasonableness: A Comment on Nita Farahany's 'Law and Behavioral Morality,'" in this volume, 191 n.19: Kathleen D. Vohs and Jonathan W. Schooler, "The Value of Believing in Free Will: Encouraging a Belief in Determinism Increases Cheating," *Psychological Science* 19 (2008): 49; Roy F. Baumeister et al., "Prosocial Benefits of Feeling Free: Disbelief in Free Will Increases Aggression and Reduces Helpfulness," *Personality and Social Psychology Bulletin* 35 (2009): 260.

150. See *Gregg Cartage and Storage Co. v. United States*, 316 U.S. 74, 79–80 (1942); Dan W. Brock and Allen Buchanan, "The Genetics of Behavior and Concepts of Free Will and Determinism," in *Genetics and Criminality* (Washington, DC: American Psychological Association, 1999), 69–75.

151. See Deborah W. Denno, "A Mind to Blame: New Views on Involuntary Acts," *Behavior Science and the Law* 21 (2003): 601, 603; Bernadette

McSherry, "Voluntariness, Intention and the Defense of Mental Disorders: Toward a Rational Approach," *Behavior Science and the Law* 21 (2003): 581, 593.

152. Some commentators share the view that the "failure of the Anglo-American criminal justice system to consider differences in individual capacities in determining blame and punishment can be viewed as a conceptual and structural flaw, which renders it fundamentally unjust and inefficient." Halleck, "Responsibility and Excuse in Medicine and Law," 127, 141.

153. See, e.g., Eugene R. Milhizer, "Justification and Excuse: What They Were, What They Are, and What They Ought to Be," *St. John's Law Review* 78 (2004): 725, 890–93 (distinguishing justifications from excuses and advocating a subjective standard including the actor's subjective perception of the circumstances to evaluate excuses to determine the validity of the excuse); V. F. Nourse, "Self-Defense and Subjectivity," *University of Chicago Law Review* 68 (2001): 1235 (demonstrating that the divide between an objective and a subjective reasonable-person standard is an artificial one); Alan Reed, "Duress and Provocation as Excuses to Murder: Salutary Lessons from Recent Anglo-American Jurisprudence," *Florida State Journal of Transnational Law and Policy* 6 (1996): 51 (comparing the English and the U.S. systems of reasonableness and advocating a subjectivization of the reasonable-person standard to include unique mental characteristics of the defendant, such as timidity); Paul H. Robinson, "Criminal Law Scholarship: Three Illusions," *Theoretical Inquiries in Law* 2 (2001): 287, 308 (explaining that although there are calls for increased subjectivization of the reasonable-person standard, it is unclear which characteristics of a defendant should be incorporated); Lauren E. Goldman, Note, "Nonconfrontational Killings and the Appropriate Use of Battered Child Syndrome Testimony: The Hazards of Subjective Self-Defense and the Merits of Partial Excuse," *Case Western Reserve Law Review* 45 (1994): 185 (proposing that psychological characteristics of abused children should be included in the assessment of reasonableness for purposes of an excuse when the focus is on the circumstances of the defendant, rather than the crime); Sarah McLean, Comment, "Harassment in the Workplace: When Will the Reactions of Ethnic Minorities and Women be Considered Reasonable?" [*Watkins v. Bowden*, 105 F.3d 1344 (11th Cir. 1997)], *Washburn Law Journal* 40 (2001): 593, 609 (claiming that the reasonable-person standard reflects a white Anglo-Saxon male bias and should be reformulated to allow the subjective perceptions of women and ethnic minorities, particularly with respect to employment discrimination claims).

154. Holmes, *The Common Law*, 51.

155. Hisham M. Ramadan, "Reconstructing Reasonableness in Criminal Law: Moderate Jury Instructions Proposal," *Journal of Legislation* 29

(2003): 233, 238 (noting that some argue that reasonableness represents societal standards of conduct and "crystallizes the norms and values of the society and incorporates them into a set of rules that govern individuals' conduct and communicates its meaning to the public frankly"). In his treatise *Criminal Law* (New York: Aspen, 1997), 21, Paul H. Robinson also describes the criminal law's role in shaping societal norms:

The real power in shaping people's conduct lies in the networks of interpersonal relationships in which people find themselves, the social norms and prohibitions shared among those relationships and transmitted through those social networks, and the internalized representations of those norms and moral precepts. . . . Criminal law, in particular, plays a central role in creating and maintaining the social consensus on morality necessary to sustain norms. In fact, in a society as diverse as ours, the criminal law may be the only single mechanism that is society-wide, transcending cultural and ethnic differences. Thus the criminal law's most important real-world effect can be its ability to assist in building, shaping, and maintaining these norms and moral principles. A central role for the criminal law and the criminal justice system, therefore, is to contribute to and harness the compliance-producing power of interpersonal relationships and personal morality.

156. John C. P. Goldberg and Benjamin C. Zipursky, "Accidents of the Great Society," *Maryland Law Review* 64 (2005): 364, 386 (explaining that law, and negligence law in torts, may help to reduce car accidents not only through pricing and prohibition—a stick—but also by helping to reify social norms of safe driving and thereby to promote "internal deterrence").

157. Nita A. Farahany and James E. Coleman Jr., "Genetics and Responsibility: To Know the Criminal from the Crime," *Law and Contemporary Problems* 69 (2006): 115, 153–54.

158. Mayo Moran, *Rethinking the Reasonable Person: An Egalitarian Reconstruction of the Objective Standard* (Oxford: Oxford University Press, 2003), 132.

159. Amanda Myers, "The Human Brainome: Genome, Transcriptome and Proteome Interaction In Human Cortex," NIH Grant, available at http://projectreporter.nih.gov/project_info_description.cfm?icde=0&aid=7727728.

160. And this is problematic when behavioral moralists introduce such evidence in the criminal courtroom, since no consensus exists as to what effect a brain abnormality should or did have on any particular individual. Early insights, however, include brain imaging and lesion studies that suggest that psychopaths may exhibit brain abnormalities in the amygdala and the orbitofrontal cortex. "Predicting Behavior," *Nature Neuroscience* 6

(2003): 647. There is also no consensus on which deficits in moral reasoning and moral action may have underlying neural correlates. See Jorge Moll et al., "The Neural Basis Of Human Moral Cognition," *Nature Reviews Neuroscience* 6 (2005): 799. But, to date, no population-wide brain-environment to behavioral linkages have been established.

161. Caspi et al., "Role of Genotype in the Cycle of Violence in Maltreated Children."

162. John Teehan, "On the Naturalistic Fallacy: A Conceptual Basis for Evolutionary Ethics," *Evolutionary Psychology* 2 (2004): 32, 33:

This provides an important lesson for understanding ethics. While the universe is value-neutral in the sense of not entailing any moral imperatives, it does contain the conditions that give rise to valuing and to creatures who make value judgments. These value judgments are not the expression of some pre-existing moral essence but rather arise from the complex interactions between individuals and the environment. In effect, morality is not "out there" waiting to be found, it is constructed by individuals-who-value, who live in an environment which provides the conditions for both satisfying and frustrating our desires, and who must live with others who may or may not value the same things, in the same way. Morality is both the result of and a contributor to complex social interactions.

163. Goldsmith and Jones, "Evolutionary Biology and Behavior," 133.

164. Jones, "Evolutionary Analysis in Law," 1225.

165. Goldsmith and Jones, "Evolutionary Biology and Behavior," 133.

166. Jones and Goldsmith, "Law and Behavioral Biology," 417.

167. Jones, "Evolutionary Analysis in Law," 1166.

168. E.g., *Hertz v. State*, 941 So.2d 1031 (Fla. 2006) (Defendant claimed ineffective assistance of counsel for failure to introduce the testimony about his brain dysfunction, in particular his frontal-lobe damage, suggesting an impulse control problem, in support of three statutory mitigating factors to the death penalty—diminished capacity, extreme mental illness, and statutory age (on the theory that his mental age was younger). The appellate court found that sufficient mitigating evidence had been presented on his behalf, and that his counsel had made strategic decisions in excluding certain expert testimony); *State v. Borchardt*, 914 A.2d 1126 (Md. App. 2007) (Defendant filed petition for postconviction relief from his death sentence claiming ineffective assistance of counsel. At sentencing, the defendant's neuropsychological expert testified regarding defendant's organic brain impairment, as verified by MRI, and his exhibited behavioral impairments, including impulsive and explosive behavior, poor judgment and reasoning, and emotional control, but, on the basis of a deal between the defense and the State, made statements about how such impairments

affect people generally rather than how it affected the defendant. The circuit court granted his petition and ordered new sentencing proceedings. The State appealed. The Court of Appeals of Maryland reversed the circuit court decision and held that counsel made reasonable, strategic decision at trial to limit the expert's testimony.).

169. 2005 WL 3131603 (Ky. 2005).

170. 965 So. 2d 1 (Fla. 2007).

171. Ibid., 16.

172. Ibid., 17.

173. *Crook v. State*, 908 So. 2d 350 (Fla. 2005) (vacating death sentence after resentencing by finding the death sentence was disproportionate in light of evidence of extreme mitigation).

174. *Crook v. State*, 813 So. 2d 68, 71 (Fla. 2002).

175. *Crook*, 908 So. 2d at 352.

176. 813 So. 2d at 75–76.

177. *Crook*, 908 So. 2d at 355.

178. Ibid., 354.

179. Ibid., 358.

180. 543 U.S. 551 (2005).

181. 536 U.S. 304 (2002).

182. 130 S. Ct. 2011.

183. John Stanton-Ife, "Strict Liability: Stigma and Regret," *Oxford Journal of Legal Studies* 27 (2007): 151, 156.

184. Ibid.

185. Ibid., 158.

186. Ibid.

187. Greene and Cohen, "For the Law, Neuroscience Changes Nothing and Everything," 1775.

5

RETHINKING *UN*REASONABLENESS: A COMMENT ON NITA FARAHANY'S "LAW AND BEHAVIORAL MORALITY"

AMANDA C. PUSTILNIK

1. Introduction

In her stimulating essay, Professor Nita Farahany defines the new movement of "behavioral morality" and situates it within a taxonomy of movements that relate human biology to moral capacities and content. As Farahany's taxonomy illustrates, there are numerous branches of inquiry that tread this field; yet, what may be genuinely novel in the work of behavioral moralists is their emphasis on relating the functions of and the activity within particular brain ensembles[1] to specific types of moral cognition and action. While she is skeptical that behavioral moralists' work on explicating causation will—or should—affect legal determinations of actors' culpability, Farahany offers an avenue through which she believes behavioral morality could contribute to criminal law doctrine: she proposes that scholars working in behavioral morality should contribute at a more general level by refining the criminal law's notion of the "reasonable person." This is a doctrinally and scientifically practicable project and potentially a highly valuable one. Refinements of the reasonable-person standard could lead to more accurate judgments within the criminal law about the typical actor and could stretch beyond criminal law to other areas, like tort law.

While Farahany proposes the utterly reasonable project of rethinking reasonableness, this comment proposes a perhaps less prudent project of rethinking *un*reasonableness. This suggestion, although put lightly, is meant seriously. Behavioral moralists are interested in explicating the general neurobiology of morality, but many behavioral moralists are at least equally interested in explicating the morally salient differences between neurotypical and nonneurotypical actors. For behavioral moralists who work in this vein, rethinking reasonableness would be but a prelude to disaggregating "reasonableness" into several dimensions and then demonstrating how particular types of aberrant internal causation might compromise performance on those dimensions.

Scholars working in the behavioral moralist mode may be interested in showing how abnormal moral cognition leads to nonconforming social performance; they further may use this as a lens through which to explore the question whether abnormal biological causation should ever lead to legal and social exculpation. Put most generally, a central behavioral morality question for law would be "Can internal causes ever exculpate?" The predominant answer in both law and legal philosophy has been "no," which is why Professor Farahany suggests that behavioral moralists direct their efforts to elucidating aggregate normalcy in the service of improving legal models thereof.

This invitation to rethink *un*reasonableness (or, really, the relationship between deviance and culpability) and Farahany's invitation to behavioral moralists to rethink reasonableness both proceed from the same impulse: one that is exploratory and constructive toward the field of behavioral morality, while remaining agnostic about the general feasibility of or specific likely outcomes of these endeavors. This comment does not itself argue for how culpability determinations within the criminal law should be modified to account for biologically rooted moral deviance. Instead, it proposes criteria that behavioral moralist arguments in favor of differentiated legal culpability for nonneurotypical actors would have to satisfy, as well as identifies some of the practical, legal, and normative barriers to the development of such criteria. Specifically, I propose that behavioral moralists will have to identify differences in morally salient perception, affect, or cognition that are stable, atypical, severe, and relevant to the particular offense the person committed. Furthermore, they must do so without merely reinscribing biological or social difference as disease ("otherizing"), since it is in theory possible to describe everything in physicalist language.

The project of rethinking unreasonableness relates to that of rethinking reasonableness in a further way: if typical moral cognition can be described biologically, as behavioral moralists propose, then certainly it should be possible to describe in biological terms deviant moral cognition (whether or not the biological level of description is the most relevant one, under the circumstances). Accepting a fully materialist account of cognition and behavior, is it possible to say that a person who is morally disordered is per se biologically disordered? More narrowly—and to take the causal arrow in the other direction—are there particular physical disorders that interfere significantly and specifically with aspects of moral cognition and performance?

These questions present as philosophical ones, but they are of particular interest to legal and policy scholars who focus on reducing antisocial behavior and promoting prosocial behavior. Interest in understanding the causes of lawbreaking conduct and the hope that causal understanding will lead to more effective legal policies and institutions have driven the law's long and varied association with the biological and social sciences. While this new area of behavioral morality is arousing intense interest among legal scholars, what remains as vexing as ever is the appropriate relationship between causal explanation and legal consequences.

This relationship is particularly fraught in the area where applications for moral biology may be the greatest: criminal law. Questions of cause and consequence are most salient in criminal law because of the criminal law's unique function of imposing not only penalties but also morally freighted judgment or "stigma," a primary concern of Farahany's piece. Imposing stigma seems just only when it is deserved. The criminal law—tracking common moral intuition—exonerates most harm-causing actions when the actor was not the volitional agent of the harm, even if he or she was its proximate cause.[2] Other branches of law, from tort to contract to property, embody and express values of efficiency.[3] Criminal law, too, has its utilitarian features, but it also deals heavily in the moral realm. Accordingly, in the criminal law, questions of the relationship between cause and moral blame become questions both of fact and of value.

Part 2 expands the definition of behavioral morality offered in Farahany's essay and then situates her specific area of concern within the broader behavioral morality field. In this section, I propose a tentative map or diagram of different scholarly positions relating internal causation with reduced moral culpability. Part 3 elucidates the important differences between behavioral moralists who take the position that any physical cause is exculpatory and those who argue that only aberrant physical causes are exculpatory. Turning in Part 4 to Farahany's invitation to rethink reasonableness, I explore why the reasonable-person standard may be a productive and practicable target for behavioral moralists.

Part 5 suggests that behavioral moralists may be most interested in rethinking unreasonableness—in explaining and possibly exculpating deviant causation. This Part suggests a series of steps that may be necessary to identify legally relevant biological causes of deviance. The intuition of behavioral moralists that such factors should reduce culpability is normatively contentious, philosophically fraught, and, at this point, still scientifically tenuous. Yet, behavioral moralists working with new neuroscientific tools at least may be better equipped than prior generations of moral philosophers to make the argument that these kinds of causes are different from others and should matter morally and legally.

2. Defining Behavioral Morality

The potential impact of behavioral morality on law and related fields depends on what behavioral morality *is*. Farahany defines behavioral moralists as the set of thinkers who claim "that deviant behavior attributable to a physical cause is either less or not at all morally blameworthy." She identifies two claims as central to behavioral morality, one positive and the other normative. The positive behavioral morality claim is that it eventually will be possible, on the basis of new brain science, to understand fully the causes of deviant and law-breaking behavior. The closely related normative claim is that knowledge of the physical causes of deviant behavior should lead to the replacement of existing punitive criminal and social responses to deviance with a therapeutic or medicalized norm. On this view, causal explanations both will and should up-end determinations of criminal culpability (moral blame/censure) and criminal responsibility (whether one may be punished for wrongdoing). Farahany proposes that behavioral moralists are motivated to make such claims because they believe criminal offenders are unfairly stigmatized by the criminal law.

Farahany's definition is provocative because it suggests that behavioral moralist thought is, at least in large part, teleological: that it is motivated by the goal of reducing stigma for offenders whose lawbreaking actions were physically caused. More radically, Farahany's description points to a project among behavioral moralists to dismantle retributive elements of the criminal law by using physical causation to negate moral culpability.

Before exploring these aspects of behavioral morality and of Farahany's argument, I want first to expand the definition of behavioral morality and to show where within the broader field the segment of behavioral morality on which Farahany focuses is located. I then propose that it would be useful to subdivide Farahany's area of focus into two further areas: behavioral moralists who claim that all physical causal explanations are exonerating and those who claim that only aberrant physical causes are exonerating. This distinction is important because there are significantly different philosophical and legal stakes, as well as issues of proof, attached to each position. The distinction also matters to Farahany's ultimate proposal, that behavioral moralists focus their attention not on the deviant actor but on refining the criminal law's model of the reasonable person.

Behavioral Morality, Expanded

"Behavioral morality" generally describes the project of understanding moral reasoning as a product of and as being predicated upon human biology in interaction with its environment. Behavioral moralists mean this in more than the basic sense in which all materialists would agree that every thought, feeling, and behavior arises from and is effectuated through an organism's biology. Rather, they explore the biological predicates of particular "moral" sentiments at the group and the individual level. Most behavioral moralists assert that forms of moral reasoning are intrinsic to the biology of human beings; some would go further to claim that particular moral sentiments are preprogrammed into people via specific neurological structures and genetic encoding.[4] Additionally, scholars in this area may investigate the impact of contextual factors and social cues on moral and normative judgments, as mediated through their effect on neurological activation patterns and neurochemical responses. Looking at the brain's facilitation of moral or normative judgment in this more dynamic, "ecologically valid" fashion helps avoid (or at least moderates the risks of) acontextually reifying cognitive and affective responses that have social dimensions and culturally conditioned components.

William D. Casebeer describes behavioral morality as the attempt to "improve our understanding of the nature of moral theory and its place in moral judgment by treating morality as a natural phenomenon subject to constraints from and ultimately reduced to the cognitive and biological sciences."[5] Similarly, Patricia S. Churchland, one of the true innovators in biological philosophy, has described the field as focusing on "basic neuroscience research" questions, such as whether the brain contains anything like a "moral module"; whether, conversely, moral reasoning is broadly distributed throughout the brain; whether areas of the brain engaged by particular moral reasoning tasks are variable across subjects and cultures; and whether what philosophers have termed "moral reasoning" constitutes a biological natural kind or rather is—in terms of underlying biological processes, at least—a set of unlike phenomena.[6] These scholars and their peers investigate the neural and physiological bases of moral cognition and the relationship between moral cognition and behavior at a level of inquiry simultaneously more basic and more abstract than that which might lead to direct legal conclusions about moral culpability for criminal wrongs.

Work on impaired subjects shows how damage to particular brain regions can alter morally relevant affect, cognition, and decision making. For example, there is now strong evidence that damage to brain regions "associated with empathy, rules compliance, and with moderating aggression or triggering inhibition" closely correlates with certain types of lawbreaking behavior.[7] Such damage may result from physical trauma but may also be caused by the more chronic (and common) deformations of "childhood maltreatment, or other stressors such as post-traumatic stress of war."[8]

Researchers have identified that damage to areas of the orbital prefrontal cortex can result in "deficit[s] in acquisition of moral and social rules."[9] Thus, research is beginning to show which brain regions subserve a subject's acquisition and comprehension of social and moral rules, which in turn influences perception, emotion, behavioral repertoire, and behavioral control.

Behavioral morality is but one of the areas of scholarship that focus on the relationship between human biology and morality; it is a close cousin of evolutionary morality. Evolutionary morality, as Farahany points out, looks at the general human capacity for moral judgment and posits that the "trait" of forming moral judgments must have conferred a survival advantage on early human groups. Evolutionary morality draws support from empirical work that shows constancy in certain moral judgments across populations and cultures and aims to describe the degrees of freedom (or constraint) that social institutions like the law may have on shaping moral intuition.[10]

Behavioral morality departs from evolutionary morality in ways that make it enticing to some legal practitioners and scholars. It can be more focused on present biological causes, rather than on prehistorical environmental constraints. Arguments that sound in behavioral morality may be more applicable or at least equally applicable to the individual subject as to the population group. Further, behavioral morality may (although it need not) focus on biological deviance, while evolutionary morality seeks to identify species-typical characteristics. For example, a behavioral morality argument might take the form of explaining at the level of mechanism how morally salient affect, cognition, and control become impaired in a person with a particular disorder, like fetal alcohol syndrome. The behavioral moralist argument might go on to draw conclusions as to whether aberrant biological causation should lead to a different ascription of moral blame and legal responsibility. Thus, behavioral morality lends itself more to direct legal advocacy than do related forms of scholarship.

In her definition of behavioral morality, Farahany emphasizes this advocacy dimension, postulating that behavioral moralists may be moved by emotional or social-justice concerns to exculpate people whose behavior can be traced to a physical cause. While scholars like Churchland and Casebeer define the field significantly more broadly, Farahany's definition captures the approach of scholars who focus on exonerating actors with identifiable biological causes of their antisocial or lawbreaking behavior.

Behavioral Morality, Mapped

As Farahany describes, certain behavioral moralists do assert that *all* physical causes of behavior are exculpatory (in the moral sense, if not the legal one). Others, however, claim that only *aberrant* physical causes, like structural or functional brain damage, are morally exculpatory. The premises and conclusions of these two groups differ in important ways.

It may be this latter group that is more motivated by the issue of stigma; the history of debate within criminal law about the punishment of people with biological deviance shows both that such people have been the targets of tremendous stigma and that advocates on their behalf are strongly moved by a perception that such stigma is unfair. Behavioral moralists may see a lawbreaking individual as the victim of disease, abuse, physical trauma, or one or more of a host of other biological or biosocial insults that impair brain function in particular ways; their intuition is that it is unjust to hold an actor responsible for deviance visited upon him by the confluence of bad environment and bad biology.[11] In identifying stigma as a motivating concern of behavioral moralists, Farahany tacitly connects behavioral moralists to a deep and varied tradition of criminal law scholarship contending that the mentally impaired are overly punished and inappropriately stigmatized.[12]

In this essay, I propose a tentative map of scholars' various positions on the relationship among moral culpability, legal responsibility, and physical cause (see figure 5.1). This map may help locate where different moral philosophy and behavioral moralist claims about the relationship between causation and moral responsibility lie. Mapping out the categories of arguments as to the relationship between cause and culpability will be helpful—I hope—in making more explicit the distinction Farahany points to among behavioral moralists. Some behavioral moralists argue that the fact of physical causation—all physical causation—is morally exculpatory. Others focus on abnormal causation only. These claims lie on different footings and lead to significantly different endpoints.

FIGURE 5.1

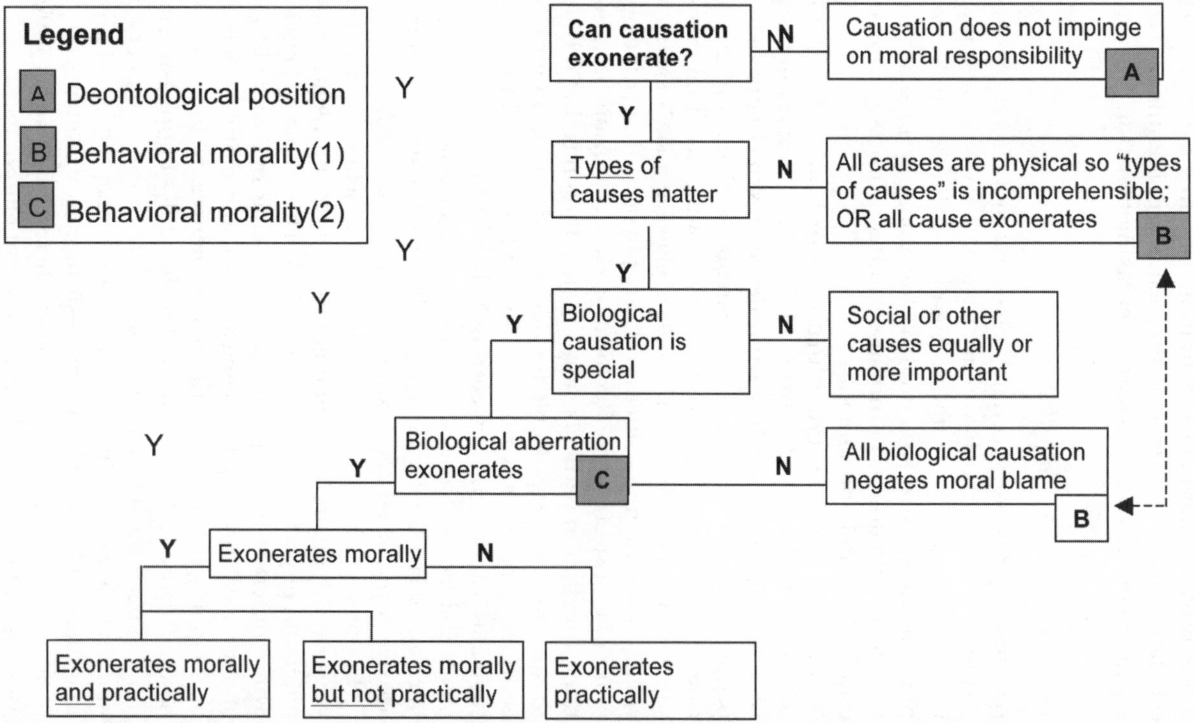

Legend

A Deontological position

B Behavioral morality(1)

C Behavioral morality(2)

Can causation exonerate?

N — Causation does not impinge on moral responsibility [A]

Y — Types of causes matter

N — All causes are physical so "types of causes" is incomprehensible; OR all cause exonerates [B]

Y — Biological causation is special

N — Social or other causes equally or more important

Y — Biological aberration exonerates [C]

N — All biological causation negates moral blame [B]

Y — Exonerates morally

Y — Exonerates morally and practically

N — Exonerates morally but not practically

N — Exonerates practically

3. Parsing Claims about Causation and Responsibility in Behavioral Morality

Revisiting Farahany's definition of behavioral morality in relation to the map in figure 5.1, we find that she states that behavioral moralist thinkers claim "that deviant behavior attributable to [any] physical cause is either less . . . or not at all morally blameworthy." This description of behavioral moralists would correspond to the [B] position in the map. She further notes that behavioral moralists might argue that "those individuals who *fall outside the norm or range* of average capacity to control their conduct ought to be held to a different level of social blame than those who can meet the capacities of the criminal law."[13] Behavioral moralists who make this claim would fall at the [C] position.

Although the [B] and [C] positions are significantly different, both are in opposition to the [A] position—the position that no internal physical causes are exculpatory. (The absence of minimal rationality may be exculpatory, but this test is causally agnostic; the presence or absence of minimal rationality can be assayed behaviorally.) The [A] position represents at a very general level the various schools of thought that assert that, although (or, agnostically, regardless of whether) all behavior is fully physically caused, legal and moral determinations of blame and punishment should be indifferent to causation.[14] In the modern era, one could look to Michael Moore's canonical tome *Law and Psychiatry*[15] and Christopher Slobogin's commentaries thereon as robust statements of this position.[16] Most recently and vigorously, Stephen Morse has defended this territory,[17] as has Michael Gazzaniga.[18] These thinkers take the position, although on varied grounds, that causal arguments are not relevant to attributions of moral blame and legal responsibility.[19]

Moving into the territory occupied by behavioral moralists, the [B] position represents scholars who argue that all behavior, including moral behavior, is fully physically caused and who conclude, on that basis, that all ascriptions of credit or blame are meaningless because a person does not have the opportunity to do otherwise.[20] Joshua Greene and Jonathan Cohen, who are among the founders of experimental moral philosophy, represent this position. They assert that, because all behavior is fully caused, legal accounts of an actor's "choice" to "control" his or her behavior in any particular context are mere storytelling. This, they assert, is equally true of all actors: like some deontologists—although from very different grounds—they argue that distinguishing between actors' relative moral culpability on the basis of whether or not they are neurotypical would not be a comprehensible project. However, their conclusion is the inverse of the deontologists': *no one*, they contend, is the proper recipient of morally infused "blame" (or "credit") for his or her actions. Rather, we need to eliminate folk psychological, retributive concepts and develop a purely harm-focused system. Such a system would evaluate the actor's potential danger to society and confine, supervise, or otherwise treat him or her appropriately. This move would go to the very roots of the criminal system, both philosophically and historically.

The behavioral moralists at [C] differ from this position because of their emphasis on differentiating the moral and legal consequences of actions carried out by functioning moral agents from those of impaired agents. These scholars contend that moral behavior is fully enabled by a physical moral apparatus but that physical cause is not in itself inimical to moral blame. When functioning within a *range of normalcy*, an individual can be judged as a moral agent. Lacking neurological and associated behavioral function within a range of normalcy, however, he or she could be judged as if he or she were an intact moral agent. From the "is" of faulty causation, behavioral moralists of this kind move to the "ought" of reduced culpability. This group of behavioral moralists does not seek to eradicate the concept of blame from all criminal punishment; instead, it seeks to preserve and even extend the criminal law's long-established distinctions in relative culpability based on excuses of mental abnormality. This may lead not to a conclusion of *no* moral agency but rather to a continuum: that agency and culpability determinations should be modified on the basis of or calibrated to the actor's kind and degree of impairment.

While this continuum or calibration approach might sound cumbersome and impracticable, there is (some) legal precedent for such distinctions: competency to stand trial differs from competency to contract; both differ from competency to make a will. What constitutes sufficient competency for a given context involves determinations *both* of the different mental skills called for by the task *and* of the different social-legal stakes, which might militate in favor of higher or lower competency standards than would be instituted by a purely physicalist system.

4. Farahany's Invitation to Rethink Reasonableness

The heart of Farahany's proposal is that behavioral moralists —both [B] and [C]—should focus on the average actor, not the deviant individual or class. She posits that, with "a more robust understanding of human behavior, the concept of reasonableness could be informed by both a scientific understanding of human behavior and the normative purposes of the criminal law."[21] Such a rethinking of reasonableness would be more practicable than attempting to mind-read as to individual actors; it also would contribute very broadly to the criminal law.

Farahany's proposal that behavioral moralists rethink reasonableness has the dual benefits of being doctrinally constructive and scientifically practicable.[22] At the level of doctrine, it is well accepted that the "reasonable person" is a convenient legal construct —not exactly a fiction, but not exactly *not* a fiction, either. As one of law's major roles is to mediate in a pragmatic way between competing social goals, it is, of course, the prerogative of the law to create useful simplifications. Yet, the reasonable-person standard is one that frequently is ill drawn, not for reasons that serve a normative or pragmatic legal purpose but simply because it incorporates flawed assumptions. To the extent that the standard is inconsistent with real peoples' behavior because it incorporates folk psychological mistakes and cultural baggage by flawed assumptions, rather than for good legal reasons (whether retributive, utilitarian, expressive, or legal realist), it is ripe for revision.

The reasonable-person standard was updated in significant ways in the late twentieth century to accommodate changed social norms and new research in psychology. For at least a hundred years, the strong belief existed in the culture and at law that the reasonable rape victim would struggle to the utmost, even to the extent of her life, and would report the attack promptly to legal authorities. Exhaustive research on the experiences and behaviors of and the social influences on real rape victims showed that victims tend not to engage in utmost physical resistance. Rather than

pursuing the prompt reporting previously deemed both expected
and reasonable, rape victims frequently delay reporting or do not
report the crime at all. Such research has filtered into law and public consciousness and has changed the general understanding of
how the ordinary or reasonable person responds to sexual assault.

Revising reasonableness would have broad legal impact and
would be culturally viable for legal scholars. Reasonableness standards are ubiquitous throughout criminal law and beyond. Modi-
fying the law's expectations of the reasonable person therefore
would have broad impact. Further, as Professor Farahany adeptly
explains, the task of revising criminal law *mental states* is effectively
out of the hands of the scientists: the Model Penal Code (MPC)
mental states of purpose, knowledge, recklessness, and negligence
are purely behavioral[23] and resist inquiry into the underlying
causes of the individual's acts. The MPC mental states take some of
the color and romance out of criminal law: inquiries into killers'
"motives" and determinations of their "wickedness" or "moral de-
pravity" live only in the realms of history and detective stories but
are dead in the modern criminal law. Accordingly, modern criminal law is (largely) indifferent to whether a person killed because
he was financially calculating, raised from birth to hate members
of a particular group, or high on drugs. Farahany takes the prudent position that, because the MPC mental states are so fully en-
trenched in modern criminal theory and practice, talk of replac-
ing them with richer models of cognition would be of only passing
theoretical interest.

5. AN INVITATION TO RETHINK *UN*REASONABLENESS

Professor Farahany has advanced the eminently reasonable proposal of rethinking reasonableness. In this Part, I offer a potentially unreasonable proposal to rethink *un*reasonableness. The
latter is not offered as a substitute for the former, which is an important and promising endeavor. I offer it in the constructive and
somewhat playful spirit of thinking through what it would mean to
take seriously the differences between behavioral moralist [B] and
[C] positions and what it then would take to construct a behavioral
morality [C] position under which the criminal law might take account of deviant causation in evaluating culpability.

The different behavioral moralist positions [B] and [C] raise interesting questions for criminal law. Are some physical causes exonerating, while others are not? If so, is there an in-principle basis for the distinction or only ad hoc distinctions derived from norms and customs? Are there valid social and legal purposes for making distinctions as to causes, even if the biological and philosophical bases are lacking? Conversely, if biological and philosophical bases for such distinctions are found, might there still be social and legal grounds on which to refuse to make distinctions? Behavioral moralists [B] argue that all internal physical causes are exculpatory, so the challenge for scholars who argue [C] is to define precisely why, if we live in a world of complete physical causation, some biological causes but not others mitigate blame.

Legal Deviance and Brain Difference

How might one begin to construct the argument that certain kinds of physical difference—but not others—should result in different treatment under the criminal law? What, generally, would be a consistent and logically coherent way of constructing the [C] argument? Although I am agnostic about whether this would be a beneficial direction for the criminal law, I offer what follows in the exploratory and constructive spirit in which Professor Farahany offered proposals for a behavioral moralist rethinking of reasonableness.

As a first step, it would be necessary for behavioral moralists [C] to define what biological difference actually means in this context: there must be a generally acceptable and reasonably stable definition for the kinds of differences that scholars working in this behavioral moralist mode would argue to be exculpatory. Next, it would be necessary for such scholars to define empirically how particular kinds of biological difference relate causally to lawbreaking —an endeavor that is scientifically challenging, as well as politically contentious. After establishing these elements, it then would be necessary to move from the descriptive to the normative argument of why such differences should affect legal consequences.

In defining the relationship between biological difference and criminality, behavioral moralists [C] might now make a twofold contribution. First, a precise delineation of morally relevant brain aberration is needed. Second, neuroscience research on aberration and morality could develop a more precise description of how and why specific types of disorders increase the likelihood of an affected subject's criminal justice involvement. What is needed is a compelling causal account of which neurological aberrations on average impair the subject's morally salient affect, perception, cognition, or control—and why.

The first question for this research program likely would be: what kinds of neurobiological difference should—and should not —matter to moral culpability, and why? Not every newly discovered brain variation is a "brain disease"—despite media neurohype to the contrary.[24] Every living human brain is individual, making the definition of "typical" and "aberrant" rife with scientific difficulty and potential normative judgment. Defining salient neurological difference for behavioral moralists' purposes requires clear definitions of disease states and some method for defining disease that is relatively insulated from norms and biases.

The neurobiological aberrations that behavioral moralists [C] may count as exonerating should, I would posit, share at least the following characteristics: stability, atypicality, severity, and relevance. I will discuss each of these in turn.

Stability is a necessary characteristic of any type of exonerating brain aberration. Stability matters as it is one criterion that differentiates between disease conditions and fleeting situational responses. This is particularly important for behavioral moralists [C] in countering the claim that, since all behavior is biologically caused, no biological cause is meaningfully different from any other—and none should be exonerating. Behavioral moralists might distinguish between functional and situational responses that merely have negative social effects (e.g., a man gets angry at another for calling him names and punches him in the nose, an incident that could be fully described in biological terms but as to which the biological level of description is less powerful than the social-contextual description) and contrast them with persistent impairments that alter the actor's morally salient perception, affect, cognition, or control.

Stability of a trait related to lawbreaking is on its own, however, insufficient. It must also be, among other things, atypical. The most obvious stable yet typical biological characteristic that correlates highly with criminal justice involvement is sex: specifically, being male. Men commit almost all violent crimes; thus, maleness is the most significant "risk factor" for violent criminality. Yet, being male would not be exonerating under the principles sketched earlier because it is not aberrant; indeed, the very commonality of maleness shows that it is insufficient to relieve one of moral responsibility for violence, since moral rules have developed over time with the average man in mind.

Stable atypicality may begin to mark out the kinds of brain difference on which behavioral moralists [C] might focus, although stable atypicality is not independently sufficient; brain difference alone does not mean disease. People who are left-handed (like this author) certainly have brains that deviate from the norm. And, this set of brain differences produces reliably different behavior—unexpectedly throw someone a ball and the relationship between right-left brain difference and behavior will be obvious. But these differences are not plausibly related to impairments in moral reasoning or moral performance. The stable, atypical brain difference must be connected in ways that are describable at the level of mechanism to morally salient impairments in perception, affect, cognition, or control.

This last example of handedness shows an additional challenge in defining brain diseases (or disorders) that relate to morally relevant conduct. That problem is how to define intact or appropriate moral performance in ways that do not merely reflect contemporary social norms and inequalities. In other words, how would it be possible to screen out normative feedback and biases in the definition of "morally salient" brain disorder? For centuries, European and American culture deemed lefthandedness a sign of wickedness; use of the left signaled sympathy with the devil, the ultimate immorality. While behavioral moralists and evolutionary moralists might view morality as relatively constant across historical time periods and cultures, examples of significant moral change over time and place abound. Areas of significant moral dissensus include all types of sexual behavior—particularly, in contemporary times, whether homosexuality and bisexuality are immoral. Homosexuality may be the lefthandedness of today: it arises at least in part from brain difference, it is stable, it is not within the statistical norm, and it is equated by some with defective moral performance. Yet, to equate these forms of difference with disease would be to engage in the worst kind of reverse reasoning: a type of behavior is defined as immoral and socially injurious, a brain-based difference related to the behavior is identified, and then the individual exhibiting the socially disfavored behaviors (and/or identity characteristics) is identified as morally diseased. Past efforts to ascribe biological bases to criminal lawbreaking provide abysmal examples of inscribing social difference as disease, so it would be particularly important to avoid such errors this time around.

The second step, elucidating the causal relationship between biological difference and lawbreaking, is equally important. This endeavor has engendered an extensive if uneven literature over the past century and a half. It has ignominious eugenic roots in the so-called biological criminology of the late nineteenth and early twentieth centuries, therapeutic roots in the asylum movements of the nineteenth century, and liberal roots in the mental health movements of the late twentieth century.

Behavioral moralists [C] may avoid the pitfalls of earlier attempts to biologize criminal deviance by reining in the field's ambition: delimiting particular biological conditions that relate to criminal deviance, rather than attempting a complete biological description for all lawbreaking behavior, may be more productive and less strewn with landmines. Certainly not all—and probably not even most—people who exhibit antisocial and lawbreaking behavior have what could be described as mental illness or brain damage.[25] Social norms, community influences, and demographic and situational factors may exert the greatest influences on whether a person commits a crime.[26] While such factors all are moderated by and processed through an individual's biological equipment, his or her response to such factors cannot be said to constitute a disorder that resides "within" the person's neurobiology (or at least that does so in any kind of stable way). And, obviously, it is not possible to make the reverse inference that lawbreaking conduct (or other kinds of socially disfavored behavior) in itself indicates biological dysfunction.[27]

Recent work in law and neuroscience has posited a return—on totally different scientific footing—to notions of "biological criminology" based on brain difference, scrupulously scrubbed of the eugenic and racial dimensions of past work in this area. Research on the relationship between mental health or mental difference and criminality shows that people who have certain forms of structural or biochemical brain dysfunction are significantly more likely to have particular limitations in perception, affect, cognition, and control that correspond with their particular form of brain damage.[28] The incidences of mental illness and brain damage in the criminal system are multiples higher than in the general population; rates of mental illness among chronic recidivists are even higher.[29]

What has eluded researchers until now is a causal explanation for how specific forms of brain difference influence or interfere with typical moral or social performance—with law-abidingness. And it is here—in the hard and detailed work of showing the mechanisms by which certain deficits impair an actor's perception, affect, cognition, or control in ways that interfere with law-abidingness—that the major contribution could be made.

At this point, I anticipate the objection that connecting particular biological deficits with lawbreaking conduct would not only be difficult but pointless: law requires no more than minimal rationality of actors, and the causes of deviant behavior are legally irrelevant provided minimal rationality is present; presumed within minimal rationality is the capacity for ordinary self-control. This certainly is the position that [A] scholars would assert, as part of the claim that internal causes are not exculpatory.[30] This view has a certain moral and philosophical purity, as well as practical appeal in that it leads to clear and implementable legal rules.

One possibility, though, is that work by behavioral moralists [C] and others may show that the concept of minimal rationality is not a standard of general legal accountability but rather a pragmatically useful legal fiction. I will attempt here an example of a domain-specific impairment that should be legally exculpatory in a particular instance. A person with a severe autism-spectrum disorder appears in court as a party or witness. This person has an average-high IQ and satisfies the requirements of minimal rationality: he has a basic understanding of cause and effect (he knows to get in out of the rain, for example), and has a cognitive understanding of reward, punishment, and consequences for action. When he addresses the court, the presiding judge tells him that he must look at the judge and must stop engaging in certain repetitive physical behaviors. The actor not only does not stop the behaviors but indeed does them more, despite the threat of a contempt sanction. The judge eventually holds him in contempt of court.[31]

Autism's deficits and differences are now fairly well defined (compared, at least, to those of other neurological developmental disorders); an autism expert could explain how the judge's threat of contempt would have increased this actor's anxiety, which would have had the effect of stoking—rather than suppressing—his repetitive physical behaviors. So, here we have an actor who has ordinary intelligence and minimal rationality; he understands what a "consequence" is, and he knows that he is supposed to do what a judge tells him. But the nature of his impairment makes his social performance less conforming, not more conforming, when he is threatened with the consequence by the judge. The judge in this example stands in for the proverbial "policeman at the elbow." If the policeman at the elbow fails here, where else might it fail?

Resistance to Differentiated Culpability

If behavioral moralists [C] could accomplish the ambitious project outlined earlier, would the criminal law then embrace differentiated culpability based upon the morally salient and stable brain differences that behavioral moralists identified? The weight of past and current scholarly argument and popular sentiment suggests not. The strong resistance to differentiating culpability on the basis of neurological difference rests in part—but perhaps only in small part—on philosophical grounds. Those who take the [A] position, sketched out earlier, oppose such differentiation for in-principle reasons. Among the majority of commentators, legal scholars, lawmakers, and citizens, however, the resistance engendered by proposals for differentiated justice may be less philosophical than they are normative, emotional, and pragmatic.

Professor Farahany contends that behavioral moralists [C] are motivated by their perception of unfair stigma against people with neurological differences. Stigma certainly may play a strongly motivating role in legal discourses about the treatment of people with disabilities. But might not the opposition to the behavioral morality [C] position be at least as normatively driven? Major sources of resistance to differentiated culpability may include the role of risk shifting in the criminal law, the immature and unreliable state of the science, pragmatic or efficiency-related concerns, and legal-doctrinal concerns. Finally, some of the resistance to behavioral morality [C] proposals may also be based in stigma against (or at least preconceptions about) lawbreakers, people with brain difference, or both.

Resistance to differentiated culpability may arise in part from the intuition that current criminal law regimes require a person with a behavioral difference to internalize the risks of his or her atypical behavior. Risk shifting is typically associated with tort law; it does not operate in any obvious way in the criminal law, framed as the criminal law is in the retributive language of moral blame and the utilitarian language of deterrence. And yet, criminal law implicitly addresses questions of which party should assume the risks and bear the costs of neurobiological difference. Let us take for example a person with severe fetal alcohol syndrome. This actor gets into a minor traffic accident; his neurobiological differences make it significantly more likely that he will become violent —in this case, he punches the other driver in the nose. We could think of the law's current treatment of this actor, under which he receives no consideration for his mental difference, as functioning to internalize the risks of the actor's disease to the actor. Why should the general right of innocent third parties to be unmolested in public be lessened by virtue of an impaired person's instability?

The nascent state of brain sciences, too, poses a hurdle to the individualization of justice. Even in cases of gross anatomical abnormality, the link between brain difference and behavioral output in any one individual remains speculative—it is probabilistic and correlative, not individually provable. Some individuals experience major brain damage but are relatively behaviorally unimpaired. Others suffer minor head injuries and yet experience protracted mood and behavioral alteration, as with postconcussion syndrome; this may be particularly true in cases of low-level but diffuse brain damage that would not even be detectable with any current neuroimaging technology. Even in cases of demonstrable brain abnormality, the question of causation remains vexed: a defendant who presented evidence that his self-control was impaired due to postconcussion syndrome still would face the hurdle of linking the abnormalcy to his specific failure of self-control on the occasion in question. This then raises the metaphysical question of the degree of control any individual ever has over his actions—a question that behavioral moralists may consider empirical but that other moral philosophers may consider not amenable to empirical determination.

Efficiency-related concerns may also underlie much resistance to individualizing justice on the basis of physical difference. These fall into two general categories, which relate to how to evaluate the offender and then how to dispose of him. First, most offenders will not have the benefits of an expert examination. Even if an expert does examine and identify in the defendant a significant structural or functional difference (and query what thresholds should be set for "significant"), it remains difficult and speculative to connect the difference to a legally relevant impairment.

If a causal connection is found, how should a court respond? The practical legal difficulties with individualized justice go further still, from evaluation to disposition: if richer mental state descriptions or other mechanisms for accounting for mental impairment were incorporated into the criminal law, what consequences would follow? The current repertoire of criminal sanctions is narrow: incarceration or supervised release. Justice individualized based on physical difference could make use of these alternatives, but this seems unlikely and unsatisfying. Expanded postconviction alternatives might be developed, like diversion to the mental health system. Yet, individualizing these postconviction alternatives would be as uncertain as individualizing the evaluative phase.

Considerations about the state of legal doctrine set up hurdles to individualizing justice on the basis of difference, as well. As Farahany aptly notes, modern criminal law does not inquire deeply into the mind of the offender; "motive" is merely a narrative device that ties together factual evidence. The evidence need only show whether the defendant committed the act and, if so, whether he knew what he was doing or disregarded a risk that his actions might cause a particular harm. These are the thinnest of mental states.[32] Attempting to substitute these MPC mental states with richer mental-state descriptions—descriptions incorporating accounts of why the defendant acted as he did and whether his perception, cognition, and affect fall within a range of normalcy

—would require a sea change of almost unimaginable proportions across every area of modern criminal law.

Opposition to differentiated justice of the kind proposed by behavioral moralists [C] also engenders resistance on normative and emotional grounds. Empirical research demonstrates again and again that jurors and lawmakers believe brain difference should be an aggravating factor, not a mitigating one. The public greets claims of brain differences with deep suspicion, particularly since the insanity defense (which is now all but nonexistent) is mistakenly perceived as a get-out-of-jail-free card. Some of the hostility to claims of brain difference could be ameliorated through the development of more reliable neurological testing. Such a process of norm change through gradual assimilation of empirical findings is likely to be slow. This takes us back to Farahany's important point of stigma: behavioral moralists [C] may (or may not) be overly influenced to "protect" people whom they perceive as victims of stigma in part because cultural stigma against people with mental illnesses is so significant.

Fairness arguments, too, have stood in the way of differentiated justice. A major argument against differentiating legal responsibility on the basis of mental disease or disability has been that doing so is unjustly underinclusive: childhood environment, trauma, abuse, demographic factors, and all of the other influences on individual development and on action-in-the-moment are just as physical and just as inexorable as mental disease. Contemporary work in cognitive neuroscience indeed is contributing to the body of evidence that growing up with severe environmental insults, whether chemical or situational, can trigger predispositions to mental illness or cause impairments equivalent to currently recognized mental illnesses. Thus, current legal excuses based on mental disease—like insanity—discriminate against people who are equally impaired but whose impairments arise from other sources. If it were to become accepted that biological impairment could, in principle, reduce moral culpability, then reduced culpability should apply to all people with valid physical conditions. Accordingly, any behavioral morality efforts to differentiate justice on the basis of physical cause may have to address the challenge that many factors traditionally labeled demographic, socioeconomic, or emotional also could be construed as physical. Principled line-drawing between these sources of difference may be the greatest challenge of all.

6. CONCLUSIONS AND FURTHER DIRECTIONS

I share Professor Farahany's conclusion that brain-based individuation of criminal justice is neither scientifically possible nor normatively desirable. Differences in individual actors' brains are too hard to assess against any reliable baseline, and the criminal justice system could not be so finely calibrated even if individual brain readings were possible. Accordingly, Farahany appropriately suggests that the right target of analysis for scholars in behavioral morality is the typical community member, not the transgressor.

Picking up from Farahany's work, this comment speculates as to whether behavioral moralists could develop an intermediate position that focuses neither on the individual disordered offender nor on the aggregate typical person but on aggregate kinds of abnormalcy—or "unreasonableness." Instead of "cause" being an all-purpose excuse—or no excuse at all—could particular aberrant causes instead become the basis of taxonomies of exculpation, of kind and degree of excuse? In addition to expectations we might have of the typical person, based on work to date in behavioral morality, what tailored expectations might we have of people who meaningfully depart from the typical? I offer the suggestions in this comment as initial suggestions of what it might mean for scholars to think about whether deviant internal causation matters in ways that are distinct from the general question of whether any form of internal causation matters.

As we understand more fully how the lived environment shapes people physically as moral agents and how biology lays the preconditions for and establishes constraints upon moral cognition, behavioral morality may require reconsideration of a society's moral responsibilities to its citizens and of people's moral obligations to each other. Behavioral morality does not suggest that individual moral character is wholly inborn or that social mores are biologically fixed. Rather, people have a fragile capacity for moral flourishing that can be developed or deformed by social and physical environment.

One important criticism of various historical and contemporary efforts to ground criminal law on a neuroscientific footing—or to develop a modern "biological criminality"—has been that they focus too narrowly on the individual in isolation—as if individuals and their constituent bits of brain were free-standing, stable entities. What we learn from behavioral morality, developmental neuroscience, behavioral economics, and situationist psychology is this: individuals' biological capacities and moral intuitions both arise from physical primes and also are shaped, constrained, and given content by the physical and social matrices in which individuals are embedded. Some biological conditions are so extreme that they render the individual indifferent to situational and social factors; a child with severe brain damage will not flourish beyond a certain level regardless of the degree of environmental enrichment. But the converse is not true: a person who starts out perfectly intact is vulnerable to becoming grotesquely cognitively, affectively, and morally deformed under the wrong environmental and social conditions. In other words, we may have more downward than upward variability—or vulnerability. The moral intuition that such factors should reduce culpability is a contentious one, by no means universally shared. But behavioral moralists at least may be equipped to make the argument that these kinds of causes are different from others, and should matter morally and legally.

NOTES

Thanks to Richard C. Boldt, Danielle A. Citron, Nita A. Farahany, James E. Fleming, Oliver Goodenough, and Sandy Levinson. Jonathan Tippens provided invaluable research assistance.

1. By "ensembles," I mean regions of the brain that become active in concert.

2. E.g., as when the actor is impelled by an external force or suffers a nonnegligent accident.

3. This is not to say that criminal law is the exclusive branch of law that expresses social norms. Law inevitably reflects the norms of its drafters or constituents; the apotheosis of economic values in various branches of law may itself be seen as normative—and different schools of economic thought may have different normative valences. However, I am

distinguishing here the criminal law's peculiar function of passing moral judgment. The purpose of a judgment in contract or tort is to reallocate resources, not to brand the loser a "bad man"; the purpose of a judgment in criminal law is, in part, to hold up the actor to public disapprobation.

4. Michael S. Gazzaniga, *The Ethical Brain* (New York: Harper Perennial, 2006).

5. William D. Casebeer, *Natural Ethical Facts: Evolution, Connectionism, and Moral Cognition* (Cambridge, MA: MIT Press, 2003). See also Jorge Moll et al., "The Neural Basis of Human Moral Cognition," *Nature Reviews Neuroscience* 6 (2005): 799 (surveying basic research; describing functional imaging and clinical evidence that "indicates that a remarkably consistent network of brain regions is involved in moral cognition").

6. William D. Casebeer and Patricia S. Churchland, "The Neural Mechanisms of Moral Cognition: A Multiple-Aspect Approach to Moral Judgment and Decision-Making," *Biology and Philosophy* 18 (2003): 169.

7. Oliver R. Goodenough and Micaela Tucker, "Law and Cognitive Neuroscience," *Law and Social Science: Annual Review of Law and Social Science* 6 (2010): 61.

8. Ibid. (citing Antonio R. Damasio, *Descartes' Error: Emotion, Reason, and the Human Brain* (New York: G. P. Putnam, 1994); Cathy Spatz Widom, "Child Abuse, Neglect, and Violent Criminal Behavior," *Criminology* 27, no. 2 (1989): 251–71).

9. Ibid. (citing S. W. Anderson, A. Bechara, H. Damasio, D. Tranel, and A. R. Damasio, "Impairment of Social and Moral Behavior Related to Early Damage in Human Prefrontal Cortex," *Nature Neuroscience* 2 (1999): 1032–37).

10. See, among many others, Margaret Gruter, *Law and the Mind: Biological Origins of Human Behavior* (Thousand Oaks, CA: Sage,1991), 53; Paul H. Robinson, Robert Kurzban, and Owen D. Jones, "The Origins of Shared Intuitions of Justice," *Vanderbilt Law Review* 60 (2007): 1633; Paul H. Robinson and John M. Darley, "Intuitions of Justice: Implications for Criminal Law and Justice Policy," *Southern California Law Review* 81 (2007): 18 (arguing that intuitions of justice are largely innate and that legal institutions that deviate from such intuitions will have high costs of compliance). Professor Farahany thoroughly surveys this ground in her essay "Law and Behavioral Morality," in this volume.

11. Farahany, "Law and Behavioral Morality," 117 (citing Joshua Greene and Jonathan Cohen, "For the Law, Neuroscience Changes Nothing and Everything," *Philosophical Transactions of the Royal Society of London B* 359 (2004): 1775).

12. Amanda C. Pustilnik, "Violence on the Brain: A Critique of Neuroscience in Criminal Law," *Wake Forest Law Review* 44 (2009): 183.

13. Farahany, "Law and Behavioral Morality," 151 (emphasis added).

14. There are numerous, robust philosophical arguments as to why causal stories should *not* impinge upon moral blameworthiness; it is the purpose of this comment not to survey or extend them but merely to note their place in the debate about the relationship between causal arguments and the claims of behavioral moralists.

15. Michael S. Moore, *Law and Psychiatry: Rethinking the Relationship* (Cambridge: Cambridge University Press, 1984).

16. Christopher Slobogin, "A Rational Approach to Responsibility: A Review of Michael Moore, *Law and Psychiatry: Rethinking the Relationship*," *Michigan Law Review* 83 (1985): 820.

17. See, e.g., Stephen J. Morse, "Moral and Legal Responsibility and the New Neuroscience," in *Neuroethics: Defining the Issues in Theory, Practice and Policy*, ed. Judy Illes (New York: Oxford University Press, 2005); Stephen J. Morse, "Determinism and the Death of Folk Psychology: Two Challenges to Responsibility from Neuroscience," *Minnesota Journal of Law, Science, and Technology* 9 (2008): 1; Stephen J. Morse, "Brain Overclaim Syndrome and Criminal Responsibility: A Diagnostic Note," *Ohio State Journal of Criminal Law* 3 (2006): 397.

18. Gazzaniga, *The Ethical Brain.*

19. They further contend pragmatically that folk psychological concepts of "choice" and "volition," whether or not they are true, are indispensable for ordering individual and social behavior. This makes sense intuitively; additionally, a growing body of empirical literature supports the conclusion that people behave better when they believe that they have control over their behavior. See, e.g., Kathleen D. Vohs and Jonathan W. Schooler, "The Value of Believing in Free Will: Encouraging a Belief in Determinism Increases Cheating," *Psychological Science* 19 (2008): 49 (finding that subjects primed with information about free will were less likely to cheat on an experimental task and those primed with information about determinism were more likely to cheat); Roy F. Baumeister et al., "Prosocial Benefits of Feeling Free: Disbelief in Free Will Increases Aggression and Reduces Helpfulness," *Personality and Social Psychology Bulletin* 35 (2009): 260.

20. Greene and Cohen, "For the Law, Neuroscience Changes Nothing and Everything."

21. Farahany, "Law and Behavioral Morality," 152.

22. The scientific aspects of this proposal are fully addressed in Farahany, "Law and Behavioral Morality."

23. Morse, "Brain Overclaim Syndrome and Criminal Responsibility."

24. Two of my favorite recent examples: music is potentially addictive because the experience of listening to it releases the same brain chemicals

as drugs and sex! Yes: the dopaminergic system is involved in pleasure and reward, but that does not mean that music = drugs or that listening to music is the brain disorder of addiction (although the triumvirate of sex, drugs, and rock and roll must have been catnip to science reporters, whose beat is usually much drier). Further, rudeness is a "neurotoxin," and people who are rude have been "infected."

25. Some scholars who work in the behavioral moralist vein, broadly construed, have asserted that brain dysfunction can be inferred from the mere fact of social deviance; there is little evidence for drawing the causal arrow in that direction and many issues with such claims. For a critique of that position, see Pustilnik, "Violence on the Brain."

26. See, e.g., Jon Hanson and Michael McCann, "Situationist Torts," *Loyola of Los Angeles Law Review* 41 (2008): 1350; Nita A. Farahany and James E. Coleman Jr., "To Know the Criminal from the Crime," *Law and Contemporary Problems* 69 (2006): 128. These social factors may also be the subject of biological inquiry; situational and environmental factors affect behavior only insofar as the individual takes them in and processes them affectively and cognitively against the background of memory and predisposition.

27. For a debunking of this reverse inference argument, see Pustilnik, "Violence on the Brain."

28. Ibid.

29. Ibid., 207 (citing Nathaniel J. Pallone and James J. Hennessy, "Brain Dysfunction and Criminal Violence," *Society* 35, no. 21 (1998): 21; Richard E. Redding, "Why It Is Essential to Teach about Mental Health Issues in Criminal Law (and a Primer on How to Do It)," *Washington University Journal of Law and Policy* 14 (2004): 407, 408–10). This is not to say that most people with severe mental illnesses in fact cross paths with the criminal justice system; they do not. And, there are many factors that influence why some people with severe mental illness do come to the attention of the criminal system—not least that the criminal system has become a hospital system of last resort for the uninsured and underinsured with mental illnesses. So the prevalence of people with mental illness and brain damage in the criminal system is not due to biological causation alone; it rests as well on interrelated political and economic factors. Nevertheless, the economic and political factors that contribute to concentrating people with mental illnesses or brain damage in the criminal system themselves show the importance of biology: in the absence of the biological problem, people with these conditions would not need political and financial resources to keep them out of prison.

30. Again, as discussed earlier, those in the [A] position may assert that only minimally rational agents may be held culpable. The focus of that

inquiry is the presence or absence of minimal rationality, not the types of rationality deficits or the causes thereof. Such an inquiry as to minimal rationality, then, is cause-agnostic. Moral behavior is fully enabled by a physical moral apparatus, which, when functioning within a range of normalcy, permits the individual to be judged as a moral agent. Farahany proposes that a person should not be judged morally if he or she is so impaired that "attributions of human agency" would be inappropriate. Farahany, "Law and Behavioral Morality," 151. I interpret this standard to be equivalent to the standard of minimal rationality.

31. We could say that this is an unrealistic example because a judge would never be such a jerk; however, it would be within the scope of the judge's power to act in this way, and only discretion would prevent it.

32. Occasionally, the mental state of criminal negligence suffices for conviction. Criminal negligence is the culpable absence of a normatively mandated mental state of due care.

6

A CASE STUDY IN NEUROSCIENCE AND RESPONSIBILITY

WALTER SINNOTT-ARMSTRONG

Several prominent criminal law theorists argue vigorously and persistently that responsibility and excuses (which are denials of responsibility) should not be based on causation. Moore, for example, opposes "the causal theory of excuses," which claims that "when an agent is caused to act by a factor outside his control, he is excused."[1] Similarly, Morse fights "the fundamental psycholegal error," which is the claim that causation per se excuses.[2]

The newest addition to this coalition is Farahany, who argues against "behavioral morality," defined as the claim that "deviant behavior attributable to a physical cause is either less blameworthy than intentional behavior or is not at all morally blameworthy."[3] To her credit, Farahany does not go all the way over to the opposite extreme, which claims that the physical and neural causes of an act are always completely irrelevant to all aspects of morality or criminal law. Instead, Farahany suggests a compromise: physical and neural causes of an action might be relevant to some legal standards, including culpability and reasonableness, but they are still not relevant to legal or moral responsibility.

Like Farahany, I reject "behavioral morality" as she defines it. Every act has some physical cause, so no agent would be fully morally blameworthy (or responsible) for any act if the mere fact that an act was physically caused were enough to excuse it or reduce its agent's blameworthiness (or responsibility). But some agents are fully morally blameworthy (and responsible)—or so I assume here with Farahany. Hence, the mere fact that an act had some physical cause is not enough to reduce its agent's blameworthiness (or responsibility).

It is still not clear how often lawyers, philosophers, or common folk make this mistake. Admittedly, some desperate defense attorneys cite neural causes to argue that their clients are not fully blameworthy or responsible.[4] However, they always present their neuroscientific evidence in the context of much more evidence, including psychological, sociological, and nonscientific evidence. Thus, they cannot fairly be accused of arguing from neural causes alone. Moreover, there need not be anything fallacious about taking norms for granted without stating them explicitly. Many fine arguments in real life have suppressed premises. Hence, arguments that assume norms cannot fairly be accused of committing the naturalistic fallacy by inferring a normative conclusion from descriptive premises alone.[5] In addition to lawyers, I also doubt that many philosophers or common folk really commit the mistake of inferring reduced responsibility from a neural cause alone without any context or normative assumptions.

Most people recognize that the real issue is not simply *whether* our acts are caused. The real issue is, instead, *how* they are caused —which *kind* of cause they have. Tom Wolfe gets to the point with his usual flair: "The conclusion people out beyond the laboratory walls are drawing is: *The fix is in! We're all hardwired!* That, and: *Don't blame me! I'm wired wrong!*"[6] According to Wolfe, then, the real issue is not whether we are wired. Nobody should deny that we are wired somehow. The real issue is instead whether we are "wired *wrong*"—which presumably means: wired in the wrong way to be fully blameworthy or responsible. Dennett, among others, has been saying this for decades.[7]

Of course, this reformulation of the issue does not help much until we specify which causes and which wiring are wrong and what exactly they are wrong for. I will not try to solve all of these problems in this short comment. Here I will merely introduce a single case in order to illustrate and illuminate some of the issues at stake.

1. INTRODUCING PEDER

An anonymous patient, whom I will call "Peder Tumkopf," was born in 1960. From adolescence on, he had a strong interest in pornography.[8] However, this interest was neither illegal nor very unusual for his culture, and it never led to any related social or marital problems. Most important, he denied that he had had any sexual attraction to children before 2000, and no evidence to the contrary was given. In 1984, he had a closed head injury, lost consciousness for two minutes, and suffered migraines for two years. This injury caused no known long-term neurological problems. Peder also had no history of psychiatric or developmental problems and no deviant sexual behavior before 2000. Peder worked as a corrections officer until 1998, when he finished his master's degree in education and became a school teacher. There is no reason to suspect that his career change was based on sexual interest in school children. Also in 1998, Peder married a woman with a daughter. It was his second marriage and was reportedly stable.

Then problems arose. During 2000, Peder "acquired an expanding collection of pornographic magazines and increasingly frequented Internet pornography sites. Much of this prurient material emphasized children and adolescents. . . . He also solicited prostitution at 'massage parlors,' which he had not previously done." He reported fighting his urges and feeling that his acts were unacceptable, but he stated that "the pleasure principle overrode" his attempts at restraint.

Later in 2000, Peder made "subtle sexual advances to his prepubescent stepdaughter." After several weeks, his stepdaughter told her mother, who discovered her husband's child pornography and reported him. Peder was removed from the home, diagnosed with pedophilia, and prescribed 10 mg/d of medroxyprogesterone (also known as Depo-Provera and used in "chemical castration"). A judge found him guilty of child molestation and ordered him to either go to jail or undergo a twelve-step in-patient program. He expressed a strong desire to avoid prison, so he entered the in-patient program.

In the program, Peder "could not restrain himself from soliciting sexual favors from staff and other clients." He was expelled from the program and had to be sent to prison. The evening before sentencing, he complained of a headache, but doctors suspected a nonphysiologic cause. Then he expressed "suicidal ideation and a fear that he would rape his landlady," and he displayed balance problems. "During a neurologic examination, he solicited female team members for sexual favors. He was unconcerned that he had urinated on himself."

Structural magnetic resonance imaging (MRI) revealed an egg-sized tumor that was displacing the right orbitofrontal area of the brain. At this time he showed no cognitive or sensory deficits but had trouble writing and drawing. After resection of the tumor in December 2000, all of his symptoms went away. He successfully completed a Sexaholics Anonymous program, so he was welcomed home seven months later, after he was found to pose no threat to his stepdaughter.

Four months later, however, "In October 2001, he developed a persistent headache and began secretly collecting pornography again. Magnetic resonance imaging showed tumor regrowth, and re-resection was accomplished in February 2002." His symptoms then went away again.

The fact that Peder's behaviors came and went with the presence or absence of the tumor is evidence that the tumor caused his behaviors. The reporting doctors see this pattern as "establishing causality" and conclude that his pedophilia was "a specific manifestation of orbitofrontal syndrome." Of course, neither the doctors nor I think that this cause operates independent of environment, that there is one and only one cause, or that everyone with a similar tumor would act the same. The relevant notion of causation is not that crude.[9]

Even if causation was clear, the specific causal mechanism was not. The doctors speculate, "The orbitofrontal disruption likely exacerbated a preexisting interest in pornography, manifesting as sexual deviancy and pedophilia," perhaps because "[t]he orbitofrontal cortex is involved in the regulation of social behavior." However, this hypothesis does not explain why Peder became interested in children, although he had never shown that particular interest before. It is not clear, then, whether the tumor created a new desire, increased a preexisting desire, or reduced Peder's

ability to restrain his behavior in the presence of a new or preexisting desire. However it worked, what matters here is that Peder's
tumor caused his misbehavior.

2. IS PEDER RESPONSIBLE?

There are many kinds of responsibility. One is causal responsibility, such as when the drought is responsible for the famine with
no moral implications at all. Another is role responsibility, such
as when parents have a responsibility to care for their children. In
contrast, as Farahany says, "Criminal responsibility focuses on the
legal liability of an individual for criminal conduct."[10] Since Peder's
acts clearly were causally responsible for harms and he clearly has
responsibilities as a stepfather, the question here is whether Peder
is criminally liable for his conduct.

The Standard View of Responsibility

Most modern criminal law systems impose criminal liability and,
hence, responsibility when and only when the agent does (1) a voluntary act (2) of a forbidden type (3) with a requisite mens rea
(4) without an affirmative defense, such as insanity. Peder seems
to meet these conditions of responsibility for two criminal acts: collecting child pornography and molesting his stepdaughter. He did
an act of each of these two types, those acts were voluntary insofar
as they resulted from conscious choices, they were also intentional
and hence done with mens rea, and he had no affirmative defense,
such as duress or insanity. Standard insanity defenses would not
apply because Peder knew what he was doing (he was not delu-
sional), he knew that it was legally and morally wrong (as shown
by his hiding his acts and trying to restrain his urges), and he had
substantial capacity to conform to law (he could have left home
or sought psychiatric help before molesting his stepdaughter). His
most extreme symptoms (such as soliciting sex from medical staff)
did not arise until after his crimes, so they do not show that he
lacked control when he first collected child pornography and mo-
lested his stepdaughter. Consequently, Peder meets the standard
legal criteria for sanity and responsibility. If we strictly apply the
criminal law as it is formulated in most modern legal systems, then

Peder should be convicted of at least two crimes: collecting child pornography and child molestation.

The usual standards also suggest that Peder should be punished severely. His crimes—child pornography and child molestation —carry long sentences of years in prison. If he is responsible for these crimes, as the usual standards suggest, then he deserves punishment, and that by itself is adequate reason to punish him, according to retributivists. This argument, then, suggests that Peder should be sent to prison for years. This retributivist line of reasoning is common among the many judges and law professors with whom I have discussed this case. Indeed, most in these groups seem to accept the view that Peder should go to prison for a long time.

Nonetheless, in my experience, many other people think that Peder should not be punished either for collecting child pornography or for child molestation, and the reason they give is usually that he is not responsible for those acts. These people might be trying to apply the usual legal standards. They might, for example, think that Peder is criminally insane or that his acts were not intentional or voluntary in the sense of resulting from decision or will. This position might rest on a different understanding (perhaps a misunderstanding) of the relevant legal standards, or it might result from a different view (perhaps a mistaken view) of the facts of the case.

Another possibility interests me here. Many people admit that the usual standards in criminal law plus the facts of Peder's case imply that he should be punished by sending him to prison for years. However, they think that this result is absurd, because Peder is neither responsible nor dangerous, so he should not be punished. They conclude that the usual legal standards of responsibility need to be revised.

Problems for the Standard View

This position rests on the claim that Peder is not responsible. Why not? This question needs to be answered in order to justify deviating from the traditional account of responsibility.

One simple (and simplistic) answer is that Peder's act was caused. Some might argue that the mere fact that Peder's act had *a* cause (the tumor) is enough to show that he was not fully responsible. However, as mentioned earlier, all acts are caused; so, if this simple argument worked in this case, it would imply that no agent is ever fully responsible for any act. That seems absurd, so mere causation by itself is not enough to justify the claim that Peder is not fully responsible. This is why I reject behavioral morality, the causal theory of excuses, and the fundamental psycholegal error, as defined earlier.[11]

A second potential answer refers not to causation in general but rather to a kind of causation: physical or mechanistic causation. Some might argue that the mere fact that Peder's act had a *physical* cause (the tumor) is enough to show that he was not fully responsible.[12] But why? The fact that an act has a physical cause (such as a tumor) might seem to imply that the act is not caused by mental states (including beliefs, desires, and decisions). Recent surveys suggest that many people believe that agents are not responsible for their acts when the causal chain "bypasses" the agent's mental states.[13] However, this argument is faulty. The fact that an act has a physical cause does not imply that it does *not* have a mental cause. One reason is that a single act can sometimes have both a physical cause and a mental cause. Indeed, a mental cause can also be a physical cause, if noneliminativist physicalism is true.[14] Another reason is that Peder's mental states were *not* bypassed. As mentioned, he knew what he was doing and consciously chose to do it. The tumor was not mental, but that cause of his acts operated through or by means of his mental states. The causal chain did not bypass mental states in the way that is often taken to remove or reduce responsibility.

A third possible answer is that the cause of Peder's act—his tumor—was outside his control and removed his capacity to do otherwise and to conform to law. Some might argue that the fact that Peder's act had such a *disabling* cause is enough to show that he was not fully responsible. A disabling cause does seem to remove responsibility. If someone bumps into you so hard that you cannot stop yourself from falling on me, then I should not and will not blame you for falling on me. In contrast, if someone bumps into you lightly and you could stop yourself from falling on me but you do not exert enough effort to avoid falling on me, then I will blame you for falling on me, because the physical cause was not disabling.

Peder's tumor, however, was not completely disabling in the same way as a very hard bump or shove. One reason is that a bump or shove happens quickly, whereas the tumor did its work slowly over a long period of time. However, this difference does not show that Peder's tumor does not reduce his control or capacity at all. Abilities come in degrees and apply only to certain types of acts and certain time periods.[15] A person with claustrophobia might lack the ability to stay in a small elevator for more than a minute but still might have the ability to enter the small elevator for ten seconds or to enter a larger elevator for a minute, though only with enough incentive of the right kind. Analogously, Peder had some control but not total control. He was able to stop himself from raping his landlady and from making blatant public advances to his stepdaughter. (Recall that his advances were subtle and private.) His ability to hide his child pornography for so long shows that he did not become wild with uncontrollable urges at moments when action would have revealed his indiscretions. In addition, he carefully chose child pornography and did not indiscriminately collect any and all pornography. In such respects, Peder's tumor was not fully disabling.

Nonetheless, Peder's tumor was disabling to some degree. Although he strongly desired to avoid prison, he "could not restrain himself from soliciting sexual favors from staff and other clients" even though he presumably knew (at least after the first time) that such acts would get him kicked out of the treatment program and land him in prison. He also presumably knew that these attempts to get sexual favors had little chance of succeeding. Doing what one knows to have little chance of benefit and large risk of great harm is classic evidence of incapacity to refrain. Similar points could be made about his solicitations and urination during the neurologic exam.

For assessing criminal responsibility, the crucial question is whether Peder had the ability to avoid collecting child pornography and molesting a child, since those are the crimes with which he was charged. Although many details are unclear, Peder does seem to have had some kinds of control relevant to those criminal acts. He seems to have controlled when he collected or used pornography, what kind he used, and whether his advances to his stepdaughter were subtle or private.

This degree of control, however, does not imply that Peder controlled whether or not he would collect child pornography or molest his stepdaughter. People who control when and how they do an act do not always control whether or not they do some act of that kind eventually. Just as an alcoholic can have some control over what and when he drinks without controlling whether he drinks any alcohol this week, so Peder might control when and how he uses child pornography and molests his stepdaughter without controlling whether he will do those acts eventually. In addition, the tumor seems to have continued growing. If Peder's ability to control his child pornography and molestation reduced as the tumor got bigger and if the tumor would have kept getting bigger until it was removed, then Peder probably would have used child pornography or committed molestation at some point.

Admittedly, headaches and lack of coordination might have led to a neurological examination and tumor resection before Peder committed any illegal acts. Moreover, as mentioned, Peder could have left home or sought psychiatric help before he reached the point where he was unable to conform to law. However, such moves might not have worked, and they would have had high personal costs, including the risk that he would lose his new family and job.

It is also relevant that Peder tried but failed to restrain himself. He said that "the pleasure principle overrode" his attempts to stop. On the one hand, this description sounds like an admission that he was seeking his own personal pleasure. On the other hand, this description suggests that he did try hard to restrain himself but was unable to control his actions.

Overall, then, it seems that Peder had some degree of control and also lacked some degree of control. Whether or not he had *enough* control to justify holding him responsible and punishing him is the crucial issue.

A Role for Causation

Although people are bound to disagree, my judgment is that Peder's lack of control by itself was not enough to excuse him. If Peder had had the same degree of control, but the neurological examination had revealed no tumor, then I would think that Peder was responsible, and I suspect that most people would agree. However, when we find that the limits in Peder's control are caused by a tumor, then I and many other people would not hold Peder responsible. This comparison suggests that the tumor makes a difference. The fact that Peder's control is reduced by a tumor raises the threshold of control that is needed for responsibility in such a way that Peder's degree of control is beneath that threshold and, hence, too low for him to be responsible.

If you disagree about Peder's case in particular, imagine different individuals with tumors that reduce or increase their control to varying extents. Then compare people with the same degree of control but without tumors. When I think about a range of such cases, there are some cases in which an agent with a certain degree of incapacity but no tumor seems responsible, whereas another agent with the same degree of incapacity caused by a tumor seems not to be responsible. If so, then the fact that a tumor causes the disability is relevant to the judgment about responsibility in at least some cases. Sometimes, the tumor adds force to the excuse by raising the threshold of control required for responsibility.

This picture of how causation can matter is not unknown in criminal law. Almost all insanity defenses from *M'Naughten* to *Durham* to the Model Penal Code include a causal requirement that the relevant mental disability must be "a result of mental disease or defect." Why? If the mental disability were enough by itself to excuse the agent, then there would be no need for the clause "as a result of mental disease or defect." Without this clause, the insanity defense would be available to a defendant with the same disability that was not "a result of mental disease or defect." But that is not how any insanity defense is written. The fact that this causal requirement is so widely accepted suggests that what matters to responsibility in cases of insanity is not only the disability but also the cause of the disability. That is close to what I am arguing. The only difference is that I would add that a certain degree of disability can excuse because it exists "as a result of *neural* disease or defect."

Compare also the voluntary act requirement. Model Penal Code section 2.01 says that guilt and liability must always be based on "conduct that includes a voluntary act," and then it adds that "conduct during hypnosis or resulting from hypnotic suggestion" is not a voluntary act. Acts resulting from hypnotic suggestion are often intentional and controlled to some extent, even if not totally. Here again, the cause of the act seems to matter to the criminal law. If the act results from hypnotic suggestion, its agent is not liable, guilty, or responsible, even though the agent would be responsible if the same act did not have that cause. Although this voluntary act requirement is distinct from the insanity defense, both cases show that it is not unprecedented for the criminal law to consider causation in formulating defenses.

If not all causation excuses, but some does, then we are back to the question raised by Tom Wolfe: which causes are the *wrong* kind? These questions are hard to answer precisely. One answer that strikes many as plausible is that mental as well as neural diseases and defects are seen as external to an agent's true or real self. Though vague and questionable, acceptance of this view might explain why so many people do not find Peder responsible. Frankfurt has argued for decades that people identify with some of their desires but not with others and that we do not and should not hold people fully responsible when their actions are caused by desires that they do not identify with.[16] This theory is controversial, but recent surveys have suggested that many common folk endorse or assume something along these lines.[17]

This view can be understood as a specification of a distinction in the law, mentioned by Farahany:

> Th[e] presumption of agency may be challenged and successfully overcome if a defendant demonstrates that his bodily movements arose from natural phenomena or *external* forces. A claim of involuntariness based on internal factors is traditionally rejected, because criminal law generally rejects a dualistic view of behavior in favor of a system that recognizes the capacity of agency.[18]

Tumors are surely "natural phenomena," but are they "external forces" or "internal factors"? That depends on where you draw the line between internal and external. Peder's tumor was inside his skull, but physical location hardly seems relevant to moral or legal responsibility, since a microchip used by an evil scientist to control an agent would surely be seen as an external force even if it happened to be put inside the skull. Thus, what makes something internal or external in the relevant way is not its physical location but, instead, its relation to the agent's true or real self. If so, the view of responsibility as depending on the true or real self is not as foreign to the law as some might claim.

All of this is controversial. It is also vague. However, this approach begins to capture many people's views about responsibility, as illustrated by Peder's case. People who are sympathetic with this general approach then have reason to reject the standard account of legal responsibility and to try to formulate an excuse for those whose acts are caused in the wrong ways.

3. Objections and Replies

Defenders of a more traditional view will have several objections against including causation in a theory of responsibility.

First, they might accuse me of misapplying traditional defenses, including the voluntary act requirement, mens rea, or the insanity defense.[19] However, I admit that Peder did commit voluntary acts of kinds that criminal law forbids, he had the requisite mens rea, and he was not eligible for an insanity defense in most jurisdictions. My argument does not apply these traditional standards, so it cannot be misapplying them. I am also not rejecting these standards. I concede that defendants who meet these conditions are not fully responsible, if they are responsible at all. Instead, my claim is that this traditional list of defenses is incomplete. I am arguing for addition, not subtraction—much less erasure—of the tradition.

Some critics might claim that nothing needs to be added, because the criminal law already has some defenses that apply to Peder. Some jurisdictions, for example, include a diminished-capacity provision that "enables a criminal defendant to claim a partial excuse for having a 'greater than normal difficulty in conforming to law.'"[20] This kind of provision seems to apply to Peder because presumably it was abnormally difficult for him to fight his mysterious and growing urges constantly for a long time. However, diminished-capacity defenses usually apply only to specific intent crimes, and they usually reduce the charges (such as from first-degree murder to manslaughter) without removing liability to severe punishment. Hence, this part of the law is not enough to satisfy those who believe that Peder should not be forced to go to prison for years.

The same goes for culpability: "In addressing culpability, the behavioral moralist acknowledges that the defendant will be held accountable for his crime but argues that he should be punished less severely than other defendants because of the causal contributions to his behavior."[21] Prominent examples of reduced culpability are recent U.S. Supreme Court decisions that ruled out the death penalty for crimes committed before the defendant reached the age of 18 and life without parole for nonlethal crimes committed before the age of 18.[22] However, the defendants in these cases were still kept in prison for many years because they were held responsible even if not fully culpable. Again, those who oppose lengthy imprisonment for Peder will not be satisfied by saying that he is not fully culpable but is still responsible and liable to severe punishment.

It is also not enough to argue that "reasonableness should be informed by emerging scientific evidence to reflect the actual average capacities of society."[23] Scientific psychology could be useful in this reform. However, reasonableness is most central to negligence, recklessness, and cases where intention is questionable. Peder's acts were clearly intentional, and he did not deny intentionality. Thus, reforming legal standards of reasonableness would not affect Peder's case.

Overall, then, there seems to be no easy way for the law to accommodate many people's intuitions that Peder is not responsible and should not be found guilty or punished much if at all. The next question is whether those intuitions are defensible.

As Farahany observes, "criminal stigma is the unnamed discomfort driving much of the debate."[24] Those who think that Peder does not deserve stigma or moral opprobrium (or that he deserves less) will think that the law needs to be reformed. Of course, they can also have other reasons for excusing Peder, including the belief that punishing him will do no good for anyone, since he is repentant, the tumor is removed and can be monitored, and his family apparently wants him back. In any case, the fundamental question is why we should punish a defendant who does not seem to deserve any (or much less) criminal or moral opprobrium or stigma.

Farahany suggests two reasons. One is that "the choice may be to free a responsible and dangerous defendant, but one for whom a juror feels less moral opprobrium."[25] However, this potential danger does not apply to Peder. He passed the sexual treatment program, and neither the court nor his family sees him as dangerous. It is troubling that Peder resumed collecting pornography when his tumor came back in October 2001, but pornography was legal, and there was no report of any inclination toward anything illegal, including *child* pornography or molestation. Peder has plenty of incentive to comply with the law; he wants to behave properly, he will be monitored closely, and repeating his acts will create serious risks.[26] Some might argue that the legal system cannot allow this safe individual to escape punishment because a law that excuses in this case will allow other dangerous individuals to escape punishment. However, it seems unfair to punish safe Peder because of dangerous Paul. Moreover, if others are dangerous, then they can be subjected to involuntary civil commitment instead of punishment.

Farahany suggests a second reason to punish Peder when she writes:

> If criminal law is intended to both enforce and create new norms of conduct, there may be a normative justification for stigmatizing individuals, even if the psychological sense of stigma turns one against it in the individual case. Norm creation itself has a normative purpose—to guide individuals in society to act in a manner deemed in the best interest of society. Stigmatizing individuals who fail to do so may serve as an effective tool for enforcing norms and creating new norms of conduct.[27]

In Peder's case, society wants to create, enforce, and stabilize norms against child pornography and molestation. To do so, it might seem necessary to express moral condemnation of Peder and of his acts, even if we feel that he does not really deserve any moral opprobrium or stigma. However, as before, it seems unfair to punish Peder just to send a message to other individuals, when Peder's acts were caused by a tumor. Moreover, there are more effective and less harmful ways to send that message. Imprisoning Peder could not do much to enforce norms against child pornography and molestation, because very few people will know about Peder's case, and most people already know about many other cases of severe punishments for child pornography and molestation. Punishing Peder is harmful not only to him and to his family but potentially also to respect for the law if many people think that he is not responsible.[28] If people do find out that Peder was punished, they might wonder how many other punished child molesters are not responsible. If the law really wants to create, enforce, and stabilize norms against child pornography and molestation, well-publicized improvements in policing, counseling, and education are better ways to solidify norms.

Critics still might object that Peder is a rare exception, and legal officials need to set legal norms for more common cases. In other cases, there might be uncertainty about neural causes, and some defendants might fake neural defects in order to get off.[29] These dangers can be serious when defenses depend on functional magnetic resonance imaging. However, there is no way to fake a tumor of the kind that structural magnetic resonance imaging found in Peder. There is also no uncertainty about the presence of the tumor, since it was removed and analyzed. The only uncertainty is about the causal link between the tumor and the behavior. As in all cases of uncertainty, the burden of proof becomes crucial. It might be fair to require defendants to prove a causal link by preponderance of evidence or even with clear and convincing evidence, as in other affirmative defenses. Adopting such procedural rules would prevent feared abuses, including faking. And Peder could meet those burdens, because the way in which his urges and behaviors came and went with the presence or absence of his tumor provides strong evidence of causation, as his doctors said.[30]

Finally, a slew of philosophical objections deserve responses. Some critics might accuse me of committing a naturalistic fallacy.[31] I plead not guilty. My claim that Peder is not responsible is not entailed by or deducible from the premise that his tumor caused his action. My argument openly depends on normative premises, as well. Second, I also do not assume dualism.[32] I am a nonreductive physicalist, but even a reductive physicalist could agree that Peder is not responsible. Physicalists need not think that every physical cause has the same normative status. Some physical causes, such as tumors, can excuse even if other physical causes, such as normal brain states, do not excuse. Physicalists do not have to eliminate the mental. They can hold that some physical states are also mental, but others are not. Third, I am also not assuming determinism.[33] I am a determinist, but determinism plays no role in my argument here. The reason that Peder's tumor excuses him is not that it determines his acts but that it is external to his true or real self (in some way that admittedly still needs to be explained). Fourth, I am not assuming incompatibilism or denying free will.[34] I am a compatibilist (of a contrastivist kind) who believes in free will.[35] To hold that some people lack free will because of how their brains operate is not to deny free will for everyone else.

That brings us to the final and, perhaps, most basic issue. The main objection that Moore raises to "causal theories of excuses," that Morse raises to "the fundamental psycholegal error," and that Farahany raises to "behavioral morality" involves generalization: every act of every agent has a physical or neural cause, so we will have to excuse everybody for everything if we excuse anyone on the basis of causation alone without reference to traditional legal excuses. I focused on Peder in order to show that we can reasonably excuse some unusual people on the basis of causation without excusing everyone on the basis of causation. Generalization can be avoided simply by pointing out that Peder's case is peculiar. Not everyone has a tumor and evidence that the tumor caused the act. That is why excusing Peder does not entail or even suggest excusing everyone.

That leaves no reason against the view that Peder is not responsible, should be excused, and should not be punished. Of course, not everyone will agree with this intuition. My main goal has been to show only that this position is defensible and plausible. Of course, many details need to be spelled out. In particular, what counts as the true or real self? I have not tried to fill in those details in this short note. Much work remains for other occasions. Still, I hope that this case study illustrates one way in which neuroscience can be relevant to law and can point toward the need for reform in the criminal law of excuses.

NOTES

For helpful comments, I am grateful to Nita Farahany and to audiences at the American Political Science Association, the University of Pennsylvania Law School, Harvard University, and Duke University.

1. Michael Moore, "Causation and the Excuses," *California Law Review* 73 (1985): 1091, 1091–149.

2. Stephen J. Morse, "Culpability and Control," *University of Pennsylvania Law Review* 142 (1994): 1587, 1592–94.

3. Nita Farahany, "Law and Behavioral Morality," in this volume, 115.

4. Ibid., 132–37.

5. Ibid., 129.

6. Tom Wolfe, "Sorry, but Your Soul Just Died," *Forbes*, December 2, 1996. Wolfe mentions being "hardwired"—suggesting an inability to change—but that term does not help because we are all hardwired to some extent, and hardwiring need not always be bad wiring.

7. Daniel Dennett, *Elbow Room: Varieties of Free Will Worth Wanting* (Cambridge, MA: MIT Press, 1984).

8. Jeffrey M. Burns and Russell H. Swerdlow, "Right Orbitofrontal Tumor with Pedophilia Symptom and Constructional Apraxia Sign," *Archives of Neurology* 60 (March 2003): 437–40. All of the facts and quotations in this section are from this article.

9. Cf. Farahany, "Law and Behavioral Morality," 128–29 and 144–45.

10. Ibid., 139. *Black's Law Dictionary* defines "responsible" as "liable" and vice versa!

11. This point also applies to the causal theory of excuses as Moore defines it, because every act is caused by some "factor outside [the agent's] control." Moore, "Causation and the Excuses," 1091.

12. The tumor is also a proximate cause (Farahany, "Law and Behavioral Morality," 128–29), but it is not clear why proximacy makes any difference to responsibility.

13. Eddy Nahmias, "Intuitions about Free Will, Determinism, and Bypassing," in *The Oxford Handbook on Free Will*, 2d ed., ed. R. Kane (New York; Oxford University Press, 2011), 555–76.

14. See my "Downward Mental Causation" (in preparation).

15. See my "Free Contrastivism," in *Contrastivism in Philosophy*, ed. Martijn Blaauw (London: Routledge, 2012).

16. Harry Frankfurt, *The Importance of What We Care About* (Cambridge: Cambridge University Press, 1988).

17. Robert L. Woolfolk, John M. Doris, and John M. Darley, "Identification, Situational Constraint, and Social Cognition," *Cognition* 100 (2006): 283–301; Chandra Sekhar Sripada, "The Deep Self Model and Asymmetries in Folk Judgments about Intentional Action," *Philosophical Studies* 151 (2010): 159–76.

18. Farahany, "Law and Behavioral Morality," 131.

19. In particular, they might object that I confuse motivation with intention (cf. ibid., 131–32). Motivation usually does not matter under traditional criminal law of excuses. However, my discussion of Peder's tumor does not depend on his motivation, which was, admittedly, pleasure. What

excuses him is not the content of that motivation but, rather, the cause of that motivation.

20. Ibid., 135 (citing *Clark v. Arizona*, 548 U.S. 735 (2006)).

21. Ibid., 148.

22. *Roper v. Simmons*, 543 U. S. 551 (2005), and *Graham v. Florida*, 130 S. Ct. 2011 (2010).

23. Farahany, "Law and Behavioral Morality," 142.

24. Ibid., 147.

25. Ibid., 149. Farahany suggests that we might understigmatize agents whose acts have known neural causes, because "It may be difficult to psychologically internalize the physical existence of both the body and the mind." Ibid., 151. However, many who would excuse Peder do not make this mistake, for they (and I) are physicalists who also recognize Peder's mental states.

26. Cf. ibid., 140 ("no incentive").

27. Ibid., 152.

28. My point here is not that "criminal law must be limited to . . . criminals who have a blameworthy cause for having engaged in prohibited conduct." Ibid., 138. It is only that criminal punishments express moral opprobrium, as Farahany admits (ibid.), so the criminal law must be moral and fair in order to be legitimate and must seem fair and legitimate in order to be effective in the long run.

29. Cf. ibid., 163 n.157.

30. Peder's doctors present the facts as "establishing causality." Burns and Swerdlow, "Right Orbitofrontal Tumor with Pedophilia Symptom and Constructional Apraxia Sign," 439. To show causation, defendants should not be required to show that *all* people with a certain neural abnormality in a certain environment would do the act. Cf. Farahany, "Law and Behavioral Morality," 144–45. Causation can be probabilistic in science and in law.

31. Cf. Farahany, "Law and Behavioral Morality," 129.

32. Cf. ibid., 140.

33. Cf. ibid.

34. Cf. ibid., 130.

35. See my "Free Contrastivism."

7

SCIENCE FICTION: SOME UNEXAMINED ASSUMPTIONS OF NITA FARAHANY'S "LAW AND BEHAVIORAL MORALITY"

JENNIFER L. CULBERT

Nita Farahany's essay "Law and Behavioral Morality" takes up several distinct but related topics concerning the application of science, specifically neuroscience, to matters of criminal law. My response to "Law and Behavioral Morality" focuses on what I take to be, at least at first glance, one of its least controversial and most sensible conclusions: the suggestion that behavioral moralists focus their energies on scientifically validating and qualifying our legal notion of reasonableness.[1] This particular conclusion reveals the centrality of the problem of judgment for Farahany's essay.

According to Farahany, behavioral moralists argue for new explanatory causes of human behavior that focus on the physical condition of the brain. In so doing, they undermine the concept of human agency and the theories of responsibility that are fundamental to our criminal justice system. Farahany recognizes the significance of the threat behavioral moralists pose to the premises of the criminal justice system and argues strongly against any use of neuroscience, behavioral genetics, and scientific studies of human behavior to explain (away) criminal behavior. Nevertheless, she values scientific insights about human capacities. Consequently, she proposes that behavioral moralists interested in the criminal justice system change the focus of the application of their argument. Instead of taking issue with causal mechanisms and thereby opening up a Pandora's box of questions about responsibility at law, Farahany suggests that behavioral moralists turn their attention to the notion of reasonableness as it informs discussions of culpability in criminal cases.

Reasonableness refers to the norms of behavior that society expects any given person to meet.[2] These norms are both "subjective" and "objective." According to Farahany, they are subjective when they "begin with a shared set of embedded values" or express "aspirational goals for members of society to meet."[3] They are "objective" when they refer to "those with which the average member of the community can comply."[4] The problem—and hence the opportunity for behavioral morality—is that it isn't clear what we can actually expect of the average member of the community. In other words, the "objective" norm to which reasonableness refers is not particularly objective. Indeed, at present "we base the average or reasonable person solely on fictional predictions of human capacities."[5] This can change, however. Farahany believes that, "[a]s neuroscience, behavioral genetics, and scientific studies of human behavior progress, these disciplines will become increasingly more relevant to societal constructs of average or normal behavior."[6] When this happens, behavioral morality can reshape "a fundamental component of criminal responsibility—the notion of reasonableness underlying it."[7] In other words, the notion of reasonableness may one day reflect not only what we know a population can do but what we can anticipate and require its individuals to do.

Although Farahany is careful not to say anything definitive about the future, she implies that the notion of reasonableness is not only susceptible to the charms of behavioral morality but also in need of the attention. She implies as much when she asks, "[O]nce we have a better understanding of human behavior, why should we base the average or reasonable person solely on fictional predictions of human capacities? Why wouldn't we use scientific information about the average person, as empirically tested and validated by science?"[8]

Why indeed?

Certain assumptions inform these questions and the argument they make by implication. In particular, these questions take for granted a clear distinction between "fictional predictions" and "scientific information." This distinction echoes the difference between the "subjective" and "objective" norms that inform the notion of reasonableness, thus reiterating and amplifying the oft-noted tension between them. As a result, the difference between subjective and objective norms, a difference that is criticized for not being sufficiently strong, is not only reiterated but also strengthened. In brief, a deficit of difference is made up. But, observing this, a question is begged. Specifically, on what was the assumption of a difference between "fiction" and "science" originally based?

If we look more closely at the references to fiction and science in "Law and Behavioral Morality," it is clear that fiction is understood to be "arbitrary" and "contingent" while science is conceived as logical and self-sufficient. Rather than reflecting or responding to the particular interests of a time and place, science works in its own precise and systematic terms to discover what is true, such as what is "actually" average or "really" normal.

This characterization of science fails to note that scientific experiments are always explicitly framed, however. That is to say, Farahany does not acknowledge how scientific experiments occur in normative settings that dictate what counts as sound methodology, good data, meaningful results, and legitimate inferences. Indeed, philosophers and historians of science have gone so far as to suggest, as Richard Lewontin does in *The Doctrine of DNA*, that "what appears to us in the mystical guise of pure science and objective knowledge about nature turns out underneath, to be political, economic, and social ideology."[9] In other words, the settings that dictate what counts as good science are normative themselves. In particular, they reflect or express particular values and aspirations; they also inform practices of scientific validation, even though they cannot be empirically tested. In this particular regard, then, science may not be so easily opposed to fiction.

For scientists like Lewontin, the loss of this opposition is no loss at all. Unlike Farahany, Lewontin rejects the idea that we should naturally privilege science or "objectivity" over fiction or "subjectivity." In fact, Lewontin sees the interdependence between science and fiction as a reflection of the intrinsically dynamic and open nature of the object of scientific inquiry. What is more, Lewontin's work, among others', suggests that although this interdependence may require us to abandon a particular kind of faith in science, it need not undermine our notion of responsibility. On the contrary, insight into interdependence may broaden and deepen that notion.

Farahany may have the best of intentions when she seeks to incorporate into the criminal justice system behavioral morality's insights. Indeed, as I read her suggestion that behavioral moralists focus their energies on establishing an empirically sound notion of reasonableness, she seeks to preserve a space where social institutions such as criminal law may continue to honor obviously problematic—from a scientific point of view—but essential—from a pragmatic and moral point of view—notions such as "agency." Yet, she undermines what she seeks to preserve in "Law and Behavioral Morality" when she expresses the idea that through genetics or neuroscience we will eventually identify a "normal" that is always already there waiting to be revealed by researchers with the proper tools and techniques.

First, given Farahany's argument, it is ironic that the insights she anticipates science will provide about what is "normal" behavior—insights that may then be used to establish an "objective" foundation for a legal notion of reasonableness—are not particularly "scientific." That is to say, claims about what is "normal" or "average" are based on statistics. Statistics generalize data collected from and about individuals, data that are collected in highly regulated and tightly controlled environments. Whatever insights statistics based on these data provide are not insights a neuroscientist or a geneticist would be competent to offer or support.

Second, and more significant from a philosophical perspective, in "Law and Behavioral Morality," Farahany embraces a "challenging" orientation toward the world. Such an orientation is akin to what Martin Heidegger calls "standing-reserve."[10] As an orientation, "standing-reserve" seeks certainty, the satisfaction of an expectation that something stands still in a world in which everything else is in flux.[11] When absolutely everything is in flux, there is no obvious way to distinguish between "subjective" and "objective" claims. In a context such as criminal law—where a distinction between arbitrary or biased opinions and rational or impartial conclusions is understood to be a distinction that is not only possible to make but also necessary to respect if there are to be fair and just decisions about culpability—it is easy to appreciate how we might turn to science to tell us what we can *actually* expect of people. Thus, Farahany's proposal for behavioral moralists is not as modest as it sounds. The power and the promise of behavioral science at law is that empirical testing and validation by practices guided by the scientific method will transform not what is judged but how what is judged is judged. Should the normative and the normal become identical as Farahany anticipates they will, the arbitrary and contingent quality of the norms that now inform the legal notion of reasonableness will no longer be able to threaten the integrity of any determination of culpability. Once the norm is revealed and called by its proper name, the normal, the decision in a criminal case will require only that the decision maker legally acknowledge or recognize what was simply always already the case about (most of) us. The practice of judgment will then be rendered completely "objective."

By reminding us how subjective and objective norms inform the practice of science as well as the practice of criminal justice, I do not mean to imply that science and criminal justice share the same subjective and objective norms. By noting how different methodologies are employed by "hard" science and social science, I also do not mean to imply that hard science is incapable of producing useful information about human beings and the world in which we exist. Rather, I mean to call attention to the fact that the problem of judgment—the problem of discerning what is "reasonable" to expect of a person in a particular set of circumstances, the problem that "scientific information" is supposed to help us with in the case of decisions about culpability in criminal trials—is what is at stake in "Law and Behavioral Morality." As Farahany describes them, behavioral moralists hold out the possibility that we may one day be able to understand human behavior on the basis of "true" rather than "fictional" accounts of what is "reasonable." However, as many have observed, science is set apart from other social activities only by its institutional procedures for overcoming particularity. So, while science may appear to overcome the conditions that limit us to "fictional" accounts of the world, behavioral genetics and population studies do not "really" solve the problem of judgment by informing us of the "actual average capacities" of members of society. Instead, a kind of positivist epistemology ends up limiting how we imagine and speak about human beings at law. Judges and jurors are charged with deciding culpability on the basis of what is always already the case about those of us who count, instead of acting as "the conscience of the community." Because "reasonableness" is a quality that is determined by context and community, a quality that can be defined neither universally nor empirically, we might nevertheless want to continue to base "the reasonable person" on a "fictitious" person and focus attention on the stories we tell ourselves about each other.

NOTES

1. Nita Farahany, "Law and Behavioral Morality," in this volume, 142–46.

2. Ibid., 142.

3. Ibid., 141.

4. Ibid., 142.

5. Ibid., 145.

6. Ibid., 144–45

7. Ibid., 141.

8. Ibid., 145.

9. R. C. Lewontin, *The Doctrine of DNA: Biology as Ideology* (London: Penguin, 1991), 57.

10. Martin Heidegger, "The Question Concerning Technology," in *The Question Concerning Technology and Other Essays*, trans. William Lovitt (New York: Harper Colophon, 1977), 3–35, 24.

11. For a discussion of this interpretation of standing-reserve, see Jennifer L. Culbert, *Dead Certainty: Capital Punishment and the Problem of Judgment* (Stanford: Stanford University Press, 2008), 130.

PART III

BIOPOLITICAL SCIENCE

8

BIOPOLITICAL SCIENCE

LARRY ARNHART

Political science could become a true science by becoming a biopolitical science of political animals. This science would be both Aristotelian and Darwinian. It would be Aristotelian in fulfilling Aristotle's original understanding of political science as the biological study of the political life of human beings and other political animals. It would be Darwinian in employing Charles Darwin's evolutionary theory as well as modern advances in Darwinian biology to explain political behavior as shaped by genetic evolution, cultural evolution, and individual judgment.

Some political scientists have complained about the deficiencies of their discipline in understanding politics. A small but growing number of political scientists have argued that a political science rooted in an evolutionary theory of human nature could overcome many of these deficiencies.[1] I will support this claim by laying out a theoretical framework for a biopolitical science that rectifies some of the defects in contemporary political science. To illustrate how such a biopolitical science accounts for the course of political history, I will show how such a science could deepen our understanding of one of the crucial turns in American political history—Abraham Lincoln's Emancipation Proclamation of January 1, 1863.

1. THE POVERTY OF POLITICAL SCIENCE

Critics of the contemporary state of political science have identified at least seven deficiencies that could be alleviated by a biopolitical science—deficiencies that come from playing down the
importance in political science of history, morality, judgment,
emotion, religion, ambition, and liberal education.

First, although *history matters* in the study of politics, because
the significance of each political event depends on its place in a
temporal sequence of events over extended periods of time, contemporary political science often ignores the historical character
of political life. So, recently, some political scientists have sought
to recover political history as an integral part of political science.[2]
Biopolitical science builds on this scholarship, while exploring
the deep history of politics over millions of years that includes not
only human beings but also other political animals, which draws
from what some historians today call "big history"—the unification of natural history and human history into a grand narrative.[3]
This evolutionary political history moves through three levels
—natural history, cultural history, and individual history. For example, to fully understand Lincoln's Emancipation Proclamation,
we need to see it as an event in the natural history of cooperation
in the human species, in the cultural history of slavery in America,
and in the individual history of Lincoln as a political actor in the
Civil War.

Second, although *morality matters* in the study of politics, contemporary political science often ignores the moral dimensions
of political life. Against the assumption of many political scientists that political behavior is motivated solely or predominantly
by the rational maximization of self-interest, some political scientists have argued for going "beyond self-interest" to recognize the
other-regarding motives of political actors that drive political controversy as a moral debate over the common good.[4] Biopolitical
science supports this position by showing how the evolved political
nature of human beings as shaped by genetic and cultural group
selection manifests not only a selfish concern for oneself and one's
kin but also a moral concern for reciprocity, fairness, and the good
of the group. *Homo politicus* combines the traits of *Homo economicus*
and *Homo moralis*. Lincoln's participation in the debate over slav-

ery and emancipation shows this moral sense in the recognition of slavery as unjust exploitation, while also showing the need to accommodate the self-interest of the slaveholder as a constraint on the pursuit of justice.

Third, although *judgment matters* in the study of politics, contemporary political science has little to say about practical judgment in politics and how to distinguish good and bad political judgment. To rectify this defect, some political scientists have contended that political science needs to recognize and explain political judgment as an intellectual and moral virtue of practical wisdom that cannot be reduced to scientific or theoretical reasoning.[5] Biopolitical science confirms Aristotle's insight about the importance of prudence or practical judgment in morality and politics. Darwinian science recognizes that brains evolved to help animals who need to make practical decisions to satisfy their desires in response to the risks and opportunities offered by their physical and social environments. Human beings and other political animals have evolved brains that allow them to make practical judgments in circumstances of social complexity where knowledge must always be uncertain and imprecise. For human beings, such judgments require deliberate reflection. But they also require worldly experience, proper habituation, intuitive insight, and emotional dispositions that go beyond purely logical reasoning. Lincoln's decision to issue the Emancipation Proclamation illustrates the intricacy—if not mystery—of practical judgment in politics.

Fourth, although *emotion matters* in the study of politics, political scientists who emphasize "rational choice" in explaining human behavior have often played down the role of emotion in political life, and generally many political scientists have assumed that emotion subverts rational decision making, particularly in democracies threatened by popular passions. And yet some political scientists have rightly argued that political decision making and rhetoric show the interdependence of reason and emotion, because human practical cognition is guided by the emotional dispositions of human nature, which is apparent, for example, in the power that emotion has in electoral behavior and political journalism.[6] Biopolitical science shows how emotion belongs to the evolved nature of human beings and other political animals. Biological psychology uncovers the neural bases of emotion in the practical judgments of political animals. The power of emotion in political rhetoric is illustrated in the passionate controversies surrounding the Civil War and Lincoln's emancipation of slaves.

Fifth, although *religion matters* in the study of politics, many political scientists have ignored the political importance of religion, particularly those who have assumed that "modernization" would bring a withering away of religious belief. In recent years, the political effects of religion have been hard to ignore, which has made "politics and religion" a vibrant field of study.[7] Even though Darwinian evolutionary thinking is sometimes associated with atheism, Darwin recognized religion's importance in the moral evolution of human beings. Following Darwin's lead, some biologists have developed an evolutionary theory of religion as a product of genetic and cultural evolution driven by group selection: religion is adaptive insofar as it helps groups to solve collective action problems and function as collective units.[8] American political culture has always been deeply shaped by biblical religion, and so a critical part of the debate over slavery was whether it was compatible with the Bible. It was crucial, therefore, for Lincoln to defend his Emancipation Proclamation as conforming to biblical morality.

Sixth, although *ambition matters* in the study of politics, many political scientists look to impersonal laws of political behavior and abstract models of rational choice in which the personal ambition of political actors falls out of view. Against this tendency, some political scientists have asserted that politics is all about the manly spiritedness of ambitious political actors competing for importance.[9] Biopolitical science recognizes such political ambition as the striving for hegemonic dominance that arises among political animals organizing themselves into hierarchies of dominance and submission. Among human beings and some other primates, this competition for dominance creates a tense balance of power between the desire of the dominant few to rule and the desire of the subordinate many to be free from exploitation. Lincoln was an example of a restlessly ambitious man who yearned to do something great in politics that would bring immortal glory to his name. His ambition was channeled and checked by the American system of constitutional government. But that constitutional system also allowed him to satisfy his ambition by winning the glory that came from issuing the Emancipation Proclamation.

Seventh, although *liberal education matters* in the study of politics, the discipline of political science has become so specialized and fragmented as to be almost completely separated not only from the natural sciences and the humanities but even from the other social sciences, and thus it cannot be integrated into the interdisciplinary activity of liberal learning. Some political scientists worry that this professional isolation of political science from general education prevents students and scholars from seeing how the study of politics ultimately requires a general understanding of the place of human beings in the universe.[10] Biopolitical science employs evolutionary thinking as a way of unifying knowledge across all the disciplines of the natural sciences, the social sciences, and the humanities to understand the evolved nature of human beings as political animals. This contributes to the intellectual project of what Edward O. Wilson calls "consilience," the unification of all knowledge through biological science broadly conceived.[11] This is illustrated by explaining Lincoln's Emancipation Proclamation as an individual political judgment constrained by the natural history of the human species and the cultural history of American politics.

The fundamental framework for biopolitical science is the theoretical analysis of political behavior as conforming to a nested hierarchy of three levels of deep history—the universal history of the species, the cultural history of the group, and the individual history of animals within the group. To fully comprehend the human nature of politics, we must understand the unity of political universals, the diversity of political cultures, and the individuality of political judgments. I will work through these three levels of biopolitical history as they are generally manifested in human politics and as they are particularly illustrated in Lincoln's decision to issue the Emancipation Proclamation.

2. Political Universals

Political universals are those stable tendencies of political behavior that characterize each species of political animal as shaped by its genetic evolutionary history. I will concentrate on political primates and particularly on human beings and on chimpanzees as the closest living primate relatives of human beings. Since the fossil record of evolution gives us little direct evidence for behavioral evolution and since our understanding of how genes influence complex behavior is limited, we are forced into indirect inferences about the genetic evolution of political behavior based on triangulation of data from studies of chimpanzees and human hunter-gatherers. This assumes that chimpanzees give us the best proxies for the common ancestors of chimps and humans and that human hunter-gatherers give us the best proxies for hominid ancestors.[12] This leaves room for plenty of controversy. My aim is only to make a plausible case.

The Ambivalent Behavioral Repertoire of Human Politics

Government and politics are universal to human beings, because they express a universal human nature as shaped by the genetic evolution of the human species.[13] I define politics as the government of a society. A society is any group of individuals who cooperate with one another. A government is any ruling coordination of a society. The universal behavioral repertoire of human politics includes social behavior and governmental behavior. The repertoire of social behavior includes egoism, nepotism, mutualism, reciprocity, and group-selected morality. The repertoire of governmental behavior includes dominance, deference, and counterdominance (or resistance to dominance). These behavioral propensities can be found in some form among many animals.[14] They belong to the list of what many anthropologists have identified as "human universals."[15]

This behavioral repertoire shows the ambivalent or contradictory character of our human political nature.[16] We are socially ambivalent animals, because our naturally egoistic propensities conflict with our naturally social propensities. We are politically ambivalent animals, because our natural propensities to dominance and deference conflict with our natural propensity to resist being dominated.

Egoism is the natural propensity of individuals to favor their own interests over those of other individuals. This arises from an evolutionary process in which individuals compete with one another for resources necessary for survival and reproduction.[17]

Nepotism is the natural propensity of individuals to cooperate more readily with their genetic relatives than with those who are not related to them. This is to be expected if individuals evolved to enhance not just their individual survival and reproduction but also the survival and reproduction of collateral relatives.[18]

Mutualism is the natural propensity of individuals to cooperate when it is mutually beneficial to do so and when the benefits are direct and immediate. To secure the benefits, individuals must cooperate; if they don't cooperate, they lose the benefits.[19]

Reciprocity is the natural propensity of individuals to cooperate with those people they expect to be cooperative in return. Direct reciprocity arises from the expectation that the beneficiaries of one's cooperation will themselves reciprocate in kind.[20] Indirect reciprocity arises from the tendency to cooperate with those who have a reputation for being cooperative.[21]

Group-selected morality is the natural propensity of individuals to cooperate with others with whom they feel an affiliative bond of group identity based either on face-to-face cooperative encounters or on a symbolic community sustained by moral norms of cooperation. This group-selected morality inclines individuals to be conditional cooperators—who cooperate as long as others are cooperating—and conditional punishers—who punish those who violate the norms of cooperation as long as others are also enforcing such sanctions.[22] Cross-cultural studies using game-theory experiments show that moral norms vary across cultures in ways that reflect the diversity in the social ecology of these cultures but that moral variability is constrained by universal propensities to fairness rooted in evolved human nature.[23] Just as human beings have an evolved language instinct that provides the universal principles for learning specific languages, they also have an evolved moral instinct that provides the universal principles for learning specific moral systems.[24]

Group-selected morality corresponds to what Darwin called "the moral sense."[25] He regarded the human moral faculty as the greatest distinction between human beings and other animals. And yet, he believed he could explain the evolution of human morality through the complex interaction of at least five factors. First, the social instincts would incline social animals to feel sympathy for other animals in their group and to cooperate with them. Second, the development of mental faculties would allow human ancestors to act in the light of past experience and future expectations, so that an animal might feel regret for betraying a fellow group member. Third, the development of language would allow human ancestors to formulate norms of good behavior for the community, so that individuals would be more inclined to act for the public good. Fourth, the development of habit or social learning allows individuals to habituate themselves to conform to the standards of the community. Finally, the competition between groups would favor those groups with cooperative members over those groups that were less cooperative.

For Darwin, then, morality is identified with the good of the group and immorality with subverting the group. Consequently, the range of good conduct depends on the extension of the moral circle. The dark side of such group morality is that, while individuals can be good toward others they perceive to belong to their group, the same individuals can be vicious toward those outside their group. Much of the history of morality turns on whether the circle of group morality is narrow or wide. This adds to the ambivalent human nature of morality. Not only does acting in one's self-interest sometimes conflict with acting for the good of one's group, but acting for the good of one's group sometimes conflicts with acting for the good of those outside one's group. Although the circle of moral concern can be extended very far, perhaps even to include some humanitarian concern for distant strangers, group-selected morality always displays some form of tribalism or us-against-them psychology.[26]

Darwin's evolutionary account of morality requires that evolutionary selection occur not only between individuals but also between groups. Group selection has been controversial among evolutionary biologists.[27] But the debate in recent years has shifted in favor of Darwin's conception of group selection as reformulated in David Sloan Wilson's "multilevel selection" theory.[28] At each level of the hierarchy of life, there is a fundamental problem—the group-level benefits of cooperating are in tension with the individual-level benefits of exploiting the group. If competition between individuals in the same group is intense, selection might favor cheating individuals over cooperative individuals. But if the competition between groups is more intense than the competition within groups, then selection might favor cooperative individuals who help their groups compete better than groups with less cooperative individuals. (The depth of this problem throughout the hierarchy of life becomes clear as soon as we recognize that what we call an "individual" or an "organism" is a biological group of cells that manages to act as a collective unit.) This problem of group selection becomes even more complex when we see the ambivalence of political behavior in the tension between dominance and deference.

Dominance is the natural propensity of individuals to seek the power over others that comes from superior rank in a group. The political life of primates is organized around dominance hierarchies in which the old tend to have dominance over the young and males tend to have dominance over females, although females also have a dominance hierarchy. This is a political universal for chimpanzees, both in the wild and in captivity, and for human beings throughout history. Winning or losing dominance is determined by patterns of coalition formation that depend on shifting circumstances and individual decisions.[29]

Deference is the natural propensity of individuals to submit to those who are dominant. As political universals, deference is the correlative of dominance. Among the various species of political primates, there are distinctive behavioral cues, both verbal and nonverbal, by which subordinates defer to dominants.

Counterdominance is the natural propensity of individuals to resist being dominated. Among some primates, subordinate individuals can resist excessive dominance and thus limit the power of dominant individuals. Subordinate individuals can form alliances to challenge those at the top of the hierarchy. The variation in this behavior creates differences in dominance style across species. Rhesus monkeys show a "despotic dominance" style in which subordinates cannot challenge dominants. But chimpanzees show an "egalitarian dominance" style in which subordinates can restrain dominants. Dominant individuals are expected to mediate conflicts within the group and to lead the group in conflicts with other groups. Among chimpanzees, dominant individuals can be challenged or even deposed if they do not properly carry out their conflict-mediation role. Like chimpanzee politics, human politics shows a dominance hierarchy that can be egalitarian in style, based on the principle that leaders are only "first among equals."[30] This egalitarianism is most evident among human hunter-gatherers who use various kinds of sanctions to punish leaders who become too despotic in their dominance. This resistance to dominance was probably a crucial part of human evolutionary history in the Pleistocene epoch (beginning about two million years ago). But, with the establishment of large bureaucratic states based on agricultural production, which began more than five thousand years ago, most states have been more despotic than egalitarian. The recent emergence of constitutional democracies—over the past two centuries—is in some ways a return to the "egalitarian dominance" of the foraging way of life in which subordinates limit the power of dominants.[31] Thus, one can see the entire history of civilization as a struggle between freedom and domination.[32]

To the old question of political philosophy as to whether human beings are naturally hierarchical or naturally egalitarian, the answer from biopolitical science is that human beings are both. Machiavelli was right to see that human political nature is torn by the tension between the propensity of the few to dominance and the propensity of the many to resist dominance.[33] The history of political practice and political thought turns on this natural ambivalence interacting over time with particular political circumstances and decisions.

While I have drawn this conclusion about the ambivalent character of the evolved nature of human beings from comparisons with chimpanzees, the conclusion would still stand if one were to look to bonobos as the primate model for human evolutionary ancestry. Bonobos or pygmy chimpanzees (*Pan paniscus*) are similar to and yet distinct from chimpanzees (*Pan troglodytes*). Although bonobos seem somewhat more peaceful than chimps, bonobos still show a tense balance between competition and cooperation. And, although bonobos seem somewhat more egalitarian than chimps, bonobos do have dominance hierarchies among both males and females. Some primatologists see female dominance over all. Others see a codominance shared by the alpha male and the alpha female.[34]

In any case, if human ancestry is traceable back to a common ancestor shared with bonobos as well as chimps, one would expect human beings to show an ambivalent balance in their nature —competition balanced against cooperation and a propensity to dominance balanced against a propensity to resist dominance.[35]

Research on the neurophysiology of social behavior suggests that the desire for status or dominance in human beings and other primates is associated with biochemical factors such as serotonin and testosterone. Those individuals in dominant positions have higher levels of serotonin and testosterone, while those in subordinate positions have lower levels.[36] Moreover, the physiological character of status is suggested by the fact that those with high status tend to have better health than those with low status.[37] The mechanisms here are complex because of the interaction of many factors in the body and with the external physical and social environment. But the evidence suggests that some people are temperamentally inclined to have a stronger dominance drive than others.

Lincoln's Leadership in the Conflict over Slavery

Here, then, is the fundamental ambivalence in the political nature of human beings. People like Abraham Lincoln naturally desire dominance, and many other people naturally defer to the dominant leadership of men like Lincoln. Even an egalitarian political regime based on the principle that the people can govern themselves cannot dispense with the leadership of ambitious men like Lincoln. But there is also a natural desire to be free from despotic dominance. In an early speech, Lincoln warned that the greatest danger to the perpetuation of the American republic would come from ambitious men seeking glory to satisfy their dominance drive. The people need such leaders. But they also need to restrain the ambitious dominance of such leaders. Lincoln, as noted, was himself an intensely ambitious man who yearned to do something great to earn immortal glory. After he signed the Emancipation Proclamation, he told one of his friends that he had finally satisfied that dream of glory that he had had since he was a young man.[38]

The great question, particularly in a republican regime, is whether egalitarianism and dominance can be reconciled through a balance of power that allows for a leadership style of egalitarian dominance. Lincoln is the model of egalitarian leadership in American political history because he found a way to satisfy his personal ambition for power by advancing the principle of equal liberty in popular government and winning the glory of emancipating the slaves.

Lincoln's handling of the slavery debate also shows a prudent recognition of the social ambivalence in human nature that comes from the conflict between human egoism and human morality. For Lincoln, the dispute over slavery showed two opposing sides of human nature. He observed:

> Slavery is founded in the selfishness of man's nature—opposition to it, is his love of justice. These principles are an eternal antagonism; and when brought into collision so fiercely, as slavery extension brings them, shocks, and throes, and convulsions must ceaselessly follow. Repeal the Missouri compromise—repeal all compromises —repeal the Declaration of Independence—repeal all past history, you still cannot repeal human nature. It still will be the abundance of man's heart, that slavery extension is wrong.[39]

Lincoln saw that the Southerners themselves were torn between their selfish interest in preserving slavery and their moral feeling that slavery was wrong.[40] He also saw that any stable political order —particularly one with a popular form of government—had to be rooted both in self-interest and in morality. That's why he accepted the constitutional protections for slavery in the South as a prudent compromise with slavery out of respect for the interests of the South. But he also looked to the "ultimate extinction" of slavery, which would be served best by restricting slavery's extension into the Western territories. In devising plans for emancipation, he repeatedly argued for a scheme of compensated emancipation with voluntary colonization of the emancipated slaves in Africa or some other land outside the United States. He explained: "Will springs from the two elements of moral sense and self-interest. Let us be brought to believe it is morally right, and, at the same time, favorable to, or, at least, not against, our interest to transfer the African to his native clime, and we shall find a way to do it, however great the task may be."[41]

Lincoln argued that human beings were naturally equal in their right not to be ruled over without their consent. Government by consent of the governed was egalitarian, not in the sense that everyone would have absolutely equal authority but in the sense that those with superior authority would derive their authority from the consent of the citizens. Rulers would be only the "first among equals."

Slavery was wrong, Lincoln believed, because it denied this principle of equal right to be governed only by one's consent. Lincoln thought: "As I would not be a slave, so I would not be a master. This expresses my idea of democracy. Whatever differs from this, to the extent of the difference, is no democracy."[42] This same idea is found in egalitarian foraging communities, where it is based on the thought that "all men seek to rule, but if they cannot rule, they prefer to be equal."[43]

Slavery could be justified, however, if there were some biologically natural difference between masters and slaves such that the slaves were naturally adapted for their slavery and the masters naturally adapted for their mastery. Citing Aristotle's comments about the possibility that some human beings were slaves by nature, American proslavery advocates argued that the black race was physically, mentally, and morally adapted by nature for enslavement. They appealed to the racial science of scientists like Samuel Morton and Josiah Nott, who claimed that the human races were actually separate species that could be ranked as superior and inferior.

Against this racial science was the argument of Darwin and others that the human races were only varieties of one human species. Darwin's science of the unity of humanity supported Lincoln's affirmation of human equality as rooted in the universal nature of all human beings.[44] In fact, one of Darwin's motivations for writing *The Descent of Man* was to refute the biological arguments for slavery. He followed closely the news of the American Civil War, and he rejoiced when the war finally brought the emancipation of the slaves.[45]

For Lincoln, conceding the morality of slavery would deny the principles of democratic republicanism, because the arguments used to morally justify slavery are the same arguments that have been made for kingship. He warned: "They are the arguments that kings have made for enslaving the people in all ages of the world. You will find that all the arguments in favor of kingcraft were of this class: they always bestrode the necks of the people, not that they wanted to do it, but because the people were better off for being ridden."[46]

For almost all political scientists today, there is no controversy here, because they agree with Larry Diamond "that democratiza-

tion is generally a good thing and that democracy is the best form
of government."[47] Biopolitical science supports this idea with the
claim that modern democracy satisfies the natural human desire
for egalitarian leadership shaped originally in the Pleistocene evolutionary history of human ancestors who lived in hunter-gatherer
groups. But human hunter-gatherer groups—like groups of chimpanzees—are typically small communities of 30 to 150 individuals bound together by face-to-face interactions. If human beings
evolved to live in such small groups, how was it possible for them
to live in bureaucratic states with large populations of individuals with no direct ties of kinship or acquaintance? And, if human
beings evolved to live in egalitarian societies, why has democracy
been so rare over the past five thousand years of political history,
in which monarchy, despotism, and slavery have been much more
common than democracy, liberty, and equality? To address these
questions, biopolitical science must move from natural history to
cultural history.

3. POLITICAL CULTURES

Political cultures are the variable patterns of political behavior of
each species of political animals as shaped by cultural evolution
and constrained by genetic evolution. Biopolitical science must
study not only the political universals that constitute the enduring behavioral repertoire of political animals but also the political cultures that diversely express that behavioral repertoire in
the cultural history of political animals. The history of government among human beings shows how human political cultures
for structuring rule evolve as constrained manifestations of the
human political universals of human political nature. This is illustrated by how Lincoln's handling of the Emancipation Proclamation was shaped by American political culture.

The Question of Animal Culture

We can define culture as "a system of socially transmitted patterns of behavior, preferences, and products of animal activities
that characterize a group of social animals."[48] By such a definition,
some nonhuman animals have culture, because many animals in

complex societies show some capacity for the social transmission of material and social traditions of culture. The evidence for culture is clear among chimpanzees, because each chimpanzee community has its own distinctive repertoire of cultural traditions.[49] This cultural uniqueness of each chimpanzee community comes into view, for example, if one reads Jane Goodall's account of the chimpanzees at Gombe; one realizes that this is a political history that manifests both the political universals that might be seen in any chimpanzee community and the political culture unique to the chimpanzees at Gombe.[50]

Culture is particularly important for human beings, and thus any biological account of human politics must include cultural evolution as well as genetic evolution. Darwin recognized that, once natural selection had shaped the social instincts and intellectual capacities of human beings, moral and political progress would depend primarily on cultural learning, which would include habituation, instruction, social traditions, individual reasoning, and religious beliefs.[51] Recently, evolutionary theorists have revived Darwin's program for studying the complex evolutionary interaction of innate propensities and cultural learning.[52]

Human cultural evolution is uniquely human insofar as it is based on information transmitted through symbolic communication.[53] Aristotle was right: human beings are not the *only* political animals by nature, but they are the *most* political animals by nature because of the political complexity of human learning through conceptual symbolism.[54] The human capacity for symbolic communication explains why human beings—unlike other primates—have moved beyond small foraging groups to form political communities with huge populations that do not depend on face-to-face interaction. Social insects like bees can live in communities with comparably large populations because of a system of chemical communication that allows a colony to function as a collective unit.[55] Human beings do this through a system of symbolic communication by which cooperating groups can be defined by symbolic markers.[56] Human rulers derive their authority from some belief system that supports the social stratification and political institutions of their community. A belief system consists of symbolic markers that hold people together in a community. Although it does not have to be religious, it usually is. For example, the Protestant Reformation was politically explosive because it challenged the Roman Catholic tradition of authority and thus altered those symbolic markers of biblical religious belief that had bound European people together into large communities. For the European Protestants who settled in America, biblical religion was foundational for their politics, as they drew even their codes of law from Mosaic law.[57]

Deep History

For any science of political cultural history, we need a typology of regimes that generalizes about the structures of political rule. S. E. Finer's magisterial *History of Government* provides a modern political typology in the tradition of Aristotle's regime analysis.[58] Finer's typological history of government is a deeper history than one usually finds among contemporary political scientists. Even those political scientists who stress the importance of political history tend to rely on a shallow history—the history of the past few centuries. At least, this is a slightly deeper history than that of those political scientists whose historical context is the last few decades! But it's still shallow compared with Finer's history of government, which begins with the first appearance of the Sumerian city-state around 3,500 B.C. And yet, even Finer's deep history is not deep enough, because he ignores the preliterate political experience of human beings. Assuming that true history begins with written records is common for historians, but it shows a remarkably narrow view of history that reflects the fundamentalist biblical notion that all human history began six thousand years ago in the Middle East.[59] Biopolitical science looks for a deeper history that embraces the entire evolutionary history of politics, from the Pleistocene to the present. The intellectual advantage of such a deep Darwinian history of politics is that it brings into view the general evolutionary patterns that are lost in shallow political history. This Darwinian history belongs to what some historians today call "big history" or "deep history."[60]

In its most expansive form, as in the work of David Christian, this deep Darwinian history encompasses the complete scientific history of the universe starting at the Big Bang thirteen billion years ago. After surveying the modern scientific understanding of the origins and history of the universe, the stars, the Earth, and life on Earth, Christian turns to human evolutionary history from the Paleolithic era to the present. He divides human history into three stages corresponding to three major eras of human social life: the foraging era (from 250,000 years ago to 10,000 years ago), the agrarian era (from 10,000 years ago to 1750 A.D.), and the modern era (from 1750 to the present). The most general pattern for Christian's history is set forth by Eric Chaisson[61]—the emergence of ever more complex levels of order requires that the flow of energy be structured to sustain order against the entropic tendency of the second law of thermodynamics. Within that cosmic pattern, human history's three eras can be seen as three levels of ever more complex order that require ever more complex means for extracting energy to sustain ever greater human populations. Foragers extract energy through hunting wild animals and gathering wild plants. Farmers extract energy through cultivating domesticated plants and herding domesticated animals. In the modern era, humans have come to rely increasingly on fossil fuels as sources of energy. This energy in plants, animals, and fossil fuels comes ultimately from the Sun.[62]

Another general pattern in human history as seen by Christian is set by the human capacity for collective learning. Although many animals have some capacity for learning, human language enhances the human capacity for learning beyond anything seen in the rest of the animal world. This permits human beings to spread widely over varying niches in their ecosystems and to construct new niches, thus extending the evolutionary niche construction carried out by other organisms.[63] The human history from foraging to farming to modernity is largely the history of human collective learning as human beings learned new ways to extract energy from their environments to sustain ever larger populations of human beings in ever more complex societies, so that now human beings live in a global system of collective learning that has transformed life on Earth.

Lincoln had some understanding of this evolutionary deep history as the context for American political history. According to William Herndon, his friend and law partner, Lincoln was persuaded to accept the idea of universal evolutionary history from his reading of Robert Chambers's *Vestiges of the Natural History of Creation*, a book first published in 1844 that Darwin later acknowledged as anticipating his own theory of evolution.[64] Lincoln had a remarkably deep view of human cultural evolution that follows the pattern of Darwinian universal history set forth by Darwin and by scientific historians like Christian. In his "Lecture on Discoveries and Inventions," his "Address to the Wisconsin State Agricultural Society," and in his meeting with some American Indian chiefs, Lincoln laid out his conception of cultural evolution as moving through three stages of society—from foraging societies to agrarian societies to societies based on commercial exchange and free labor.[65] Like Aristotle, Darwin, and Christian, Lincoln believed that human beings were unique in the animal world because of the human capacity for symbolic speech, which allowed for collective learning in the artful domination of nature for the material, moral, and intellectual improvement of human life. Originally, all human beings lived by foraging, a way of life still manifested in Lincoln's day among some of the Native American Indians. The invention of agriculture supported human civilization as an advance beyond the savage life of foragers. But, despite the progress in civilization in agrarian states, such states were founded on slavery and other forms of coerced labor, so that rulers lived by exploiting peasant labor. Lincoln saw that the Industrial Revolution based on commercial exchange and free labor was bringing a new revolution in human cultural evolution that promised the physical, moral, and intellectual liberation of labor. He saw the abolition of slavery as a crucial move toward this new state of society, which would bring a "new birth of freedom" in which all human beings would have a fair chance in the "race of life."

The History of Regimes

The clearest pattern in the Darwinian history of politics is a movement through these three stages or ways of life—the foraging way, the agrarian way, and the modern way.[66] Throughout the Pleistocene epoch, until about eleven thousand years ago, all human beings lived in small foraging or hunter-gatherer bands that resembled chimpanzee bands in size and structure. But then the development of agriculture based on the domestication of plants and animals brought the emergence of larger, more settled societies and, eventually, large bureaucratic states, beginning in Mesopo-tamia, Egypt, India, China, and Mesoamerica. Over the past five thousand years, hunter-gatherer bands have dwindled in number and eventually disappeared from most parts of the world. During this period of bureaucratic states, as Finer shows, the most com-mon form of regime has been the "Palace," in which the domi-nant ruler might be variously identified as a king, an emperor, a prince, a tyrant, or a dictator—one person, with an aristocratic bureaucracy and military support, who rules in an often despotic manner.[67] By contrast, the "Forum"—a regime open to "the peo-ple" and public debate—was extremely rare, emerging in ancient Athens, the Roman Republic, the medieval European city-states, and Renaissance Italy. But, then, in seventeenth- and eighteenth-century Europe, the authority of kings was challenged by ap-peals to the authority of the people. This brought a radical shift in claims to legitimacy toward the assumption that every regime —even a monarchy—had to claim some authorization from the people.[68] In the modern history of regimes, the mandate to rule had moved from the king's Palace to the people's Forum. A true science of politics must explain this pattern in the history of gov-ernment and what it suggests about the future of government. A biopolitical science explains this through the complex interaction between genetic political history and cultural political history.

The biopolitical scientist sees the genetic evolution of human ancestors in the Pleistocene as shaping the behavioral repertoire of human political nature as adapted for the hunter-gatherer or foraging way of life. Human beings are by nature socially ambiv-alent, being both selfish and social, and politically ambivalent in both desiring dominance and desiring not to be despotically dom-inated. Hunter-gatherers enforce an ethic of cooperative sharing, but this breaks down in times of conflict when their natural selfish-ness is displayed. They enforce an ethic of egalitarian leveling, but this requires stringent sanctions against the natural tendency of some to dominate. Although there is no formal or enduring struc-ture of dominance, there is informal and episodic leadership by those individuals with personal qualities that earn them more pres-tige than others.[69]

Bureaucratic states with often despotic regimes based on kingly and oligarchic rule offered many benefits over hunter-gatherer societies.[70] Most important, bureaucratic states were militarily powerful and thus favored in cultural group selection over political communities that could not sustain great military power. And yet, biopolitical science suggests that liberal democracies conform better than bureaucratic states to the evolved social and political nature of human beings.[71] Liberal democracy approximates some of the central traits of a foraging society—individual liberty, social solidarity, and an egalitarian dominance structure in which the desire of the few to dominate is checked by the desire of the many to be free from despotic dominance. The natural appeal of liberal democracy to the multitude of human beings was largely frustrated for thousands of years, until modern social and political conditions shifted in favor of democratic regimes.

In the modern world, many innovations of political culture—as surveyed by Finer—favored the growth of modern constitutional republicanism.[72] The idea of limited monarchy was invented in the ancient Jewish kingdoms and then transmitted through the Bible into the political thought of Europe.[73] The ideas of the citizen (as opposed to the subject), of democracy, and of government as accountable to the governed were invented in ancient Greece. The ideas of checks and balances and government by rule of law were invented in ancient Rome. These political ideas from Greece and Rome were transmitted throughout Europe as part of a tradition of republican political thought. The idea of representation as invented in medieval Europe was added to this republican tradition. In the American colonial and early national experience, all of these inherited ideas of republican political culture were combined with new political inventions that favored republican government—a written constitution, federalism, the presidency, and judicial review.[74] These institutional innovations are human inventions. They are artificial, not natural. And yet, their success depended on their satisfying the social needs and desires of evolved human nature in the cultural conditions of the modern world. As one constitutional scholar has observed, "constitutionalism is a human creation that results from the interaction between human nature and the brute facts of social existence in a postneolithic world."[75]

John Adams, James Madison, Alexander Hamilton, and others among the American founders recognized that popular governments for thousands of years had suffered from serious defects that prevented them from competing with monarchic regimes. Democracies and republics tended to be too small in territory and population to withstand the military power of monarchic empires. Democracies and republics also tended to lack the energetic leadership possible in monarchic regimes. The American founders combined the new ideas of republicanism so as to join liberty and power and to unite local governments into a large national union. For example, the American presidency was a novel cultural invention that combined much of the energetic leadership of a monarch with the limitations on power that come from a written constitution with checks and balances.[76] The office of the presidency was designed to attract people of restless ambition, those moved by the love of fame and glory. But their ambition would be channeled through a constitutional system in which ambition would counteract ambition, and thus the presidency would be turned away from the despotic excesses of monarchic power. Madison and others hoped that such institutional novelties would provide "a republican remedy for the diseases most incident to republican government."[77]

The American founders foresaw that the political offices in the new American republic would attract the "natural aristocracy" of those people moved by ambition and avarice to seek to rule, and the problem would be how to structure and check their desire for domination.[78] John Adams insisted that human nature would always tend toward societies with three social orders—a deferential multitude, an oligarchic few, and one leader at the top. Adams thought that such social ranking could be found among many animals, because it satisfied the natural desire for status or distinction. A well-designed constitution should balance these three natural orders—the one, the few, and the many—so that they check one another and their passions are directed to the public good.[79]

If such a structure of rule is rooted in evolved human nature, then the aim of those friendly to democratic government should be not to abolish all dominance hierarchy but to channel and restrain it. The same conclusion seemed to follow from the great twentieth-century debate among political scientists over elite theory and pluralism. If even the most radical of socialist democrats cannot abolish the "iron law of oligarchy," then a realistic conception of democracy might have to combine elite rule and democratic accountability through a republican regime of balanced and limited powers.[80] Biopolitical science explains this as showing that equality of rank without any hierarchy at all is contrary to evolved human nature.[81]

Lincoln's Ambition and the Emancipation of Slaves

To see how the political culture of a constitutional republic can reconcile dominance and democracy, consider, again, the political career of Lincoln and particularly his decision to issue the Emancipation Proclamation. By 1854, Lincoln saw the debate over slavery as providing him the national stage on which he could display his talents and satisfy his quest for glory. He looked a lot like that "towering genius" he had described in his Lyceum Address of 1838—"it thirsts and burns for distinction; and, if possible, it will have it, whether at the expense of emancipating slaves, or enslaving freemen."[82] But, in American constitutional government, such desire for dominance is structured by the Constitution. Although Lincoln was always clear in condemning slavery as morally wrong, he recognized that the constitutional framers had provided constitutional protection for slavery in the South, even as they hoped for the "ultimate extinction" of slavery. So he was neither an abolitionist nor proslavery. But, while the Constitution protected slavery in the South, he thought, there was no constitutional duty to allow for slavery to be introduced into the Western territories. Restricting the Western expansion of slavery was important to sustain the principle that slavery was wrong—as contradicting the principle of equality in the Declaration of Independence—although "practical necessity" might dictate tolerating it in the existing slaveholding states.[83]

During the first year of the Civil War, Lincoln began to consider whether he might use his presidential power in war to emancipate the slaves in the South. His power to do that was constrained by all of those principles of republican political culture that had been put into the Constitution.[84] As president, he could not violate the constitutional protections for slavery. But he was constitutionally invested with all the powers of the commander in chief in time of war. And therefore he might constitutionally issue an emancipation order if it could be justified as a military necessity. The final

Emancipation Proclamation was carefully worded to apply only to the states or parts of states that were still in rebellion against the Union as of January 1, 1863. The rationale was that this would promote military victory for the North by allowing Union troops to advance into the South with the promise of emancipation for the slaves, who might then be recruited as soldiers. Lincoln needed congressional support for his decision. He was also constrained by federalism in that the border states fighting on the side of the Union—Maryland, Kentucky, and Missouri—were slave states. And he had to worry about whether judicial review would allow federal courts to overturn his decision. He made it clear that the permanent abolition of slavery would require the passage of the Thirteenth Amendment. He also had to consider whether public opinion was ready for this, because he foresaw that the Democrats would use this as an issue against the Republican Party in the congressional elections of 1862. He also had to anticipate the possibility of being defeated for reelection in 1864. In all of these ways, his presidential power for emancipating slaves was circumscribed by the constitutional system.

In the final Emancipation Proclamation, Lincoln appealed to five principles: "And upon this act, sincerely believed to be an act of justice, warranted by the Constitution, upon military necessity, I invoke the considerate judgment of mankind, and the gracious favor of Almighty God."[85] As we have seen, a crucial part of human political culture is the use of symbolic communication to bind people into large groups and then persuade them to work together for the common good. Here and elsewhere, we can see Lincoln's rhetorical skill in the use of moral, political, and religious symbolism to persuade his audience to act collectively. He appeals not only to legal and pragmatic considerations—the Constitution and military necessity—but also to higher principles of justice, the universal judgment of mankind, and Divine Providence.

For Lincoln, the "philosophical basis" of American political culture was stated in the Declaration of Independence—the principle of natural human equality of rights as dictating government by the consent of the governed, a principle rooted not just in American history but in human nature.[86] The real issue at the foundation of the American regime, Lincoln believed, was the universal conflict in political history between the desire of some human beings for despotic dominance and the desire of the rest of humanity to be free from such despotic dominance.

It is the eternal struggle between these two principles—right and wrong—throughout the world. They are the two principles that have stood face to face from the beginning of time; and will ever continue to struggle. The one is the common right of humanity and the other the divine right of kings. It is the same principle in whatever shape it develops itself. It is the same spirit that says, "You work and toil and earn bread, and I'll eat it." No matter in what shape it comes, whether from the mouth of a king who seeks to bestride the people of his own nation and live by the fruit of their labor, or from one race of men as an apology for enslaving another race, it is the same tyrannical principle.[87]

For Lincoln, the alternative to kingly dominance was popular government by the consent of the governed, in which the dominance of the few would be checked by popular consent. He thought that such principles as stated in the Declaration of Independence should be the ground for uniting all regions of the country—North and South—into one Union. But this was hard to achieve, because the United States was divided into distinctive cultural traditions traceable back to different British folkways.[88] The Civil War as interpreted by Lincoln's rhetoric was a crucial turning point in the cultural political evolution of the United States, because it brought smaller social units into a national union bound together by shared symbolic norms of republican liberty and equality of opportunity.

Lincoln knew that one fundamental element of America's shared political culture was the commitment to biblical religion. Although Lincoln revealed his atheism in some private conversations with a few friends, he was careful to conceal this in public, and he often invoked the Bible as an authoritative text for American political culture.[89] Unfortunately, the Bible did not clearly resolve the debate over slavery.[90] In his Second Inaugural Address, Lincoln vividly conveyed the theological problem dividing the two sides in the Civil War: "Both read the same Bible, and pray to the same God; and each invokes His aid against the other."[91] Many passages in the Bible support slavery. But some of the general teachings of the Bible—such as the equality of all human beings as created in God's image—could be used to condemn slavery. Lincoln's rhetoric is full of biblical references and imagery, and he had to read the Bible as clearly teaching the wrongness of slavery.[92] And yet, if the Civil War was a theological crisis over the interpretation of the Bible, as Mark Noll has observed, "it was left to those consummate theologians, the Reverend Doctors Ulysses S. Grant and William Tecumseh Sherman, to decide what in fact the Bible actually meant."[93]

This reminds us that, while the cultural evolution of politics through group selection can turn on intricate moral and religious debates, these debates are often resolved by force of arms. The biopolitical study of political cultural evolution must include the evolutionary history of war. Recent research confirms Darwin's claim that group selection through warfare created the conditions among human ancestors for social cooperation and morality.[94] This research also supports Thucydides's observation that human beings go to war when fear, interest, or honor move them to fight for their community against opposing communities.[95] As Winston Churchill observed, "Great battles, whether won or lost, change the entire course of events, create new standards of values, new moods, new atmospheres, in armies and in nations, to which all must conform."[96]

Of course, when Lincoln decided in 1862 to issue the Emancipation Proclamation, he could not know the outcome of the war or the ultimate consequences of his Proclamation. That's generally true of political judgments—political actors must decide what to do under conditions of such uncertainty that they cannot know whether they have made the right decision. A biopolitical science must account for such practical reasoning.

4. POLITICAL JUDGMENTS

Political animals must make political judgments. To understand politics, we must understand the political judgments of individual political actors as they navigate their way through the unique circumstances of their political lives. The problem, however, is that political judgment is not usually governed by any precise and rigorous formulations of logical proof, and therefore it is not clear that political judgment can be explained through the scientific methods of modern political science. This problem underlies the old debate as to whether the study of politics is properly a science or an art. The debate turns on the distinction between two kinds of knowledge, with proponents of the "scientific study of politics" favoring the knowledge that comes from methodical rationalism and their critics favoring the knowledge that comes from practical wisdom. The critics—people like Isaiah Berlin,[97] Michael Oakeshott,[98] and Leo Strauss[99]—insist that the technical rationality of modern scientific methodology cannot rightly grasp the practical reality of politics as it appears to citizens and statesmen, because this practical knowledge of politics requires the particular insights of prudential judgment, rather than the abstract generality of theoretical science. These critics of modern political science suggest that we need to revive an older tradition of political science as rooted in Aristotle's recognition of prudence as the practical wisdom required for politics.[100] This debate poses a stark choice between placing the study of politics in the realm of natural science and placing it in the realm of humane knowledge.

Biopolitical science pursues a third alternative. If the choice is between the physical sciences and the humanities, then the study of politics surely belongs with the humanities. But, if biology is the natural science that includes all of life, including human life, then the study of politics should be seen as a biological science of political animals that is both a natural science and a humanistic art. Such a biological political science must understand politics as it is understood by citizens and statesmen, in which political knowledge requires political judgment.

The Prudence of Political Animals

Political judgment is manifested in the communities of chimpanzees and bonobos studied by primatologists.[101] These primate studies provide social and political biographies based on the life histories of the animals in each community. Each must begin with a "who's who" of personalities, because each animal is a unique individual in a unique community. Each animal's distinctive personality arises from a combination of inherited and acquired tendencies. One cannot fully understand the behavior of these animals unless one knows the life history of each individual as it interacts with the other individuals. These animals need practical intelligence, because they need to make decisions from moment to moment about how to work their way through a complex social network of ever-changing relationships of kinship, friendship, and hierarchy. To succeed, they must understand the making and breaking of alliances and coalitions. To do this, they must understand how to interpret and employ a complex repertoire of verbal and nonverbal signals that convey emotional and factual information about their social environment. The ranking of individuals in the community depends on a complex range of factors, including age, sex, temperament, intelligence, and contingent events. Among chimps, the males seem to be more dominant than the females. But de Waal has seen coalitions of females among captive chimps that can challenge the alpha male. And, among the bonobos, there is an alpha male, but his dominance seems to be embedded within a social network of matriarchal dominance.

Some of these animals are low ranking because they seem not to care much about striving for dominance. Others show an intense dominance drive. Success in reaching the top depends on many factors. Goodall observes: "Factors other than age, which determine the position of a male in the dominance hierarchy include physical fitness, aggressiveness, skill at fighting, ability to form coalitions, intelligence, and a number of personality factors such as boldness and determination."[102] The intricacy of chimpanzee social life requires a complex social awareness. Thus, Goodall concludes: "There is no doubt whatsoever that a chimpanzee is capable of assessing the complexities of the ever-changing social environment and planning his own behavior accordingly."[103]

Until recently, Lody has been the alpha male in the bonobo group in the Milwaukee County Zoo, which has the largest collection of bonobos in captivity. After ten years of careful study, the human observers have concluded that Lody shows "good judgment" and "evidence of wisdom, in the Aristotelian sense: the ability to see life in all its aspects and to act in a way that benefits others."[104] Aristotle might have agreed, because he indicated in his biological writings that some animals show prudence insofar as they learn from experience and use forethought in judging what is good for their lives, and he also recognized that the apes were the animals most closely related to human beings.[105]

Lincoln's Prudence

Like other political primates, human beings need leaders with practical judgment, and someone like Lincoln exemplifies such leadership. Explaining Lincoln's leadership—as in his Emancipation Proclamation—requires that biopolitical science move through many levels of analysis. At the level of the natural history of political universals, we could explain Lincoln's political life as manifesting the sort of dominance drive or political ambition that one sees throughout political history in every political community. At the level of the social history of political cultures, we could explain Lincoln's political life as shaped by the peculiar political culture of nineteenth-century America, which would include the constitutional framework of American government and the problem of slavery in American politics. Finally, at the level of the individual history of political judgment, we could see how Lincoln's Emancipation Proclamation was constrained by the political universals of political ambition and the political culture of American political institutions. But this would still not fully explain Lincoln's political judgment in deciding to issue the Emancipation Proclamation.

As Aristotle indicated, political judgment is an exercise in prudence, which is an intuitive capacity of moral character to judge what should be done in particular circumstances where it is impossible to infer any right answer by general rules or logical proof. The historical contingency and complexity of political life make it necessary to rely on such practical wisdom in circumstances where it is impossible to determine the right answer by purely logical means. We can see this in the debate over Lincoln's decision to issue the Emancipation Proclamation, a debate that began in Lincoln's lifetime and continues today among historians and social scientists, some of whom dispute the wisdom of his decision,[106] while others defend him.[107] I agree with those scholars who argue that Lincoln's decision manifests his Aristotelian prudence, because it shows Lincoln acting to enforce enduring moral principles within the constraints of his practical circumstances so as to avoid the extremes of unprincipled opportunism on the one hand and moralistic absolutism on the other.[108]

Studying prudential judgment is difficult, because it's a form of practical reasoning and moral temperament that cannot be explained simply as an exercise in pure logic or abstract generalization.[109] Figuring out how human beings make judgments in practical situations of irreducible uncertainty and inevitable error is one of the fundamental problems in the social sciences.[110] We can study it best by considering particular examples of it, as in the biographies of prudent moral and political leaders like Lincoln. The political biographies of political actors—human and nonhuman—are an essential part of biopolitical science.

If prudence, like all mental activity, is ultimately an exercise of the brain and nervous system, then we can deepen our study by exploring the ever-advancing knowledge that comes from neuroscience, which can illuminate the character of political judgment as rooted in the brain. This research in neuroscience indicates the dependence of judgment on worldly experience, emotional dispositions, intuitive insights, and narrative thinking, confirming Aristotle's account of political prudence and rhetorical persuasion.[111]

Neuroscience helps us to understand prudence as a natural moral faculty rooted in the human brain as shaped by human evolutionary history for solving moral problems.[112] Neuroscientific and evolutionary theories of moral judgment confirm Aristotle's insight that "thought by itself moves nothing," because moral motivation is driven by moral emotions.[113] Such research into the neural grounds of moral and political judgments must be part of biopolitical science.

5. OBJECTIONS AND REPLIES

I can anticipate at least three objections to my proposal for a biopolitical science. First, some critics will object to what they see as an unreasonable reductionism. They will say that in joining Wilson's project for "consilience," based on a unification of all knowledge through biology, I am reducing political life to physical and biological causes in a way that leaves no room for those modes of understanding politics that come from the humanistic disciplines, such as history, philosophy, and rhetoric. Second, some critics will worry that a biopolitical science assumes a biological determinism that denies human freedom. They will say that human political actors are capable of deliberate choices that cannot be explained by the deterministic causes of biology. Finally, a different group of critics

—those who agree that political science should be a natural science—will complain that the biopolitical science I have sketched
lacks the predictive power necessary for a true science. After all,
they might say, the ultimate aim of a true science of politics is not
just to interpret political events in the past (like Lincoln's Emancipation Proclamation) but to predict the future course of political
events through scientific laws of political behavior.

Emergent Complexity

There is plenty of evidence for the charge that Wilson's vision of
consilience is strongly reductionistic. "The central idea of the consilience world view," he declares, "is that all tangible phenomena,
from the birth of stars to the workings of social institutions, are
based on material processes that are ultimately reducible, however long and tortuous the sequences, to the laws of physics."[114]
But, against this idea of consilience through strong reductionism,
which I find unpersuasive, Wilson often recognizes an alternative
idea of consilience through emergent complexity, which I find
more persuasive and which I regard as a fundamental idea for biopolitical science.[115]

The simplest expression of the idea of emergence is that a
whole can be greater than the sum of its parts. Emergent phenomena are those complex wholes with properties that we could not
explain or predict from our knowledge of the parts. For example,
we see emergent properties in water that we could not have predicted from the properties of hydrogen and oxygen. The emergent evolution of novelty is manifested throughout the evolution
of the universe.[116]

The idea of emergent evolutionary complexity supports biopolitical science as a nonreductive science that explains political order as the joint product of natural propensities, cultural traditions,
and individual judgments. The natural propensities as shaped in
the genetic evolution of human beings will constrain but not determine the cultural traditions of political life. These natural propensities and cultural traditions will then constrain but not determine the practical judgments of political actors about what should
be done in particular cases, as in Lincoln's decision to issue the
Emancipation Proclamation. To explain this complex interaction

of nature, culture, and judgment, biopolitical science will draw pertinent knowledge from all the intellectual disciplines—the natural sciences, the social sciences, and the humanities.

Emergent Freedom

Biopolitical science recognizes that the emergent evolution of the human brain gives human beings a uniquely human freedom of thought and action, which should allay the fear of biological determinism. The human mind is an emergent product of the evolution of the primate brain once it passed a critical threshold of size and complexity in the neocortex, particularly in the frontal lobes. With the evolution of ever larger and more complex frontal lobes, primates have more behavioral flexibility than other animals. They have the capacity for voluntary action, in the sense that they can learn to alter their behavior in adaptive ways in response to complex and ever-changing circumstances in their social and physical environments. That's why it's not unreasonable to speak of chimpanzees as exercising judgment or prudence. In human evolution, the evolution of the primate brain passed a critical threshold, enabling human beings to use words and images to compare alternative courses of action through mental trial and error.[117] Consequently, human beings are capable not just of voluntary action but of deliberate choice by which they self-consciously choose present courses of action in the light of past experiences and future expectations to conform to some general plan of life.

As a matter of common experience, we all know that we can exercise free choice by deliberately reflecting on the choices before us and then concentrating our mental force to execute the choice that we desire. A big part of becoming a mature adult is learning how to do this and habituating ourselves to do it well. Having a normally functioning human brain makes this possible.

Modern neuroscience is beginning to explain how this works. Using brain-imaging technology, we can now see how mental concentration changes the neuronal activity of the brain. The mind that emerges from the human brain can change the brain itself.[118] This emergent power of the brain for mental attention enables human freedom, which supports the freedom of human political actors in exercising judgment.

Predicting Patterns

Because of the complexity and freedom of human political behavior, any science of politics must be a science of history based on historical narratives. By contrast with nonhistorical sciences, historical sciences have only limited predictive power. At best, political science can make general predictions about political patterns. But it cannot make specific predictions about political events. Biopolitical science deepens the historical narratives of political science by grounding them in the evolutionary history of political animals, which moves through three kinds of historical narratives: natural history, cultural history, and biographical history. And yet, this biopolitical history cannot provide the precise predictions that are possible in the nonhistorical sciences.[119]

Evolutionary biology and the social sciences are historical sciences of emergent complexity. By contrast, physical sciences such as physics and chemistry are nonhistorical sciences of reductive simplicity.[120] Except for historical disciplines such as cosmology and geology, physical scientists study physical phenomena without reference to their history. Many social scientists—particularly economists—have taken physics as the model for all science, and they have tried to unify the social sciences as founded on a social physics free from historical contingency.[121] But biopolitical science rejects this approach. Biopolitical science recognizes that social phenomena are necessarily historical, and therefore they can be explained only through historical narratives, which cannot have the predictive precision that is achieved through the deterministic laws of the physical sciences. Pursuing social physics sacrifices accuracy for the sake of precision, because it ignores the fuzzy complexity of social reality. Pursuing biopolitical history sacrifices precision for the sake of accuracy, because it recognizes that fuzzy complexity.[122]

Although biopolitical science cannot provide deterministic laws, it can provide probabilistic regularities, which support falsifiable but fuzzy predictions of behavioral patterns. For example, evolutionary game theory has developed formal models of the natural behavioral repertoire that I have laid out, and those models can generate falsifiable predictions that can be tested through experimental game playing. This research shows a complex interaction among natural history, cultural history, and individual history. There are some universal behavioral patterns that manifest a natural history of the human species that has shaped human beings to be both self-regarding and other-regarding. But there is great cultural variation in that behavior that manifests a cultural history that has shaped some societies to be quite different from others. And yet, there is also great variation across individuals that cannot be precisely predicted from what we know about natural and cultural history.

Consider, for instance, the playing of the "ultimatum game." In this game, there are two players under conditions of anonymity. Both players are told that there is a specified sum of money to be divided between the two players. One player is told to propose a division of the money to the other player. The responding player can either accept or reject the proposal. If the responder accepts the proposal, the money will be divided as proposed. If the responder rejects the proposal, then neither player receives any money. Assuming that human beings are purely self-regarding egoists, rational-choice theorists will predict that the responder will accept any proposed division, because any money is better than none, while the proposer will want to take most of the money and give the responder as little as possible. But Darwinian evolutionary theorists, who think human beings have evolved to have other-regarding moral concerns, will predict that responders will indignantly reject unfair offers, and proposers will feel obligated to offer fair divisions of the money, somewhere around an even split. The Darwinians predict that human beings will on average show a sense of fairness in reciprocity by their willingness to punish those who make unfair offers, even when inflicting the punishment is costly to the punisher.

The experimental play of the ultimatum game generally confirms the predictions of the Darwinians—in most cases, responders reject unfair proposals, and proposers feel compelled to offer fair divisions. But, while this evidence suggests that a sense of fairness is part of the natural behavioral pattern of most human beings, a substantial portion of the participants in these experiments (about one quarter) behave in a purely selfish manner.[123] And, in a few societies—particularly, in small-scale societies where there is no experience with market exchange to cultivate a culture of reciprocal fairness—almost everyone behaves in a purely selfish manner.[124] So, although we can't make specific predictions based on deterministic laws, we can make general predictions based on probabilistic propensities.

Similarly, political scientists could not have precisely predicted Lincoln's signing of the Emancipation Proclamation. But political scientists could have predicted that chattel slavery would provoke resistance from those who saw that it violates the natural moral desire for justice as reciprocity, and political scientists might have predicted that the cultural circumstances of American constitutionalism would create opportunities for ambitious political actors to satisfy their desire for glory by promoting the ultimate extinction of slavery. Once Lincoln issued the Proclamation, political scientists could begin a debate over what kind of historical narrative best accounts for that political event. Biopolitical science contributes to that debate by providing a broad theoretical framework for such a historical narrative as moving through the natural history of slavery, the cultural history of slavery in America, and the biographical history of Lincoln as the political actor who won his glory in becoming the Great Emancipator.

6. CONCLUSION

The biopolitical science of political animals overcomes many of the defects of contemporary political science. Biopolitical science recognizes that *history matters*, because it provides a deep history of politics embracing the natural history of political universals, the social history of political cultures, and the individual history of political judgments. It recognizes that *morality matters*, because it studies the natural biological roots of the human moral sense manifested in political controversy. It recognizes that *judgment matters*, because it studies political judgments as cultural and individual expressions of evolved human nature. It recognizes that *emotion matters*, because it shows how the evolved emotional dispositions of human nature shape political action and thought. It recognizes that *religion matters*, because it explains religion as an evolutionary adaptation that helps political groups work together as collective units. It recognizes that *ambition matters*, because it studies political ambition as expressing the evolved striving for dominance. Finally, it recognizes that *liberal education matters*, because it employs evolutionary biology to study politics in a way that integrates ideas and methods from the natural sciences, the social sciences, and the humanities. With biopolitical science at the center of a Darwinian liberal education, we can better understand how human beings as political animals find their home in the order of living nature.

NOTES

This chapter is a revised version of "Biopolitical Science," *Politics and the Life Sciences* 29 (2010): 24–47. I am grateful to the Association for Politics and the Life Sciences for permission to republish this paper.

1. John R. Alford and John Hibbing, "The Origin of Politics: An Evolutionary Theory of Political Behavior," *Perspectives on Politics* 2 (2004): 707–23; Larry Arnhart, "The New Darwinian Naturalism in Political Theory," *American Political Science Review* 89 (1995): 389–400; Larry Arnhart, *Darwinian Natural Right: The Biological Ethics of Human Nature* (Albany: State University of New York Press, 1998); Robert Blank and Samuel Hines, *Biology and Political Science* (London: Routledge, 2001); Peter Corning, *The Synergism Hypothesis: A Theory of Progressive Evolution* (New York: McGraw Hill, 1983); Peter Corning, *Holistic Darwinism: Synergy, Cybernetics, and the Bioeconomics of Evolution* (Chicago: University of Chicago Press, 2005); Gary R. Johnson, "The Evolutionary Origins of Government and Politics," in *Human Nature and Politics*, ed. Albert Somit and Steven A. Peterson (Greenwich, CT: JAI Press, 1995), 243–305; Roger D. Masters, *The Nature of Politics* (New Haven: Yale University Press, 1989); Roger D. Masters, *Beyond Relativism: Science and Human Values* (Hanover, NH: University Press of New England, 1993); Albert Somit and Steven A. Peterson, *The Failure of Democratic Nation Building: Ideology Meets Evolution* (New York: Palgrave Macmillan, 2005); Bradley A. Thayer, *Darwin and International Relations: On the Evolutionary Origins of War and Ethnic Conflict* (Lexington: University Press of Kentucky, 2004); James Q. Wilson, *The Moral Sense* (New York: Free Press, 1993).

2. Karen Orren and Stephen Skowronek, *The Search for American Political Development* (Cambridge: Cambridge University Press, 2004); Paul Pierson, *Politics in Time: History, Institutions, and Social Analysis* (Princeton: Princeton University Press, 2004).

3. David Christian, *Maps of Time: An Introduction to Big History* (Berkeley: University of California Press, 2004).

4. Jane Mansbridge, ed., *Beyond Self-Interest* (Chicago: University of Chicago Press, 1990); Elinor Ostrom, "Collective Action and the Evolution of

Social Norms," *Journal of Economic Perspectives* 14 (2000): 137–58. Elinor Ostrom, "Policies That Crowd Out Reciprocity and Collective Action," in *Moral Sentiments and Material Interests: The Foundations of Cooperation in Economic Life*, ed. Herbert Gintis, Samuel Bowles, Robert Boyd, and Ernst Fehr (Cambridge, MA: MIT Press, 2005), 253–75.

5. Ryan Patrick Hanley, "Political Science and Political Understanding: Isaiah Berlin on the Nature of Political Inquiry," *American Political Science Review* 98 (2004): 327–39; Michael Oakeshott, *Rationalism in Politics and Other Essays* (Indianapolis: Liberty Press, 1991); David Ricci, *The Tragedy of Political Science* (New Haven: Yale University Press, 1985); Leslie Paul Thiele, *The Heart of Judgment: Practical Wisdom, Neuroscience, and Narrative* (Cambridge: Cambridge University Press, 2006).

6. Michael Billig, "Political Rhetoric," in *Oxford Handbook of Political Psychology*, ed. David O. Sears, Leonie Huddy, and Robert Jervis (New York: Oxford University Press, 2003), 222–50; George Marcus, W. Russell Neuman, and Michael MacKuen, *Affective Intelligence and Political Judgment* (Chicago: University of Chicago Press, 2000); George Marcus, *The Sentimental Citizen: Emotion in Democratic Politics* (University Park: Pennsylvania State University Press, 2002); George Marcus, "The Psychology of Emotion and Politics," in *Oxford Handbook of Political Psychology*, ed. David O. Sears, Leonie Huddy, and Robert Jervis, 182–91; W. Russell Neuman, George E. Marcus, Ann N. Crigler, and Michael MacKuen, eds., *The Affect Effect: Dynamics of Emotion in Political Thinking and Behavior* (Chicago: University of Chicago Press, 2007); Maria Elizabeth Grabe and Erik Page Bucy, *Image Bite Politics: News and the Visual Framing of Elections* (Oxford: Oxford University Press, 2009).

7. Ted G. Jelen and Clyde Wilcox, eds., *Religion and Politics in Comparative Perspective: The One, the Few, and the Many* (Cambridge: Cambridge University Press, 2002); Pippa Norris and Ronald Inglehart, *Sacred and Secular: Religion and Politics Worldwide* (Cambridge: Cambridge University Press, 2004).

8. David Sloan Wilson, *Darwin's Cathedral: Evolution, Religion, and the Nature of Society* (Chicago: University of Chicago Press, 2002); David Sloan Wilson, "Human Groups as Adaptive Units: Toward a Permanent Consensus," in *The Innate Mind*, vol. 2: *Culture and Cognition*, ed. Peter Carruthers, Stephen Laurence, and Stephen Stich (New York: Oxford University Press, 2006), 78–90.

9. Harvey Mansfield, *Manliness* (New Haven: Yale University Press, 2006); Harvey Mansfield, "How to Understand Politics," *First Things*, no. 175 (August/September 2007): 41–47.

10. Larry Arnhart, "Darwinian Liberal Education," *Academic Questions* 19 (2006): 6–18; Ricci, *Tragedy of Political Science*.

11. Edward O. Wilson, *Consilience: The Unity of Knowledge* (New York: Knopf, 1998).

12. Christopher Boehm, *Hierarchy in the Forest: The Evolution of Egalitarian Behavior* (Cambridge, MA: Harvard University Press, 1999); Alexandra Maryanski and Jonathan H. Turner, *The Social Cage: Human Nature and the Evolution of Society* (Stanford, CA: Stanford University Press, 1992); John Tooby and Irven DeVore, "The Reconstruction of Hominid Behavioral Evolution through Strategic Modeling," in *The Evolution of Human Behavior: Primate Models*, ed. Warren G. Kinzey (Albany: State University of New York Press, 1987), 183–237.

13. Johnson, "Evolutionary Origins of Government."

14. Lee Alan Dugatkin, *Cooperation among Animals: An Evolutionary Perspective* (New York: Oxford University Press, 1997); Martin A. Nowak, *Evolutionary Dynamics: Exploring the Equations of Life* (Cambridge, MA: Harvard University Press, 2006); Martin A. Nowak, "Five Rules for the Evolution of Cooperation," *Science* 314 (2006): 1560–63.

15. Donald Brown, *Human Universals* (Philadelphia: Temple University Press, 1991).

16. Boehm, *Hierarchy*; Masters, *Nature of Politics*.

17. Richard Dawkins, *The Selfish Gene*, 2d ed. (Oxford: Oxford University Press, 1989).

18. William D. Hamilton, *Narrow Roads of Gene Land: The Collected Papers of W. D. Hamilton* (Oxford: W. H. Freeman, 1995).

19. Corning, *Synergism*, 84–88, 103–20, 254–58; Dugatkin, *Cooperation*, 31–34.

20. Robert Axelrod, *The Evolution of Cooperation* (New York: Basic Books, 1984); Robert Trivers, "The Evolution of Reciprocal Altruism," *Quarterly Review of Biology* 46 (1971): 35–57.

21. Richard Alexander, *The Biology of Moral Systems* (Hawthorne, NY: Aldine de Gruyter, 1987); Karl Sigmund, *The Calculus of Selfishness* (Princeton: Princeton University Press, 2010).

22. Herbert Gintis, Samuel Bowles, Robert Boyd, and Ernest Fehr, "Moral Sentiments and Material Interests: Origins, Evidence, and Consequences," in *Moral Sentiments and Material Interests*, ed. Herbert Gintis, Samuel Bowles, Robert Boyd, and Ernst Fehr, 3–40; Natalie Henrich and Joseph Henrich, *Why Humans Cooperate: A Cultural and Evolutionary Explanation* (Oxford: Oxford University Press, 2007); Ernst Fehr and Urs Fischbacher, "Third Party Sanction and Social Norms," *Evolution and Human Behavior* 25 (2004): 63–87; Ernst Fehr and S. Gachter, "Altruistic Punishment in Humans," *Nature* 415 (2002): 137–40; Sigmund, *The Calculus of Selfishness*.

23. Joseph Henrich, Robert Boyd, Samuel Bowles, Colin Camerer,

Ernst Fehr, and Herbert Gintis, eds., *Foundations of Human Sociality: Economic Experiments and Ethnographic Evidence from Fifteen Small-Scale Societies* (New York: Oxford University Press, 2004).

24. Arnhart, *Darwinian Natural Right*; Marc Hauser, *Moral Minds: How Nature Designed Our Universal Sense of Right and Wrong* (New York: Harper-Collins, 2006).

25. Charles Darwin, *The Descent of Man*, 2d ed. (London: Penguin Books, 2004), 119–72, 679–82; Charles Darwin, *Charles Darwin's Notebooks, 1836–1844*, ed. P. H. Barret, P. J. Gautrey, S. Herbert, D. Kohn, and S. Smith (Ithaca, NY: Cornell University Press, 1987), 617–29.

26. David Berreby, *Us and Them: Understanding Your Tribal Mind* (New York: Little, Brown, 2005).

27. George C. Williams, *Adaptation and Natural Selection: A Critique of Some Current Evolutionary Thought* (Princeton: Princeton University Press, 1966); George C. Williams, *Natural Selection: Domains, Levels, and Challenges* (Oxford: Oxford University Press, 1992).

28. Elliott Sober and David Sloan Wilson, *Unto Others: The Evolution and Psychology of Unselfish Behavior* (Cambridge, MA: Harvard University Press, 1998); Wilson, "Human Groups as Adaptive Units"; David Sloan Wilson, *Evolution for Everyone: How Darwin's Theory Can Change the Way We Think about Our Lives* (New York: Delacorte Press, 2007); David Sloan Wilson and Edward O. Wilson, "Rethinking the Theoretical Foundation of Sociobiology," *Quarterly Review of Biology* 82 (2007): 327–48.

29. Boehm, *Hierarchy*; Jane Goodall, *The Chimpanzees of Gombe: Patterns of Behavior* (Cambridge, MA: Harvard University Press, 1986); Alexander H. Harcourt and Frans de Waal, eds., *Coalitions and Alliances in Humans and Other Animals* (New York: Oxford University Press, 1992); Arnold Ludwig, *King of the Mountain: The Nature of Political Leadership* (Lexington: University Press of Kentucky, 2002); Allan Mazur, *Biosociology of Dominance and Deference* (Lanham, MD: Rowman and Littlefield, 2005); Frans de Waal, *Chimpanzee Politics: Power and Sex among Apes* (New York: Harper and Row, 1982); Frans de Waal, *Good Natured: The Origins of Right and Wrong in Humans and Other Animals* (Cambridge, MA: Harvard University Press, 1996).

30. De Waal, *Good Natured*, 125–32.

31. Boehm, *Hierarchy*.

32. Alexander Rustow, *Freedom and Domination: A Historical Critique of Civilization* (Princeton: Princeton University Press, 1980); James C. Scott, *The Art of Not Being Governed: An Anarchist History of Upland Southeast Asia* (New Haven: Yale University Press, 2009).

33. Niccolo Machiavelli, *Discourses on Livy*, trans. Harvey Mansfield and Nathan Tarcov (Chicago: University of Chicago Press, 1996), 1.4–5, 1.16.

34. Takayoshi Kano, *The Last Ape: Pygmy Chimpanzee Behavior and Ecology* (Stanford, CA: Stanford University Press, 1992); Ian Parker, "Swingers," *The New Yorker*, July 30, 2007, 48–61; Jo Sandin, *Bonobos: Encounters in Empathy* (Milwaukee: Zoological Society of Milwaukee and the Foundation for Wildlife Conservation, 2007); Frans de Waal and Frans Lanting, *Bonobo: The Forgotten Ape* (Berkeley: University of California Press, 1997); Richard W. Wrangham and Dale Peterson, *Demonic Males: Apes and the Origins of Human Violence* (Boston: Houghton Mifflin, 1996).

35. Frans de Waal, *Our Inner Ape* (New York: Penguin Books, 2005).

36. Douglas Madsen, "Serotonin and Social Rank among Human Males," in *The Neurotransmitter Revolution: Serotonin, Social Behavior, and the Law*, ed. Roger D. Masters and Michael T. McGuire (Carbondale: Southern Illinois University Press, 1994), 146–58; Allan Mazur and Alan Booth, "Testosterone and Dominance in Men," *Behavioral and Brain Sciences* 21 (1998): 353–63; James M. Dabbs and Mary Godwin Dabbs, *Heroes, Rogues, and Lovers: Testosterone and Behavior* (New York: McGraw-Hill, 2000); Peter T. Ellison, "Social Relationships and Reproductive Ecology," in *Endocrinology of Social Relationships*, ed. Peter T. Ellison and Peter B. Gray (Cambridge, MA: Harvard University Press, 2009), 54–73.

37. Michael Marmot, *The Status Syndrome: How Social Standing Affects Our Health and Longevity* (New York: Henry Holt, 2004).

38. Abraham Lincoln, *The Collected Works of Abraham Lincoln*, ed. Roy P. Basler, 9 vols. (New Brunswick, NJ: Rutgers University Press, 1953), 1:8, 108–15; William H. Herndon, *Herndon's Life of Lincoln* (New York: Da Capo Press, 1983), 172, 422–23.

39. Lincoln, *Collected Works*, 2:271.

40. Lincoln, *Collected Works*, 2:263–64.

41. Lincoln, *Collected Works*, 2:409.

42. Lincoln, *Collected Works*, 2:532.

43. Boehm, *Hierarchy*, 105.

44. Arnhart, *Darwinian Natural Right*, 189–208.

45. Adrian Desmond and James Moore, *Darwin's Sacred Cause: How a Hatred of Slavery Shaped Darwin's Views on Human Evolution* (Boston: Houghton Mifflin Harcourt, 2009); Adam Gopnik, *Angels and Ages: A Short Book about Darwin, Lincoln, and Modern Life* (New York: Knopf, 2009); James Lander, *Lincoln and Darwin: Shared Visions of Race, Science, and Religion* (Carbondale: Southern Illinois University Press, 2010).

46. Lincoln, *Collected Works*, 7:500.

47. Larry Diamond, *Developing Democracy: Toward Consolidation* (Baltimore: Johns Hopkins University Press, 1999), 2.

48. Eva Jablonka and Marion J. Lamb, *Evolution in Four Dimensions:*

Genetic, Epigenetic, Behavioral, and Symbolic Variation in the History of Life (Cambridge, MA: MIT Press, 2005), 160.

49. William McGrew, *The Cultural Chimpanzee: Reflections on Cultural Primatology* (Cambridge: Cambridge University Press, 2004); A. Whiten, J. Goodall, W. C. McGrew, T. Nishida, V. Reynolds, Y. Sugiyama, C. E. G. Turin, R. W. Wrangham, and C. Boesch, "Cultures in Chimpanzees," *Nature* 399 (1999): 682–85; A. Whiten, J. Goodall, W. C. McGrew, T. Nishida, V. Reynolds, Y. Sugiyama, C. E. G. Tutin, R. W. Wrangham, and C. Boesch, "Charting Cultural Variants in Chimpanzees," *Behaviour* 138 (2001): 1481–1516; Andrew Whiten, "The Identification and Differentiation of Culture in Chimpanzees and Other Animals from Natural History to Diffusion Experiments," in *The Question of Animal Culture*, ed. Kevin N. Laland and Bennett G. Galef (Cambridge, MA: Harvard University Press, 2009), 99–124.

50. Jane Goodall, *Chimpanzees of Gombe.*

51. Darwin, *Descent of Man*, 121–22, 158, 163, 167, 169, 688–89.

52. Peter J. Richerson and Robert Boyd, *Not by Genes Alone: How Culture Transformed Human Evolution* (Chicago: University of Chicago Press, 2005); Joseph Henrich and Richard McElreath, "Dual-Inheritance Theory: The Evolution of Human Cultural Capacities and Cultural Evolution," in *The Oxford Handbook of Evolutionary Psychology*, ed. R. I. M. Dunbar and Louise Barrett (Oxford: Oxford University Press, 2007), 555–70.

53. Terence W. Deacon, *The Symbolic Species: The Co-evolution of Language and the Brain* (New York: Norton, 1997); Kim Hill, "Animal 'Culture'?," in *The Question of Animal Culture*, ed. Kevin N. Laland and Bennett G. Galef (Cambridge, MA: Harvard University Press, 2009), 269–87; Jablonka and Lamb, *Evolution.*

54. Aristotle, *History of Animals*, 488a7–14; *Politics*, 1253a1–18; Larry Arnhart, "Aristotle, Chimpanzees, and Other Political Animals," *Social Science Information* 29 (1990): 479–559; Larry Arnhart, "The Darwinian Biology of Aristotle's Political Animals," *American Journal of Political Science* 38 (1994): 464–85.

55. Jurgen Gadau and Jennifer Fewell, eds., *Organization of Insect Societies: From Genome to Sociocomplexity* (Cambridge, MA: Harvard University Press, 2009); Bert Holldobler and E. O. Wilson, *The Ants* (Cambridge, MA: Harvard University Press, 1990); Bert Holldobler and E. O. Wilson, *The Superorganism: The Beauty, Elegance, and Strangeness of Insect Societies* (New York: Norton, 2009); Thomas D. Seeley, *Honeybee Democracy* (Princeton: Princeton University Press, 2010).

56. Henrich and Henrich, *Why Humans Cooperate*; Peter Turchin, *War and Peace and War: The Rise and Fall of Empires* (New York: Penguin Books, 2006).

57. Donald S. Lutz, *The Origins of American Constitutionalism* (Baton

Rouge: Louisiana State University Press, 1988); Eric Nelson, *The Hebrew Republic: Jewish Sources and the Transformation of European Political Thought* (Cambridge, MA: Harvard University Press, 2010).

58. S. E. Finer, *The History of Government*, 3 vols. (Oxford: Oxford University Press, 1997).

59. Daniel Lord Smail, *On Deep History and the Brain* (Berkeley: University of California Press, 2008).

60. Christian, *Maps of Time*; Ian Morris, *Why the West Rules—For Now: The Patterns of History, and What They Reveal about the Future* (New York: Farrar, Straus and Giroux, 2010).

61. Eric Chaisson, *Cosmic Evolution: The Rise of Complexity in Nature* (Cambridge, MA: Harvard University Press, 2001).

62. Oliver Morton, *Eating the Sun: How Plants Power the Planet* (New York: HarperCollins, 2008).

63. F. John Odling-Smee, Kevin N. Laland, and Marcus W. Feldman, *Niche Construction: The Neglected Process in Evolution* (Princeton: Princeton University Press, 2003).

64. Herndon, *Life of Lincoln*, 354; Robert Chambers, *Vestiges of the Natural History of Creation*, ed. James A. Secord (Chicago: University of Chicago Press, 1994).

65. Lincoln, *Collected Works*, 2:437–42, 3:356–63, 3:471–82, 6:151–52; Eugene F. Miller, "Democratic Statecraft and Technological Advance: Abraham Lincoln's Reflections on 'Discoveries and Inventions,'" *Review of Politics* 63 (2001): 485–515; Lander, *Lincoln and Darwin*, 7–13; Larry Arnhart, "Abraham Lincoln's Biblical Liberalism," *St. John's Review* 36 (Summer 1985): 25–40.

66. Gerhard Lenski, *Ecological-Evolutionary Theory* (Boulder, CO: Paradigm, 2005; Ted C. Lewellen, *Political Anthropology: An Introduction*, 3d ed. (Westport, CT: Praeger, 2003); Chris Scarre, ed., *The Human Past: World Prehistory and the Development of Human Societies*, 2d ed. (London: Thames and Hudson, 2009).

67. Finer, *History*, 1:34–87.

68. Reinhard Bendix, *Kings or People: Power and the Mandate to Rule* (Berkeley: University of California Press, 1978).

69. E. Adamson Hoebel, *The Law of Primitive Man: A Study in Comparative Legal Dynamics* (Cambridge, MA: Harvard University Press, 1954); Richard B. Lee, *The !Kung San: Men, Women, and Work in a Foraging Society* (Cambridge: Cambridge University Press, 1979), 343–50, 457–61; Allen W. Johnson and Timothy Earle, *The Evolution of Human Societies: From Foraging Group to Agrarian State*, 2d ed. (Stanford, CA: Stanford University Press, 2000), 54–89; Robert L. Kelly, *The Foraging Spectrum: Diversity in Hunter-Gatherer Lifeways* (Washington, DC: Smithsonian Institution Press,

1995), 295–97; Doron Shultziner, Thomas Stevens, Martin Stevens, Brian A. Stewart, Rebecca J. Hannagan, and Giulia Saltini-Semerari, "The Causes and Scope of Political Egalitarianism during the Last Glacial: A Multi-Disciplinary Perspective," *Biology & Philosophy* 25 (2010): 319–46.

70. Lewellen, *Political Anthropology*; Masters, *The Nature of Politics*; Roger Masters, *Machiavelli, Leonardo, and the Science of Power* (South Bend, IN: University of Notre Dame Press, 1996).

71. Boehm, *Hierarchy*; Maryanski and Turner, *The Social Cage*; Mark F. Grady and Michael T. McGuire, "The Nature of Constitutions," *Journal of Bioeconomics* 1 (1999): 227–40; Paul Rubin, *Darwinian Politics: The Evolutionary Origin of Freedom* (New Brunswick, NJ: Rutgers University Press, 2002).

72. Finer, *History*, 1:87–94.

73. Daniel J. Elazar, *Covenant and Polity in Biblical Israel* (New Brunswick, NJ: Transaction, 1995); Yoran Hazony, "Does the Bible Have a Political Teaching?," *Hebraic Political Studies* 1 (2006): 137–61; Nelson, *Hebrew Republic*.

74. Bernard Bailyn, *The Ideological Origins of the American Revolution* (Cambridge, MA: Harvard University Press, 1967); Paul Rahe, *Republics Ancient and Modern: Classical Republicanism and the American Revolution* (Chapel Hill: University of North Carolina Press, 1992).

75. Donald S. Lutz, *Principles of Constitutional Design* (Cambridge: Cambridge University Press, 2006), 26.

76. Charles C. Thach, *The Creation of the Presidency, 1775–1789* (Baltimore: Johns Hopkins University Press, 1969).

77. Alexander Hamilton, James Madison, and John Jay, *The Federalist*, ed. Jacob E. Cooke (Middletown, CT: Wesleyan University Press, 1961), 65.

78. Bernard Bailyn, ed., *The Debate on the Constitution: Federalist and Antifederalist Speeches, Articles, and Letters during the Struggle over Ratification*, 2 vols. (New York: Library of America, 1993), 1:53, 1:78, 1:84, 1:321, 1:409–10, 2:760.

79. John Adams, *The Works of John Adams*, ed. Charles Francis Adams, 10 vols. (Boston: Little, Brown, 1851), 4:285–86, 4:379–400, 5:90, 6:165–66.

80. Robert Michels, *Political Parties: A Sociological Study of the Oligarchical Tendencies of Modern Democracy* (New York: Free Press, 1962); Kenneth Prewitt and Alan Stone, *The Ruling Elites: Elite Theory, Power, and American Democracy* (New York: Harper and Row, 1973).

81. Albert Somit and Rudolf Wildenmann, eds., *Hierarchy and Democracy* (Carbondale: Southern Illinois University, 1991).

82. Lincoln, *Collected Works*, 1:114.

83. Lincoln, *Collected Works*, 2:247–83, 2:398–410, 3:522–50.

84. Doris Kearns Goodwin, *Team of Rivals: The Political Genius of Abraham Lincoln* (New York: Simon and Schuster, 2005); Allen C. Guelzo, *Lincoln's*

Emancipation Proclamation: The End of Slavery in America (New York: Simon and Schuster, 2004).

85. Lincoln, *Collected Works*, 6:30.
86. Lincoln, *Collected Works*, 2:245, 2:265–71, 4:17.
87. Lincoln, *Collected Works*, 3:315.
88. D. H. Fischer, *Albion's Seed: Four British Folkways in America* (Oxford: Oxford University Press, 1989).
89. Lander, *Lincoln and Darwin*, 7–11, 40–57.
90. Elizabeth Fox-Genovese and Eugene D. Genovese, *The Mind of the Master Class: History and Faith in the Southern Slaveholders' Worldview* (Cambridge: Cambridge University Press, 2005); Mark Noll, *The Civil War as a Theological Crisis* (Chapel Hill: University of North Carolina Press, 2006).
91. Lincoln, *Collected Works*, 8: 333.
92. Arnhart, "Abraham Lincoln's Biblical Liberalism"; Joseph Fornieri, *Abraham Lincoln's Political Faith* (DeKalb: Northern Illinois University Press, 2003).
93. Noll, *Civil War*, 50.
94. Samuel Bowles, "Did Warfare among Hunter-Gatherers Affect the Evolution of Human Social Behaviors?," *Science*, 324 (2009): 1293–98.
95. Azar Gat, *War in Human Civilization* (Oxford: Oxford University Press, 2007); Malcolm Potts and Thomas Hayden, *Sex and War: How Biology Explains Warfare and Terrorism and Offers a Path to a Safer World* (Dallas: Benbella Books, 2008); Stephen Peter Rosen, *War and Human Nature* (Princeton: Princeton University Press, 2005); Raphael D. Sagarin and Terence Taylor, eds., *Natural Security: A Darwinian Approach to a Dangerous World* (Berkeley: University of California Press, 2008).
96. Winston S. Churchill, *Marlborough: His Life and Times*, 2 vols. (London: George G. Harrap, 1947), 2:381.
97. Isaiah Berlin, *The Sense of Reality* (New York: Farrar, Straus and Giroux, 1996).
98. Oakeshott, *Rationalism in Politics*.
99. Leo Strauss, "Epilogue," in *Essays on the Scientific Study of Politics*, Herbert Storing, ed. (New York: Holt, Rinehart and Winston, 1962), 305–27.
100. Aristotle, *Nicomachean Ethics*, 1140a24–1145a11.
101. Goodall, *Chimpanzees of Gombe*; Sandin, *Bonobos*; De Waal, *Chimpanzee Politics*; De Waal, *Good Natured*; De Waal and Lanting, *Bonobos*.
102. Goodall, *Chimpanzees of Gombe*, 415.
103. Ibid., 568.
104. Sandin, *Bonobos*, 51.
105. Aristotle, *History of Animals*, 502a16–b27, 611a11–618a30; *Parts of Animals*, 648a6–13, 689b1–35; *Metaphysics*, 980a27–b25; *Nicomachean Ethics*, 1141a22–29.

106. Thomas DiLorenzo, *The Real Abraham Lincoln, His Agenda, and an Unnecessary War* (Roseville, CA: Prima, 2003); Thomas DiLorenzo, *Lincoln Unmasked: What You're Not Supposed to Know about Dishonest Abe* (New York: Crown Forum, 2006).

107. Thomas L. Krannawitter, *Vindicating Lincoln: Defending the Politics of Our Greatest President* (Lanham, MD: Rowman and Littlefield, 2008).

108. Joseph Fornieri, "Lincoln and the Emancipation Proclamation: A Model of Prudent Leadership," in *Tempered Strength: Studies in the Nature and Scope of Prudential Leadership,* ed. Ethan Fishman (Lanham, MD: Lexington Books, 2002), 125–50; Guelzo, *Emancipation Proclamation.*

109. Douglas Den Uyl, *The Virtue of Prudence* (New York: Peter Lang, 1991).

110. Kenneth R. Hammond, *Human Judgment and Social Policy: Irreducible Uncertainty, Inevitable Error, Unavoidable Injustice* (New York: Oxford University Press, 1996).

111. Thiele, *Judgment;* Larry Arnhart, *Aristotle on Political Reasoning: A Commentary on the "Rhetoric"* (DeKalb: Northern Illinois University Press, 1981).

112. Arnhart, *Darwinian Natural Right;* Jonathan Haidt, "The New Synthesis in Moral Psychology," *Science* 316 (2007): 998–1001; Hauser, *Moral Minds.*

113. Jonathan Haidt, "The Emotional Dog and Its Rational Tail: A Social Intuitionist Approach to Moral Judgment," *Psychological Review* 108 (2001): 814–34; Jonathan Haidt, "The Moral Emotions," in *Handbook of Affective Sciences,* ed. R. J. Davidson, K. R. Scherer, and H. H. Goldsmith (Oxford: Oxford University Press, 2009), 852–70; Joshua D. Greene, "The Cognitive Neuroscience of Moral Judgment," in *The Cognitive Neurosciences,* 4th ed., ed. Michael S. Gazzaniga (Cambridge: MIT Press, 2009), 987–99.

114. Wilson, *Consilience,* 266.

115. Ibid., 55, 67–68, 70–71, 83–86, 109, 162–65, 167, 172–73, 240, 255, 263, 266, 276–77, 297–98; Larry Arnhart, *Darwinian Conservatism: A Disputed Question,* ed. Kenneth C. Blanchard Jr. (Exerter, UK: Imprint Academic, 2009), 104–11.

116. David Blitz, *Emergent Evolution* (Boston: Kluwer Academic, 1992); Philip Clayton, *Mind and Emergence* (Oxford: Oxford University Press, 2004); Harold Morowitz, *The Emergence of Everything: How the World Became Complex* (Oxford: Oxford University Press, 2002); Corning, *Holistic Darwinism.*

117. R. E. Passingham, *The Frontal Lobes and Voluntary Action* (Oxford: Oxford University Press, 1992); Deacon, *Symbolic Species;* Georg F. Striedter, *Principles of Brain Evolution* (Sunderland, MA: Sinauer Associates, 2005); Jablonka and Lamb, *Evolution.*

118. Jeffrey M. Schwartz and Sharon Begley, *The Mind and the Brain: Neuroplasticity and the Power of Mental Force* (New York: HarperCollins, 2002); Normon Doidge, *The Brain That Changes Itself* (New York: Viking, 2007).

119. Larry Arnhart, "The Behavioral Sciences Are Historical Sciences of Emergent Complexity," *Behavioral and Brain Sciences* 30 (2007): 18–19.

120. Ernst Mayr, *What Makes Biology Unique? Considerations on the Autonomy of a Scientific Discipline* (Cambridge: Cambridge University Press, 2004).

121. Philip Mirowski, *More Heat Than Light: Economics as Social Physics, Physics as Nature's Economics* (Cambridge: Cambridge University Press, 1989); Geoffrey M. Hodgson, *How Economics Forgot History: The Problem of Historical Specificity in Social Science* (London: Routledge, 2001); Geoffrey M. Hodgson and Thorbjorn Knudsen, *Darwin's Conjecture: The Search for General Principles of Social and Economic Evolution* (Chicago: University of Chicago Press, 2010).

122. Hubert M. Blalock Jr., *Basic Dilemmas in the Social Sciences* (Beverly Hills, CA: Sage, 1984).

123. Gintis et al., "Moral Sentiments and Material Interests."

124. Joseph Henrich, Robert Boyd, Samuel Bowles, Colin F. Camerer, Ernst Fehr, Herbert Gintis, and Richard McElreath, "Overview and Synthesis," in *Foundations of Human Sociality: Economic Experiments and Ethnographic Evidence from Fifteen Small-Scale Societies*, ed. Joseph Henrich, Robert Boyd, Samuel Bowles, Colin Camerer, Ernst Fehr, and Herbert Gintis (Oxford: Oxford University Press, 2004), 8–54; Joseph Henrich et al., "Markets, Religion, Community Size, and the Evolution of Fairness and Punishment," *Science* 327 (2010): 1480–85.

9

COMMENT ON LARRY ARNHART, "BIOPOLITICAL SCIENCE"

DANIEL LORD SMAIL

On the eve of the invasion of Iraq in March of 2003, the faculty and students of Fordham University in the Bronx, where I was teaching at the time, came together for an evening forum to discuss the looming war. I have vivid memories of the atmosphere: walking through the gathering dusk to the inviting brightness of the hall; the nervous laughter; the frustrations, the anxieties and, yes, the sense of fellowship, regardless of one's politics. The event had been organized by a colleague of mine in political science, and the issues raised are the familiar ones. All of the students wanted to voice their ideas about the "real" causes of the war. It was about oil. It was about American political dominance in the Middle East. There was concern about tyranny and the worrying possibility of weapons of mass destruction.

I listened to this with a certain detachment because I, of course, knew *exactly* how to explain the push to war. When I am not writing about the deep history of humanity, my field of study includes the history of vengeance and emotion in medieval Europe. An emotional framework suffuses medieval accounts of conflict, ranging from private feuds to great wars and crusades. In this framework, one can detect an explicit political philosophy used to account for conflict, for the authors of contemporary chronicles and histories knew that kings and princes go to war for much the same reason that private families go to feud: to avenge humiliation and repair a wounded honor. Postmedieval histories written about medieval events typically discount this political philosophy. Historians instead are held captive to the rationalizing perspective that has dominated political discourse since the days of Machiavelli and Descartes. We imagine that the real reasons that medieval kings and princes and popes went to war are the strategic ones: to expand dominions, increase tax revenues, and dominate internal enemies, motivations that can perhaps be grouped under the rubric of the rational maximization of self-interest. But these are just the usual Cartesian façades. Adapting these lessons, we can see that the invasion of Iraq, ultimately, had nothing to do with oil or democracy and especially the effort to eliminate weapons of mass destruction. It was, instead, the lashings out of an injured alpha-nation guided by a simmering desire to avenge both the perceived humiliation of the first President Bush and a decade of taunts issued by an unrepentant Saddam Hussein. Our political culture no longer acknowledges vengeance as a legitimate motivation: hence the need for ex post facto rationalization.

Okay, these thoughts are just the ramblings of a medieval historian with fantasies of relevance. I mention them only to show how warmly predisposed I am to Larry Arnhart's challenge to the status quo in the study of politics.[1] Emotion really does matter, as he points out. This goes for the remainder of the seven challenges enumerated at the outset of the chapter. Since I have already taken the biological turn, I take these perspectives very much for granted these days. What I find remarkable about Arnhart's essay is that he *doesn't* take them for granted. In an effort to define the lineaments of a biopolitical science, he has synthesized a formidable bibliography, clarified important matters, and pointed a way forward by means of a case study. This last point is especially important. The question facing us now is not whether biology and neuroscience are relevant to fields like politics, economics, and history but how they are going to be relevant. One of the many things I admire about this essay, therefore, is that Arnhart has offered us an example of biopolitical science in action. The proof, as they say, is in the pudding, and this is a rich offering indeed. That my own tastes run to different kinds of pudding will become clear enough in the remarks that follow. So let me acknowledge here that I am substantially in agreement with the model that Arnhart has proposed and that I offer these remarks on the assumption that spirited disagreement on points of interpretation is the highest form of praise.[2]

Political science, like any discipline, wants to be able to explain events, trends, and patterns. In his chapter, Arnhart hopes to explain Abraham Lincoln's Emancipation Proclamation of January 1, 1863. At the outset, he notes that some political scientists have been complaining about the deficiencies of their discipline, and the main target of the seven-point critique that follows is the principle of the rational maximization of self-interest.[3] The alphatheory of political science, he suggests, cannot account for the evidence that humans go "beyond self-interest" and act in moral ways (point 2). It fails to appreciate that intuitive judgment plays as big a role in decision making as scientific or theoretical reasoning (point 3). The emphasis on "rational choice" obscures the role of emotion in political life (point 4)—as any medieval observer, his power of observation unbefuddled by Descartes, could have told you. Religion, that *ne plus ultra* of irrationality, guides ideas of morality (point 5). And ambition, if I can summarize the point succinctly, is just testosterone (point 6).

Although Arnhart never says it in so many words, the implication of this critique is that the principle of the rational maximization of self-interest would do a poor job of accounting for the Emancipation Proclamation. Hence the need for a biopolitical science and the more robust understanding of human nature that such a science can offer. In the body of the chapter, Arnhart develops the theoretical outlines of this biopolitical science at a more leisurely pace. Most of this is excellent and well grounded in the literature. Certain elements, I believe, leave room for debate. This is notably the case with the tension that exists between Arnhart's treatment of ambivalence[4] and flexibility[5] on the one hand and some of his invocations of the "natural" on the other. To take one example, consider the claim that there is "a natural desire to be free from despotic dominance."[6] I suspect that this is not true, but in any case Arnhart's understanding seems to embrace the idea that a natural inclination like this is always turned on. This is emphatically not the case. In all social species, natural inclinations have to be capable of being turned off, notably where juveniles and other subordinate individuals are concerned. This is also the case for individuals suffering from stress. One of the functions of the stress system is to temporarily shut off natural desires for sex, dominance, and even, at times, food.[7] It is the oscillation between "turned on" and "turned off" that leads to the ambivalence and flexibility that Arnhart emphasizes elsewhere in the chapter.

Some of my concerns about the general theoretical approach will become clear in the remarks that follow. But I am singularly unqualified to comment on the viability and future prospects of a biopolitical science. For the purposes of this comment, therefore, I would like to focus on how Arnhart puts his model into practice, beginning with this simple question: why did Arnhart choose the Emancipation Proclamation as his case study?

In principle, any event could have served equally well. Reading the chapter, I found myself idly speculating about other events that have flitted across my attention in the past few weeks: the proclamation of Pope Urban II at the Council of Clermont in 1095, say, or the slayings of the three civil rights activists in Philadelphia, Mississippi, in 1964, or, for that matter, the 2003 decision to invade Iraq. Arnhart chose the Emancipation Proclamation, I believe, because elements of the case lend themselves readily to the points Arnhart wanted to make about intuitive judgment, morality, emotion, religion, and ambition. The Emancipation Proclamation was an act of the highest altruism, exactly the kind of event that an assumption of rational self-interest would, I imagine, have the greatest difficulty explaining. One could, like the supporters of an Earth-centered solar system, invoke epicycle upon epicycle in the effort to make the older theory match the evidence. But, faced with the specter of a tortured logic, isn't it better to chuck the paradigm entirely and start from scratch? Isn't it better to consult biologists and neuroscientists, the experts on human nature, while building a paradigm that can account parsimoniously for an event like the Emancipation Proclamation? The unstated claim of the chapter is that, in the Darwinian competition between two views of human nature, the biological perspective, red in tooth and claw, will easily outcompete the rational-choice perspective.

Maybe this works well if you lob yourself a softball like the Emancipation Proclamation. What about the 1964 murder of civil rights activists? There's not much altruism there. Or, since I am a medieval historian, what about the speech of Pope Urban II at the French town of Clermont in the year 1095? This was the infamous proclamation calling for a crusade against the enemies of Christendom. Remarkably, we have five separate accounts of this speech, a sure sign that it was a memorable event.[8] But, even though the accounts vary considerably, the recurrence of key adjectives, including "vile," "despised," "base," and "accursed," allow us to make a reasonable inference about Urban's attitude toward the Turks and the Arabs. The tenor of this speech, I have to say, was mild compared to some of the invective cast in both directions during the period.

How well could a Darwinian understanding of human nature account for a circumstance like this, so clearly lacking even the tiniest whiff of compassion and altruistic feeling? Quite well, as it turns out. As Arnhart observes later in the essay, "we are politically ambivalent animals," and Urban's proclamation is in fact a rich illustration of Arnhart's claim that "the dark side of . . . group morality is that, while individuals can be good toward others they perceive to belong to their group, the same individuals can be vicious toward those outside their group."[9] Urban, in other words, went over to the dark side. Let's call him the Darth Vader of medieval Europe. The Darwinian understanding of human nature, perhaps unlike the perspective of rational choice, is flexible enough to accommodate the whole spectrum of moral stances.

This flexibility is part of the beauty of the model but, at the same time, a potential weakness. Rational choice, in the hands of its proponents, was a universal solvent, purporting to cut through every event or trend to reveal the singular motivation that underlies all political behavior. The biological understanding of human nature offers us instead an array of particular solvents. Reach for this one if you want to dissolve the context of Emancipation Proclamation and penetrate through to the underlying altruism. If presented with Urban's proclamation at Clermont, however, you will need to use a different solvent. Given the existence of choice among explanatory models, aren't we open to the accusation of cherrypicking the one needed for our particular explanation? By any biological understanding of human nature, moreover, it would have been perfectly natural if Lincoln had favored his own group, white people, at the expense of black people. But he didn't. So, when push comes to shove, a biological understanding of human nature alone cannot actually explain why Lincoln was Lincoln rather than Urban. Ergo, a biopolitical science cannot explain the Emancipation Proclamation a priori. Unlike heliocentrism, quantum physics, plate tectonics, or perhaps even the principle of the rational maximization of self-interest, it cannot be predictive. This is why I think of the biological understanding of human nature not as a competing paradigm that vitiates all others but as an optic that exists comfortably alongside other optics.[10]

But I do not believe that Arnhart's essay actually tries to account for the Emancipation Proclamation. Again and again, the argument flips the explanatory direction. Consider these passages:

- "Lincoln's participation in the debate over slavery and emancipation shows this moral sense" [i.e., that humans go beyond self-interest][11]
- "Lincoln's decision to issue the Emancipation Proclamation . . . illustrate[s] the intricacy . . . of practical judgment in politics."[12]
- "The power of emotion in political rhetoric is illustrated in the passionate controversies surrounding the Civil War and Lincoln's emancipation of slaves."[13]
- "Lincoln was an example of a restlessly ambitious man [a seeker of dominance]."[14]
- "We can study [prudential judgment] best by considering particular examples of it, as in the biographies of prudent moral and political leaders like Lincoln."[15]

Throughout the essay, as in these examples, biopolitical science is not used to explain the Emancipation Proclamation. Instead, the Emancipation Proclamation is used to illustrate the truths of biopolitical science. What we learn about Lincoln is that he was a leader and a statesman whose egalitarian and altruistic desire to emancipate the slaves was uncannily in tune with the biological understanding of human nature.[16] This raises one of several objections: wasn't Pope Urban II equally in tune with human nature? Didn't he, like some of the political figures of our own day, intuitively grasp that there is no better way to bind your group and promote solidarity than to demonize your enemies?

I believe in the need for a biopolitical science. Where I differ with Arnhart, at least so far, is that I am not yet convinced that such a science can easily be brought to bear on specific events like the Emancipation Proclamation. At the very least, I think Arnhart will need to test these ideas against two or more cases and use comparison as a platform for addressing questions that cannot be asked in the context of a single case.

Let me now turn to the historical model presented in the chapter. Throughout, Arnhart invokes the idea of a deep history of politics. It may seem odd to harness the perspectives of deep history to the task of explaining an event that took place in the nineteenth century, but as a point of general principle I would defend his instinct. A deep history of humankind is more than just a history of everything that preceded the first cities. Archaeologists and paleoanthropologists, after all, have been writing humanity's paleohistory ever since Darwin. Deep history is instead a mode of interpretation that insists that the grand historical interpretations undergirding all the social sciences and humanities are fundamentally altered when we stretch the canvas of history beyond Sumeria. In his essay, Arnhart offers a salient example of the salutary effects of taking a deep historical perspective. One of the most deeply ingrained of all historical myths is the belief that human history, everywhere, reveals a trend from hierarchy and tyranny in the past to democracy and egalitarianism in the present. This illusion of direction is utterly confounded when one grafts several million years of foraging egalitarianism onto the front end of this narrative. Using this basic insight, Arnhart has argued forcefully that history matters.

Amen to that. But how does history *actually* matter to his essay? In other words, how does Arnhart use history? Let us take a look at this question, beginning with Lincoln's relationship to the age that preceded him.

Arnhart develops a robust argument about the oscillation from foraging egalitarianism to the tyranny and despotism of bureaucratic states, beginning in the Sumerian city-states some 5,500 years ago and back to the egalitarianism evinced by Lincoln and Emancipation Proclamation.[17] The accuracy of this model needs some refinement. Among other things, recent archaeological research has suggested that a foraging economy in rich marine or riverine environments, such as Natufian sites in the Near East or sites on the Pacific coast and the Mississippi valley in North America, can sustain relatively large villages or towns marked by fixed hierarchies and oligarchical political forms. The lesson is clear: it is population density that makes oligarchy, not any quality inherent in agricultural economies, such as the need to organize labor with maximal efficiency. In addition, there is some question as to whether foraging egalitarianism is at all similar to the putative egalitarianism of the large political societies of the present day (Arnhart, I noted in several spots, is aware of this).

Leaving this aside, a Darwinian perspective necessarily treats any political form, whether despotic or egalitarian, as equally natural, where any oscillation between them is driven by force of circumstance. There are scintillating examples of this to be found in the natural world, beginning with the relatively rapid evolution of the political society characteristic of North American bison from resource-defense polygyny—a system where dominant and solitary bulls staked out territories and lured females to the richness of the resources they controlled—to the herd structure, with its more egalitarian access to reproductive opportunities, that became the norm several thousand years ago. The most vivid example of the plasticity of animal political forms that I know concerns a population of olive baboons in which the despotic males all died after consuming tainted food at a garbage dump. What emerged in the wake of this event was an enduring female-centered political hierarchy.[18] Baboon political societies are in fact noteworthy for the variety of political forms they can take; the amazing feature of this example is that observers were able to witness the actual process of transformation. No genetic predisposition was violated in the process simply because genes do not micromanage political structures to that degree.

In light of these observations, consider this passage:

> Bureaucratic states with often despotic regimes based on kingly and oligarchic rule offered many benefits over hunter-gatherer societies. . . . And yet, biopolitical science suggests that liberal democracies conform better than bureaucratic states to the evolved social and political nature of human beings. Liberal democracy approximates some of the central traits of a foraging society—individual liberty, social solidarity, and an egalitarian dominance structure in

which the desire of the few to dominate is checked by the desire of the many to be free from despotic dominance. The natural appeal of liberal democracy to the multitude of human beings was largely frustrated for thousands of years, until modern social and political conditions shifted in favor of democratic regimes.[19]

Let me reduce this claim to simple terms. For several million years, human societies were democratic and free from tyranny. Then something went badly wrong, and a multitude of humans suffered in frustration for 5,500 years. The despotic kings who governed during this long purgatory reduced whole populations to slavery and other forms of coerced labor.[20] Other parts of the chapter suggest that, like slavemaking ants, these despots "lived by exploiting peasant labor."[21] The period of despotism began to yield, in turn, to democratic regimes within the past 250 years, and the Emancipation Proclamation was the ultimate expression of this return to natural democracy.

This is not good biology. Parasitism, or "exploitation," as we call it among ourselves, is a perfectly natural phenomenon. Neither is the model good history, for it suffers from what I call the fallacy of Edenism. Edenism is not just the tendency to romanticize the distant past, though there is some of that in Arnhart's chapter. The fallacy of Edenism is the desire to locate human origins in a distant and unchanging utopia, postulate an expulsion from this utopia, and then treat the ensuing millennia as the dark period during which humanity has yearned to find its way back to Eden. Finally, I have to point out that this is not a new history. It is the old history dressed up in new clothing. This basic narrative—the loss of goodness, followed by a period of darkness—was initially laid down by Edward Gibbon between 1776 and 1789 in *The History of the Decline and Fall of the Roman Empire* and later became calcified in the historical narratives retold by twentieth-century historians of the Renaissance and the Enlightenment. From my perspective as a historian, there is nothing new to be learned from this example of biopolitics in action.

Does any of this vitiate the possibility of a biopolitical science? Emphatically not. What Arnhart and I would argue about here are issues of detail and interpretation. I think that a biopolitical science cannot emphasize chimpanzee politics at the expense of bison and baboons. As Aristotle understood, there are lessons to be learned from all comparisons. A biopolitical science has to be far more sensitive to the fact that there were changes in human society across the Paleolithic period and that these changes are relevant to the deep political history that we are trying to write. The development of identity objects and status markers, beginning with the origin of the species some 160,000 to 190,000 years ago and particularly in the past 50,000 years (or more), is a crucial component of any deep political history. So is the development of techniques to exploit marine environments and the later invention of effective hunting weapons, since these developments changed the flow of calories in human societies and allowed for demographic increase, as did the out-of-Africa migration 50,000 years ago. A deep political history needs to be sensitive to the demographic and economic aspects of the shift to agriculture. Finally, I think the explanatory power of the model is unnecessarily hobbled by the tendency here to imagine that the five-thousand-year period of agrarian states was an unnatural deviation from a natural human inclination toward egalitarianism. By offering these amendments, I hope to make it clear that I am using my own version of biopolitics whenever I think about the past and that, like Arnhart, I am exhilarated by how much enlightenment this model can bring.

NOTES

This comment was prepared for "Evolution and Morality, Perspectives from Political Science," a panel sponsored by the American Society for Political and Legal Philosophy at the 2008 annual meeting of the American Political Science Association, August 28–31, in Boston. I would like to express my warm appreciation to Sandy Levinson of the University of Texas Law School for the invitation to participate and to the organizers, including Joel Parker, for their assistance and welcome.

1. Larry Arnhart, "Biopolitical Science," in this volume.
2. For more background to these remarks, see my *On Deep History and the Brain* (Berkeley: University of California Press, 2008).
3. Arnhart, "Biopolitical Science," 222–25.
4. Ibid., 226–31, 239.
5. Ibid., 251.
6. Ibid., 231.

7. Robert M. Sapolsky, *Why Zebras Don't Get Ulcers*, 3d ed. (New York: Times Books, 2004).

8. See http://www.fordham.edu/halsall/source/urban2-5vers.html, accessed 22 August 2008.

9. Arnhart, "Biopolitical Science," 226, 228.

10. Richard Dawkins wrote about the extended phenotype as an optic, comparing it to a Necker cube, that well-known visual allusion in which the orientation of a cube pops from one state to another and back again. See Richard Dawkins, *The Extended Phenotype: The Long Reach of the Gene* (Oxford: Oxford University Press, 1982).

11. Arnhart, "Biopolitical Science," 222–23.

12. Ibid., 223.

13. Ibid., 224.

14. Ibid.

15. Ibid., 249.

16. Ibid., 237–38. I detect here the operations of a rhetorical sleight of hand, because there is no better way to legitimize a stance than to attribute it to a figure of reverence.

17. Ibid., 236–38.

18. Robert M. Sapolsky and Lisa J. Share, "A Pacific Culture among Wild Baboons: Its Emergence and Transmission," *PLoS Biology* (April 2004).

19. Arnhart, "Biopolitical Science," 239–40 (citations omitted).

20. Ibid., 238–42.

21. Ibid., 238.

10

ARNHART'S EXPLANATORY PLURALISM

RICHARD A. RICHARDS

Larry Arnhart, in his "Biopolitical Science," argues for a comprehensive, integrative approach to political science.[1] According to Arnhart, this "biopolitical" framework of a "science of political animals" moves through three main levels of "deep" political history—a universal political history of the human species; a cultural political history of groups; and individual political history—and incorporates multiple explanatory factors based on, in his terms, natural and social history, morality, judgment, emotion, religion, ambition, and liberal education. Arnhart illustrates this approach through his explanation of Abraham Lincoln's Emancipation Proclamation of 1863 in terms of the natural history of the human species, the cultural history of America, and the individual history of Lincoln. The details of Arnhart's specific example are beyond my expertise, and I will not comment on them. The basic substance and method of his approach are, however, of considerable philosophical and methodological interest. I will here sketch out, first, what I take to be the virtues of Arnhart's biopolitical approach; second, the challenges in employing such an approach; and, third, a contrast with other methodological stances.

I endorse both the substance and the method of Arnhart's biopolitical approach. The *substance* of his approach lies in its reliance on what we know from science—biology and evolution, in particular—to understand human political behavior. On such a biopolitical approach, for instance, we can understand human political behavior partly on the basis of similarities between humans and their closest primate relatives; partly on the basis of what we know about the evolutionary history of the human lineage; and partly on the basis of what we know about brain functioning and development.

The *method* of his approach is pluralistic and empirical. It is pluralistic in two ways. First, it is pluralistic in terms of the "explananda"—what is being explained—the political history of the species; the cultural political history; and the individual political history. On this approach, what we need to understand is not just the actions of individual actors and the particular culture in which they act but also certain behavioral patterns of humans in general, across cultural and natural environments, and over time periods that transcend cultural idiosyncrasies. Second, it is pluralistic in terms of the "explanans"—the causal factors employed in explanation. Arnhart advocates the use of multiple kinds of explanations in his list of relevant factors—in terms of natural and social history, morality, judgment, emotion, religion, ambition, and education. Finally, Arnhart's approach is empirical in that he advocates reliance on the observationally based methods of science. The well-confirmed theories of evolutionary biology, anthropology, and the brain sciences provide the explanation "store"—the causal mechanisms that can potentially function in an explanation of political behavior.

Arnhart argues that his approach to political science is in the methodological tradition of Aristotle and Darwin. This is certainly plausible. Aristotle saw humans as political animals, and in his *Metaphysics* he famously argued for a pluralism within the framework of his four causes: formal, efficient, material, and teleological. The specific explanations of human political behavior that Aristotle employed were often based on the same principles he might use to explain the behavior of other creatures—even if humans were nonetheless unique by the possession of various capacities not possessed by other creatures or not possessed to the same degree. Darwin was, if anything, even more committed to this sort of continuity in the understanding of human behavior, including political behavior, on the same principles that we can understand nonhuman animal behavior. But Darwin's pluralistic framework (as developed in his *Origin* and then in the *Descent of Man*) also explained human behavior by reference to natural selection and sexual selection, as well as evolutionary history, the effect of the environment, use and disuse, and the correlation of parts. While the substance of Arnhart's approach may not be precisely the same as Darwin's—since evolutionary theory and biology have changed dramatically in the past 150 years—the fundamental commitments seem to be in the same spirit.

One disadvantage of such a pluralistic approach is that it is very complicated. Isn't simplicity a scientific value? Wasn't Newton's hypothesis of universal gravitation good precisely because it unified different phenomena under a single explanation—a centripetal force that varies in proportion to mass and in inverse proportion to distance? On a pluralistic approach, different phenomena may require different explanations, and each of these explanations may in turn appeal to multiple factors. And, if the various factors are difficult to tease apart, then it is difficult to determine the effects of each factor. For instance, there are difficulties when we try to tease apart the various genetic and environmental factors in development. Actual developmental outcomes of organisms and traits typically depend on multiple genes, affected by multiple factors in multiple levels of cellular and external environments. The complexity of Arnhart's biopolitical approach is even more striking, as evidenced by his list of relevant factors from natural and social history to emotion, ambition, and more.

A second disadvantage of explanatory pluralism is that it requires some knowledge of all these factors. If, for instance, we are to give a fully adequate explanation of the development of any particular human, we need to know more than his or her genotype. We need to know what constituted the cellular and external environments and the operation of the various causal factors in these environments. This presents a challenge to anyone undertaking a pluralistic, empirical approach. And, given the recent explosion of information about biological processes, the demand for knowledge can be daunting. To apply a biopolitical approach, we would ultimately need to know not just the cultural history and the psychology of those involved but also the biology, the evolutionary history, and more. In an academic world that values specialization, this is a demand not often met.

Nonetheless, the advantages of a pluralistic approach outweigh the disadvantages. As Aristotle emphasized, the approach to an inquiry depends on the nature of the subject. Astrophysics may be served by the simplicity of Newton's theory of universal gravitation, but biology, psychology, and political science may not be well served by a similar simplicity. If there are in fact multiple causal factors for some phenomenon, then pluralism is not just preferred but required. This is illustrated by a disagreement in evolutionary biology. Darwin recognized multiple forms of selection—most significant, natural and sexual selection. For Darwin, which mechanism was explanatory depended on circumstances. Features that were advantageous for *survival* were to be explained in terms of natural selection. Features that were advantageous for *reproduction* were to be explained in terms of sexual selection. The tail of a peacock, for instance, is clearly not an advantage for survival in the struggle against predators, but it is an advantage in attracting a mate. Recently, though, evolutionary biologists have defined natural selection simply as a change in gene frequencies over time. Genes that increase in frequency in a population are therefore to be explained as products of natural selection. This is simpler than Darwin's framework, but it cannot distinguish traits that are an advantage in survival from those that are an advantage in reproduction. More precisely, it cannot distinguish traits that are an advantage in reproduction but not in survival from those that are an advantage in survival but not in reproduction.[2] Here, a pluralistic framework has greater explanatory resolution. This is not an isolated case. In biology, climatology, natural history, and the social sciences, there are typically multiple causes, and simplicity is therefore often a vice, rather than a virtue.

There is another advantage to Arnhart's biopolitical approach. That is its empirical stance. This empirical stance is most obvious in his willingness to appeal to scientific theories and observation. How science is empirical and, consequently, how Arnhart's biopolitical stance is empirical are far beyond the scope of discussion here. I don't mean to imply that, because of its empirical basis, science is somehow infallible. Nonetheless, few of us really doubt the power of natural science in its more rigorous forms to give us understanding of the world. We fly on huge airplanes, take antibiotics and vaccines, and get MRIs and genetic testing because we have confidence in the conclusions of science. This is all true in spite of the recent postmodern challenges to the authority of science. Surely we want some of this authority for the human and social sciences.

1. Challenges for a Pluralistic "Biopolitical" Framework

Our recognition of the virtues of a biopolitical approach does not require that we overlook the challenges. The first and most obvious challenge lies in getting the science right. This is more difficult than it might initially seem. We cannot just look to the most recent scientific theories for scientific truth. The history of science is filled with theories taken by consensus to be the final word, only to be later shown as false. In fact, it may seem that the history of science is really a story of one false theory followed by another. Philosophers of science have noted this and highlighted it in the "pessimist's induction," whereby the established falsity of each historical theory provides evidence that the current theory or future theories will also be shown false. The failures of Aristotelian, Cartesian, and Newtonian mechanics, for instance, seem to provide evidence for the ultimate failure of relativistic mechanics. We find this problem in the biological sciences as well. *Homo habilus* and *Homo erectus*, once thought to be ancestors of *Homo sapiens*, are now often taken by many to be on other branches of the primate lineage.[3] If so, they are not our ancestors. And it may be that the human environment of the Pleistocene was not quite what we thought it was and that the operation of natural selection was therefore not just as we thought.

This fallibility of science cannot be ignored. And the pessimistic puzzle about scientific progress—how one false theory can replace another yet still be an improvement—is not easily or simply solved. Nonetheless, we have abundant practical evidence that science is still the best way to arrive at an understanding of natural phenomena, and not just in its efficacy to give us airplanes that fly, vaccines that protect us against disease, computers that get smaller and faster, and procedures to identify and correct deficits in brain functioning. Science also has a theoretical power—a power to give us the causal mechanisms that make its practical success possible. It is not just that we have the ability to control nature in these ways but that we have seemingly uncovered the underlying mechanisms. It is these causal mechanisms that make explanation and understanding of nature—and human political nature—possible. What this all implies is that, just as a scientific account of nature in general is fallible and subject to revision, so is a biopolitical account of human nature. Nonetheless, our understanding of the causal mechanisms is enriched by the appeal to scientific theories.

There are other challenges for a pluralistic, biopolitical approach as well. Arnhart gives us a list of factors that he takes to be relevant to a biopolitical explanation. His list includes: natural and social history, morality, judgment, emotion, religion, ambition, and liberal education. Within each of these categories there is a set of explanatory factors. We can, I think, ask how he arrived at this list of categories and how he identified the explanatory factors within each category. If I understand him correctly, this is to be an empirical process. But even a little reflection suggests that this empirical process is not simple or straightforward. Some factors are on this list because of how they fit into scientific theories, and they get their explanatory power in part from the power of their respective theories. Explanations based on brain functioning, for instance, get their power to explain in part because they are formulated in the terms of a well-confirmed empirical theory about how the brain works that has successfully explained other cases.

But other explanations look very different. They are based not on scientific theories but on what we might call "folk theories." These explanations appeal to the ways that we explain human (and animal) behavior in prescientific or everyday terms. When we explain the actions of a politician, for instance, in terms of his or her ambition, we are appealing not to a scientific theory about physical causation but to a folk theory about the politician's desires and goals.[4] Similarly, when we explain an action in terms of a belief and a desire, such as we see in Arnhart's explanation of Lincoln's actions, we are using a folk theory to understand that action. There are some obvious questions lurking here. What is the status of these "folk explanations"? How can they be combined with scientific explanations into an overarching framework?

We can, I think, understand the problem in terms of what are sometimes described as "intentional explanations." Intentional explanations are explanations formulated in terms of intentional states. Intentional states are states with content. The belief that one action is better than another, for instance, is intentional because it has content—the proposition that "one action is better than another." The first problem with intentional explanations is that they seem to rely on a different kind of causal mechanism than physical causes. How can the *content* of a belief or a desire play a causal role within an empirical, scientific framework? We cannot obviously associate a physical mechanism with the content of a belief. This is a problem that has plagued philosophy of mind for some time. Different people can have the same intentional state by virtue of having the same *content* of a belief or desire but still have different physical states that fit into the causal framework in different ways. This worry is amplified by consideration of the difficulty in measuring and verifying intentional content. How do we *verify* the presence of a belief with particular content? And how can we *measure* things like the degrees of belief "that something" or a desire "for something"? The worry here is that folk theories and intentional states are not easily incorporated into a scientific framework that is based on physical mechanisms and looks for quantifiable data.[5] This is a problem that has yet to be solved.

There is yet another challenge for a pluralistic, empirical biopolitical theory. First, on what basis can we decide which factors are relevant? We have causal factors based on theories in the natural sciences. We have causal factors based on theories in the social sciences. And we also have folk theories. A pluralistic framework has to give us the resources to decide which factors are most relevant to an explanation. Is a particular event best explained in terms of a scientific theory or in terms of a folk theory, or both? The answer to this, in my opinion, varies depending on what is to be explained and the state of scientific understanding. If we have a well-confirmed scientific theory that can explain an action, *perhaps* we start there. For instance, if we know enough about brain functioning to explain why a particular sensory input has a particular motor output, then this should be our starting point. But, if we lack such information, we may be forced to give a folk explanation in terms of what we think a person sees, believes, and desires— or saw, believed, and desired. Similarly, if we lack the information about the specifics of a particular event, we may need to revert to a folk explanation. We simply have no information about the physical state of Lincoln, for instance, so we cannot apply a scientific theory that requires such information. In these cases, we have a *contextual* and pragmatic criterion to help us choose between kinds of explanations: use what information you have, and apply the best explanatory strategy given that information.

But, even within a particular kind of explanation, the choice of explanations is still open. Often, there are competing theories with competing explanations. There are a variety of empirical criteria here that can help us though. An explanatory factor that has a history of success has some justification, especially in comparison with one that does not have that history of success. An up-and-coming theory has perhaps more support than one in decline. So an explanation based on an up-and-coming theory is perhaps better supported empirically. Furthermore, we might also generally prefer explanations that are more empirical—and that employ mechanisms that can be relatively easily observed or connected to observation. I can only gesture toward all the important issues here, but what I think is ultimately most important is that what counts as a good explanation in a biopolitical framework should be empirical in some way or another. That is we cannot decide a priori what factors should be used in any particular explanation.

2. COMPARING APPROACHES

It might be easy to get the impression here that, with all the challenges I have outlined, a pluralistic, empirical "biopolitical" approach is unworkable. I am far from suggesting this. As I have already indicated, I fully endorse the substance and method of Arnhart's approach. We should, however, also understand the difficulties in such an approach, and I believe there are many. But, just as we typically judge scientific theories by comparing them with competing theories, so should we judge methodological approaches by comparing them with other approaches. The alternatives to an empirical pluralism, in my view, are clearly inferior. One alternative is based on the substance and rejects the assumption that science, biology in particular, can really explain human behavior. The second alternative is based on method and applies an a priori approach to explanation.

The first alternative, based on substance, has a very long history and is committed to the view that, because human nature is unique in some way, humans are exempt from the laws of nature that apply to other creatures. Consequently, human behavior cannot be explained on the same grounds that we use to explain the behavior of other creatures. One "ontological" version of this exemptionalism undoubtedly had its origins in an earlier, religious stance, but it gets clear presentation in the philosophy of Descartes. Descartes argued in his *Meditation VI* that there are two kinds of substances, a material, extended substance and an immaterial, thinking substance. For humans, these substances are joined together—a physical, extended body joined with an unextended thinking substance or soul. As students in introductory philosophy courses learn, this leads to a problem in mind/body causal interaction. First, it is not obvious how an extended, material substance can cause effects in a nonmaterial, nonextended thinking substance or, in turn, be affected by it. Second, because the laws of nature apply only to the extended, material substance, the nonextended, immaterial part of human nature—the soul—is not subject to the laws of nature. (In contrast, for Descartes, nonhuman creatures are only of material body and not thinking substance and therefore are fully subject to these laws.) On the Cartesian account, then, humans fit into the causal nexus of the world in a very different way from other creatures. The downside is the difficulty in seeing how humans can causally interact with the world, but the upside is that, because we have a nonmaterial soul, we can act in ways that are outside the normal patterns of cause and effect. We, unlike other creatures, can transcend the laws of nature! This ontological dualism thus leads to a *causal exemptionalism*. It also reflects a deep tendency for humans to see themselves as somehow unique and exempt from the laws of nature.

There are other ways to be an exemptionalist about humans. One related approach, also with a very long history that goes back at least to Plato and his tripartite conception of the soul (as laid out in Book IV of *The Republic*), is to see humans as different from other creatures on the basis of their reason: the capacity for humans to self-consciously think about themselves and the world, represent the world, and have beliefs, preferences, desires, and fears about the world. The philosopher Christine Korsgaard seems to argue for such a *rationalistic exemptionalism* (that she identifies

with Kant) in response to the arguments of the primatologist Frans
de Waal that we can understand human moral behavior by analogy
with that of other primates.

> A form of life governed by principles and values is a very different
> thing from a form of life governed by instinct, desire and emo-
> tion—even a very intelligent and sociable form of life governed
> by instinct, desire and emotions. . . . We have ideas about what we
> ought to do and to be like and we are constantly trying to live up to
> them. Apes do not live in that way. . . . Even if apes are sometimes
> courteous, responsible and brave, it is not because they think they
> should be.[6]

According to this sort of rationalistic exemptionalism, human behavior has a different and unique set of causes—causes based on
self-conscious commitment to "principles and values," as opposed
to "mere" instinct and emotion. Therefore, human behavior cannot be explained on the same naturalistic principles we use to explain the actions of other creatures. Our reason allows us to transcend the laws of nature!

Another form of exemptionalism can be found in the approach
that emphasizes the importance of culture for humans. According
to this *cultural exemptionalism* (usually associated with the views of
the cultural anthropologist Ruth Benedict but shared by many in
the social sciences), humans have escaped their biology by virtue
of their lives being a product of the cultures they create, and that
in turn "creates" them. On this view, humans—unlike other creatures—create a culture in which they grow and live, a culture that
determines their beliefs, attitudes, values, and goals. It does this,
in part, through the language associated with a particular culture.
Language, on this version of exemptionalism, "constructs" a reality
that is independent of mere nature. Culture and language therefore make us exempt from the laws of nature. The anthropologist
Loren Eisley is explicit: "The mind of man, by indetermination, by
the power of choice and cultural communication, is on the verge
of escape from the blind control of that deterministic world with
which the Darwinists had unconsciously shackled man."[7]

The first problem with these exemptionalisms is that they seem
to depend in part on ignorance of the nonhuman animal world
and, in consequence, on an anthropocentrism that is not sup-

ported by the science. The Cartesian claim that only humans have a "thinking substance" is not just problematic in its metaphysics but also dismissive of much of what we know about animal cognition. There are clear analogs of human thinking in other animals, particularly our primate relatives. Chimps and bonobos may not think *just* as humans think, but they do something similar.[8] Similarly, they may not have a *human* political behavior, but they have a *primate* political behavior that shares much with the human.[9] An analogous ignorance about human cognition is required to follow Korsgaard in treating humans as motivated just by principles and reason and not by emotion and instinct. Human cognition, like much animal cognition, seems to be a product of a complex mix of deliberation, instinct, and emotion.[10] It may be a mix with a different emphasis, but it is a mix, nonetheless. Finally, while we can trivially claim that only humans have *human* culture, it would be the height of anthropic arrogance to claim that nothing like culture can be found in other primates, some mammals, and even birds.

Even more problematic is the exemptionalist implication that human behavior is somehow "miraculous" by virtue of its occurring outside the natural causal framework. In the theological tradition, an event is a miracle if it was caused by something beyond the normal causal framework—the intervention of a supernatural God. Likewise, if human action occurs outside the normal causal framework by virtue of its basis in rationality, culture, or language, it is just as miraculous as if caused by a supernatural God intervening in the natural world. Moreover, if there *are* interventions into the normal causal framework, whether on the basis of reason, culture, language, or a God, then the causal regularities assumed by scientific law seem unjustified. If human action in the natural world is *not* governed by the causal framework of nature, then the assumption that the world is governed by causal regularities seems itself problematic. The laws of nature cannot be constantly countervened by reason, culture, and language and still be true laws of nature. The point is this: if the exemptionalists are right, nature cannot have the causal regularities science assumes it has. One can be scientific or an exemptionalist, but not both.

The alternative to a biopolitical approach based on method is one that begins with an a priori explanatory framework. This is a framework that is accepted on a commitment to certain kinds of explanations independent of empirical investigation. Arnhart mentions one such framework that seeks to explain political behavior in terms of "rational self-interest." There are other a priori approaches as well, most notably those based on one of the holy trinity—race, class, and gender. The idea is that we might adopt the "lens" or "analytic framework" of class and then look at the events of interest in terms of class interest. And we could adopt similar approaches based on gender, race, or rational self-interest.

There are some obvious problems with these a priori approaches. First, if we adopt one of these analytic frameworks, we can seemingly explain everything in terms of the causal factors allowed by the framework. They can explain too much. Just as adaptationism produced a flurry of "just so" stories that seemed to trivially confirm the all-importance of natural selection, these a priori explanations based on rational self-interest, race, class, and gender seem to trivially confirm the assumptions of the approach, through their own versions of "just so" stories. To be clear, we need not reject the *potential* relevance of the explanatory factors in any of these frameworks based on rational self-interest, race, class, and gender—if our empirical methods suggest relevance. But there is more than a whiff of circularity here: assume some factor or set of factors, construct an explanation based on this set of factors, conclude on the basis of explanatory success that the assumed factors are the correct explanation.

There is much more to be said about the exemptionalist and a priori approaches. Advocates of these approaches may see my characterization as unfair. Perhaps, in actual application, these alternatives are not always as exemptionalist or a priori as I have described. Nonetheless, there is a real difference between a framework that tells us to look at all plausible explanations—including those from science—and a framework that begins by looking at just a single factor or a few factors. There is also a real difference between an approach that rejects scientific explanations of human behavior and one that embraces them.

There is also much more to be said about Arnhart's pluralistic, biopolitical approach to political science. We can look more closely at each of the factors on his list of things that matter. We can look at "morality," for instance. Beginning with Darwin, there is a long tradition in science and philosophy of trying to understand the biological origins and social functioning of systems we associate with morality. There has been a recent flurry of efforts to understand human morality in biological terms.[11] Some of the questions asked are designed to understand how emotion, self-conscious deliberation, and moral judgment function in social behavior. We can also look at genetics and development for understanding the origins of our moral emotions and self-conscious deliberation.[12] An empirical, pluralistic approach such as Arnhart's biopolitical framework can potentially lead us to ask new questions and, in the process of answering those questions, develop and extend our theoretical frameworks. One of the great virtues of this approach is its fertility. By contrast, the exemptionalist and a priori approaches seem to cut off inquiry, in particular by excluding that most successful way of understanding ourselves and the world—science.

NOTES

1. Larry Arnhart, "Biopolitical Science," in this volume.

2. Richard A. Richards, "Sexual Selection: Its Possible Contribution to Recent Human Evolution," in *Encyclopedia of Life Sciences* (Hoboken, NJ: John Wiley and Sons, 2010). DOI: 10.1002/9780470015902.a0021788.

3. Matthew J. Rossano, *Evolutionary Psychology: The Science of Human Behavior and Evolution* (Hoboken, NJ: John Wiley and Sons, 2003).

4. For an introduction to this distinction, see Alexander Rosenberg, *Philosophy of Social Science* (Boulder, CO: Westview Press, 1995), 28–56.

5. Ibid.

6. Christine M. Korsgaard, "Morality and the Distinctiveness of Human Action," in *Primates and Philosophers: How Morality Evolved*, ed. Frans de Waal (Princeton: Princeton University Press, 2006).

7. Steven Pinker, *The Blank Slate: The Modern Denial of Human Nature* (New York: Penguin Books, 2002).

8. Rossano, *Evolutionary Psychology*, 334–47.

9. Frans de Waal, "Anthropomorphism and Anthropdenial," in *Primates and Philosophers: How Morality Evolved*, ed. Frans de Waal (Princeton: Princeton University Press, 2006).

10. Rossano, *Evolutionary Psychology*, 137–86.

11. For just two of many examples, see William S. Casebeer, *Natural Ethical Facts: Evolution, Connectionism, and Moral Cognition* (Cambridge, MA:

MIT Press, 2003), and Scott M. James, *An Introduction to Evolutionary Ethics* (Malden, MA: Wiley-Blackwell, 2011).

12. Joseph LeDoux, *The Emotional Brain* (New York: Simon and Schuster Paperbacks, 1996).

PART IV

NATURE, CONSERVATISM, AND PROGRESSIVISM

11

AGAINST NATURE

ELIZABETH F. EMENS

Progressive arguments on behalf of subordinated social groups often embrace social models of group identity. In other words, these arguments treat identity categories, based on race or sex or disability, as socially constructed. Relatedly, progressives tend to resist naturalizing models of group difference—what we might call "nature talk"—and to view claims that group identity is "natural" as conservative efforts to preserve the status quo.

We can see this resistance and a concomitant embrace of social explanations in various contexts: for example, in the feminist response to the invocation by Lawrence Summers, then president of Harvard, of biological explanations of gender differences in scientific aptitude, in disability advocates' embrace of the *social model* over the *medical model* of disability, and in race progressives' reaction to discussions of the so-called slavery hypothesis for African American rates of hypertension, among other examples.

This essay seeks to understand this progressive resistance to nature talk. Why the concern, where it arises, about natural accounts of group difference? The essay addresses this question by tracing key themes in the rhetoric of the nature-versus-culture debate across five identity categories:[1] sex, disability, sexual orientation, age, and race. No essential similarity links these categories or the subgroups organized around them. (Indeed, differences abound, some of which will be crucial to the discussion, particularly of sexual orientation.) For my purposes, the most important similarity

that links these categories is that each category inspires some progressive reformers on behalf of the proclaimed subordination of
some people based on this axis of identity. In this essay, I use the
terms "progressive" and "reforming" to refer to efforts to counter
subordination of particular social groups, and I use "conservative"
and "traditional" to refer to positions and attitudes hostile to such
group-based antisubordination efforts.

Reflecting on the role of nature in the rhetoric of identity-
group politics reveals a series of recurring assumptions about nature. In particular, three ideas about nature seem to undergird
these discussions, making nature talk seem threatening to social
change: *immutable nature,* the idea that nature cannot be changed;
normative nature, the idea that nature should not be changed; and
guiltless nature, the idea that nature need not be changed because
it is no one's fault. These assumptions operate in some areas, so
that a claim that, say, a gender difference in math skills is biologically based seems to imply that this difference can't be changed,
that it shouldn't be changed, and that its effects aren't society's
responsibility to address. Progressive wariness of nature talk seems
understandable in this light. Nature works as a conversation stop-
per, as a claim that, if true, seems to presuppose certain conclusions supportive of the status quo.[2]

Yet, looking closely within and across categories also reveals instability and inconsistency in these assumptions. We see that nature is not always immutable, that it is not always assumed to be
something we shouldn't change, and that natural disasters are not
always deemed less deserving of intervention than socially created
ones.[3] Moreover, slicing these categories along the theme of nature shows several interesting relationships among these groups.
For instance, progressive arguments about sexual orientation and
about age both evince less resistance to nature, but for opposite
reasons, as I will discuss. These instabilities make our assumptions
about nature no less robust where they operate. But the instabilities show the frailties in these arguments, as well as set into relief
discontinuities in the cultural understanding of the core antidiscrimination categories. The final section of the essay turns more
squarely to law, tracing these assumptions in discussions of the
immutability criterion in constitutional equal protection doctrine
and in cases requiring plaintiffs to mitigate their disabilities to ob-

tain protection under the Americans with Disabilities Act. But the bulk of the essay focuses on the broader rhetorical landscape of each identity category.

A note before beginning: to discuss many categories at once inevitably requires schematizing; for every category, there will be positions and arguments that contradict the story I am telling. Moreover, there are fascinating histories to the categories and concepts under discussion, which this schematic approach neglects. I nonetheless discuss these categories together—despite the resulting omissions and simplifications—because tracing one theme across identities can teach us about these key categories of antidiscrimination law and theory and provide insights that we cannot see when we look at a single category in isolation, as does so much writing about discrimination. This essay does not purport to make empirical claims about how reformers and their opponents view the world but rather aims to show how certain arguments seem more or less appealing with regard to these different identity categories—in ways that help us better understand these identity categories, their relation to one another, and the shifting roles that nature plays in debates about their significance.

1. NATURE: THREE RECURRING ASSUMPTIONS

Why does the rhetoric of identity group politics tend to associate social models with progress and natural models with preservation of the status quo? Several common assumptions about nature seem to undergird these debates:

- *Immutable nature:* First, there is the assumption that nature is impossible to change (strong form of the argument) or at least that it is harder to change than culture (weak form). Thus, those who want to change the existing societal order may prefer cultural explanations of group-based differences to natural explanations.
- *Normative nature:* Alternatively, or in addition, there is the assumption that nature shouldn't be changed. People may believe that the aspects of our social order that are the product of nature (or God) should not be changed, as a normative matter.[4] Under this view, society, which we

created, is subject to no such proscription. Accounts that attribute difference to society are thus more attractive premises for arguments in favor of changing the circumstances of difference.

- *Guiltless nature:* Finally, there is the idea that society has no responsibility for differences caused by nature, because society didn't create these differences. Inequalities created by culture, however, are society's responsibility to change, because we created them. More specifically, we might think of this assumption that biology lets society off the hook as Guiltless Societal Nature. (In the sexual-orientation context, we will see a variant on this idea: Guiltless Personal Nature, which is the idea that biology lets the individual off the hook.)

These assumptions, as the rest of the essay will elaborate, do not apply consistently across or, sometimes, even within identity groups. But they often play an important role in these arguments nonetheless, steering the debate to a dispute about the origins of group-based differences, as if that will determine policy conclusions.

Note that two main slippages tend to occur in these discussions, to which I will generally accede in the essay. One is between biology and nature. Sometimes, these two terms are used interchangeably, even though their scope is not coterminous. Think of disabilities acquired through automobile accidents, for instance, which are now biological differences although their origins were societal not natural.[5] The second slippage is between culture and society, also two terms with distinctive, yet overlapping meanings. Society can make decisions, pass laws, and institute changes that stand opposed to dominant cultural understandings. For instance, the Supreme Court's willingness to strike down laws implicating race might be understood as (one institution in) society attempting to change the cultural meanings and functions of race. Despite such differences, in the nature-versus-culture debates, the terms "society" and "culture" are both loosely set in opposition to nature. The distinctions within both sets of terms—biology and nature, society and culture—are generally elided in these debates, and, in tracing this rhetoric, I will generally embrace, rather than parse, these elisions.

2. Sex: Who's Afraid of Larry Summers?

So, I think, while I would prefer to believe otherwise, I guess my experience with my two and a half year old twin daughters who were not given dolls and who were given trucks, and found themselves saying to each other, look, daddy truck is carrying the baby truck, tells me something.

—Lawrence Summers[6]

In January 2005, Harvard's then-president, Lawrence Summers, suggested to an audience at the National Bureau of Economic Research that biological differences between men and women might be one reason that relatively few women excel in science and engineering at elite levels.[7] His remarks created an uproar, and he faced both formal and informal criticism, as well as calls for his resignation.[8]

Contextual details of Summers's remarks certainly fueled the controversy. Commentators sympathetic to Summers emphasized that he ranked the biological differences *below* some cultural factors—such as gender differences in work-family choices and responsibilities—in terms of relative importance to the gender gap.[9] He also queried why elite institutions such as Harvard subsidize the college educations of faculty children but don't help to fund day care.[10] Summers's critics countered that Summers nonetheless ranked other cultural factors—namely discrimination and socialization—as less important than biological differences.[11] Moreover, some criticized Summers for speaking casually and anecdotally (as in this section's epigraph) about a sensitive subject on which he is not an expert, particularly a subject whose study is, according to many scholars, heavily influenced by cultural assumptions.[12] Undoubtedly, Summers's institutional position contributed to the notoriety of his remarks:[13] a claim of biological difference assumes particular significance when made by the president of Harvard in a discussion of why women are underrepresented in certain fields.[14] I will return to this last point shortly.

Though the context of Summers's statement matters, for the purposes of this analysis the associated uproar also points to a broader aspect of sex-based advocacy. It is, I think, still the case that claims of biological differences between the sexes are often understood as contrary to the goals of sex equality.[15]

I say "still" because it might seem puzzling that feminist resistance to biological arguments remained so strong in 2005, even after the gender and queer theory of the 1990s. These theories challenged the feminist enthusiasm for separating sex (i.e., biological difference) and gender (i.e., cultural construction of difference) and for trying to put all differences between men and women in the gender/culture box. Efforts to separate sex from gender are fruitless, such theories suggest, either because there is no sex (nature) separate from gender (culture) or because, epistemologically, there is no way to know the difference.[16] More important for this discussion, I read this work to critique these efforts as poignantly naïve, to the extent that they depend on optimism about our (relatively greater) ability to change culture. As Eve Sedgwick wrote nearly twenty years ago:

> [C]ulture, unlike nature, is assumed to be the thing that can be changed; the thing in which "humanity" has, furthermore, a right or even an obligation to intervene. This has certainly been the grounding of, for instance, the feminist foundation of the sex/gender system . . . , whose implication is that the more fully gender inequality can be shown to inhere in human culture rather than in biological nature, the more amenable it must be to alteration and reform. I remember the buoyant enthusiasm with which feminist scholars used to greet the finding that one or another brutal form of oppression was not biological but "only" cultural! I have often wondered what the basis was for our optimism about the malleability of culture by any group or program.[17]

Sedgwick continues by questioning not only the assumed ease of changing culture but also the assumed difficulty of changing nature.[18]

I think one could understand Sedgwick's point in this way (though Sedgwick might not):[19] if you were presented with a given individual and asked if you thought you could more easily change his sex or his gender, you might well think that current medical technology would make it easier to change his sex.[20] These days, to turn a man into a woman (or even vice versa) might well seem less daunting than to turn a feminine man into a masculine one or a butch woman into a femme.[21] Whether one agrees that sex would be easier to change than gender, presumably few would find the prospect of trying to change gender particularly promising. (By this thought experiment, I do not mean to suggest that sex and gender are not intertwined; on the contrary, they are intimately intertwined, if they can even be meaningfully separated, such that some might say changing biology would be the most effective way to change gender.)[22] Moving beyond the microlevel of culture as an individual's gender, we can equally say that it might be easier, at present or in the near future, to change a person's sex than to eradicate sexism from society. Thus, at the very least, it seems not impossible to change sex (undermining the strongest form of the Immutable Nature argument), and it may not even be easier to change culture than to change nature in this domain (undermining the weaker version of the Immutable Nature argument as well).

So what accounts for the persistence of a feminist response that arguments from biology are dangerous and arguments from culture appealing? One possible answer is that the gender theory of the 1990s had little impact on feminism. But, in fact, the ongoing feminist reaction to arguments from biology makes sense even if 1990s gender theory did influence feminism, because feminists seek political change. Arguments from culture, as opposed to biology, may seem to be the only available arguments for change if the traditional assumption is that nature should not, as a normative matter, be tampered with. In short, even if it's true that we *could* more easily change someone's (biological) sex than her (cultural) gender, would there be the political will to do so? Likely not. In other words, Sedgwick's argument addresses the Immutable Nature explanation but, in order to effect political change, feminists must tangle with the Normative Nature explanation.

Note here that changing sex need not mean a "sex change" per se. Imagine that estrogen, if given in small doses to stereotypically masculine (straight) men, tended to soften some of their more stereotypical traits—and the outcomes included improved relations with their wives and children. Would there be the political will to encourage men to take the drug? Unlikely. The mere suggestion would probably provoke a public outcry or, perhaps more damning, laughter.[23] And this response is not merely, I suspect, due to concerns about the state's overreaching into personal matters: if, instead of hormones, therapy had the same effect, the response to state support of it would likely be different—if not favorable, at least less outraged.[24] This distinction reflects a Normative Nature background assumption.[25]

For sex, then, reformers often embrace a cultural view, what is sometimes framed as a constructivist rather than an essentialist view.[26] They do so against a backdrop of the conservative's biological essentialism—a view that gender differences are rooted in natural, biological difference. And that traditional descriptive view is coupled with a normative attitude that we should not change nature—that whenever we identify something natural, we should leave it be. With this Normative Nature backdrop, it makes sense that those seeking change might prefer explanations of difference rooted in culture, in social construction, to those based in biology.

Finally, returning to the context of Summers's remarks, we can also see concerns about the Guiltless Nature argument at play. For the president of Harvard to say that biological differences may explain the gender gap in math and science at elite institutions—and that socialization and discrimination are less important factors—may seem to let Harvard off the hook. If institutions are understood to be responsible only for the inequalities they cause, then a biological explanation of difference says Harvard has no responsibility for the gender gap. Moreover, to locate the problem not in early childhood socialization, for instance, but instead in biology might seem to let society in general off the hook. If there is no associated questioning of the merit regime in which women do less well, then Summers's remarks embrace a hierarchy between men and women along one axis—with a greater number of men than women capable of superior work in these areas. If the common background assumption is that we are not responsible for that which nature rather than society caused, then to blame nature is to disclaim responsibility.

3. DISABILITY: THE GOOD OF THE SOCIAL MODEL

Society is shown to *disable* people who have impairments because the way it has been set up prevents disabled people from taking part in everyday life. It follows that if disabled people are to be able to join in mainstream society, the way society is organised must be changed.
—Disability Wales Policy Statement:
The Social Model of Disability[27]

Theoretical and political writings on disability rights generally take the social model of disability as a starting point. The social model is the idea that disability results not from individual medical problems, as is assumed in the traditional medical model, but instead inheres in the interaction between an impairment and the social environment. As Michael Stein puts it, "[t]he social model of disability asserts that contingent social conditions rather than inherent biological limitations constrain individuals' abilities and create a disability category."[28]

Many questions and doubts might be raised about the social model.[29] Is it plausible that, as an unqualified social model seems to suggest, all variations in biological capacities are relevant only because of social practices and that there is actually no such thing as impairment? If impairment does exist, how much does impairment, as opposed to environment, contribute to the disability? Most of those who endorse the social model embrace a qualified version, acknowledging that impairments do exist and that impairments may limit some people's lives, regardless of the social environment. But, even thus qualified, the social model aims to shift society's focus from medical conditions that inhere in an individual to social interactions that cause those medical conditions to limit the individual's capacities. As a fine example of this shift in focus, the writer and activist Simi Linton, who uses a wheelchair, asks her students, "If I want to go to vote or use the library, and these places are inaccessible, do I need a doctor or a lawyer?"[30]

For purposes of this essay, the question is why the social model appeals to reformers who seek social change on behalf of people with disabilities. What do reformers think they gain from adopting the social model? It has recently been argued that the social model of disability has no necessary normative implications.[31] This argument might be understood as a variation on the insight that etiology doesn't determine treatment: as behavioral psychologists have argued for decades, even if a psychological disorder is caused by early childhood trauma, it doesn't necessarily follow that the best treatment is talking about the early childhood trauma; the best treatment might be medication or short-term behavioral therapy, rather than years of psychoanalysis. Similarly, even if disabilities are caused partially or fully by the social environment, it doesn't necessarily follow that we should change that environment by, for example, enacting a law like the Americans with Disabilities Act.

As a matter of logic, this argument is surely right. Nonetheless, for disability rights advocacy, the social model seems an important advance over the medical model. Why might reformers favor the social model?

One possibility is that biology is impossible to change or at least is harder to change than society—the Immutable Nature possibility. We saw this assumption in the context of sex. But, as we also saw with sex, this assumption does not necessarily hold; indeed, sometimes the opposite is true. With disability, depending upon the impairment, the environment, and the number of people with the impairment, changing biology is often not impossible (contradicting the strong version of Immutable Nature), and either biology or culture may be more difficult or more costly to alter than the other (leaving uncertain the weak version). Though the point is not crucial here, we might note that making changes to the environment in response to disability may also be broadly beneficial, in addition to or instead of costly, in some cases.[32]

Another possibility is that normative presuppositions make biology harder to change than society. Perhaps we think not that we can't change nature (the Immutable Nature argument) but, rather, that we shouldn't change nature (the Normative Nature argument).

Disability presents a markedly different outcome on this score than sex, however. The Normative Nature argument does not appear to be the background assumption in the context of disability. On the contrary, the conservative's approach to disability—the medical model—is all about altering (i.e., "fixing") nature. The focus is on, wherever possible, curing the medical impairment that creates the disability.

Nonetheless, although conservatives embrace neither the Immutable Nature argument nor the Normative Nature argument in the realm of disability, the reformers' model is social constructivist. This is at least in part because of the Guiltless Nature argument: if the problems are purely natural, the argument goes, then society has no responsibility to solve those problems. The conservative view to which disability advocates are responding is naturalizing or biological in focus, in the sense that it emphasizes that medical rather than social problems are underpinning the category of disability. And that conservative medical model tends to assume that society's approach to disability should be to find cures for the medical problems. Disability advocates are not necessarily opposed to cures (though some are),[33] but they focus instead on the social causes and social cures, rather than on the medical origins and medical cures; they do so in part to battle the Guiltless Nature argument.

We see here a striking difference in the contours of the debate about disability, as opposed to sex. Many advocates—from both feminist and disability rights circles—embrace cultural over biological arguments, and both against a backdrop of dominant biologizing of their respective categories. But a difference appears in the traditionalists' normative stance on nature across these categories. With sex, the traditional attitude is that biological difference should *not* be changed—that is, the traditional attitude embraces the Normative Nature argument. In contrast, the traditional attitude toward disability (i.e., the medical model) is that biological difference *should* be changed—that is, the traditional attitude rejects the Normative Nature argument. Thus, the traditionalist views sex differences as positive aspects of nature to be embraced and views disabilities as negative aspects of nature to be fixed, whereas the reformers see differences of sex and disability as problems of culture.

In this light, it is interesting to note one distinctive aspect of disability relative to sex (and race and age): even from a traditional viewpoint, there are multiple points of entry into disability. Those human variations that we call impairments are understood to come, for example, from genes, from fetal conditions, from events during birth, and from diseases and accidents of varying causes. Acquired impairments may come from an individual's behavior (skiing) or from events beyond her control (collapse of a building) or beyond human control (falling trees in a hurricane).[34] These multiple entry points might contribute to the sense that disability isn't subject to the Normative Nature assumption, because not all disability comes from nature, in the sense of natural forces beyond our human control.[35] And, yet, the traditionalist perspective tends not to distinguish these events relative to Normative Nature; disability, whether a "defect" of birth or an impairment inflicted by the self, society, or the natural world, seems subject not to Normative Nature but to the hope, the race, for the cure.

The next section identifies both overlapping and distinctive strands in conflicts over sexual orientation and discusses some links to the rhetoric of psychiatric disability.[36] But, first, a further note on the question of why disability advocacy tends toward the social model. One part of the answer is that the social model shifts attention—from the individual who can be cured—to the society that surrounds her. Even if not logically necessary as a normative move, as a matter of emphasis, this shift seems to do at least two things.

First, for at least some individuals with disabilities, the social model provides psychological breathing space—an entrée into greater self-regard and diminished self-blame or pity—while attention is redirected from medical (internal) investigations to structural (external) scrutiny.[37] This individual response seems to stem from the social model's disabling of the Guiltless Nature argument (for society). If society is responsible when subordination is society's fault, rather than nature's fault, then the individual can feel relieved of some personal weight of responsibility or blame for her subordination.

Second, for some outsiders to disability, encountering the social model seems to produce an "aha!" moment, a moment of insight, in which the current shape and structure of the world is denaturalized.[38] Anecdotally, the social model seems to make such people imagine for at least a moment how the world would need to change to make various disabilities less disabling. It is interesting to speculate about how the social model might allow this insight. Perhaps, by making disability less of a natural disaster or unfortunate act of God—both in cause and in valence—the social model may make disability seem closer but also less threatening. People often fear and resist—rather than empathize with—those whose counternormative lives are imaginable, familiar, close to home.[39] This is, of course, the premise of homophobia: the internalized phenomenon (latent homosexuality) makes the outside incarnation (the homosexual) frightening and hateful. So, too, with disability; the actual disabled person may remind other people of their own susceptibility to disability (through accident or ailment).[40] This is what Harlan Hahn has termed the existential anxiety prompted by people with disabilities.[41] (More on sexual orientation in a moment.)

Perhaps the social model can help to pave a less angst-ridden way for people without disabilities to encounter disability. The social model denaturalizes the world in a way that can open up nondisabled people's imaginative possibilities without entirely unsettling them. If the social model allows a nondisabled person to see that there is nothing natural about stairs[42] and that ramps can transform the landscape of possibility, then it may also allow that person to see disability as less of an individual curse or affliction. The social model may even allow an outsider to see how disability advocacy could someday help to alter the structure of the world on behalf of anyone who might need it, even oneself. Disability advocacy may, in this light, seem less marginal and more like a social insurance policy for everyone, given that anyone could become disabled. That reassurance may be enough to suspend, for a moment at least, the conservative impulse to resist, as unfamiliar or frightening, the prospect of disability. Of course, the social model has been around for some time, and the world has not instantly transformed in its wake, so I do not mean to overstate its potential impact. I do hope, however, to capture the effect that the social model has on some outsiders, which may contribute to the reasons that so many advocates deem it a potent force.

4. Sexual Orientation: In Search of the Gay Gene

The biology reinforces what gay people know about themselves: that their homosexuality is an integral, defining aspect of their being and that an assault on their homosexuality is an assault, not just on their behavior, their rights, or their pride, but on their very selves.

—Simon LeVay[43]

Biology, my ass.

—Karla Mantilla[44]

Proponents of gay rights count many social constructivists among their numbers.[45] Indeed, the gender and queer theory moment of the 1990s, discussed earlier—which combined a kind of radical constructivism with a critique of mainstream constructivism—was driven largely by scholars writing at the intersection of sex/gender and sexual-orientation issues. The distinctive rhetorical move I focus on here in relation to sexual orientation, however, is the robust strand of pro-gay biologism.[46] This is exemplified in some gay-rights advocates' enthusiastic embrace of the efforts of Dean Hamer, Simon LeVay, and others to find a genetic or hormonal basis for homosexuality.[47] Their work has been much criticized on scientific and nonscientific grounds;[48] my interest lies in its reception by gay-rights advocacy.

Biologists' work to isolate a genetic or hormonal root for homosexuality tries to locate a natural, rather than a social, cause. Pro-gay enthusiasts for this work share the aim of the work's pro-gay critics—to change society so that it accepts gays—but the biology enthusiasts embrace a very different kind of rhetoric from the sex and disability advocates we've been discussing: these pro-biology gay-rights advocates engage in nature talk. Indeed, they long for biology to get better at explaining group-based difference.

This disparity is largely explained by the backdrop against which these pro-biology gay-rights advocates operate. Most notably, those who embrace a biological explanation of homosexuality are trying to counter a background assumption that homosexuality is socially caused—a set of (sinful) acts and not a real identity at all—and so can be socially changed—perhaps even at the level of individual choice.[49] These pro-biology advocates reply to the conservatives' argument—that homosexuality is in some sense not real—by trying to point to a biological basis for homosexuality.[50] These advocates want to say: "Look! There's a biological basis for gayness! We're real, we're part of nature, and it's not a matter of choice!" Moreover, situating themselves as part of nature helps the gay-biology enthusiasts resist a religious reading of gay sex as sin by instead locating gayness in God's natural world. Gay-biology enthusiasts thus hope that identifying a biological basis for sexuality will prompt conservatives to respond as they do to biological facts in the sex/gender realm: with the Normative Nature and Immutable Nature arguments. That is, the enthusiasts say, because gayness is a natural, biological fact, we should not and, indeed, cannot change it.

By contrast, some other gay-rights advocates criticize the pro-biology gay-rights advocates. These antibiology advocates argue that locating a biological source for homosexuality will give conservative opponents of gay rights a way to eliminate homosexuality biologically.[51] For example, finding a gay gene could result in screening to abort fetuses with that gene—or, eventually, perhaps, gene "therapy" to alter or eliminate the gay gene. Thus, the constructivist critics of the pro-biology advocates argue that the dominant response to a biological source of homosexuality would not be to adopt the Immutable Nature or Normative Nature argument, as traditionalists have with sex, but rather would be akin to the dominant response to disability, that is, that the personal characteristic of gayness, like the personal characteristic of disability, can and should be changed. In other words, the constructivists are telling the pro-biology advocates, "You think that, if you can find a biological basis, conservative forces will view you as they do sex (i.e., gayness is here to stay), but, actually, they'll view you as they do disability (i.e., gayness can and should be fixed)."

A related point may be made about the increasingly visible advocates for intersex individuals (i.e., those who are born with reproductive or sexual anatomy that in some way combines male and female features).[52] Intersex advocates want to stop medical interventions at birth—that is, at the moment of birth, they want intersexuality to be given the benefit of the Immutable Nature and Normative Nature arguments, like sex, rather than being treated as it has been treated, which is like disability.[53] These advocates often want the choice to keep or to change sex to be left to the individual once he or she is older. This emphasis on later individual choice places the intersex category somewhere between disability and sex because of advocates' recognition that medical intervention might (or might not) be later sought.

Returning to the pro-gay biology enthusiasts, we can see another way that the meaning of nature-versus-culture arguments is different for individuals in the context of gayness as opposed to disability. For (some) individuals with disabilities, the appeal of the social model is that it points to a *societal* cause for disability, which makes it possible to say, "It's not my fault; the fault lies elsewhere (i.e., with society)." By contrast, for (some) gays, claiming a *biological* basis of homosexuality serves a similar freeing function, as it provides a way to say that "it's not my fault that I'm gay; the fault lies elsewhere (i.e., with my biology)." In the case of disability, looking outward to society can allow a release from self-blame (for those who experience such self-blame), whereas, in the case of sexual orientation, looking inward to biology allows a release from self-blame (again, for those who experience it). Either nature or culture may serve this function, depending on the context. This presents a twist on the conservative Guiltless Nature argument—the argument that society is not responsible for that which nature creates—by suggesting that reformers may sometimes seek to cast blame on individual nature, where the alternative is blame cast upon individual choice. We might think of this variant as the Guiltless Personal Nature argument, a pro-biology reformer's variant on the Guiltless Societal Nature argument that we have been discussing throughout. In either case, biology is invoked to take responsibility from somewhere else: pro-gay reformers say gays are not guilty because biology is to blame; disability and sex conservatives say society is not guilty because biology is to blame.

Finally, psychiatric disability looks more like sexual orientation than physical disability under this account. As with sexual orientation, advocacy around psychiatric disability often incorporates a robust form of nature talk. The search for biological bases of psychiatric impairments is fueled not just by the drug companies but by the different starting point for psychiatric, as opposed to (most) physical, disabilities:[54] that is, psychiatric disabilities are less often believed to be actual impairments (to be *real*) and are more likely than physical disabilities to be viewed as bad behavior under a fancy name. As with sexual orientation, this disavowal of the individual's deeply felt experience generates an impetus for grounding difference in features of the self more widely accepted to be real, to be natural—thus, in biology. And so Guiltless Personal Nature operates in this arena too. For individuals with psychiatric disabilities, the fact of a diagnosis, particularly one explained through brain chemistry, can sometimes be a relief. The diagnosis may allow the individual to feel less responsible for her behavior. She's not choosing to behave badly or atypically; that's just her biology. In part for this reason, I think, the social model of disability tends to have somewhat less purchase with psychiatric disabilities than with physical disabilities. Just as there are constructivist theorists of sexual orientation, there are proponents of social-model type approaches in the realm of psychiatric disabilities.[55] But psychiatric disability and sexual orientation are both traditionally understood in ways that make nature talk relatively more appealing to advocates than it is with regard to sex and physical disability.

5. AGE: THE MOST NATURAL ACT

We believe that people lose hope and the social fabric frays if society is indifferent to the inevitability of aging and loss of capacity.
—The National Senior Citizens Law Center[56]

Another secret we carry is that though drab outside—wreckage to the eye, mirrors a mortification—inside we flame with a wild life that is almost incommunicable.
—Florida Scott-Maxwell[57]

Age also inspires competing accounts among reformers, but against a very different backdrop from sexual orientation. A conventional understanding of age is reflected in the quotation from the National Senior Citizens Law Center (NSCLC)—the idea that aging is an inevitable decline in capacity. More colloquially, this idea arises in exhortations to grow old "gracefully."[58] Such urging seems to imply accepting the biological effects of time's passing, yielding youth in favor of maturity. Here age is an unavoidable fact of life, the quintessence of Immutable Nature. Exhortations to grow old gracefully suggest we accept that fact—that we embrace a Normative Nature stance and not try to fight biology.

By contrast, there are those who instead frame age as a matter of cultural interpretation or of mindset. One brief in a case arguing age discrimination in forced retirement asserted, "If any lesson emerges from the study of mandatory retirement, it is that there simply is no correlation between age and ability."[59] Likewise, and more lightly, Elizabeth Arden is quoted as saying, "I'm not interested in age. People who tell me their age are silly. You're as old as you feel."[60] This idea of age as purely a matter of mindset seems radically constructivist; it seems against nature. Indeed, it seems ridiculous to most.

A few writers nonetheless make such arguments, claiming that age is meaningless and that no distinctions should be drawn on its basis.[61] They point out, for instance, that we are required to "act our age"—a command that suggests there is a natural way to behave for every age and yet simultaneously demonstrates the gap between being an age and acting or performing it.[62] The idea of age as an "act" shows the social pressure surrounding this category, the ways we are forced to conform to set notions of a particular age stratum. This kind of radical constructivism, while rare, seems more common among reformers concerned with youth advocacy than among advocates for older people. And, among the youth advocates, constructivism is more the domain of those who advocate for young people under the banner of equal rights—the so-called youth liberationists—than of those who call for special protections —the so-called protectionists.[63] For instance, as part of the (seemingly ridiculous) argument that the rights and privileges of adulthood be extended to any person of any age, one youth-liberation classic describes "the institution of childhood" as "a Great Divide in human life" that has "made us think that the people on opposite sides of this divide, the Children and the Adults, are very different. Thus we *act* as if the differences between any sixteen-year-old and any twenty-two-year-old were far greater and more important than the differences between someone aged two and someone aged sixteen, or between someone aged twenty-two and someone aged seventy."[64] Such radical constructivism is uncommon even among youth liberationists.

And among those who advocate for the aged—the group most commonly associated with a fight against "ageism"—radical constructivism is nearly nonexistent. Philosophers, professional and otherwise, may speak of age as notional. (Pithy quotations to this effect, such as Arden's, are innumerable.) These advocates emphasize more the disjunction between the body's decline and the spirit's youthfulness. The biological inferiority of the older body is not denied, at least not to the extent that the strong constructivists in the domains of sex and disability reject claims of meaningful biological difference. Scott-Maxwell's quotation in the epigraph nicely captures this pro-aged image of the gap between inner and outer—between biology and psychology—with her contrast between the "wreckage" outside and the "wild life" inside.

Some do attempt to change nature—to reverse the effects of aging. Indeed, most people presumably engage in some efforts to resist the onset of old age. Everything from exercise and diet to cosmetic surgery can be understood as efforts to combat the natural process of aging.[65] In these ways, Normative Nature seems weaker in relation to aging than to other areas, such as sex, where individual attempts to make changes are permitted in some places, but largely grudgingly; by contrast, if people can find ways to resist aging, then that seems a good thing. Public health campaigns don't hesitate to urge practices that will slow the aging process, such as exercising or improving one's diet. In this way, age is comparable to disability in that traditional assumptions permit or encourage efforts to resist nature.[66]

Yet, there nonetheless exists a robust cultural assumption of Immutable Nature with age. Even if some of the effects of aging can be slowed down in various ways, the idea that aging is a fact of life that will confront everyone is widespread. And Normative Nature has some purchase here, in contrast to disability. Broadly, Normative Nature arises in the exhortations, mentioned earlier, to accept one's age, to grow old gracefully, not to fight it. Specifically, some types of efforts to combat aging are more acceptable than others. Different efforts to combat aging are understood as relatively "natural" or "unnatural"—with diet and exercise generally viewed as positive ways for anyone to fend off aging and cosmetic surgery a more contestable, even derided, practice.[67]

Reformers with a political agenda for the aged thus have good reason to avoid bold claims that age is entirely a matter of social construction. For one thing, age is so widely understood to be a fact of life that to assert otherwise seems very much out of touch. Radical constructivism with regard to age seems to most people absurd.[68] With age, there is an additional political reason for reformers' reluctance to embrace a constructivist position. The politics surrounding age bridge antidiscrimination campaigns; think here of the Age Discrimination in Employment Act (ADEA) and social service and support campaigns (such as Medicare).[69] Even the so-called critical gerontologists seem disinclined to deny the body's trajectory in all of this—and understandably so.[70] Age-advocacy groups seek better benefits, better health care, and better treatment for aging and all of its effects, even as they campaign for equal treatment at work.

Age advocates therefore tend to negotiate this tension by emphasizing the individual. Individuals age at different rates and in different ways. Thus, stereotyping and generalization are the key forms of discrimination in this domain.[71] Age advocates argue that such generalizations must be prohibited, even to the point of out-lawing mandatory retirement. But they tend to do so without deny-ing that age-based generalizations may have statistical merit, since those same generalizations are so widely accepted and may be nec-essary to underpin special services. Age advocacy therefore entails a subtle dance around the role of nature—with age advocates tak-ing less of an explicit stance against nature talk than do advocates around sex and disability (and race, our next topic) and even ac-knowledging the effects of aging. Reforming arguments therefore leave the role of nature implicit or present it as part of a symbiotic relationship with culture and attitudes,[72] careful not to deny na-ture's significance in aging.

Age also sheds new light on the Guiltless Nature argument. Un-der the societal version, Guiltless Nature says that society isn't re-sponsible for that which is caused by nature. Interestingly, society expends substantial resources on support services for the aged—suggesting some sense of responsibility for the effects of the natu-ral process of aging.[73] Funding to combat discrimination on the ba-sis of age—a societal problem—is less forthcoming. For instance, the ADEA is an unfunded mandate for antidiscrimination efforts to counteract social discrimination against people past forty.[74] And federal spending for efforts to combat discrimination on the basis of age (and all other protected classes combined) is far lower than spending on services and supports for older citizens.[75] One might posit that funding for public support of aging is a function of the numbers and political power of older voters. This is surely true. But the U.S. government also funds research into treatment and cures for disabilities—and apparently at a much higher rate than we fund antidiscrimination efforts—suggesting again a sense of collective responsibility for naturally occurring disability, for which society cannot be blamed.[76] I do not mean to make too much of the funding levels. They vary across time and location, and these gross comparisons can be complicated in numerous ways. But sim-ply noting the substantial sums that we spend on social programs, even for concerns with presumptively biological causes, suggests some chinks in the Guiltless Nature argument.

Finally, we see an interesting alignment of groups here: age ad-vocates seem most like sexual-orientation advocates in their will-ingness to embrace biology, yet the reasons for this commonality are opposite. Advocates campaigning for gay rights embrace nature talk (where they do) because they are trying to counter the conservative assumption that gayness is a matter of culture, of choice, of sin—that gayness is not natural. By contrast, advocates organizing around age (at least older age) often embrace or accept nature talk because age is so widely understood to be a biological fact of life, an inescapable property of nature, that it would seem ridiculous to deny it. Moreover, the degree of public sympathy for the two groups differs—perhaps relatedly—with gays having no federal antidiscrimination legislation and with older people having a wide array of social services and federal antidiscrimination protection in the form of the ADEA. Society's intervention on behalf of gays does not even extend to protecting against workplace discrimination; Guiltless Societal Nature couldn't come into the picture because at this point there's no comparable acknowledgement of group-based disadvantage and no question of blaming society. By contrast, society intervenes on behalf of older persons both to protect against discrimination and to provide affirmative supports for disadvantage. From these very different positions, reformers on sexual orientation and age stand together—and apart from other groups—in their willingness to embrace nature talk, the former because conservatives assume it to be unnatural and the latter because conservatives—and nearly everyone else—think it so natural as to be uncontestable.

6. RACE: BIOLOGY IS HIERARCHY

Americans are deeply attracted to and readily accept racial narratives—especially when they are produced by biology.
—Evelynn M. Hammonds[77]

Biological accounts of racial difference tend to spark the most controversy. Think of the response to the publication, in the mid-1990s, of *The Bell Curve*, which asserted that there are racial differences in intelligence.[78] More recent controversies have been generated by *New York Times* articles touting what some have called the new science of race, for instance, Sally Satel's "I Am a Racially Profiling Doctor," reporting that she gives African American patients smaller initial doses of Prozac for depression because 40 percent of them metabolize it more slowly than white patients and therefore suffer greater side effects,[79] and Armand Marie Leroi's "A Family Tree in Every Gene," claiming that the "consensus" that "human races are only social constructs" is "unraveling."[80] Both articles prompted a slew of replies, including a Social Science Research Council forum that involved more than a dozen academics who responded to the latter.[81] In 2007, *The New Republic* published online a three-part dialogue in response to a reference on the *Oprah Winfrey Show* to the so-called Slavery Hypothesis of African American hypertension, the idea that blacks have higher rates of hypertension because those who retained sodium at higher rates were more likely to survive the lack of water on slave ships.[82] That a topic as relatively uncontroversial as hypertension can become the source of such controversy merely through an association with race shows the social significance of nature talk in this area.[83]

The idea that race is a social construct is arguably a central tenet of the contemporary U.S. left. Barbara Flagg has suggested, however, that many Americans on all sides of the political spectrum think that there is a biological "there there" to race—but just won't say so.[84] Such a disjunction between belief and discourse could help to explain how writers such as Satel and Leroi can present themselves as brave knights wielding the sword of truth—in the form of their race-as-biology arguments—in a dark age of political correctness. To read their rhetoric, one would think that Galileo had come to argue the sun's centrality against the religious ideologues.

That the race-as-biology adherents feel embattled is no surprise. To argue biological explanations of racial difference is to court a charge not merely of conservatism but possibly of racism as well. The political stakes of biological arguments are arguably greater in race than in any other area. But what is so objectionable about such arguments?

One possibility is that these arguments are simply wrong. The responses to the race-as-biology arguments—in particular, the race-as-meaningful-genetic-rubric arguments—set out a plethora of counterarguments. Prominent among them is the widely accepted point that there is more intraracial genetic variation than interracial genetic variation, and thus race is not a meaningful rubric.[85] But, even if the science of race were simply bad science—and it is not my aim nor within my expertise to come down on this—the inadequacy of the science wouldn't alone explain the strength of the reaction. What makes the nature talk seem so dangerous? Some responses emphasize practical consequences. What of the 60 percent of African Americans with depression who are given something lower than the initial recommended dose of Prozac because the other 40 percent will metabolize it differently from whites? Relatedly, some authors have argued that the dangers of overparticularism by race in clinical medicine are greater than the dangers of overgeneralism because of the fact, just noted, that individuals are more similar across race than within it.[86] Critics of race-based diagnostics have also warned that the salience of race in our culture will lead doctors to overvalue race relative to other factors—or to be misled by myths or other unsubstantiated racial diagnostics. Sally Satel—the self-proclaimed racially profiling doctor—includes an erratum on her webpage, correcting one of the very few specific clinical race proxies touted as useful in her article.[87]

More broadly, some critics worry that emphasizing genetic racial factors will mask cultural explanations of racial disparities. Note here that there are some thoughtful efforts to suggest how studies might include race as a factor without falling into these traps: for instance, by making sure to explain clearly how the study defines and determines race; to articulate why race is being used in the particular study; and to measure also the range of variables that might overlap with race, such as socioeconomic status, stress, and discrimination.[88] But, more generally, we're again encountering the left's preference for cultural to biological explanations. What's going on?

As in other domains, each of the arguments outlined in the introduction sheds light on why reformers prefer culture talk to nature talk. First, Immutable Nature: the idea that biology is impossible to change, or at least harder to change than culture. Is that true with race? Before exploring that matter, we must note that, true or not, the Immutable Nature assumption is robust where it arises. Its strength may be reason enough for those seeking change to prefer to locate difference outside nature.

So does Immutable Nature obtain with regard to race? This depends, of course, on what one means by the biology of race.[89] Aspects of the biology associated with race—such as skin color—can be altered. For skin lightening, various products are marketed to women of color and apparently used widely at least in some parts of the world, causing concerns about side effects and potential long-term damage.[90] For skin darkening, the drug Methoxsalen modifies the body's absorption of UV rays; the drug is probably best known for its role in John Howard Griffin's memoir of passing as a black man in the South to expose race discrimination, *Black Like Me*.[91]

Griffin commented on the ambiguous morphology of race in describing the early stages of his racial transformation:

> First I did not think I could possibly pass; because, although I had the skin color, I did not have the kind of bone structure or facial conformation or color of eyes that we think of as "Negroid." Yet I did not have to be in the black community, as a black man, for more than an hour to see what I had never before noticed as a white man. . . . I saw black people with every kind of bone structure, every type of facial conformation, and every density of pigment. . . . I saw black people with blue eyes, with green eyes, with gray eyes.[92]

Griffin came to call this lack of seeing "selective inattention,"[93] akin to the problems in cross-race recognition documented by psychologists.[94] Griffin's point about the observer's perspective aside, aspects of the morphology associated with race can also be physically changed, as the doctors who make their living altering eyelids can attest.[95]

If race is defined by genetic heritage, then race cannot be changed retrospectively. But race can be altered prospectively. That is, racial engineering can occur at the individual or the group level. How that changes race all depends, of course, on how race is defined. If the world is carved up into white and nonwhite and one drop of blood defines nonwhite, then nonwhites can never genetically engineer themselves into whiteness. Whites could, however, extinguish the exclusively white race. In a brief thought experiment, Geoffrey Stone explores this kind of social engineering, as a future congressional solution to the perceived impossibility of eradicating race discrimination in the form of a Mandatory Miscegenation Act of 2100.[96] Softer versions of the same idea are imaginable,[97] but, however framed, efforts to change the biology of race—even at the level of individual choice—are likely to find few adherents. This brings us from the descriptive point—that race under biological accounts is, in various ways, alterable—to the normative.

Second, the Normative Nature argument: is it wrong in the realm of race to tamper with nature but not with culture? It's hard to imagine a direct race corollary to the sex hypothetical of men taking small amounts of estrogen (rather than going to therapy) to improve their family relations, since it's hard to conjure a racial equivalent of estrogen. But trying to generate such a hypothetical need not detain us. It seems fair to assume that school integration —even if it involves more strenuous efforts than are typically required or perhaps even permitted in the United States today—is more palatable to (almost) everyone than biological or eugenic efforts to change anyone's race, white or black. This difference may be a reason, then, for race progressives to favor cultural over biological explanations of racial difference. If we're more willing to change culture than nature, then locating difference in culture opens up more possibilities for change.

Finally, perhaps race progressives fear nature talk as conservative because, under the Guiltless Nature argument, society is more likely to remedy that which is cultural out of a greater feeling of responsibility for its production. Thus, any kind of affirmative action—societal action to remedy racial disparities—may seem more justified if society, rather than biology, caused the disparities the action is meant to remedy.

It initially appears, then, that each of the three attitudes toward nature limned here—Immutable Nature, Normative Nature, and Guiltless Nature—might press race reformers to find culture arguments appealing and biology arguments threatening. Recall, though, that these attitudes to nature are not universal. As we saw in the realm of disability, the traditional model of disability—the medical model—is all about changing biology, about curing nature. And recall from the discussion of age that our society seems happy in some circumstances to expend substantial public resources to fund social services for disadvantage caused by biology, not culture. Likewise, we surely spend more on social security for the aged than on reparations for social injustices in the realm of race. Any kind of reparations for slavery have been slow in coming, to say the least, and are typically rejected as a basis for affirmative action. Recent scholars, such as Ira Katznelson, have tried to point to more recent government action privileging whites, to demonstrate a closer causal link to societal responsibility, not separated by so many years and intervening events.[98] But even narratives of the U.S. government's exclusion of African Americans from the nation's major social programs of the twentieth century have not inspired efforts at rectification. By contrast, Medicare and research into treatment and cures of various ailments, presumably including those that (some say) particularly afflict African Americans, are relatively well funded.[99]

So, while these positions on race seem fairly robust, when considered in relation to other categories, the relation to nature falters. Looking at these other categories highlights ways that the position on nature is not entirely predictable in the racial context, either. But, then, why do reformers resist so vigorously nature talk in the domain of race? This is true even if the nature talk seems to entail no necessary hierarchy—for example, racial theories of hypertension rates or clinical responses to treatment of depression. One part of the explanation is surely the longstanding association of biological accounts of race, of nature talk about race, with justifications for subordination.[100] The social salience of race seems closely tied to stories of racial hierarchy underpinned by accounts of biological inferiority and superiority. This is true in other domains, such as sex and disability, though not in identical ways.

Moreover, in the domain of race, as in others, an argument from biology, or nature talk, seems to stop theoretical progress, to trump all other theories. There seems to be some kind of societal yearning for biological narratives—exemplified by what Ruth Hubbard has called "genomania."[101] When we find these biological narratives, we seem to forget how to speak any other language. Social change, law reform, discrimination—all become eclipsed by the biological stories, perhaps particularly so with race.

7. LAW: A NOTE ON IMMUTABILITY AND MITIGATION

Clearly, the size of an internal organ, such as the brain, cannot be humanly controlled.

—Kari Balog[102]

This analysis of the rhetoric of nature across categories helps to illuminate aspects of law's relation to these categories. This section traces these themes through two such areas: the notion of immutability in equal protection doctrine and of mitigation under the Americans with Disabilities Act. Looking first at constitutional law, we see intriguing assumptions about identity groups and their relationships to immutability and biology. Immutability as a term and concept enters constitutional law in the Supreme Court's elaboration of equal protection doctrine, under which courts closely scrutinize statutes that distinguish people on the basis of certain suspect classifications, such as race. In the early 1970s, the Court set forth a series of criteria, or factors, that contribute to the determination of whether a particular classification is suspect (or quasi-suspect).[103] These "traditional indicia of suspectness" include a "history of purposeful unequal treatment," relative "political powerlessness" of the group, and "immutab[ility]" of the trait.[104] The Court's heightened-scrutiny doctrine in general—and the immutability prong in particular—has been much criticized.[105] My aim is not to rehearse or to answer these critiques but, rather, to highlight a few features of courts' and commentators' discussions of immutability in light of the foregoing analysis.[106]

The first suspect class was, of course, race.[107] The term "immutability" enters the heightened-scrutiny analysis to link sex to race and thus to justify making sex a suspect class. In *Frontiero v. Richardson*, the plurality opinion written by Justice Brennan mentions immutability in striking down the federal Armed Services benefit statutes that automatically granted dependency benefits to wives, but not to husbands, of uniformed service members.[108] Justice Brennan wrote:

> [S]ince sex, like race and national origin, is an immutable characteristic determined solely by the accident of birth, the imposition of special disabilities upon the members of a particular sex because of their sex would seem to violate "the basic concept of our system that legal burdens should bear some relationship to individual responsibility."[109]

In the last part of this quotation we see Guiltless Personal Nature at work: the idea that individuals are not responsible for that which is biologically given to them, and so law should not burden them on that basis. The first part of the quotation seems to assume Immutable Nature, because, while not everything immutable is natural (for example, national origin), the phrase "accident of birth" implies that birth lands you in a particular physical place (national origin) with a particular physical body (sex and race). To assume that your physical body, your biology, cannot be changed is the essence of Immutable Nature. As we've seen, both sex and race are not so immutable as commonly thought. But, while the Court has recognized, in a different doctrinal area, that race may be a social construct,[110] the Court did so by recognizing that race is largely not biological; it has not questioned the assumption that what is in fact biological is immutable.[111]

When the Court decided, in *Murgia v. Massachusetts Board of Retirement*, that discrimination based on age did not warrant strict scrutiny,[112] it did not expressly consider the immutability factor.[113] (One of the critiques of the immutability component of the heightened-scrutiny analysis is that it appears only sometimes.)[114] Scholars who have considered the question reach opposite conclusions as to whether age is immutable for purposes of equal protection analysis.[115] Their disagreement may be understandable, as the answer seems to depend on what one thinks the purpose of the immutability factor is and thus what immutability means here. If immutability determines whether your group is isolated and likely subject to empathy failures from others in the political process—if immutability helps show you are part of a "discrete and insular" group, as *Murgia* emphasizes[116]—then age is not immutable.[117] It changes over a lifetime, with "old age" "mark[ing] a stage that each of us will reach if we live out our normal span."[118] (Note, too, that these discussions of age are marked by the definitional confusion that confronted the Court in *Cline*, where the Court held that the ADEA protects against discrimination only in favor of young over old, not the reverse; there the Court faced the ambiguity in the ADEA as to whether "age" refers to a special time of life (old age) or refers to whatever age you are (years of age).)[119] This emphasis on our potential for empathy is Ely's, as well as the Court's; Ely writes, "the fact that all of us once were young, and most expect one day to be fairly old, should neutralize whatever suspicion we might otherwise entertain respecting the multitude of laws . . . that comparatively advantage those between, say, 21 and 65 vis-à-vis those who are younger or older."[120] But Ely admits that this idea "is not quite the same thing as immutability, of course."[121]

So what else might immutability mean? If it, instead, refers to whether your classification along this axis is within your control, whether you are responsible for it, then age seems deeply immutable.[122] In other words, if we recall the language from *Frontiero*—"an immutable characteristic determined solely by the accident of birth"—then a person's age seems the ultimate "accident of birth." *Frontiero* told us that this lack of control mattered because of " 'the basic concept of our system that legal burdens should bear some relationship to individual responsibility.' "[123] With age, a person controls neither the fact of getting into it—that's the "accident of birth"—nor the fact of its progression.[124] There's no turning back. Thus, the subcategory of old age, once entered, can never be evaded during a lifetime. (This is, of course, a difference from youth.) As one scholar puts it, "Once a person [turns forty], age becomes an immutable characteristic because one is forever in the protected class, just as people who are born a particular race or sex."[125] Indeed, more so, it seems, than for race or certainly sex. As we have seen, age is the category for which the assumption of Immutable Nature seems most robust.

Disability has not been found to warrant heightened scrutiny, at least not in the limited contexts in which the Supreme Court has considered the question.[126] One might expect that, if disability is to be excluded from the quasi-suspect classes, then mutability might be the reason. At least some disabilities are mutable at both the front end and the back end; that is, you can fall into them (e.g., through an accident of life, as opposed to birth), and you can be cured out of them (e.g., through surgery).[127] On the contrary, however, in *City of Cleburne*, the Court seemed to consider the immutability of mental retardation as part of a reason *not* to grant it heightened scrutiny.[128] The Court wrote, "those who are mentally retarded . . . are thus different, *immutably* so, in relevant respects, and the States' interest in dealing with and providing for them is plainly a legitimate one."[129] One might think that immutability arises in this case only because it involves mental retardation, which is generally (though questionably) thought not amenable to "cure."[130] Perhaps physical disability would be treated differently.[131] Indeed, later in the opinion, the Court included "the disabled" in a list of other groups "who have *perhaps* immutable disabilities."[132] But the Court quoted, in a footnote, a passage from Ely that uses the immutability of physical disability, as well as intelligence, to show the limits of immutability analysis:

> As Dean Ely has observed, "Surely one has to feel sorry for a person disabled by something he or she can't do anything about, but I'm not aware of any reason to suppose that elected officials are unusually unlikely to share that feeling. Moreover, classifications based on physical disability and intelligence are typically accepted as legitimate, even by judges and commentators who assert that immutability is relevant. The explanation, when one is given, is that those characteristics (unlike the one the commentator is trying to render suspect) are often relevant to legitimate purposes. At that point there's not much left of the immutability theory, is there?"[133]

There is much to discuss in this passage, but our focus here is immutability. Why would physical disability be a prime example of immutability, given its mutability in many cases? The association may stem in part from an assumption about disability as an unappealing category that one necessarily wants out of. That is, if you could cure it, you would; so, if you're in it, you must be stuck in it. Of course, this is not always the case. People may choose to remain (or even become) disabled for political or community reasons (think Deaf culture), or they may not opt for treatment because of cost or reasonable or unreasonable concerns about the risks or side effects of treatment (think, on the former, of a country without health insurance or, on the latter, of the risks of anesthetic or the side effects of psychotropic medication).[134] But, more basically, the association of disability with immutability may stem from the Immutable Nature assumption. If disability is readily thought of as biological and we assume biology can't change, then disability seems like something that can't change.[135]

The Supreme Court has not addressed the question of whether sexual orientation warrants heightened scrutiny,[136] and nearly all the lower federal courts that have done so have either rejected the proposition or been reversed on appeal or en banc.[137] Since nothing in the Court's equal protection analysis has undone the presumed link between biology and immutability, advocates for heightened scrutiny for homosexuality have sometimes been drawn to arguments from biology.[138] While, as Suzanne Goldberg has shown,[139] there may be good practical reasons for litigators to argue from biology, as a conceptual matter such arguments may be problematic. Proponents of heightened scrutiny for gays can be found making striking statements such as, "Clearly, the size of an internal organ, such as the brain, cannot be humanly controlled."[140] Tell that to a brain surgeon or to a surgeon of any kind, whose job involves making physical alterations to an individual's body.[141] Such thinking assumes the strong form of the Immutable Nature assumption—the idea that nature *cannot* be changed—which, as we've seen, is problematic in varying degrees across groups but is nonetheless a robust feature of the rhetoric of nature.

In addition, Normative Nature does not always obtain in the legal domain. Turning to a statutory context, we can see this in the handful of court decisions effectively requiring disabled plaintiffs to "mitigate" their disabilities in order to bring claims under the Americans with Disabilities Act.[142] As one court put it, in finding against a plaintiff who failed to take steroid medication to correct her asthma out of concern that it would aggravate another medical condition, "A plaintiff who does not avail herself of proper treatment is not a 'qualified individual' under the ADA."[143] This is not, in my view, the correct interpretation of the Americans with Disabilities Act, for reasons that are beyond the scope of this essay.[144] But courts have nonetheless found it to be so, as have thoughtful scholars.[145]

A legal requirement to alter nature may not be wholly surprising in the realm of disability, where Normative Nature does not generally obtain as a social matter. But courts have also effectively required transsexual litigants to alter their sexual biology in order to be recognized as the sex with which they identify.[146] Normative Nature is relatively robust in the area of sex, so this requires more explanation. Perhaps, when plaintiffs depart from the norm for sex, this departure casts them from the sex rubric to the disability rubric, where Normative Nature does not apply. If so, this move should give further cause for concern to pro-biology pro-gay reformers. It may be an additional reason to think that a biological basis for homosexuality, if identified, would be treated like disability (Cure it!) rather than like sex (Don't tamper with it!).[147] In sum, courts' willingness to find a duty to mitigate disability and to require interventions in biology for trans litigants demonstrates a willingness—even as a matter of law—to require some individuals to tamper with nature.

8. CONCLUSION

> All Nature is but Art, unknown to thee;
> All Chance, Direction, which thou canst not see;
> All Discord, Harmony, not understood;
> All partial Evil, universal Good:
> And spite of Pride, in erring Reason's spite,
> One truth is clear, "Whatever IS, is RIGHT."
>
> —Alexander Pope[148]

Nature, it seems, is not a constant. This is true, first, in the sense that nature changes; nature can change, and nature can be made to change. As we saw especially in relation to sex, disability, and race, there is nothing about defining difference as natural or biological that means that it definitely cannot, as a descriptive matter, be changed. Immutable Nature is not so immutable, after all.

But, nature is also not a constant because there is nothing constant about how nature is treated, as we see by looking at how arguments from nature apply or fail to apply to different subordinated groups. Normative Nature—"Whatever is, is right"—obtains in some areas (sex, race) but not others (disability). In still others, most notably age, efforts to combat nature's course are widespread, yet so is a sense that nature cannot be overcome.

The notion that group-based differences rooted in biology are unchangeable, that nature is immutable, is often thought the conservative one, except in the area of sexual orientation, where some reforming advocates hope to establish the immutability of this group through biology. What will happen if a convincing biological basis is found is highly uncertain—as it could be treated like sex (here to stay) or like disability (ripe for change). Moreover, even legal decision makers are at times willing to require changes to biology, as shown by some of the cases on mitigation under the ADA. The shifting terrain of courts' treatment of biology and culture should give advocates pause in assuming that biology can be relied upon as a solid foundation for group identity, as various scholars have noted.[149] Moreover, identifying social causes for group-based subordination does not necessarily spur social efforts to rectify that subordination. Sometimes biological causes prompt social action, as the social supports for aging suggest. While an assumption of Guiltless Nature may seem daunting to reformers, particularly in areas requiring some kind of affirmative action, biological problems may prompt either social or biological efforts at remedies. Where "Pride" and "Reason" find flaws with the status quo, they cannot afford to assume that nature is a constant enemy.

Looking across groups in this way thus demonstrates three things about the rhetoric of nature. First, nature has no constant meaning, as it relates to group identity and arguments for social change. Rather, nature is sometimes understood to be immutable, sometimes not; nature is sometimes understood to be something we shouldn't change, but sometimes not; and nature is sometimes thought to let society off the hook for problems and inequalities, though sometimes not. Second, these assumptions do not always even hold up in the areas to which they commonly apply; think here, on the Immutable Nature point, of sex changes or of modifications to traits that signal race. Third, though, these three assumptions about nature—Immutable Nature, Normative Nature, and Guiltless Nature—nonetheless have some background purchase. Thus, reformers' arguments about nature as it pertains to particular identity categories may well reflect sensible assessments of the hurdles to social change for each group.

This schematizing has helped to shed light on the relations among the identity categories. For the primary antidiscrimination categories, race and sex, the fact of their immutability is rarely questioned (rightly or wrongly), so redirecting attention to social causes of group difference seems appealing and not so dangerous to group recognition. Disability advocates—at least for recognized disabilities—seek to join this move, emphasizing the social causes of group difference, particularly in light of widespread medicalizing of group identity. For age, emphasizing social causes of discrimination may be useful, but the role of nature is so widely assumed that it must be acknowledged for group credibility and for the claim to services society is willing to provide to address nature's toll. For a group whose mere existence beyond individual choice or sin is questioned—gays—the first step may seem to be to establish the group through the alluring call of nature. And the rights currently sought with regard to sexual orientation do not encompass the question of what affirmative steps society should take to alleviate group-based difference, so there seems no countervailing need to turn attention to social causes to avoid Guiltless Nature's excuses. For each category, progressive rhetoric must respond to the prevailing assumptions in order to permit us to imagine that "whatever is, is not right." To compare the rhetorical moves with particular appeal for each identity category helps us along that path, allowing us to see the overlapping, yet distinct locations of these groups all seeking protection against this thing we call discrimination.

NOTES

For comments on earlier versions and helpful conversations, I thank Kathryn Abrams, Kerry Abrams, Noa Ben-Asher, Sujatha Baliga, Mary Anne Case, Moon Duchin, Robert Ferguson, James Fleming, Suzanne Goldberg, Kent Greenawalt, Seth Harris, Olati Johnson, Sarah Lawsky, Jacob Levy, Linda McClain, Henry Monaghan, Martha Minow, Susannah Pullvogt, Michael Rembis, Barbara Schatz, Katharine Silbaugh, Rachel Smith, Richard Squire, Susan Sturm, Cass Sunstein, John Witt, and participants in discus-0sions of this work in progress at the Colloquium on Research in Gender, Law, and Policy, Boston University School of Law; the Law and Humanities Workshop, University of Virginia School of Law; the Henderson Center for Social Justice Colloquium, UC Berkeley School of Law; and a 10-10 workshop at Columbia Law School. For research assistance, I thank Andrew Brantingham, Roberto Concepcion, Alex Feerst, Leah Godesky, Michelle Hull, Jacob Meyer, and Christopher Wilson. This essay was largely written in 2008, and the sources and ideas have not, for the most part, been updated.

1. In this way, my subject is what Janet Halley has called "strong essentialism": "attribution of [any irreducible and therefore constitutive] characteristic that is also natural or biological." Janet Halley, "Sexual Orientation and the Politics of Biology: A Critique of the Argument from Immutability," *Stanford Law Review* 46 (1994): 503, 548. While her aim in that foundational article was to show that essentialism didn't require naturalism and thus to show common ground between constructivists and essentialists, ibid., 568, my aim is to understand the resistance to naturalism itself. Note also that when I use the term "socially constructed" in this essay, I am echoing the language of these debates, not taking a stand on the question of whether there is any essence beyond the social, or whether essentialism

and constructivism can be separated. See, e.g., Diana Fuss, *Essentially Speaking: Feminism, Nature and Difference* (New York: Routledge, Chapman and Hall, 1989); Edward Stein, *The Mismeasure of Desire: The Science, Theory and Ethics of Sexual Orientation* (New York: Oxford University Press, 1999).

2. Natural and biological are not the same thing, but the distinctions are typically elided in these debates, as I discuss in the next section.

3. The reference to natural disasters is not meant to imply that the subgroups of any of these categories are disasters (though the conditions of subordination sometimes are); it is meant to evoke the sense of public concern and responsibility to act that (sometimes) accompanies natural disasters.

4. This view is sometimes referred to as the *naturalistic fallacy*, that is, the attempt "to derive ethical conclusions from empirical facts." See Stein, *The Mismeasure of Desire*, 300. In his essay "Nature," Mill points out and assails the frequent reliance on nature as a source of moral authority. His particular target is the invocation of nature as a sign of God's intention, and his conclusion, which I do not share, is the opposite of the common wisdom: "the duty of man is the same in respect to his own nature as in respect to the nature of all other things, namely not to follow it but to amend it." John Stuart Mill, *Nature, the Utility of Religion and Theism* (Elibron Classics 2005, 1874): 54.

5. Each of these terms, perhaps especially the term "nature," has numerous senses, frequently blurred. See, e.g., Mill, *Nature, the Utility of Religion and Theism*, 3; *cf.* Howard R. Pollio et al., "Cultural Meanings of Nature: An Analysis of Contemporary Motion Pictures," *Journal of Psychology* 137 (2003): 117 (examining the range of thematic meanings attributed to nature).

6. Lawrence Summers, "Remarks at Conference on Diversifying the Science & Engineering Workforce: Women, Underrepresented Minorities, and Their S&E Careers in Massachusetts," co-sponsored by the National Bureau of Economic Research and the Alfred P. Sloan Foundation (Jan. 14, 2005) (transcript available at http://www.president.harvard.edu/speeches/summers_2005/nber.php).

7. See ibid.

8. See Daniel Hemel, "Summers' Comments on Women and Science Draw Ire: Remarks at Private Conference Stir Criticism, Media Frenzy," *Harvard Crimson*, January 14, 2005, http://www.thecrimson.com/article/2005/1/14/summers-comments-on-women-and-science/; Letter from the Harvard Faculty of Arts and Sciences' Standing Committee on Women, to Lawrence Summers (Jan. 19, 2005), http://www.boston.com/news/education/higher/articles/2005/01/19/harvard; Press Release, American Association of University Women, http://www.aauw.org/newsroom/

presskits/harvard.cfm; Letter from the Association for Women in Mathematics to the New York Times (Jan. 28, 2005), http://www.awm-math.org/response.html). On March 15, 2005, members of the Harvard Faculty of Arts and Sciences, which instructs graduate students in the Graduate School of Arts and Sciences and undergraduates in Harvard College, passed, by a vote of 218–185, a motion of "lack of confidence" in Summers's leadership.

9. He sorted the explanations of gender differences in science and engineering into three groups, in descending order of importance in his view: (1) the different choices by men and women with regard to family and high-intensity career paths; (2) biological differences in aptitude, particularly in variance; and (3) discrimination and socialization. It was in discussing the second explanation that he made the infamous "daddy truck" and "baby truck" reference, quoted in the epigraph. Summers, "Remarks at Conference on Diversifying the Science & Engineering Workforce."

10. See ibid.

11. See ibid.; see also, e.g., Derrick Z. Jackson, "Summers's Tortured Logic," *Boston Globe*, January 19, 2005, at A15; "The AAUP's Committee on Women Responds to Lawrence Summers," *For the Record* 91, no. 4 (July–August 2005): 59, http://www.aaup.org/AAUP/comm/rep/Summers Response.htm.

12. See Jackson, "Summers's Tortured Logic"; see also Marcella Bombardieri, "Summers' Remarks on Women Draw Fire," *Boston Globe*, January 17, 2005 ("Here was this economist lecturing pompously [to] this room full of the country's most accomplished scholars on women's issues in science and engineering.").

13. In a letter to Summers, the Harvard Faculty of Arts and Sciences' Standing Committee on Women wrote, "[i]t is obvious that the president of a university never speaks entirely as an individual, especially when that institution is Harvard and when the issue on the table is so highly charged." Marcella Bombardieri, "Harvard Women's Group Rips Summers," *Boston Globe*, January 19, 2005, http://www.boston.com/news/education/higher/articles/2005/01/19/harvard_womens_group_rips_summers.

14. At least one avowed defense—an op-ed entitled "Summers Is Right" and penned by Harvard economics professors Claudia Goldin and Lawrence Katz—specifically lauded the fact that "the President of Harvard, an economist," was calling attention to the gap in men's and women's scientific achievement. Without noting any departure from Summers's remarks, however, the authors also flipped the order of the concerns Summers raised, to put discrimination and socialization up top; they then mentioned different family/career choices and only then possible differences in ability. They dismissed the last as unhelpful "not because it

is politically incorrect to talk of gender differences in ability, but because research shows that men and women of similar ability have different career outcomes, particularly in science and engineering." Claudia Goldin and Lawrence F. Katz, "Summers Is Right," *Boston Globe*, January 23, 2005, at E11, http://www.boston.com/news/globe/editorial_opinion/oped/articles/2005/01/23/summers_is_right/. It is not my aim here to debate the merits of Summers's presentation in form or substance.

15. This image of feminism remains popular, I think, despite important feminist work—including some (though not all) versions of difference feminism or cultural feminism—that embraces (or at least does not resist) more biologizing accounts of difference. The kind of sex differences under discussion affects the type of feminist responses that arise. One intriguing possibility is that feminists are more willing to talk about differences as natural when the difference is an absolute (or nearly absolute) one—such as pregnancy—rather than something both groups can do, but with varying success on some measures—such as mathematics. I thank Kerry Abrams for this suggestion.

16. Compare Judith Butler, *Gender Trouble: Feminism and the Subversion of Identity* (New York: Routledge, 1999), with Judith Butler, *Bodies That Matter: On the Discursive Limits of "Sex"* (New York: Routledge, 1993).

17. Eve Kosofsky Sedgwick, *Epistemology of the Closet* (Berkeley: University of California Press, 1990), 41.

18. Ibid., 43 ("[J]ust as it comes to seem questionable to assume that cultural constructs are peculiarly malleable ones, it is also becoming increasingly problematical to assume that grounding an identity in biology or 'essential nature' is a stable way of insulating it from societal interference.").

19. Sedgwick might well resist the thought experiment that assumes, even temporarily, the separability of sex and gender in this way.

20. Even judicial opinions have noted the possibility of changing sex. See, e.g., *Tanner v. Oregon Health Sci. Univ.*, 971 P.2d 435, 446 (Or. App. 1998) ("Both alienage and religious affiliation may be changed almost at will. For that matter, given modern technology, so also may gender.").

21. Of course, this depends on what definition one gives to sex, for which the definitions vary, under law as well as other discourses. See, e.g., Dean Spade, "Documenting Gender," *Hastings Law Journal* 59 (2008): 731.

22. And given the interrelatedness of mind and body, perhaps changes in gender performance alter the physiology of sex (e.g., hormone production). More generally, some might say that it's meaningless to speak of sex and gender as separate categories. Cf., e.g., the sources cited in note 1; Brady Dunklee, Jenny Reardon, and Kara Wentworth, *Race and Crisis*, SSRC Forum, http://raceandgenomics.ssrc.org/Reardon/ (June 7, 2006) (making a related point in the context of race science debates).

Throughout this essay, however, I am using categories that are culturally salient, despite being subject to deconstruction.

23. Of course, the idea of biological attempts to change an individual's group status is not at all absurd in reality. Such attempts have been imposed on some groups in the past—to try to change sexual orientation, for instance—and continue for children with disabilities and intersex status. See, e.g., Kenji Yoshino, "Covering," *Yale Law Journal* 111 (2002): 769 (reviewing efforts at psychological and biological conversion for gays); see also notes 142–45 and accompanying text.

24. Note that this contrast—between using therapy and using hormones to change people—formally distinguishes biology from culture in the form of treatment used, rather than in the account of the origins. This hypothetical, therefore, rests on the common (though often unsupported) assumption that, if we can change something biologically, then it is biologically, not culturally, based and that, if we can change something culturally, then it is culturally, not biologically, based. Etiology and treatment need not be mirror images, as I discuss in the next section, not least because culture and biology are not so distinct as often assumed. But, for purposes of the hypothetical, the assumed link between etiology and treatment allows us to use a contrast between possible treatment types to help show the contrast in attitudes toward changing biology and culture.

25. Cf. Cass R. Sunstein, "Moral Heuristics and Moral Framing," *Minnesota Law Review* 88 (2004):1556, 1577 (discussing "don't tamper with nature" as a common heuristic).

26. For contrary views, see sources cited in note 1. Essentialism need not be rooted in nature or biology, however; for instance, someone can think that a person's sexual orientation is fixed and immutable, with the cause in the person's upbringing. See Stein, *The Mismeasure of Desire*. Essentialism is often used to mean biological essentialism. See also Halley, "Sexual Orientation and the Politics of Biology." To keep the focus on the natural and biological, though, I rarely use the term "essentialism" here.

27. Manchester City Council, Disabled People: The Social Model of Disability (last visited Jan. 7, 2011), http://www.manchester.gov.uk/info/200041/equality_and_diversity/106/disabled_people/5. The social model has British origins—see Michael Oliver, *Understanding Disability: From Theory to Practice* (New York: St. Martin's Press, 1996), 19–42 (defining the "social model" as distinct from the "individual model")—but it now holds an important place in U.S. disability studies and advocacy. See, e.g., Samuel R. Bagenstos, "Subordination, Stigma, and 'Disability,'" *Virginia Law Review* 86 (2000): 397, 428–29.

28. Michael Ashley Stein, "Disability Human Rights," *California Law Review* 95 (2007): 75, 85.

29. Many of these questions have been or are being raised by disability studies scholars, who have been critiquing and complicating the social model for some time. See, e.g., Oliver, *Understanding Disability*, 33–41 (discussing some of these critiques).

30. Simi Linton, *My Body Politic: A Memoir* (Ann Arbor: University of Michigan Press, 2006), 120.

31. Adam Samaha, "What Good Is the Social Model?," *University of Chicago Law Review* 74 (2007): 1251.

32. See Elizabeth F. Emens, "Integrating Accommodation," *University of Pennsylvania Law Review* 156 (2008): 839 (discussing the third-party benefits of some disability accommodations).

33. Opponents of cochlear implants among the Deaf community are among the most prominent examples of this. See, e.g., Jeannette Cox, "Crossroads and Signposts: The ADA Amendments Act of 2008," *Indiana Law Journal* 85 (2008): 187, 217–18 (citing sources).

34. See ibid. Thus, given this point and the availability of "cures" and other forms of mitigation, disability can be understood as sometimes mutable on either the front end or the back end. For discussion of this in relation to the immutability factor in equal protection analysis, see notes 126–35 and accompanying text.

35. To speak of the diverse causes of disability, as I do here, is different from the way that we might talk about the different types of accounts of what makes up a category such as race. The point here is not about how many different ways we might understand disability but, rather, about how many different ways someone might become disabled under an account of disability as a biological impairment or difference (a difference that, on the social model, society renders disabling).

36. See Ben-Asher, note 53 and accompanying text.

37. Cf. Oliver, *Understanding Disability*, 41–42 ("I cannot explain how significantly all this was turned around when I came into contact with the notion of the social model of disabilities, rather than the medical model which I had hitherto lived with. Over a matter of months, my discomfort with this secret beast of burden called epilepsy . . . completely changed. I think I went through an almost evangelical conversion as I realised that my disability was not, in fact, epilepsy, but the toxic drugs with their denied side-effects; the medical regime with its blaming of the victim; the judgment through distance and silence of bus-stop crowds, bar-room crowds and dinner-table friends; the fear; and, not least, the employment problems. All this was the oppression, not the epileptic seizure at which I was hardly (consciously) present."); Samaha, "What Good Is the Social Model of Disability?," 1283 (making this point and citing sources).

38. Note the power of the word "denaturalized" in this context: em-

bedded within it, I think, are Immutable Nature and Normative Nature assumptions. If something is denaturalized, we no longer think it must be as it is, because we can change it and we may change it.

39. See, e.g., Kenji Yoshino, "Assimilationist Bias in Equal Protection: The Visibility Presumption and the Case of 'Don't Ask, Don't Tell,'" *Yale Law Journal* 108 (1998): 485, 512; Elizabeth F. Emens, "Monogamy's Law: Compulsory Monogamy and Polyamorous Existence," *New York University Review of Law and Social Change* 29 (2007): 277, 345–46.

40. The claim is not that the feelings are precisely the same with regard to homosexuality and disability, only that they share a similar combination of identification and resistance. Among other differences, the concept of homophobia implies latent desire for the other, in a way that Hahn's existential anxiety does not. See note 41. In addition, homophobia concerns fears about one's own inclinations, which applies only to some disabilities. For instance, while fears of an unknown genetic predisposition for a disability seem rather similar to fears that one has frightening desires lurking within, fears of disability by accident do not involve this fear of what's inside. Finally, for some religious traditions, sexual orientation, of course, has a distinctive association with sin, though there is also a history of disability being treated as a sign of God's disfavor. See, e.g., Herbert C. Covey, "Western Christianity's Two Historical Treatments of People With Disabilities or Mental Illness," *Social Science Journal* 42 (2005): 107.

41. See Harlan Hahn, "The Politics of Physical Differences: Disability and Discrimination," *Journal of Social Issues* 44 (1988): 39, 43–44.

42. Note here an almost metaphorical function of the term "natural," which also imports the Immutable Nature and Normative Nature assumptions that give "denaturalize" its meaning. Cf. note 38 (discussing "denaturalize").

43. Simon LeVay, *Queer Science: The Use and Abuse of Research into Homosexuality* (Cambridge, MA: MIT Press, 1996), 295.

44. Karla Mantilla, "Biology, My Ass," *Off Our Backs*, 1999, http://web.archive.org/web/20040105072257/http://staffweb.lib.uiowa.edu/ktonella/oob/features/Biology.htm#_Toc433523802 (last visited Dec. 7, 2010). I quote Mantilla's title here, because it's a terrifically evocative line, not because of an intention to endorse Mantilla's arguments in the cited article or elsewhere.

45. See, e.g., Halley, "Sexual Orientation and the Politics of Biology," 505 (discussing the "pro-gay constituencies eager to deny the claim that homosexuality is biologically caused"). I use the term "gay" here to mean gay men and lesbians, and I decline the more common acronym of LGB or LGBT (lesbian, gay, bisexual, transgender), because the biologizing move I'm discussing tends to be more about L and G than B, and T raises its own

set of interesting issues that deserve distinct attention; see note 53. (Also, to the extent that "gay" is both an umbrella term that can include lesbians and a term that also seems to foreground gay men, the term's emphasis is consistent with the predominantly male focus of the biologizing advocacy I'm discussing here.)

46. By "pro-gay," I mean something like Janet Halley's definition— "those who believe that homosexuality is good or value neutral and should be celebrated or tolerated"—though with more emphasis on "good" and "celebrated" than on "tolerated," which can imply holding one's nose to endure something unpleasant. Ibid., 516. Pro-gay may best be defined as the opposite of "anti-gay," meaning "those who believe that homosexuality is bad or harmful and should be punished, hidden, or restrained." Ibid.

47. See, e.g., Simon LeVay, "The Biology of Sexual Orientation," http://www.simonlevay.com/the-biology-of-sexual-orientation (summarizing this work); Andrew Sullivan, *Virtually Normal* (New York: Knopf, 1995).

48. See, e.g., Melanie Blackless and Anne Fausto-Sterling, "How Sexually Dimorphic Are We? Review and Synthesis," *American Journal of Human Biology* 12 (2000): 151, 161; Halley, "Sexual Orientation and the Politics of Biology"; Edward Stein, "Born That Way? Not a Choice? Problems with Biological and Psychological Arguments for Gay Rights," 13 (unpublished manuscript, on file with author); Stein, *The Mismeasure of Desire*, 33 (analyzing thoroughly and critiquing the science, as well as the ethical presumption that a biological basis for orientation could ground rights to conduct); but see Martha C. Nussbaum, "Millean Liberty and Sexual Orientation: A Discussion of Edward Stein's 'The Mismeasure of Desire,'" *Law and Philosophy* 21 (2002): 317, 331. Stein's sophisticated work on this issue reckons with many nuances, including the distinction between "born that way" arguments and "not a choice" arguments, that this brief essay glosses over. As noted earlier, Janet Halley's work critiquing the science of sexuality and demonstrating the points of overlap between essentialist and constructivist positions shows that essentialism doesn't require naturalism; in this essay, I am concerned, however, with the varying attractions and resistances to naturalism. See Halley, "Sexual Orientation and the Politics of Biology."

49. The alternatives to a biologizing idea of homosexuality encompass a range of views: from, for instance, a belief that homosexuality is fixed by parents or other early childhood experiences to a belief that it is simply a matter of individual behavioral choice.

50. Empirical work suggests a correlation between believing that homosexuality is biologically based or not chosen and supporting gay rights. See Stein, *The Mismeasure of Desire*, 45 n.146 (citing sources). As Stein points out, the correlation could point in a direction the reverse of the

one commonly assumed, with supporting gay rights leading to adopting a view that homosexuality is biologically based or with both spurred by a third factor. Ibid.

51. See, e.g., ibid., 46; Halley, "Sexual Orientation and the Politics of Biology," 523.

52. Estimates of how many people fall into this category are controversial, in part because they depend on how intersex is defined. One study estimates that one to two of every one thousand births receive surgery to "normalize" genital appearance. Blackless and Fausto-Sterling, "How Sexually Dimorphic Are We?," 161.

53. Noa Ben-Asher elegantly elaborates the paradoxical emphases of intersex versus transsex advocates: transsex advocates emphasize cultural gender as the key self to which biology must be made to conform (when an individual so desires, and with public funding); in contrast, intersex advocates emphasize biological sex as crucial and not to be tampered with by medical professionals at birth. Noa Ben-Asher, "The Necessity of Sex Change: A Struggle for Intersex and Transsex Liberties," *Harvard Journal of Law and Gender* 29 (2006): 51. In a move resonant with the constructivists' stance against nature, she ultimately concludes that a general move away from biological and medical accounts is desirable—in favor of an emphasis on the positive and negative liberties of trans and intersex individuals, respectively.

54. Exceptions include physical disabilities that are relatively new or contested diagnostic categories that are hard for others to perceive, such as fibromyalgia, chronic fatigue, or back pain. In these instances, a diagnosis, particularly one that offers a physiological explanation for symptoms, can be a relief from doctors' or others' suggestions that it's "all in your head." As with psychiatric disability and sexual orientation, locating experience in physical biology can make even physical symptoms more real and seem less the fault of the individual. Here, again, the physical, the biological, is weightier—it counts more—than the mental, the emotional, or the relational, and correspondingly Guiltless Personal Nature operates to make nature talk relatively appealing to the individual. (Obesity also operates in interesting ways here, because the weight is widely perceived, but disagreements arise as to the cause of the weight.)

55. Activism and scholarship around autism provide a striking example (though even classifying autism as psychiatric is contested, as it is generally perceived as a hybrid): the neurodiversity movement seeks to relativize autism and other neurological difference by placing all of us, including those with autism, on the neurodiversity spectrum. See, e.g., Judy Singer, "Why Can't You Be Normal for Once in Your Life? From a 'Problem with No Name' to the Emergence of a New Category of Difference: The Autistic

Spectrum," in *Disability Discourse*, ed. Mairian Corker and Sally French (Philadelphia: Open University Press, 1999), 59, 64 ("The rise of Neurodiversity takes postmodern fragmentation one step further. Just as the postmodern era sees every once too solid belief melt into air, even our most taken-for granted assumptions . . . that we all more or less see, feel, touch, hear, smell, and sort information, in more or less the same way, (unless visibly disabled) . . . are being dissolved."). Moreover, thinking about the social model in relation to mental disability can be fruitful across a range of contexts; for instance, a social-model perspective can make more visible and more plausible ways to change the environment to reduce conflict surrounding a mental disability. Cf., e.g., *Groner v. Golden Gate Apts.*, 250 F.3d 1039 (6th Cir. 2001) (considering but dismissing as unreasonable the idea of soundproofing apartments to address a conflict between neighbors, one of whom screams and slams doors at night, behavior that both parties concede stems from his schizophrenia).

56. The National Senior Citizens Law Center (NSCLC), "Our Mission," http://www.nsclc.org/NSCLC/about-us/whoweare.

57. Florida Scott-Maxwell, *The Measure of My Days* (New York: Penguin Books, 1968), 32.

58. See, e.g., CyberNation International, Age and Aging: Quotes to Inspire, http://www.cybernation.com/victory/quotations/subjects/quotes_ ageandaging.html ("It is a rare and difficult attainment to grow old gracefully and happily.") (quoting R. Palmer).

59. Brief for Legal Services for the Elderly Poor, the National Council of Senior Citizens et al., as Amici Curiae Supporting Respondent at 14, Massachusetts Board of Retirement v. Murgia, 427 U.S. 307 (1976) (No. 74-1044), 1975 WL 173591.

60. Gretchen B. Dianda and Betty. J. Hofmayer, eds., *Older and Wiser* (New York: Fawcett Books, 1995).

61. See, e.g., sources cited in note 64.

62. See Cheryl Laz, "Act Your Age," *Sociological Forum*, March 1998, at 85.

63. See Elizabeth F. Emens, "Aggravating Youth: *Roper v. Simmons* and Age Discrimination," *Supreme Court Review* 51 (2005) (explaining the distinction between youth liberationists and protectionists and discussing examples of youth liberationists going so far as to oppose an age-based cutoff for the death penalty because such line drawing is paternalistic).

64. John Holt, *Escape from Childhood* (Boston: Dutton, 1974), 25–26; see also Brian A. Dominick and Sara Zia, "Young and Oppressed: Revolution Kid Style," *Liberating Youth*, November 13, 2008 (Behind Enemy Lines Publications 1996), http://www.zcommunications.org/young-and-oppressed -revolution-kid-style-by-brian-dominick ("*Youth* is not necessarily possessed

only by those who are young in age. It is a state of mind which can be attained by anyone, was once possessed by everyone, but is rarely present in anyone beyond adolescence.").

65. See, e.g., The American Society for Aesthetic Plastic Surgery, http://www.surgery.org/consumers/consumer-resources/news-and-trends/Despite-Recession-Overall-%20Plastic-Surgery (documenting nearly three million Botox procedures in 2009).

66. Whether those traditional assumptions *permit* or *encourage* such efforts seems to turn in part on the gender of the ager. Women are more likely to be criticized for failing to combat the aging process; in common parlance, a woman may be accused of "letting herself go." I thank Kathy Abrams for this point.

67. See, e.g., Anne Bloom, "Life in Plastics: Law, Medicine and Aesthetics," 4 (unpublished manuscript, on file with author) (observing that plaintiffs bringing suits against plastic surgeons fare worse than plaintiffs in other medical malpractice suits because juries appear to blame the victim for trying to "mess with nature" in the first place); see also Anne Bloom, "To Be Real: Sexual Identity Politics in Tort Litigation," *North Carolina Law Review* 88 (2010): 357, 390; Victoria Pitts-Taylor, *Surgery Junkies: Wellness and Pathology in Cosmetic Culture* (New Brunswick, NJ: Rutgers University Press, 2007).

68. That some might find their claims absurd doesn't stop some advocates in other areas, such as sex/gender, but the spectrum of what might be plausibly considered cultural rather than biological seems much wider with sex.

69. Of course, the same is true for disability, yet a more robust social model seems to have more uptake with advocacy arguments surrounding disability.

70. E.g., Thomas R. Cole, Preface to *Voices and Visions of Aging: Toward a Critical Gerontology*, ed. Thomas R. Cole et al. (New York: Springer, 1993), xxxix.

71. See, e.g., W. Willard Wirtz, The Older American Worker: Age Discrimination in Employment, Report of the Secretary of Labor to Congress 5–9 (June 1965) [hereinafter "Wirtz Report"]; *Smith v. City of Jackson*, 544 U.S. 228 (2005); *General Dynamics Land Systems, Inc. v. Cline*, 540 U.S. 581 (2004).

72. See, e.g., United Nations Programme on Ageing, "New Age for All Ages," http://www.un.org/esa/socdev/ageing/society_newage.html ("It is helpful to think of the individual and society as two entities living in a symbiotic relationship. And just as individual lives are changing, so too is group life, whether this be the family, neighborhood, extended community or nation. Ageing and migration are factors changing group demographic

structures. And the evolution of values as, for example, regarding the advancement of women, is having a profound impact on the various roles and relationships within social groups."); Robert Venne, United Nations Programme on Ageing, "Mainstreaming the Concerns of Older People into the Social Development Agenda," http://www.un.org/esa/socdev/ageing/mainstreaming.html ("Age is one of the characteristics of social differentiation. While being a biological fact, the perception of age is nevertheless socially constructed.").

73. Budget figures for 2010 are nearly $1.6 billion for the Administration on Aging and $450 billion for Medicare, which covers people age sixty-five and older and people with certain disabilities. See Administration and Aging Homepage: Legislation and Budget, http://www.aoa.gov/AoARoot/About/Budget/docs/AoA_Appropriation_FY2010.pdf; Office of Management and Budget Homepage: Department of Health and Human Services, http://www.whitehouse.gov/sites/default/files/omb/budget/fy2011/assets/health.pdf.

74. Age Discrimination in Employment Act of 1967, 29 U.S.C. §§ 621–634 (2000).

75. Antidiscrimination spending is in the millions, rather than the billions. Recent figures for federal civil rights and antidiscrimination efforts (for all covered groups) suggest total spending of less than $800 million, in contrast to the billions spent on disease control and prevention, Medicare, and other aging support (see note 73). Budget requests of relevant agencies involved in antidiscrimination efforts (for FY 2011, unless stated otherwise), as reported on their websites, were as follows: DOJ: Civil Rights Division ($114 million), HHS: Office for Civil Rights ($44 million), EEOC ($385 million), U.S. Commission on Civil Rights ($8.8 million; from 2008), HUD ($48 million), DOE Office for Civil Rights ($105 million; 2011 request), DOL Office of Federal Contract Compliance Programs ($113 million; 2011 request).

76. Compare FY 2010 Centers for Disease Control and Prevention Justification of Estimates for Appropriation Committees, http://www.cdc.gov/fmo/topic/Budget%20Information/appropriations_budget_form_pdf/FY2011_CDC_CJ_Final.pdf (citing the budget for the Centers for Disease Control for fiscal year 2011 at a total of $10.6 billion, a similar number to the budgets from 2010, which exceeded $10 billion); with note 75 (describing funding for antidiscrimination efforts).

77. Evelynn M. Hammonds, "Straw Men and Their Followers: The Return of Biological Race," Social Science Research Council (June 7, 2006), http://raceandgenomics.ssrc.org/Hammonds/.

78. Richard J. Herrnstein and Charles Murray, *The Bell Curve: Intelligence and Class Structure in American Life* (New York: Free Press, 1996). On

the controversy, see, among many other examples, the dedicated issue of *The New Republic.* Adrian Wooldrigde, "Bell Curve Liberals," *The New Republic,* February 27, 1995, at 22.

79. Sally Satel, "I Am a Racially Profiling Doctor," *New York Times,* May 5, 2002, at 56.

80. Armand Marie Leroi, "A Family Tree in Every Gene," *New York Times,* March 14, 2005, at A1.

81. See Social Science Research Council, "Is Race 'Real'?," http://race andgenomics.ssrc.org.

82. See, e.g., Merlin Chowkwanyun and Justin Shubow, *A TNR Debate: Race Riot, The New Republic* (online), June 13–15, 2007. Although the slavery hypothesis to explain hypertension rates has been widely discredited as a scientific matter (*see* Chowkwanyun, ibid.) (citing sources), the argument continues to arise in popular contexts. See, e.g., *Black in America: The Black Woman and Family,* CNN (aired July 23, 2008).

83. The apparent lack of "prejudice" associated with hypertension seems to have made it an appealing choice for Ely in explaining why not all invisible traits warrant the judicial solicitude that he thinks homosexuality warrants. See John Hart Ely, *Democracy and Distrust* (Cambridge, MA: Harvard University Press, 1980), 162. The ADA has rightly made hypertension more controversial, in part through the Court's failure to recognize just how many jobs exclude those who have it. See *Murphy v. UPS,* 527 U.S. 516 (1999) (where a mechanic, who was fired because he had hypertension that prevented him from obtaining necessary health certification for operation of commercial vehicles, was not "regarded as" disabled for purposes of the ADA); Bagenstos, "Subordination, Stigma, and 'Disability,'" 511–12.

84. See Barbara Flagg, "The Souls of White Folk" (unpublished manuscript dated Dec. 19, 2007, on file with author); see also Stein, *The Mismeasure of Desire,* 46 ("It is widely believed—despite significant evidence to the contrary—that race is biologically based."). The phrase "there there," used in this way, is generally attributed to Gertrude Stein, *Everybody's Autobiography* (New York: Vintage Books, 1973).

85. See, e.g., starting with R. C. Lewontin, "Confusions about Human Races," Social Science Research Council, June 7, 2006, http://raceand genomics.ssrc.org/Lewontin/; see also note 110 (quoting the Supreme Court's favorable rendering of this argument).

86. See Jacqueline Stevens, "Eve Is from Adam's Rib, the Earth Is Flat, and Races Come from Genes," Social Science Research Council, June 7, 2006, http://raceandgenomics.ssrc.org/Stevens/.

87. See SallySatelMd.com, *Erratum,* http://www.sallysatelmd.com/ html/a-nytimes3.html. The correction was of a colleague's assertion that

African Americans tend to salivate more, so he gives them a drying agent during intubation, the process of inserting a breathing tube in a windpipe. Apparently, there's no basis for this asserted racial difference.

88. See, e.g., Judith B. Kaplan and Trude Bennett, "Use of Race and Ethnicity in Biomedical Publication," *Journal of the American Medical Association* 20 (2003): 2709–16; Adolph Reed Jr, "Making Sense of Race, I.: The Ideology of Race, the Biology of Human Variation, and the Problem of Medical and Public Health Research," *Journal of Race and Policy* 7 (2005): 11–42 ; Nancy Krieger, "If 'Race' Is the Answer, What Is the Question?— On 'Race,' Racism, Health: A Social Epidemiologist's Perspective," *Social Science Research Council*, June 7, 2006, http://raceandgenomics.ssrc.org/ Krieger/.

89. Thoughtful accounts of the social construction of race abound, but this section discusses only biological accounts of race, because the question here is whether race, if it could be understood as biological, would be immutable.

90. See, e.g., Thomas Fuller, "A Vision of Pale Beauty Carries Risks for Asia's Women," *New York Times*, May 14, 2006, http://www.nytimes.com/ 2006/05/14/world/asia/14thailand.html. These tend to work by inhibiting melanin, absorbing UV rays, or burning off outer lays of skin with acid. Potential side effects include ochronisis (dark patches) and leukoderma (pink patches, resulting from skin's losing its ability to produce pigment). More serious effects are less certain but may include mercury poisoning or cancer. See S. Allen Counter, "Whitening Skin Can Be Deadly," *Boston Globe*, December 16, 2003, http://www.boston.com/news/globe/health _science/articles/2003/12/16/whitening_skin_can_be_deadly/; Mawusi Afele, "Women in Ghana Ignore Warnings about Dangers of Bleaching Skin," *Chicago Sun-Times*, November 13, 1988, http://www.highbeam.com/ doc/1P2-3914043.html.

91. John Howard Griffin, *Black Like Me* (New York: Penguin Books, 1961); Robert Bonazzi, *Man in the Mirror: John Howard Griffin and the Story of Black Like Me* (New York: Orbis Books, 1997). Fictional uses of darkening pills appear in Armistead Maupin's *Tales of the City* (San Francisco: Chronicle, 1978) and in the film *Soul Man* (New World Pictures, 1986).

92. Bonazzi, *Man in the Mirror*, 38–39 (quoting John Howard Griffin, *Racial Equality: The Myth and the Reality*, Iowa University Center for Labor and Management (1970)).

93. Bonazzi, *Man in the Mirror*, 38.

94. Psychologists disagree as to whether cross-race facial identification problems are symmetrical or asymmetrical and in what direction, as well as on the cause of cross-racial misrecognition. See, e.g., Daniel T. Levin, "Race as a Visual Feature: Using Visual Search and Perceptual

Discrimination Tasks to Understand Face Categories and the Cross-Race Recognition Deficit," *Journal of Experimental Psychology* 129 (2000): 559.

95. Blepharoplasty, also known as eye-widening or double-eyelid surgery, is surgery to put a pretarsal crease in eyes that are smooth rather than folded; approximately 50 percent of Pacific Asians have a pretarsal crease. Charles S. Lee, Blepharoplasty, Asian, WebMD, February 13, 2008, http://www.emedicine.com/plastic/topic425.htm. The surgery costs approximately $2000. According to the American Academy of Facial, Plastic and Reconstructive Surgery, approximately 125,000 blepharoplasty procedures were performed in 2000 in the United States, and the numbers have been increasing; it is the most popular form of plastic surgery in Asia. See also Sandy Kobrin, "Asian-Americans Criticize Eyelid Surgery Craze," *We-News*, August 15, 2004, http://www.womensenews.org/article.cfm/dyn/aid/1950/context/cover/.

96. Geoffrey R. Stone, Commentary, "If America Only Had One Mixed Race," *Chicago Tribune*, March 30, 1999, at 17 (reprinting Stone's University of Chicago Centennial Contribution).

97. See Elizabeth F. Emens, "Intimate Discrimination: The State's Role in the Accidents of Sex and Love," *Harvard Law Review* 122 (2009): 1307, 1382–85 (elaborating, though not endorsing, a range of such alternatives).

98. Ira Katznelson, *When Affirmative Action Was White: An Untold History of Racial Inequality in Twentieth-Century America* (New York: Norton, 2005).

99. See notes 73–76 (discussing funding levels for agencies that support aging and disease, as opposed to expenditures for antidiscrimination efforts).

100. See, e.g., Cheryl I. Harris, "Whiteness as Property," *Harvard Law Review* 106 (1993): 1709, 1738; Lisa C. Ikemoto, "In the Shadow of Race: Women of Color in Health Disparities Policy," *University of California at Davis Law Review* 39 (2006): 1023, 1041 n.63.

101. Ruth Hubbard, "Genomania and Health," *American Scientist* 83 (Jan./Feb. 1995): 8.

102. Kari Balog, Note, "Equal Protection for Homosexuals: Why the Immutability Argument Is Necessary and How It Is Met," *Cleveland State Law Review* 53 (2005–2006): 545, 564.

103. See, e.g., Suzanne Goldberg, "Equality without Tiers," *Southern California Law Review* 77 (2004): 481 (discussing and critiquing the doctrine); Halley, "Sexual Orientation and the Politics of Biology," 507 (discussing them as "factors," not "requirements"). The heightened-scrutiny analysis is notably inexact, as many scholars have noted. See, e.g., Cass R. Sunstein, "Homosexuality and the Constitution," *Indiana Law Journal* 70 (1994): 1; Yoshino, "Assimilationist Bias in Equal Protection."

104. The first three quotations come from *San Antonio Indep. Sch. Dist.*

v. Rodriguez, 411 U.S. 1, 28 (1973) (rejecting a challenge by poor families to a state education system supported by property taxes as implicating neither a suspect classification nor a fundamental right). Immutability, so called, first appeared in *Frontiero v. Richardson,* 411 U.S. 677 (1973) (plurality opinion); see text accompanying notes 108–9.

105. See, e.g., Goldberg, "Equality without Tiers"; Sunstein, "Homosexuality and the Constitution," 9 (characterizing immutability as neither necessary nor sufficient for suspect-class status); Laurence H. Tribe, "The Puzzling Persistence of Process-Based Constitutional Theories," *Yale Law Journal* 89 (1980): 1063, 1073 (same, for "features like immutability"); Yoshino, "Assimilationist Bias in Equal Protection"; Stein, *The Mismeasure of Desire,* 3 n.8 (arguing that the Court essentially embraces Ely's critique of immutability in *Cleburne* and "has rarely even mentioned immutability as a factor in equal protection analysis" since *Cleburne*); Halley, "Sexual Orientation and the Politics of Biology."

106. To discuss the immutability analysis might seem a poor use of pages, given that ten years earlier a discussion of immutability was described as "tantamount to cataloguing new ways to flog a dying horse." Yoshino, "Assimilationist Bias in Equal Protection," 491; see also Stein, *The Mismeasure of Desire,* 3 n.8. But, while it may still go too far to say it is "a live issue at the litigation level," as it was in 1998 (Yoshino, "Assimilationist Bias in Equal Protection," 491 n.19), immutability continues to be debated in the courts in recent years. See, e.g., *In re Marriage Cases,* 43 Cal.4th 757 (2008) (discussing the immutability prong in a decision holding that sexual orientation is a suspect classification under the California Constitution and noting that, while immutability "is not invariably required" under the California Constitution's equal protection clause, sexual orientation is "so integral an aspect of a person's identity [that] it is not appropriate to require a person to repudiate or change [it] to avoid discriminatory treatment").

107. See *Korematsu v. United States,* 323 U.S. 214, 216 (1944).

108. *Frontiero v. Richardson,* 411 U.S. 677 (1973) (plurality opinion).

109. *Frontiero,* 411 U.S. at 686 (quoting *Weber v. Aetna Casualty & Surety Co.,* 406 U.S. 164, 175 (1972)).

110. See *Saint Francis College v. Al-Khazraji,* 481 U.S. 604, 610 n.4 (1987) ("Many modern biologists and anthropologists . . . criticize racial classifications as arbitrary and of little use in understanding the variability of human beings. . . . The particular traits which have generally been chosen to characterize races have been criticized as having little biological significance. It has been found that differences between individuals of the same race are often greater than the differences between the 'average' individuals of different races. These observations and others have led some, but

not all, scientists to conclude that racial classifications are for the most part socio-political, rather than biological, in nature.").

111. Occasional lower courts have recognized the potential mutability of sex and race. See *Tanner*, 971 P.2d at 446 ("Both alienage and religious affiliation may be changed almost at will. For that matter, given modern technology, so also may gender."); *Watkins v. U.S. Army*, 847 F.2d 1329, 1347 (9th Cir. 1988) ("People can have operations to change their sex. . . . Lighter skinned blacks can sometimes 'pass' for white, as can Latinos for Anglos, and some people can even change their racial appearance with pigment injections."), *superseded by* 875 F.2d 699 (9th Cir. 1989) (en banc).

112. The Court considered this question before the introduction of intermediate scrutiny.

113. *Murgia v. Mass. Bd. of Retirement*, 427 U.S. 307 (1976) (per curiam).

114. See, e.g., Ely, *Democracy and Distrust*, 150; *Watkins*, 847 F.2d at 1347 (citing cases that do not mention immutability).

115. Compare, e.g., Tribe, "Puzzling Persistence," 1073 n.51 ("Old age is an immutable characteristic"), and Alison Barnes, "Envisioning a Future for Age and Disability Discrimination Claims," *University of Michigan Journal of Law Reform* 35 (Fall 2001/Winter 2002): 263, 264 n.7 ("Age and disability also differ from race in that individuals may move into the category, while race is immutable."); and text accompanying note 125.

116. *Murgia*, 427 U.S. at 313.

117. The fact of sharing a trait or potentially sharing a trait with a subordinated group does not necessarily lead to empathy, however. See, e.g., Yoshino, "Assimilationist Bias in Equal Protection," 510–18; text accompanying note 41 (discussing Harlan Hahn's notion of existential anxiety in relation to disability); Emens, "Aggravating Youth," 98–100.

118. *Murgia*, 427 U.S. at 313–14.

119. See *General Dynamics Land Systems, Inc. v. Cline*, 540 U.S. 581 (2004); see also note 71.

120. Ely, *Democracy and Distrust*, 60.

121. Ibid.

122. Age seems immutable at least with regard to one's years of age and any notion of old age that depends on a particular age cutoff. If one understands old age to concern what age someone "acts" or even one's health status, then that person may have some effect on it. *Murgia* involved a mandatory retirement age of fifty, so a cutoff was involved.

123. *Frontiero*, 411 U.S. at 686 (quoting *Weber*, 406 U.S. at 175). Ely and others also discuss this idea of whether a trait is in your control as importantly related to whether laws can be understood to be rationally trying to incentivize the trait. See Ely, *Democracy and Distrust*, 154 ("It would not make sense, however, to defend a law disadvantaging blacks on the ground

that we are trying to discourage people from being black."); see also Janet E. Halley, "The Politics of the Closet: Toward Equal Protection for Gay, Lesbian, and Bisexual Identity," *University of California Los Angeles Law Review* 36 (1989): 915, 927–29.

124. One may, however, affect the timing of getting out of it, through suicide or through the care taken with one's health and life.

125. D. Aaron Lacy, "You Are Not Quite as Old as You Think: Making the Case for Reverse Age Discrimination," *Berkeley Journal of Employment and Labor Law* 26 (2005): 363, 397.

126. *City of Cleburne, Tex. v. Cleburne Living Center*, 473 U.S. 432 (1985) (mental retardation); see also *Schweiker v. Wilson*, 450 U.S. 221 (1981) (obliquely, mental illness); *Bd. of Trustees of the Univ. of Alabama v. Garrett*, 531 U.S. 356, 366 (2001) (favorably revisiting the reasoning in *Cleburne*).

127. See also notes 34–35 and accompanying text. There are, of course, other means of entering and exiting disability, which are within one's control or not to varying degrees. For instance, a car accident could be entirely one's fault, not at all, or partially; cancer could be due to genetics or a toxic environment or smoking.

128. As Justice Marshall points out, the Court's conclusion that the classification does not warrant heightened scrutiny is dictum; because the Court struck down the ordinance, it did not need to reach the question. See *Cleburne*, 473 U.S. at 473–75 (Marshall, J., concurring in part and dissenting in part).

129. *Cleburne*, 473 U.S. at 442 (emphasis added). On this division of the world into "two classes of persons, normal and abnormal," see Martha Minow, "When Difference Has Its Home: Group Homes for the Mentally Retarded, Equal Protection and the Legal Treatment of Difference," *Harvard Civil Rights-Civil Liberties Law Review* 22 (1987): 111, 120–21.

130. Determinations of intelligence and related functioning can be meaningfully affected, however, by various educational techniques and contextual factors. See, e.g., Anita Silvers and Michael Ashley Stein, "Disability, Equal Protection, and the Supreme Court: Standing at the Crossroads of Progressive and Retrogressive Logic in Constitutional Classification," *University of Michigan Journal of Law Reform* 35 (2001): 81, 107.

131. And the Court favorably invoked the reasoning in *Cleburne* in considering Title I of the ADA's application to the states in *Garrett*, which involved physical disabilities. *Bd. of Trustees of the Univ. of Alabama v. Garrett*, 531 U.S. 356, 366 (2001).

132. *Cleburne*, 473 U.S. at 442, 445–46 (emphasis added) ("[I]f the large and amorphous class of the mentally retarded were deemed quasi-suspect for the reasons given by the Court of Appeals, it would be difficult to find a principled way to distinguish a variety of other groups who have

perhaps immutable disabilities setting them off from others, who cannot themselves mandate the desired legislative responses, and who can claim some degree of prejudice from at least part of the public at large. One need mention in this respect only the aging, the disabled, the mentally ill, and the infirm."). The Court later referred to this passage as "prescient." *Garrett*, 531 U.S. at 366.

133. *Cleburne*, 473 U.S. at 445 (quoting Ely, *Democracy and Distrust*, 150). Interestingly, disability is frequently Ely's example to show the outer limits of heightened scrutiny. See, e.g., Ely, *Democracy and Distrust*, 154–55, 156, 163.

134. See Jill Elaine Hasday, "Mitigation and the Americans with Disabilities Act," *Michigan Law Review* 103 (2004): 217. On choosing to remain or become disabled, see, for example, Elizabeth Loeb, "Cutting It Off: Bodily Integrity, Identity Disorders, and the Sovereign Stakes of Corporeal Desire in U.S. Law," *Women's Studies Quarterly* 36 (2008); Emens, "Intimate Discrimination," 1347; note 33.

135. The Court's ease in implying that mental illness is not necessarily immutable reflects the divide between the unreality attributed to mental illness and the reality assumed of physical disability, discussed earlier. *Schweiker*, 450 U.S. at 229 n.11 ("The [district] court also *acknowledged* that '[i]t is debatable whether and to what extent the mental illness is an immutable characteristic determined solely by the accident of birth.'" (citations omitted; emphasis added)). See note 54.

136. This category, along with mental retardation, has been the occasion for the Court to strike down statutes (or particular applications, in the case of *Cleburne*) using so-called rational basis with teeth. For a discussion of the narrow scope of *Cleburne*, see Silvers and Stein, "Disability, Equal Protection, and the Supreme Court."

137. See, e.g., Stein, *The Mismeasure of Desire*; Goldberg, "Equality without Tiers," 485–86, 502 n.84 (reviewing cases); see also, e.g., *Watkins v. U.S. Army*, 847 F.2d 1329 (9th Cir. 1988) (finding heightened scrutiny for sexual orientation), *superseded by* 875 F.2d 699 (9th Cir. 1989) (en banc). In the recent federal challenge to California's ban on same-sex marriage, the district judge stated that strict scrutiny applies, both because the marriage ban implicates the fundamental right to marry and because the ban relies on the suspect classification of sexual orientation. The judge went on to conclude, however, that strict scrutiny review was "unnecessary," because the ban would fall even under rational-basis review. *See Perry v. Schwarzenegger*, 704 F. Supp. 2d 921, 997 (N.D. Cal. 2010), aff'd *Perry v. Brown*, 671 F.3d 1052 (9th Cir. 2012). On the state level, the California Supreme Court has held that sexual orientation warrants strict scrutiny under the state constitution. *In re Marriage Cases*, 43 Cal.4th 757 (2008).

138. The Supreme Court has, however, given meaningful credit to arguments that sexual orientation is historically contingent. See *Lawrence v. Texas*, 539 U.S. 558, 568–69 (2003).

139. Suzanne B. Goldberg, "On Making Anti-Essentialist and Constructivist Arguments in Court," *Oregon Law Review* 81 (2002): 629, 657 (arguing that courts respond better to arguments of biological or essential difference, at least for traits that are not readily apparent to courts, because arguments that difference is socially constructed make courts uncomfortably aware of their own role in creating the category).

140. See, e.g., Balog, "Equal Protection for Homosexuals," 565. As has been noted elsewhere, some litigators have pointedly avoided arguing from biology. See, e.g., Stein, *The Mismeasure of Desire* (discussing, inter alia, the decision in *Baker v. State*, 744 A.2d 864, 867 (Vt. 1999)).

141. In other words, a surgeon could make the brain smaller, most simply by cutting out part of it.

142. See, e.g., *Hewitt v. Alcan Aluminum Corporation*, 185 F.Supp.2d 183, 188–89 (N.D.N.Y. 2001) (concluding that a plaintiff who could mitigate PTSD by taking medication and chooses not to do so is not a "qualified individual with a disability" for purposes of protection under the statute); *Johnson v. Maynard*, No. 01 Civ. 7393 (AKH), slip op. at 4 (S.D.N.Y. Feb. 20, 2003) ("Since plaintiff had medication available to her, and knew that she could function normally if she took it, she cannot be said to have been substantially impaired if she neglected to avail herself of such corrective measures."); *Mont-Ros v. City of West Miami*, 111 F. Supp. 2d 1338, 1356–57 (S.D. Fla. 2000) ("Additionally, Plaintiff's sleep apnea condition is treatable and can be corrected with either of the following: (1) weight loss, (2) use of a nasal CPAP machine, and/or (3) the UPPP surgical procedure"). Thus, because Plaintiff's sleep apnea condition is treatable and can be corrected with the use of a CPAP machine at night, Plaintiff cannot demonstrate that he is "substantially limited in a major life activity."); see Hasday, "Mitigation and the Americans with Disabilities Act, " 237–39 (citing cases).

143. *Tangires v. Johns Hopkins Hosp.*, 79 F.Supp.2d 587 (D. Md. 2000), aff'd 230 F.3d 1354 (4th Cir. 2000) (unpublished opinion).

144. I plan to discuss this issue and the relation between accommodation and mitigation in a future project, provisionally entitled "Disability's Work." Though my view was based on the ADA as originally enacted, these mitigation cases are further undermined by the ADA Amendments Act of 2008, which seeks "to reject the requirement enunciated by the Supreme Court in Sutton v. United Air Lines, Inc., 527 U.S. 471 (1999) and its companion cases that whether an impairment substantially limits a major life activity is to be determined with reference to the ameliorative effects of mitigating measures," and the statute does so, with an exception for "ordinary

eye glasses or contact lenses." See ADA Amendments Act, S. 3406 (2008), http://www.govtrack.us/congress/billtext.xpd?bill=s110-3406.

145. See Hasday, "Mitigation and the Americans with Disabilities Act," 237–40 (citing cases and arguing for a mitigation requirement on a reasonableness standard). For a recent articulation of a contrary view, see, for instance, Jeannette Cox, " 'Corrective Surgery' and the Americans with Disabilities Act," *San Diego Law Review* 46 (2009): 113.

146. See, e.g., *In re Marriage of Simmons*, 355 Ill. App. 3d 942, 949 (2005) ("According to [the doctors], the sex change procedure is still 'in process' and has not been completed, and there are still other procedures which must be done in order to complete the sex reassignment or change. Therefore, the mere issuance of a new birth certificate cannot, legally speaking, make petitioner a male."). Altering biology isn't always sufficient; Yoshino identifies a particular kind of essentialism that frames some courts' acceptance of trans litigants' postoperative sex as their sex—an essentialism that has "shifted from body to soul." Yoshino, "Covering," 922.

147. See text accompanying note 51.

148. Alexander Pope, "Essay on Man," *in Poetry and Prose of Alexander Pope*, ed. Aubrey Williams (Boston: Houghton Mifflin, 1969), 130.

149. See note 105 (citing sources); Halley, "Sexual Orientation and the Politics of Biology."

12

NATURE, CULTURE, AND SOCIAL ENGINEERING: REFLECTIONS ON EVOLUTION AND EQUALITY

LINDA C. MCCLAIN

1. INTRODUCING THE PROBLEM

In the United States, evidence of the success of legal feminism's equality project is visible in the constitutional commitment to equal opportunity and prohibitions against legislating based on fixed notions about gender roles,[1] as well as in the move toward greater sex equality in family law and other areas of private law.[2] However, sex inequality persists, and substantive equality remains elusive.[3] Social cooperation between women and men in various domains of society is assumed to be a fundamental and necessary building block of society, but it proves hard to secure on terms of equality.

Why is sex equality so hard to achieve? One answer is that feminist quests for equality in private and public life are a form of misguided social engineering that ignores natural sex difference, hardwired by evolution, as it were, into male and female brains. This chapter examines arguments that nature constrains feminist law reform. Appeals to *nature* argue that brain science and evolutionary psychology find salient differences between women and men, limiting what social engineering can achieve in fostering sex equality or reforming family law. These contemporary claims,

347

cast in the language of hardwired brain circuitry, may signal a new form of the sameness-difference debate: that is, what are the real differences between the sexes, and what difference does difference make for law and policy? As such, they invite scrutiny by legal feminists.

This chapter points out a curious feature in some appeals to natural difference: even as critiques of feminist social engineering invoke nature, problems posed by nature feature as a reason to embrace social engineering in the form of the social institution of marriage. This view of nature is distinct from the conservative religious argument that, because marriage—"the natural family" —*reflects* the created order, feminist social engineering of the family is dangerous.[4]

The appeal to differences between "male" and "female" brains as "hardwired" and a potent explanation for the persistence of gender differences and sex inequality garners charges of "neurosexism." Critics offer as cautionary tales many historical examples of claims that basic differences between the male and female brain explained the basic inferiority of females and their unsuitability for many male-occupied spheres.[5] They also criticize the underlying studies and experiments on which claims about sex differences and their implications rest. For legal scholars, these historical examples resonate with classic examples of how jurists appealed to basic differences between women and men to rationalize women's exclusion from full participation in society. As a legal scholar, I shall not attempt to assess the adequacy of the science of sex differences. Instead, I shall draw on careful work by scientists and philosophers that reveals the flaws of this body of work. Dichotomies with profound implications for assessing sex roles and the possibility of social engineering rest on startlingly flimsy evidence. Such flimsy foundations for far-reaching claims about sex difference are of obvious concern when the question is whether hardwired, natural differences between men and women doom any feminist efforts at social engineering to promote greater equality. Neuroscience, the philosopher Cordelia Fine argues, gives a "fresh zing" to "old stereotypes."[6]

I link recent popularizing accounts of male and female brains with accounts of evolutionary science concerning human mate selection and parenting because evolution often features in accounts of the origin of sex differences. Popularizing works such as neuropsychiatrist Louann Brizendine's companion books, *The Female Brain* and *The Male Brain*, refer repeatedly to how our "Stone Age" brains and their ancient "circuitry" shape our contemporary desires and behaviors.[7] Deterministic language about brains being on "autopilot" or nature just "taking its course" envisions men and women being driven by processes that operate at an unconscious level. A common element is appeal to difference rooted in evolution to explain persistence of sex inequality and to sound a cautionary note about social engineering. Supposed hardwired brain differences feature in explanations for all manner of social practices and for why equality is hard to attain. My focus is primarily on gender relations with respect to egalitarian marriage and work/life balance (or work/family conflict). I observe the tension between the view that intractable, and likely innate, gender differences doom efforts at social engineering to change gender roles and the view that, in light of changing economic and demographic trends, men, in particular, should adapt and that public policy can employ social engineering to encourage the evolution of new understandings of manhood, fatherhood, and masculinity.

2. Appeals to Nature as a Constraint on Equality

Male and Female Brains and Evolutionary Psychology

The appeal to *nature* as a constraint on equality enlists brain science and evolutionary psychology, which reportedly find salient differences between women and men, linked to different reproductive biology and reproductive strategies. These differences limit what social engineering can achieve.

In the 1990s, a flurry of books, including Robert Wright's *The Moral Animal*[8] and David Buss's *The Evolution of Desire*,[9] introduced basic concepts of evolutionary psychology and sociobiology, proposing that science shed light on sex difference, why men and women had different views about the harm of rape and sexual harassment, and why they made different choices about work-family balance.[10] Wright criticized feminist legal theorists for avoiding science. He argued that "many of the differences between men and women are more stubborn than most feminists would like, and complicate the quest for—even the definition of—social equality between the sexes."[11] In the early twenty-first century, brain science rivets popular attention. Once again, evolution presents limits to social engineering and affirms sex difference. Enthusing about Brizendine's work in popular science, *The Female Brain*,[12] the journalist David Brooks opined: "Once radicals dreamed of new ways of living, but now happiness seems to consist of living in harmony with the patterns that nature and evolution laid down long, long ago."[13]

What are these differences, and what patterns do they prescribe? Brizendine declares that "more than 99 percent of male and female genetic coding is exactly the same," but the 1 percent difference "influences every single cell in our bodies."[14] The inside flap of the book cover of *The Female Brain* promises neurological explanations for such sex differences as these:

- "A woman uses about 20,000 words per day, while a man uses about 7,000."
- "A woman knows what people are feeling, while a man can't spot an emotion unless somebody cries or threatens bodily harm."
- "Thoughts about sex enter a woman's brain once every couple of days but enter a man's brain about once every minute."

Brizendine turns to evolutionary theory to explain the roots of brain differences. However, she is not quietist about human nature. Biology need not be destiny *if* we understand how evolutionary, biological, and cultural forces shape us. Social engineering *informed* by biology holds promise:

> Biology powerfully affects us but does not lock in our reality. We can alter that reality and use our intelligence and determination both to celebrate and, when necessary, to change the effects of sex hormones on brain structure, behavior, reality, creativity—and destiny.[15]

What does this interplay of biology and human will suggest about social cooperation on terms of equality? I focus on Brizendine's use of evolutionary theory to interpret brain difference and its implications for intimate and family life. (I do not here assess whether Brizendine gets the science of brain difference right, though later in the chapter I will discuss criticisms by scientists that she does not.)[16]

The "Stone Age" Female Brain

Contemporary females, Brizendine asserts, inherit the "ancient circuitry" of "our most successful foremothers."[17] Teenage girls' drive for social connection with each other has biological and hormonal reasons. Intimacy "activates the pleasure centers in a girl's brain," triggering a near-orgasmic "major dopamine and oxytocin rush."[18] Girls are motivated "on a molecular and a neurological level" to "ease and even prevent social conflict" and to "maintain . . . the relationship at all costs."[19] These findings sound similar to those made by Carol Gilligan and her colleagues on how girls work to maintain connection.[20]

Connection among females has evolutionary roots as a strategy of protection against aggressive males, evident in studies of female mammals that develop stress responses to "tend and befriend" and to form social groups "that promote safety and reduce distress for the self and offspring."[21] "These female networks" also share infant care and "information about where to find food" and model "maternal behavior for younger females."[22] Social connectedness, thus, contributes to reproductive success.[23] Today's teen females, as they "reach" optimal fertility, undertake similar strategies.[24]

Competition is as hardwired as cooperation. Brizendine attributes the "biology of mean girls"—the harsh tactics of teen-girl cliques—to a "survival" strategy of "sexual competition" for the best male mates, a "biological imperative to compete for sexual attractiveness."[25] Success, for both sexes, requires "some aggression," and relevant hormone levels rise during puberty.[26]

Our "Stone Age brains" also shape mate selection, sex, and motherhood.[27] Brizendine repeats evolutionary psychology's familiar story of the male who chases and the female who chooses, claiming that it is "not sex stereotyping" but "the brain architecture of love, engineered by the reproductive winners in evolution."[28] Contemporary couples proceed "down an ancient pair-bonding path," over which they have "little control."[29]

Brizendine draws on Buss's influential work on the different qualities women and men seek in mates.[30] Women are "less concerned with a potential husband's visual appeal and more interested in his material resources and social status" and prefer a slightly older partner.[31] "Scientists conclude" that these "universal" mate preferences are part of the "inherited architecture of the female brain's mate-choice system" and are "presumed to serve a purpose."[32]

What purpose? Brizendine turns to the evolutionary biology scholar Robert Trivers, who explains female mate selection as a sound investment strategy stemming from women's limited number of eggs and their greater investment than men in bearing and raising children. A man "can impregnate a woman with one act of intercourse and walk away"; a woman is "left with nine months of pregnancy, the perils of childbirth, months of breast feeding," and "trying to ensure that child's survival."[33] Ancient necessities led females to seek long-term male partners to ensure reproductive success; those who "faced these challenges alone were less likely to have been successful in propagating their genes."[34] Brizendine is skeptical about whether contemporary "single motherhood . . . will succeed," noting that, even today, "in some primitive cultures," a father's presence enhances a child's survival rates, making a female's "safest bet" a long-term male partner to offer protection and improved access to "food, shelter and other resources."[35] In effect, women's need for protection and provision explains the so-called sex contract posited by evolutionary theorists.

Men's ancient brain circuitry, Brizendine reports, drawing on Buss, leads them to seek wives who are "physically attractive, between ages twenty and forty," and with "clear skin, bright eyes, full lips, shiny hair, and curvy, hourglass figures."[36] These traits are "strong visual markers of [female] fertility," which offers men "the biggest reproductive payoff for *their* investment."[37] But "the most reproductively successful males also need to pick women who will mate only with them," ensuring their paternity.[38]

Men's concern with paternity supposedly explains their concern with women's social reputation. Brizendine explains that if a woman had sex with a man on a first date or "showed off" about former bed partners, "his Stone Age brain might have judged that she would be unfaithful or had a bad reputation."[39] But male "seduction and abandonment" is an old problem.[40] Thus, male and female reproductive strategies put them at odds. Evolution, in effect, explains the sexual double standard. High paternal investment requires men's certainty of paternity.

However, this model suggests that men have little to lose in random and casual sexual encounters. Why wouldn't they care about any potential offspring they father, if their strategy is to maximize their reproductive success? The premise implies that if men spread around enough genes, even if they do not personally invest in parental care for all offspring, some may survive because of the mother's efforts.

Male sexual jealousy, thus, has evolutionary roots and "adaptive functions"—preventing infidelity and ensuring paternity;[41] it also has enormous costs, evident in domestic violence.[42] Drawing on evolutionary science, Judge Richard Posner argues the "biology of sex" explains men's mate-guarding behaviors such as "physical sequestration of wives, disparagement of female sexuality," and female genital mutilation.[43] The sexes are in conflict, rather than in cooperation; these male behaviors subvert female choice.[44]

The "Ancient" Male Brain

In *The Male Brain*, a shorter, companion volume to *The Female Brain*, Brizendine carries forward her basic themes of how ancient brain circuitry shapes men and women differently. I shall summarize the discussion most pertinent to this chapter—how "the ancient mating brain" and "daddy brain" work—and then discuss criticisms of Brizendine's claims. Because imagery can be so evocative, it is worth observing the differences in the cover art: a brain formed by telephone cord graces the cover of *The Female Brain*; a brain made of duct tape, the cover of *The Male Brain*. Book jacket copy makes the message explicit: "Women . . . have a lean, mean communicating machine"; "the male brain . . . is a lean, mean, problem-solving machine."[45]

There is a polemic and a plea for accepting difference: on the basis of her clinical practice and on the "vast new body of brain science," Brizendine is convinced that "the unique brain structures and hormones of boys and men create a male reality that is fundamentally different from the female one and all too frequently oversimplified and misunderstood."[46] There is an ambivalence over whether biology is destiny and over the degree of human agency. On the one hand, "if we know how a biological brain state is guiding our impulses, we can choose how to act, or to not act, rather than merely following our compulsions." On the other hand, when she speaks of the book as enabling female readers to "help your sons and husbands to be truer to their nature," it sounds as if the best course is not to resist nature.[47] Similarly, she suggests that brain science confirms the common saying "boys will be boys," noting that scientists find that "gender-specific toy preferences have roots in the male brain circuitry of both boys and male monkeys."[48] Describing herself as "part of the generation of second-wave feminists who had decided that we were going to raise emotionally sensitive boys who weren't aggressive or obsessed with weapons and competition," she seems to throw up her hands in the face of evidence of "innate brain wiring."[49] She concludes the book with a hope that men will have "a sense of relief at finally being understood" and that there can be a reduction in conflict between men and women that is "fueled by unrealistic expectations that stem from failing to grasp each other's innate differences."[50]

As in *The Female Brain*, Brizendine explains "what makes a man a man"—and male attitudes and behaviors—by reference to various hormones, as well as to specific regions of the brain, assigning such unscientific labels as the male brain's "sexual pursuit area" and "lust center." I shall focus on her account of mate selection and parenting. In a chapter called "The Mating Brain: Love and Lust," she follows one couple (drawn from her clinical practice), explaining how "Ryan" is "following the commands of his ancient mating brain" as his "sexual-pursuit area" lights up and sends him to meet "Nicole." Evolution features in explaining mate selection: men today "have been biologically selected over millions of years to focus on fertile females"; they have "[e]volved to zoom in on certain features that indicate reproductive health," such as an "hourglass figure." Throughout, her language is deterministic: nonverbal flirtations are "preprogrammed deep in the human brain"; Ryan is "prewired" to notice "women with hourglass shapes."[51] Smells and sounds (the voice) "trigger" the male brain to react.[52] While Ryan and Nicole consciously converse, much happens at the level of the unconscious, including the "secret" sending of information about health and genes. (As in *The Female Brain*, there is no attention whatsoever to how the brain and evolution shape women's and men's sexual attraction to and romantic love for someone of their own sex.)

Evolution features in Brizendine's account of men's imperative for reproductive success: "to a man, winning the mating game means getting his DNA and genes into the next generation," and, thus, the "instinctual part of his brain knows that the more women he has sex with, the more offspring he's likely to have."[53] As in *The Female Brain*, the complementary female mating strategy is to be coy, "cautious," and careful, with "the female brain trying to discern whether a man has what it takes to be a good protector and provider."[54] Indeed, Brizendine interprets Nicole's positive reaction to Ryan's paying for dinner by reference to (what primatologists have dubbed) the "meat-for-sex principle" observed in primates: "females have more sex with males who bring them meat."[55]

Sexual reticence—not being too sexually available too soon—is part of the female sexual strategy that signals to Ryan that Nicole would be a good long-term mate. But how does a male whose "ancient mating brain" favors a reproductive strategy of more sex/more partners/more success become committed to just one woman? The answer, evidently, is frequent sex with one woman: "the more Ryan and Nicole made love, the more addicted their bodies and brains became."[56] Brizendine explains "the male brain in love" with deterministic language about the force of chemical cocktails that trigger addiction. The release of dopamine sets the "love train" in motion; the "addicting fuel" of hormones keeps it going.[57] Then, Ryan enters the realm of "mate-guarding," making sure his friends don't "poach."[58]

Brain differences also explain why, although Ryan is fiercely possessive and easily jealous, Nicole should be understanding when he notices attractive women. In an often-quoted passage, Brizendine explains: "the lust center in the male brain automatically directs men to notice and visually take in the details of attractive females . . . . Ryan couldn't have stopped his eyes from looking at [another woman's breasts] even if he'd tried."[59] Meanwhile, a man's fear of loss or rejection can drive him to "pop the question" of marriage.[60]

Interestingly, it is Ryan's "deeply passionate feelings" that "can

lead to enduring commitments." Societal institutions play very little role in Brizendine's account. By contrast to portrayals of marriage (as I discuss later) as channeling heterosexuality and disci-
plining otherwise unruly sexual impulses, Brizendine's model has
the brains themselves doing the directing. With the aid of the right
hormonal processes, the brain merges love and lust into commitment without any evident outside assistance from the pressures
brought to bear by social institutions.

How do men's brains turn them into fathers? Brizendine's
chapter "The Daddy Brain" chronicles how men come to bond
with infants. Some popularizing accounts of human attachment
stress the mother-child bond. By contrast, in explaining how new
parents Tim and Michelle fall in love with their baby, Brizendine
includes both mother and father when she speaks of Mother Nature forging a "nearly unbreakable biological bond between parent and child."[61] The same brain circuits involved in falling in love
are "hijacked" to make sure parents fall in love with their child.[62]

Once again, in contrast to accounts that stress maternal bonding, Brizendine states: "The tending instinct is prewired into all
human brains, not just mothers.' "[63] Tim's brain circuits, including
his "reward center," pulse with the "joy of fatherhood." This is self-
reinforcing: the more he tends to his infant, the more the brain is
stimulated to reinforce his "tending instinct."[64] However, Brizendine returns to the theme of difference soon enough: infants detect differences between mom and dad, and it's "hard to match
the biological force of the love bond between Mommy and baby,"
in part because of women's role in breastfeeding. Another gender difference Brizendine reports, pertinent to the issue of work/
family conflict (to be discussed later), is mothers' tendency to be
reluctant to entrust infants to their fathers' care and to believe
that fathers will be less competent. Brizendine explains that such
mothers are "unknowingly operating on ancient brain circuitry"
that tells them "that female kin" were the ones to "look [to] for
help."[65] Fortunately for Tim, Michelle doesn't expect him to fill
the "ancient shoes" of "all her female kin" and encourages him to
"be a dad," strengthening her marriage in the process.[66]

Thus, in the midst of an otherwise very deterministic account of
how our ancient brains shape our mating and parenting, Brizendine shows recognition of the role of environmental factors—such

as a mother's positive reinforcement—in turning men into dads. She attributes certain features of child well-being to father-child interactions. Here, her inattention to the role of social construction of masculinity, and to whether such constructions warrant criticism, is discouraging. For example, while "daddy's little girl steals his heart," and while he is (supposedly) infinitely and patiently willing to drink tea at her tea parties or to do things to help her, when it comes to sons, fathers "help" by "making the boys stronger and tougher" so they can "survive as a man in the real world." This may mean that fathers "inhibit displays of affection in favor of rougher handling."[67]

The same lack of criticism features in Brizendine's chapter, "Manhood: The Emotional Lives of Men," in which she states that males learn, "from childhood on," that "[a]cting cool and hiding their fears are the unwritten law of masculinity."[68] This echoes her earlier description of how male teens must hone the "[a]ncient male survival skills of facial posturing and bluffing," "learning to hide their emotions."[69] Here is an interesting mixture of nature and nurture. Studies show that when men are viewing emotionally provocative photos, their facial muscles are initially "more emotionally reactive" than women's, but then their facial muscles become "less emotionally responsive," leading researchers to conclude that men "consciously—or at least semiconsciously—suppressed showing their emotions on their faces."[70] Men aren't hardwired to be less emotionally responsive, but they are socialized to be so, this experiment suggests.

Is there an evolutionary explanation for emotional differences? Brizendine states that, "through hundreds of thousands of years, our female and male brain circuits have been fine-tuned to run on different hormones."[71] But she doesn't give an explicit evolutionary explanation for why this might be so. One of the basic differences Brizendine reports is between "emotional empathy" and "cognitive empathy." In the former, someone feels "the same emotional pain" another feels. Women, we learn, excel at this. By contrast, men's brains have a preference for "cognitive empathy," where the male brain's "analyze-and-fix-it circuits" are activated to find a solution to someone's problem.[72] When Danielle wants sympathy but her husband Neil offers an analytical response of how to solve the problem, she is "trapped in her female brain circuit loops," just as he is "trapped in his male brain circuit loops." His brain is not "designed to wallow in anguish"; the male "express train" brain wants to get to its final destination. By contrast, her female friends will remain in their "emotional empathy system" and share Danielle's emotions.[73]

What about aggression, long claimed to be one genuine area of difference between men and women? Once again, Brizendine turns to specific features in the male and female brain, explaining that Joe blew up at a cab driver because his "brain area for suppressing anger," the septum, is smaller than in the female brain. The male "anger-aggression circuits" are formed before the male is born and are "behaviorally reinforced during childhood and hormonally reinforced during the teen years."[74] But is there an evolutionary explanation? Yes, Brizendine explains to her patients, Joe and his wife, Maria, that "Joe's male brain biologically saw the cab driver's actions as a challenge to his territory and dominance, and his brain responded with a series of chemical changes, prompting his aggressive behavior."[75] Distinguishing explanation from justification, Brizendine adds: "This brain biology doesn't give men permission to be uncivilized, but it does provide insight into why they defend their manhood so vigorously." Joe's "hormone cocktail" in his "male brain" underpins his aggression and anger, an explanation Joe readily accepts.[76]

Brizendine never discusses physical violence directed by men against intimate partners and children, just as she never discusses forms of male jealousy and mate-guarding that harm women. Joe looks "stricken" when he learns that his anger scares Maria, telling her, "But you know I'd never hurt you." Joe's surprise is not unusual, Brizendine says. But she does report that "high-testosterone men, like Joe, more than low-testosterone men, have a need to dominate others, and so they react dramatically to being challenged." Here Brizendine includes reference to primate studies showing that "dominant males whose status is consistently challenged maintain higher levels of testosterone and are more aggressive than subordinate males."[77] But the battleground here is the home, and the implication is that it is his, rather than her, territory. Brizendine seems to view Maria's reactions to Joe's dominance as a provocation to his further anger: "When Maria glared at Joe or shouted back at him, she was unknowingly challenging his dominance, thus increasing the testosterone."[78] Is the implication that she should accept his dominance? She agrees to "stop glaring back" if he will "promise to walk away before he gets so mad that he can't shut up."[79]

A "stable marriage" and "a stable social hierarchy," Brizendine contends, are social conditions that help to "dial down" men's testosterone and cortisol and, hence, their tendency to anger and aggression. But is a stable marriage one in which women simply accept male dominance? In discussing the importance of stable hierarchy, Brizendine turns explicitly to evolutionary biology to explain that "behaviors like bluffing, posturing, and fighting have evolved to protect males, especially from opponents within their own species." Male-male "competition and hierarchical fighting is driven by both hormones and brain circuits."[80] The "one-upmanship and drive for status seeking . . . found in men worldwide" are "not just a habit or a cultural tradition but more like a design feature of the male brain."[81] For example, competition at work that leaves men threatened with losing face and "forfeiting [their] place in the hierarchy" triggers men to become obsessed with "defending[their] territory," and testosterone puts men in "fight mode," prepared for "War."[82]

Critiques of Brizendine as Exemplifying "Neurosexism"

The philosopher Cordelia Fine argues that Brizendine's *The Female Brain* and similar "popular and influential books arguing for fundamental and 'hardwired' differences in male and female psychology" are illustrative of "the popular new genre of neurosexism."[83] In this genre, where "gender stereotypes [are] dressed up as neuroscience," "scientific accuracy and commonsense are often casualties in the ugly rush to cloak old-fashioned sexism in the respectable and authoritative language of neuroscience."[84] Fine suggests that such explanations may be so appealing because "[t]he answer, 'Oh, it's the brain,' offers a tidy justification for accepting the status quo with clear conscience."[85] If current social arrangements reflect fundamental, hardwired differences, perhaps trying to bring about alternative arrangements is futile.

In a book-length treatment of the "seductive allure" of neurosexism, *Delusions of Gender: How Our Minds, Society, and Neurosexism*

Create Difference, Fine situates the current appeals to neuroscience as the explanation of "hardwired" differences in the historical context of earlier diagnoses of differences in male and female brains. Doing so is quite instructive on the topic of evolution, equality, and social engineering because it counsels a healthy skepticism about contemporary claims. Fine offers as cautionary tales many historical examples of claims that basic differences between the male and female brain explained the basic inferiority of females and their unsuitability for many male-occupied spheres.

Neurologists from earlier centuries argued that "fundamental differences" in the brains of the sexes had concrete implications for men's and women's places in society. "In 1915, the illustrious neurologist Dr. Charles Dana" wrote an opinion piece in the *New York Times* concluding that these "structural differences . . . in the two sexes" will not "prevent a woman from voting," but "they will prevent her from ever becoming a man, and they point the way to the fact that women's efficiency lies in a social field and not that of political initiative or of judicial authority in a community's organization."[86] In the late nineteenth century, the evolutionary biologist and physiologist George Romanes wrote that, because women's brain weight was "about five ounces less than that of men," "on merely anatomical grounds we should be prepared to expect a marked inferiority of intellectual power in the former." He concludes: "In actual fact we find that the inferiority displays itself most conspicuously in a comparative absence of originality, and this more especially in the higher levels of intellectual work."[87] Fine further observes that when women did achieve at what were deemed male spheres of accomplishment, they "acted above their sex," with commentators attributing it to their having, in effect, "male" brains and "abnormal" development.[88]

For legal scholars, such historical examples will resonate with classic examples of how jurists appealed to basic differences between women and men to rationalize women's exclusion from full participation in society. The most famous example is the concurring opinion of Justice Bradley in *Bradwell v. Illinois* (1872), in which Myra Bradwell unsuccessfully appealed to the U.S. Supreme Court for admission to the Illinois bar to practice law. Justice Bradley explained how civil law limiting women's participation in society properly reflected nature and divine order:

[T]he civil law, as well as nature herself, has always recognized a wide difference in the respective spheres and destinies of man and women. Man is, or should be, woman's protector and defender. The natural and proper timidity and delicacy, which belongs to the female sex evidently, unfits it for many of the occupations of civil life. The constitution of the family organization, which is founded in the divine ordinance, as well as in the nature of things, indicates the domestic sphere as that which properly belongs to the domain and functions of womanhood. The harmony, not to say, identity, of interests and views which belong, or should belong, to the family institution is repugnant to the idea of a woman adopting a distinct and independent career from that of her husband. So firmly fixed was this sentiment in the founders of the common law that it became a maxim of that system of jurisprudence that a woman had no legal existence separate from her husband, who was regarded as her head and representative in the social state.[89]

In the late twentieth century, the U.S. Supreme Court repudiated this vision of naturally rooted and divinely ordained sex inequality. What once seemed to be innate differences between the sexes now seemed to be unconstitutional "archaic" stereotypes, "fixed notions" rather than "real differences" between men and women. Such views had no relationship to women's actual ability to contribute to and participate in the life of the nation. Justice Sandra Day O'Connor, the first women appointed to the Court, and Justice Ruth Bader Ginsburg, who litigated the cases that led to the transformation of the Court's equal protection jurisprudence, often refer to Bradley's concurrence in noting this transformation of the Court and of the larger society.[90] Such views of the Constitution and of women's place in the family and society are now "discredited" and at odds with contemporary constitutional understandings of women's liberty and equality.[91]

With good reason, then, skepticism is in order concerning contemporary claims about "hardwired" differences between the sexes. Fine aptly poses the question whether "early twenty-first-century neuroscientific explanations of inequality" are "doomed to join the same garbage heap as measures" used in earlier centuries, and her own suspicion is that they will.[92] Even though historical examples of scientific explanations of sex inequality counsel skepticism about contemporary neuroscience claims, it is still important to take a critical look at the claims themselves—especially if hardwired differences should make us more humble about the possibilities for social engineering to promote equality. Fine, as noted earlier, labels this kind of scientific argument "neuorosexism." As a legal scholar, I shall not attempt here to assess the underlying merits of the scientific claims Brizendine and others make. Instead, I shall draw on the work of Fine, Melissa Hines, and other scholars who do carefully criticize the underlying studies and experiments on which claims about sex differences and their implications rest.

Brizendine's hugely popular books are not without some favorable reviews in scholarly journals for providing a helpful "roadmap" for understanding how hormones shape brains.[93] However, scholars have offered trenchant critiques of her books. For example, in *Nature* magazine, Rebecca Young and Evan Balaban label *The Female Brain* a work in "psychneuorindoctrinology" and conclude:

> despite the author's extensive academic credentials, *The Female Brain* disappointingly fails to meet even the most basic standards of scientific accuracy and balance. The book is riddled with scientific errors and is misleading about the processes of brain development, the neuroendocrine system, and the nature of sex differences in general.[94]

One serious criticism of Brizendine's work is that her dramatic claims about gender differences are not supported by the sources she cites. Perhaps the most widely discussed example is about use of language: "A woman uses about 20,000 words per day, while a man uses about 7,000," a claim driving home her vivid contrast between the "communicating machine" on the one hand and the "problem-solving machine" on the other. Mark Liberman, the author of the online *Language Log*, searched unsuccessfully—among Brizendine's sources and elsewhere—to find any support for this claim. He warns that books like Brizendine's "tend to confirm our culture's current stereotypes and prejudices, and the science they cite is often overinterpreted, and sometimes seems simply to have been made up."[95]

Other reviews cite her "careless" research, including the error of citing "unrelated research" to support a dramatic claim about brain difference. One reviewer, Nicole Else-Quest, notes such problems as the use of unscientific language (like the image of female brains "marinating in estrogen"), overgeneralizations about non-human animal research to support her theory, and Brizendine's practice of ignoring research "that directly and clearly refutes her speculation." Such books, she notes, feed the endless "public hunger for scientific evidence that confirms men and women to be of different species," and such hunger—not "large meaningful gender differences in brains or behavior—must be acknowledged as the impetus for *The Female Brain*."[96]

There is not yet as extensive a critical literature on Brizendine's more recent book, *The Male Brain*, but some reviews point out similar problems. One review says of Brizendine's "breezy, incautious account of how the brain, urged on by hormones, makes men and women act completely differently": "you'd never know from reading Brizendine that beneath the sea she blithely sails are depths that researchers have only just begun to chart."[97] Another review faults Brizendine's reliance on MRI data to claim that men's "sexual pursuit area" is 2.5 times larger than that in the female brain. This, the reviewer notes, begs the question: "Where exactly is this 'pursuit area'?," a question to which an answer with scientific validity is unlikely because "in all likelihood no such 'area' exists."

Scientists caution against letting "dubious science" give credibility to stereotypes and ignore "decades of legitimate findings" about male and female similarity.[98] "Inflated claims of gender differences," they warn, have costs to children, adults, and society, as they "reify stereotypes," limit opportunity, and ignore that "males and females are similar on most, but not all, psychological variables."[99] These concerns echo questions about sameness, difference, and stereotypes long posed by feminist legal theory.[100] Critics of Brizendine and other popularizing accounts of brain difference do not deny that there are *some* differences between male and female brains. But they urge caution against overinterpreting such differences. For example, Brizendine's account of fundamentally different male and female brains relies heavily on the proposition that prenatal exposure to hormones is the source of these differences. Such research supposedly demonstrates that early hormonal exposure "organizes" the brain to "channel our fundamental interests into masculine or feminine directions."[101] Rebecca Jordan-Young, who exhaustively reviewed all the relevant studies on brain organization theory, characterizes Brizendine's *The Fe-male Brain* as offering "the most extreme claims about sex differ-ences in the human brain that I've seen in some time."[102] Jordan-Young concludes that "evidence that human brains are hormon-ally organized to be either masculine or feminine turns out to be surprisingly disjointed, and even contradictory—and the stakes involved in prematurely promoting this theory to a 'fact' of human development are high, both for the advancement of science and for social debates that draw on science."[103] She offers the example of aggression, which is linked with "a presumed masculine interest in social domination" and which is viewed by evolutionary psychol-ogists as having "adaptive significance because it encourages suc-cess in competition with other males for female sexual partners." She states: "The link between male dominance and reproductive success is almost an article of faith in evolutionary psychology, but it is not consistently supported by empirical research on either hu-mans or other primates."[104]

Sometimes, major conclusions about sex difference and how it translates into social structure rest on highly problematic ex-periments. For example, Fine talks about the significance given to an experiment that underlies Simon Baron-Cohen's distinc-tion between men as "system-builders" and women as "empathiz-ers." Baron-Cohen and colleagues studied babies who were one and a half days old to compare how long they looked at a human face versus at a mobile (presented one at a time): "empathizing versus systematizing."[105] Popularizers of brain difference draw on this work to argue that "girls are born prewired to be interested in faces while boys are prewired to be more interested in moving objects" and to draw implications for career choices. Yet, critics of this study point out a number of flaws in its design and execution, with perhaps the most "striking design flaw" being that it was not gender neutral: the experimenter knew the sex of the baby, which, in our society, may well have shaped the way she or he looked at the infant or held the mobile.[106]

Critics contend that language about "hardwired" gender differ-ences is misleading and inapt when applied to the brain. Hines uses the evocative phrase "engendering the brain" to capture the idea that "expectations and beliefs, as well as hormones, can en-gender the brain." Rather than draw a sharp—and "false"—line between biological and social/cultural causes, we should instead, she contends, recognize that:

> All of our psychological and behavioral characteristics . . . have a biological basis within our brain. No matter whether hormones or other factors, including social factors, caused us to develop in a certain way, the hormonal or social influences have been translated into physical brain characteristics, such as neurons, snyapses, and neurochemicals. Thus, the distinction between biological and social/cultural causes is false.[107]

By contrast, work like Brizendine's, which stresses a fundamentally different "male reality" and "female reality" fixed, as it were, by hormones, minimizes such social influences.

Skeptics of such gender essentialism in the brain offer a different model of "neuroplasticity" that seeks to capture the idea that brain circuits are a product of the interplay of the physical, social, and cultural environments: "what we experience and do creates neural activity that can alter the brain, either directly or through changes in gene expressions."[108] Here, Fine quotes Anna Fausto-Sterling on the idea that the steady interplay of the biological and the social means that "components of our political, social and moral struggles become, quite literally, embodied, incorporated into our very physiological being."[109] Similarly, Hines concludes that "our gender schemas, or stereotypes about sex differences and their causes, have sometimes led us to believe that hormones have behavioral influences where none exist, or that, where they do exist, they are more immutable and limiting than is the case." Instead, "recent research suggests that the adult brain is remarkably responsive, even in terms of its structure, to experience, as well as to hormones."[110]

Why does this matter for a consideration of obstacles to securing greater equality in society? As noted earlier, Fine warns that "neurosexism" is harmful because it encourages us to throw up our hands in the face of "hardwired" and innate differences. Social engineering seems futile and wrongheaded in the face of "stability and unchangeability."[111] The risk of neurosexism, Fine argues, is that it can shape how people view male and female potential, as well as the status quo and the possibility or desirability of change. This also presents ethical concerns. Merely presenting theories of gender difference as "biological, stable, and immutable"—as scientifically established "facts," rather than as claims "under debate in the scientific community"—can lead people to "more strongly endorse biological theories of gender difference, to be more confident that society treats women fairly, and to feel less certain that the gender status quo is likely to change."[112] Moreover, gendered expectations attributed to "innate, biological, and genetic difference" can shape performance, which, in turn reinforces claims about hardwired differences.[113] Fine concludes that "our minds, society, and neurosexism create difference" and "wire gender," but "the wiring is soft, not hard," and "flexible, malleable, and changeable."[114]

3. Evolutionary Psychology and Marriage Law and Policy

Two ways evolutionary psychology and sociobiology feature in contemporary discussions of family law and policy are through (1) arguments about why promoting "healthy marriage" and restoring a "marriage culture" are an appropriate task for government; and (2) arguments against redefining marriage to include same-sex marriage.[115] This embrace of social engineering is intriguing: because the social institution of marriage is necessary to address basic problems presented by nature, law and culture should reinforce it. Marriage is fundamental, yet fragile. Thus, marriage movement[116] authors criticize work like mine for ignoring sex difference and the purposes of marriage.[117]

These authors argue that marriage civilizes men by channeling them into socially productive roles as fathers and husbands.[118] Marriage addresses men's inclination toward procreating without taking responsibility for children and women's inclination toward procreating and rearing children, even in the absence of adequate resources and commitment by fathers.[119] Marriage is the social institution that *uniquely* addresses the regulation of heterosexuality and its procreative consequences, ensuring that children have a mother and a father to care for them.[120]

The marriage movement appeals to evolutionary psychology's account of men's and women's differential investment in offspring and conflicting reproductive strategies to explain society's vital interest in marriage. Marriage "closes this gap between a man's sexual and fathering capacities."[121] National Marriage Project Director David Popenoe testified in a congressional hearing on marriage promotion that the father-child bond is weaker than the mother-child bond and that men naturally tend to stray from mothers and children without the commitment of marriage.[122]

A rationale that marriage movement authors offer for limiting marriage to one man and one woman is marriage's role in ensuring maternal *and* paternal investment in children. This argument stresses family law's channeling function[123] and warns against altering marriage's social meaning. This argument has migrated into amici curiae briefs and some judges' opinions in litigation over challenges by same-sex couples to state marriage laws.

One example is a dissent in *Goodridge v. Department of Public Health*,[124] where the Massachusetts Supreme Judicial Court opened the door to same-sex marriage. The *Goodridge* majority rejected the state's argument that, because procreation was the central purpose of marriage, excluding same-sex couples from marriage was rational. It identified "exclusive and permanent commitment," rather than procreation, as marriage's indispensable feature.[125] The majority argued that the state had facilitated avenues other than marital sex for "bringing children into a family."[126] Dissenting, Justice Cordy contended that "the institution of marriage has systematically provided for the regulation of heterosexual behavior, brought order to the resulting procreation, and ensured a stable family structure in which children will be reared, educated, and socialized."[127] Although in contemporary society "heterosexual intercourse, procreation, and child care are not necessarily conjoined," an "orderly society requires some mechanism for coping with the fact that sexual intercourse commonly results in pregnancy and childbirth."[128]

The institution of marriage is, in effect, a form of social engineering that "fills a void" in nature: a process for "creating a relationship between the man and a woman as the parents of a particular child."[129] The marriage movement agrees that marriage resolves the "biologically based sexual asymmetry" between the sexes and "the problematic of fatherhood" by meeting the mother's and the child's needs respectively for a mate and a father and by giving men a family role. It "helps create a greater equality between parents than nature alone can sustain."[130]

Regulating the consequences of heterosexuality also features in the majority and concurring opinions in *Hernandez v. Robles*,[131] where New York's high court upheld as constitutional the exclusion of same-sex couples from marriage. The majority stated that the legislature could rationally conclude that same-sex couples do not need marriage as much as heterosexuals do because they are less sexually unruly and because their sexual unions do not *naturally* have procreative consequences. Moreover, the majority argued that, since most children are born as a result of heterosexual relationships, which are "too often casual or temporary," the state could "choose to offer an inducement—marriage and its attendant benefits—to opposite couples making a long-term commitment to each other."[132]

By contrast, because same-sex couples must deliberately plan parenthood, they—and their children—do not need the added security and stability marriage affords because they are more likely to have family stability.[133] This apparent reversal of past prejudices about homosexuals as promiscuous and irresponsible led law professor Kenji Yoshino to quip that gays and lesbians are "too good for marriage."[134]

Marriage movement arguments about "conjugal" marriage's evolutionary significance and fragility also feature in *Lewis v. Harris*, where the Appellate Division of New Jersey rejected the constitutional challenge brought by several same-sex couples.[135] Judge Parrillo, concurring, wrote that the purpose of marriage is "not to mandate procreation but to control or ameliorate its consequences" and that the "deep logic" of gender should remain as a "necessary component of marriage."[136] Quoting the marriage movement scholar Daniel Cere, Parrillo contended that *Goodridge*'s characterization of the essence of marriage as a permanent and exclusive commitment misses that, historically, marriage has embraced:

> the fundamental facets of [traditional] conjugal life: the fact of sexual difference; the enormous tide of heterosexual desire in human life, the massive significance of male-female bonding in human life; the procreativity of heterosexual bonding; the unique social ecology of heterosexual parenting which bonds children to their biological parents; and the rich genealogical nature of heterosexual family ties.[137]

Marriage is "conjugal," not just a "close personal relationship," because of pair-bonding's evolutionary significance. Allowing same-sex couples to marry would strip marriage of this richer meaning so that it would become "non-recognizable and unable to perform its vital function."[138]

These arguments against same-sex marriage are not persuasive.[139] They rest on assumptions about sameness and difference —between men and women and between opposite-sex and same-sex couples. Allegedly, marriage ameliorates sex difference for the sake of children and has "nothing to do" with sexuality that does not have natural reproductive consequences. But courts ruling in favor of opening up civil marriage to same-sex couples reach different conclusions about sameness and difference and eschew such a narrow focus on marriage's purposes. In *Hernandez*,[140] Chief Justice Judith Kaye dissented that the state "plainly has a legitimate interest in the welfare of children" and appropriately links "tangible legal protections and economic benefits" to marriage. "The state's interest in a stable society is rationally advanced when families are established and remain intact irrespective of the gender of the spouses."[141] Family law's channeling function is served by expanding the reach of marriage to same-sex parents. Indeed, in 2011, when New York's legislature passed the Marriage Equality Act, opening up civil marriage to same-sex couples, legislators stressed marriage's role in securing not only personal happiness but also social stability – by providing a "comprehensive structure of state-sanctioned protections, benefits, and mutual responsibilities for couples who are permitted to marry": in so doing, "the institution of marriage produces incalculable benefits for society, by fostering stable familial relationships. . . . Granting legal recognition to these relationships can only strengthen New York's families."[142]

These issues also feature in the newest wave of challenges to state marriage laws: whether the creation of a legal status alternative to marriage, such as civil unions, provides equality to same-sex couples. In *Kerrigan v. Commissioner of Public Health*,[143] the Supreme Court of Connecticut concluded that civil unions did not afford same-sex couples equal protection and that their exclusion from civil marriage lacked constitutional justification. The court determined that same-sex couples "share the same interest in a committed and loving relationship" and "in having a family and raising their children in a loving and supportive environment" as opposite-sex couples.[144] The legislature recognized these "overriding similarities" when it enacted the civil union law,[145] and, even though same-sex couples "cannot engage in procreative sexual conduct," the method of conceiving children is an insufficient difference to negate "fundamental and overriding similarities."[146]

Notably, the state did *not* appeal to procreation or optimal child rearing as rationales. However, the court noted that the procreation rationale raised by several amici did not satisfy an "exceedingly persuasive justification requirement": allowing same-sex couples to marry "in no way undermines any interest that the state may have in regulating procreative conduct between opposite sex-couples."[147] The court also argued that expanding marriage will not "diminish the validity or dignity of opposite-sex marriage" but instead reinforce "the importance of marriage to individuals and communities."[148] Citing to these amici's procreative-purpose argument, dissenting Justice Zarella disagreed: "The ancient definition of marriage as the union of one man and one woman has its basis in biology, not bigotry."[149]

This examination of case law and of marriage movement writings illustrates how biology, sex difference, and evolution are used to argue against expanding the definition of marriage. Because marriage is a form of social engineering that addresses problems posed by nature, it is a fundamental and fragile institution. I now turn to consideration of how some work in evolutionary science that more squarely asks "the woman question"[150] may aid feminist legal theorists pondering how best to respond to these kinds of arguments. This scientific work may help with identifying different "facts" about human nature and human society.

4. NATURE AND THE POLITICS OF PREHISTORY

In this chapter, I can sketch only a few ways that feminist or female-centered work on evolutionary science may challenge the presentation of nature and evolution in popularizing accounts and in public policy arguments. Feminist legal theory should heed the politics of prehistory, or how certain gender biases or stereotypes may shape the study of human origins and impose a "paleolithic glass ceiling."[151] Too often, females feature only as passive participants in accounts of human origins, rather than as "agents of evolutionary change."[152] As more female scientists study human origins, they have corrected this misconception and helped in evaluating contemporary appeals to evolution both to oppose and to support social engineering.

For example, the marriage movement stresses the pair bond, noting female and infant dependency on male help, just as evolutionary science has asserted female dependency upon male provisioning.[153] However, the assumption of a prehistoric pair bond is "a projection back in time to a narrow Western view of marriage and mating, a formulation too rigid to account for the variation that exists cross-culturally."[154] The Man as Provisioner thesis assumed that, to increase the human population by having a lesser interval between births, "females reduced their mobility, stayed near a home base, and became dependent upon males who provisioned their own mates and offspring," since they could be relatively certain about paternity.[155] This model seems "preoccupied with questions/anxieties about male sexuality" at the expense of recognizing females' roles in human evolution.[156] Female scientists have noted flaws in this model in light of fossil evidence and studies of contemporary primate and human hunter-gatherer societies.[157] The pair bond may have less to do with male provisioning than with solving the problem of male mate competition, freeing a female to care for her offspring.

As primatologists put females more at the center of evolutionary study, the image of female primates has been "fleshed out to include much more than just their roles as mothers and sexual partners of males."[158] Scientists have studied "the significance of female bonding through matrilineal networks," "female sexual assertiveness, female long-term knowledge of the group's local environment, female social strategies, female cognitive skills, and female competition for reproductive success."[159] This "female-centered 'world view'" among primatologists makes sense: "many primate societies are female-bonded; thus kin-related females are the permanent core of the social group."[160] These facts were "not immediately recognized by primatologists," but they are now "facilitating a strong focus on females as well as attracting more women to the discipline."[161]

Sarah Blaffer Hrdy's book *Mothers and Others: The Evolutionary Origins of Mutual Understanding* proposes that the human species is more adept at cooperation than other species because of the evolution of "cooperative breeding": the pattern of relying on "allomothers" or "alloparents" to help mothers care for their children.[162] An "alloparent" is any nonparent who helps parents raise their young.[163] While stories of human origins stress competition, Hrdy looks at cooperation.

The marriage movement ponders the male-female problematic; Hrdy identifies her own "perplexing paradox":[164]

> If men's investment in children is so important, why hasn't natural selection produced fathers as single-minded and devoted to children as [in some species]? And given that male care is so idiosyncratically and contingently expressed, how could natural selection have favored human mothers who invariably produced offspring beyond their means to rear alone?[165]

While the marriage movement stresses the problem of fatherlessness and looks to marriage as the solution, Hrdy looks at the way that human and nonhuman mothers enlist alloparents to assist in raising young. "These alloparental safety nets provided the conditions in which highly variable paternal commitment could evolve."[166] "Evolutionary interpretations of male behavior," she observes, have an "obsessive focus" on certainty of paternity as a prerequisite to paternal investment, but there is wide variation among men with "relatively high certainty of paternity" in terms of actually engaging in "direct care" of infants, as well as instances where men who do not share a child's genes invest in child care.[167]

Evolutionary theory tends to project the nuclear family back in time. By contrast, Hrdy describes "the typical or natural Pleistocene family" as "kin-based, child-centered, opportunistic, mobile, and very, very flexible."[168] Brizendine worries about single mothers and their lack of male protection and provision. Hrdy frames the issue differently: "[a]s always, . . .mothers still need a tremendous amount of help to successfully rear their kin," but in the modern postindustrial era, they face greater challenges in finding adequate alloparents and social supports (such as high quality paid child care) to ensure the nurture of children.[169] She worries whether the human species, as a whole, may be "losing the art of nurture," that is, rearing children so that they develop empathy and understanding and other "prosocial tendencies" that foster human survival.[170] Indeed, "the preeminence of the man-the-hunter/sex-contract paradigm, with its accompanying stereotypes about nuclear families and maternal caregiving," has offered "obstacles" to recognizing the evolution of cooperative breeding.[171] Removing these obstacles came in part from the efforts of Hrdy and other sociobiologists ("many of us women") to "expand evolutionary theory to include selection pressures on both sexes," including postmenopausal females.[172] The "grandmother hypothesis" is that "new opportunities to help kin generated selection pressures favoring longer lifespans among postmenopausal women."[173]

The assumption that hominids and early humans were patrilocal has hindered appreciation of the extent to which early residence patterns may have been matrilocal.[174] As starting assumptions of "evolutionary-minded anthropologists" about residential patterns changed, it became possible to ask new questions about cooperative breeding and the role of alloparents.[175] Studies indicate the preeminence of grandmothers among alloparents: "having a grandmother nearby has a significant impact on the child-rearing success of younger kin" and may sometimes more greatly enhance child well-being than the presence of a father.[176] In patrilocal societies, a paternal grandmother's contribution may be more important to her son's success, measured in shorter intervals between births; the presence of maternal grandmothers seems to correlate more with greater child well-being.[177] Hrdy also refers to young human females' adeptness at communication and making friends, linking it not only to tending and befriending to obtain support but also to the need to manufacture allomothers: "Whether consciously or not, women seek 'sisters' with whom to share care of our children."[178]

On the conflict between male and female reproductive interests, Hrdy speaks of "patriarchal complications since the Pleistocene," suggesting that earlier practices were less patriarchal than more modern ones.[179] Concern with ensuring paternity and preserving the patriline leads to "practices detrimental to the well-being of mothers (and children too)"; she mentions sequestering women and genital infibulations.[180]

Hrdy's hypothesis about the evolution of cooperative breeding

offers a corrective to evolutionary psychology's emphasis on competition and on male and female strategies. The focus on an ag-
onistic struggle between the sexes that is bridged only through
marriage detracts from a broader focus on the range of social
networks and supports that contribute to successful child rearing
and well-being. While the marriage movement stresses the integration of sexual and parenting bonds, some feminist legal theorists
argue that focusing on the "sexual family" diverts attention from
the family's important intergenerational caretaking function.[181] It
takes, Hrdy paraphrases, alloparents to raise a child. A prominent
contemporary example is available: First Lady Michelle Obama's
mother, Marion Robinson, moved into the White House because
of her crucial role in caring for the Obama children.[182] Hrdy's emphasis on the role of alloparents could support arguments made in
favor of greater family diversity—it is not the genetic tie so much as
providing nurture to children that contributes to their well-being.

5. NATURE, MARRIAGE, AND EQUALITY

Egalitarian Marriage

Popularizing accounts of "ancient" male and female brain circuitry
contend that men and women—universally—seek certain qualities in mates that complement their different reproductive strategies. Such accounts, we have seen, marshal evolutionary psychology. Marriage movement appeals to evolution stress that the social
institution of marriage solves certain natural, sex-based problemat-
ics and asymmetries. In this section, I consider the import of such
appeals to brain difference for the ideal of egalitarian marriage.
I also consider how recent sex scandals involving married male
political leaders trigger appeals to evolution and hardwiring to
explain why men stray. I then turn to another area in which the
appeal to male and female differences often features as a supposed limit on social engineering: work/family conflict and the
continuing problem of women doing more caregiving and housework than men. Here, I note how portrayals of recent economic
conditions (dubbed the "he-cession") stress the need for men to
"adapt" or "evolve" in ways that seem resonant with feminist social
engineering goals.

Does marital happiness require inequality? Evolutionary accounts of mate selection stress men's and women's diverging criteria. However, more recent studies of marriage patterns suggest the growing practice of "assortative mating": rather than marrying up or down, well-educated and economically resourceful people choose to marry their peers.[183] Meanwhile, lower-income men and women may cohabit rather than marry because they want a threshold level of economic resources before they marry.[184]

Egalitarian or "peer" marriage is a more just form of marriage, from a feminist or liberal perspective, than traditional marriage and is more likely to be happy and stable.[185] Marriage equality is a factor that contributes to marriage quality, particularly for women.[186] However, other scholars point out that marriages with a traditional gendered division of labor may also be quite stable so long as spouses' expectations do not change.[187] Spouses may also accept an unequal division of labor even if they think it is unfair.[188] Thus, considerable disagreement exists about whether social cooperation best takes place on terms of equality or inequality.

This debate over the desirability of egalitarian marriage surfaced in 2008 when New York's governor, Eliot Spitzer, resigned after disclosure that he was a customer of a high-priced prostitution service. Spitzer apologized for his "failings" and spoke of the need to heal himself and his family as his wife, Silda Wall Spitzer, stood by his side. The image of Spitzer's wife by his side during this scandal was in stark contrast to a photo of the two of them that previously appeared on the cover of the magazine *02138*: "Power Couples: See What Happens When Harvard Meets Harvard."[189] Love between equals can work and can even be fun and sexy, the story and the accompanying photos seemed to announce.

After the scandal, a model for happy marriage different from that of the power couple was offered by the conservative self-help author, Dr. Laura Schlessinger. Stunning her host on the *Today* show, Schlesinger laid the problem of men's cheating at the door of any wife who failed to make her husband feel "like a man . . . like a success . . . like her hero," so that he was "very susceptible to the charm of some other woman." Schlessinger held women "accountable" for not giving "perfectly good men" the love, kindness, respect, and attention they need, charging that "these days, women don't spend a lot of time thinking about how they can give their men what they need."[190] In Silda Wall Spitzer's case, this diagnosis seems particularly inapt, given that she put her own career aside to help her husband in his. But it does suggest cultural resistance to equality. Dr. Laura is a provocateur, and her comments drew criticism; however, she is also a popular author. Her book *The Proper Care and Feeding of Husbands* indicts the women's movement as a "core destructive influence" and advises wives to treat their husbands with respect, reinforce them as head of the household, and celebrate difference.[191] Admiration and deference will yield a wife more power and happiness than direct challenge. Harvey Mansfield also speaks about admiration—"look[ing] up to someone in control"—as a proper response to manliness.[192]

In this view, equality is a turn-off. Inequality is sexy. In the wake of recent infidelity scandals involving prominent politicians, some commentators look to evolutionary science's hypothesis that men's "philandering increases their reproductive success."[193] The Spitzer scandal also played as a story of marital failure and a cautionary tale to wives about how to keep their marriages sexy and their men from straying. However, resistance to this diagnosis may be evident from many women finding "a catharsis" in South Carolina First Lady Jenny Sanford's "hard hitting" public statements about Governor Mark Sanford's confessed infidelity—and her absence from his press conference.[194]

With each new wave of sex scandals involving prominent male politicians (former governor Arnold Schwarzenegger, Representative Chris Lee, and Senator John Ensign), actors (Jesse James), and athletes (Tiger Woods), media pundits seem to return again to evolution, nature, and the male brain for explanation. For example, David Buss explains that men crave "sexual variety. . . . They've evolved the desire to be with different women." Because their reproductive strategy is to mate with as many women as possible, thus creating as many offspring as possible, with a higher "payoff" (than women have) from a "short-term mating strategy, this has forged in the male brain a desire for sexual variety."[195] Marital unhappiness and the easy availability of extramarital sex are other factors. But power is a big factor. An evolutionary psychologist reports on NPR: "There's good evidence that men with great power and status are, in fact, more prone to affairs."[196] To get at the "why" of cheating, an evolutionary psychologist explains that "power has been and will forever be entangled with corruption for various reasons," and leaders have "more opportunities for corruption and for lying-cheating-stealing behaviors."[197] Moreover, Buss adds, "women are attracted to men who have power and status, so public figures usually have plenty of opportunity."[198] At least Buss acknowledges that men have some agency in not acting on such desires, "because they don't want to jeopardize social reputations or marriages."[199]

Media efforts to get at the "why" of powerful men's marital infidelity also turn to Brizendine's account of the male brain. Brizendine explains, in one story: "The way Mother Nature made us, the man's job on the planet is to look for, search for and seek out fertile females to mate with."[200] Women need to understand that a man watches attractive women because "this is how he is wired," and so ogling women (which is within the "normal range of behavior") does not mean he will be like Woods or James, whose behavior was "pathological" and "crossed over the line."[201] One news story, "Why Powerful Men (Like Arnold) Cheat," provides a link to a related story, "10 Things Every Woman Should Know about a Man's Brain," drawn largely from Brizendine's pop science claims (for example, "Hard-wired to check out women").[202]

In the midst of so many appeals to evolution to explain dramatic failures of marital happiness, it is important to recognize cultural evolution toward an ideal of egalitarian marriage as a firm foundation for marital happiness. It is striking, for example, that a recent *Time* magazine article, "Who Needs Marriage?," led with the contrast between the marriage of Britain's Prince Charles and Lady Diana Spencer and the more recent royal wedding between their son William and Catharine Middleton.[203] The gist of the article is that, by contrast to the earlier royal couple, William and Catharine are similar in age (she is six months older) and education (she went to the same university as William and would be the first English queen with a university degree). "[T]heirs is a union of equals" and, as such, reflects "the changes in the shape and nature of marriage that have been rippling through the Western world for the past few decades."[204] The historian Stephanie Coontz notes how this basic equality between the partners in this new royal union signals the emergence of a "more modern, egalitarian version of the love match," in which persons choosing mates "increasingly sought

shared interests rather than adherence to rigid gender roles."[205]
She observes that the very fact that they are close in age and education conduces to marital stability, rather than divorce. A recent
Pew Research Center report, *The Decline of Marriage and Rise of New
Families*, reports that social norms about spousal roles and what
makes for a more satisfying marriage have changed, with public
opinion, in 2010, "endors[ing] the modern marriage in which the
husband and wife both work and both take care of the household
and children."[206] (However, as I discuss later, there is still a strong
belief that men—more than women—should be providers.) Strikingly, by contrast to the gender differences stressed as "universals"
by evolutionary psychologists, the report finds remarkable similarity in views of what qualities make one a good husband/partner
and a good wife/partner.[207]

Work-Family Conflict

Another illustration of cultural limits concerning egalitarian marriage is the continuing issue of work-family conflict and the division of labor in the home. Laws and policies have moved us closer
to a world where mothers and fathers have equal rights and responsibilities, as a legal matter, for their children and where, as a
matter of social norms, women work outside the home and men
play an active role in nurturing children. But the division of labor
in families remains a flashpoint, as is evident from reports that,
in the home, women still do more child care (or care work) and
household work than men.[208] This is true within the United States
and more globally, leading a recent United Nations report on men
in families to conclude: "one of the core enduring symptoms of
gender inequality globally is the unequal work-life divide—stemming from the fact that men are generally expected to be providers and breadwinners (who work outside the home) and women
and girls are generally expected to provide care or to be chiefly
responsible for reproductive aspects of family life."[209] Moreover,
within the United States, news stories appear every several months
about the so-called opt-out revolution, where highly educated
women are choosing to stay home rather than pursue professional success. Generations of feminist legal theorists have devoted

attention to these issues about care, work, and family; my focus is on what the debate suggests about cultural limits.

One cultural limit is that while workplaces have come a long way toward recognizing that workers may have caretaking responsibilities, cultural perceptions of male workers still differ from those of female workers. Many men aspire to a more flexible balance between family life and work but may rationally perceive that they will pay a higher cost in terms of questions about their commitment to the job if they take advantage of employment policies designed to help parents.[210]

Part of the unfinished business of feminism is that men's lives have changed to a lesser degree than women's. Some feminist theorists argue that, instead of pushing the state for more public policy changes, wives and mothers should direct their energy toward persuading men to change.[211] The legal feminist Mary Anne Case argues for directing effort toward a redistribution of responsibility from women to men, rather than to employers or the state.[212] Certainly, government is not the only relevant actor when it comes to advancing sex equality. Thus, the political theorist Nancy Hirschmann raises a useful question: how can men be persuaded to change, and how can women be persuaded to insist on that change?[213] This is a basic premise of "how to" books such as Joshua Coleman's *The Lazy Husband: How to Get Men to Do More Parenting and Housework*.[214] While Dr. Laura's book promises marital happiness if women will accept role differentiation and resist feminist ideology, Coleman's book promises to save marriages and increase marital happiness by *increasing* equality.

Mansfield proposes a different cultural limit: manliness. Manly men have a disdain for women's work, including housework. "Manliness prevents men from giving equal honor to women: this is the issue behind inequality in housework."[215] If this is the case, then it suggests limits to feminist social engineering. On the other hand, alternative models of men's relationship to the home and to family life may suggest that the feminist project has had greater success. The marriage movement itself identifies women's discontent with the household division of labor as a reason why young women are less optimistic than young men about having happy marriages and why women today are more willing to exit marriages.[216] While some marriage proponents argue that a "cultural script" of a gendered division of labor in the home is better than "endless negotiation" over roles, others support "equal rights and responsibilities" inside and outside the home.[217]

Equality is important to marriage quality and to addressing work-life conflict. After the death of Betty Friedan, some commentators asked if feminism was a failure because women were choosing to stay home, rather than juggle career and family. One response was that women were making a *choice*, and wasn't feminism, after all, about women being able to make choices? No, said the feminist scholar Linda Hirshman, arguing that women who were opting out were in fact making bad choices not to be celebrated as a feminist triumph.[218] This debate about feminism's goals suggests one complication in theorizing and achieving equality. Friedan's emphasis on women getting out of the home and having careers, while paid household workers took up the slack, risked devaluing the importance of family and home life and suggested only one model of a good life to which women should aspire. However, when feminists assess the issue of choice, questions such as how cultural expectations for boys and girls shape their life prospects, whether social institutions make it equally possible for women and men to pursue certain life plans, and whether problems of unequal bargaining power constrain the exercise of choice are appropriate concerns.

6. Conclusion

Responding to assertions that "natural" differences or cultural imperatives limit the possibility of equality or necessitate particular institutional forms for the family requires that feminist theorists generate and contribute to well-informed visions of the interplay of nature and culture.[219] We should ask what sorts of social cooperation are possible and valuable in the areas of sexuality, reproduction, and parenting. Appeals to "bridging the gender divide" in ordering human society invite feminist counternarratives. As such narratives theorize about the proper role of social engineering and institutions, a feminist commitment to substantive equality should remain a guiding ideal. Perhaps a fitting coda to this essay on evolution and equality is an observation that, even in the comparatively brief time period on which this essay focuses (that is, comparatively brief when compared to the processes of evolution!), it is possible to detect what may be the beginning of a pendulum swing away from skepticism about feminist social engineering in the name of hard-wired differences and evolutionary constraints and toward the view that feminist social engineering may actually work and be beneficial for society. I refer to calls, in the wake of the present economic recession (dubbed the "hecession" or "man-cession" because men have lost more jobs than women) for men to "man up!" by becoming more like women in the workplace and in the home and for public policy to help them do so.[220] Journalists, aided by pundits, prescribe that "it's time to reimagine masculinity at work and at home," by which they mean that men should seek out more "girly" jobs in the economy (less vulnerable to the recession) and do more parenting and housework at home (to make them more desirable intimate partners). Most pertinent to this essay, American observers look to Sweden and other Western European countries for examples of successful social engineering—"smart" public policies (such as the "daddy month") that nudged new fathers to take time off work by a use-it-or-lose-it approach to paid leave.[221] Public policy, these observers conclude, actually can shift social expectations about men's roles at work and at home, leading a newer generation of young men to "feel competent at child-rearing" and to "simply expect to do it."[222] Public policies, these reports suggest, can and do lead to shifts in the culture, so that employees and employers have different expectations about gender roles.[223] Thus, the United Nations report to which I referred above notes the impact of the global economic recession on men, who "globally derive their identities and chief social function from their role as providers," while also noting that "social expectations about men's involvement in the care of children, reproduction in general and fatherhood are also changing, albeit slowly." It stresses the important role of public policy in "supporting" these "evolving roles of men in families."[224]

NOTES

This chapter incorporates a revised portion of my chapter in Martha Albertson Fineman, ed., *Transcending the Boundaries of Law: Generations of Feminism and Legal Theory* (New York: Routledge, 2010), 66–82.

1. Mary Anne Case, "Feminist Fundamentalism and Constitutional Citizenship," in *Gender Equality: Dimensions of Women's Equal Citizenship*, ed. Linda C. McClain and Joanna L. Grossman (New York: Cambridge University Press, 2009); *United States v. Virginia*, 518 U.S. 515 (1996).

2. Linda C. McClain, *The Place of Families: Fostering Capacity, Equality, and Responsibility* (Cambridge, MA: Harvard University Press, 2006).

3. Martha Albertson Fineman, "Why Marriage?," *Virginia Journal of Social Policy and the Law* 9 (2001): 239; Martha Albertson Fineman, "Equality: Still Illusive after All These Years," in McClain and Grossman, eds., *Gender Equality*, 251; Linda C. McClain, "Child, Family, State, and Gender Equality in Religious Stances and Human Rights Instruments: A Preliminary Comparison," in *What's Right for Children? The Competing Paradigms of Religion and Human Rights*, ed. Martha Albertson Fineman and Karen Worthington (Farnham, England: Ashgate, 2009), 19.

4. McClain, "Child, Family, State, and Gender Equality in Religious Stances and Human Rights Instruments."

5. Cordelia Fine, *Delusions of Gender: How Our Minds, Society, and Neurosexism Create Sex Difference* (New York: Norton, 2010). See discussion of examples in Part 2.

6. Ibid., 147.

7. Louann Brizendine, *The Female Brain* (New York: Morgan Road Books, 2006); Louann Brizendine, *The Male Brain* (New York: Broadway Books, 2010).

8. Robert Wright, *The Moral Animal: Why We Are the Way We Are: The New Science of Evolutionary Psychology* (New York: Vintage Books, 1995).

9. David M. Buss, *The Evolution of Desire: Strategies of Human Mating* (New York: Basic Books, 1994).

10. Robert Wright, "Feminists, Meet Mr. Darwin," *The New Republic*, November 28, 1994, 34–36.

11. Ibid., 34.

12. Brizendine, *The Female Brain*.

13. David Brooks, "Is Chemistry Destiny?," *New York Times*, September 17, 2006, http://www.rolereboot.org/system/storage/153/4b/b/122/is_chemistry_destiny.pdf (discussing Brizendine, *The Female Brain*, 14).

14. Brizendine, *The Female Brain*, 1.

15. Ibid., 6.

16. Mark Liberman, "Neuroscience in the Service of Sexual Stereotypes," *Language Log* (2006), http://158.130.17.5/~myl/languagelog/archives/003419.html; Carly Rivers and Rosalind C. Barnett, "The Difference Myth," *Boston Globe*, October 28, 2007, http://www.boston.com/news/globe/ideas/articles/2007/10/28/the_difference_myth/.

17. Brizendine, *The Female Brain*, 42.

18. Ibid., 37.

19. Ibid., 40.

20. Carol Gilligan, *Making Connections: The Relational Worlds of Adolescent Girls at Emma Willard School* (Cambridge, MA: Harvard University Press, 1990).

21. Brizendine, *The Female Brain*, 42.

22. Ibid., 42–43.

23. Ibid., 43.

24. Ibid.

25. Ibid., 54.

26. Ibid., 55.

27. Ibid., 60.

28. Ibid., 59–60.

29. Ibid., 60.

30. Buss, *The Evolution of Desire*.

31. Brizendine, *The Female Brain*, 61.

32. Ibid., 62.

33. Ibid.

34. Ibid.

35. Ibid.

36. Ibid., 63.

37. Ibid.

38. Ibid., 64.

39. Ibid.

40. Ibid., 64–65.

41. Buss, *The Evolution of Desire*, 125–29; Richard A. Posner, *Sex and Reason* (Cambridge, MA: Harvard University Press, 1992), 97.

42. Buss, *The Evolution of Desire*.

43. Posner, *Sex and Reason*, 97, 112.

44. Mary Batten, *Sexual Strategies: How Females Choose Their Mates* (New York: Jeremy P. Tarcher/Putnam Book, 1994).

45. Brizendine, *The Female Brain* (book jacket); Brizendine, *The Male Brain* (book jacket).

46. Brizendine, *The Male Brain*, 2.

47. Ibid., 7.

48. Ibid., 19.

49. Ibid., 18.

50. Ibid., 131.

51. Ibid., 52.

52. Ibid., 54–55.

53. Ibid., 57.

54. Ibid.

55. Ibid., 58.

56. Ibid., 63.

57. Ibid., 62–63.

58. Ibid., 65.

59. Ibid., 64.

60. Ibid., 66.

61. Ibid., 82.

62. Ibid.

63. Ibid.

64. Ibid., 84.

65. Ibid., 87.

66. Ibid., 87–88.

67. Ibid., 93.

68. Ibid., 99.

69. Ibid., 39.

70. Ibid., 100.

71. Ibid., 101.

72. Ibid., 97.

73. Ibid., 98. This resonates with the "you just don't understand" type of books by Deborah Tannen, where men want to help women by solving their problems, not realizing that women want to engage in a certain amount of "troubles talk." See Deborah Tannen, *You Just Don't Understand: Women and Men in Conversation* (New York: William Morrow, 1990).

74. Brizendine, *The Male Brain*, 102.

75. Ibid., 104.

76. Ibid.

77. Ibid., 107.

78. Ibid.

79. Ibid.

80. Ibid., 110.

81. Ibid.

82. Ibid., 111.

83. Cordelia Fine, "Will Working Mothers' Brains Explode? The Popular New Genre of Neurosexism," *Neuroethics* 1 (2008): 69–72.

84. Ibid., 69, 70.

85. Ibid., 71.

86. Fine, *Delusions of Gender*, 131 (quoting George J. Romanes, evolutionary biologist and physiologist (1887)).

87. Ibid., 141.

88. Ibid., xix–xx.

89. *Bradwell v. Illinois*, 83 U.S. 130, 141 (1872).

90. Sandra Day O'Connor, "Portia's Progress," *New York University Law Review* 66 (1991): 1546–58; Ruth Bader Ginsburg, "Constitutional Adjudication in the United States as a Means of Advocating the Equal Statute of Men and Women under the Law," *Hofstra Law Review* 26 (1997): 263–71; Ruth Bader Ginsburg, "Sex and Unequal Protection: Men and Women as Victims," *Journal of Family Law* 11 (1971–72): 347–62 (criticizing Bradley's "now notorious concurring opinion").

91. *Planned Parenthood v. Casey*, 505 U.S. 833 (1992). In *Gonzales v. Carhart*, 550 U.S. 124, 185–86 (2007), Justice Ginsburg warned, in an impassioned dissent, that the majority opinion's paternalistic picture of protecting women from abortion decisions they may regret by banning a procedure was a "way of thinking" that "reflects ancient notions about women's place in the family and under the Constitution—ideas that have long since been discredited" (citing, inter alia, to Justice Bradley's concurrence in *Bradwell*).

92. Fine, *Delusions of Gender*, 154.

93. For example, Susan A. Albrecht, "An Owner's Manual for Women . . . and Men," *Sex Roles* 61 (2009): 286–87; Lay See Ong, "Book Review: A Roadmap of the Male Brain," *Evolutionary Psychology* 8 (4) (2010): 776–78, http://www.epjournal.net.

94. Rebecca M. Young and Evan Balaban, "Psychneuroindoctrinology" (reviewing Brizendine, *The Female Brain*), *Nature* 44 (2006): 634.

95. "Neuroscience in the Service of Sexual Stereotypes," *Language Log*, August 6, 2006, http://itre.cis.upenn.edu/~myl/languagelog/archives/003419.html. For another refutation of this claim, see Matthias R. Mehl et al., "Are Women Really More Talkative Than Men?," *Science* 317 (2007): 317, http://www.sciencemag.org.

96. Mehl et al., "Are Women Really More Talkative Than Men?," 322.

97. Emily Bazelon, "A Mind of His Own," *New York Times*, March 28, 2010, Book Review, 17.

98. Rivers and Barnett, "The Difference Myth."

99. Janet Shibley Hyde, "The Gender Similarities Hypothesis," *American Psychologist* 60 (2005): 581–89.

100. *Mississippi University for Women v. Hogan*, 458 U.S. 718 (1982). Christine A. Littleton, "Reconstructing Legal Equality," *California Law Review* 75 (1987): 1279–1337.

101. Rebecca M. Jordan-Young, *Brain Storm: The Flaws in the Science of Sex Differences* (Cambridge, MA: Harvard University Press, 2010), 198–99.

102. Ibid., 50.

103. Ibid., 3.

104. Ibid., 210.

105. Fine, *Delusions of Gender*, 112.

106. Ibid., 113–14.

107. Melissa Hines, *Brain Gender* (New York: Oxford University Press, 2004), 214.

108. Fine, *Delusions of Gender*, 236.

109. Ibid.

110. Hines, *Brain Gender*, 228.

111. Fine, *Delusions of Gender*.

112. Ibid., 185.

113. Fine cites a study in which women "given a journal article to read that claimed that men are better at math because of innate, biological, and genetic differences performed worse on a GRE-like math test than women shown an essay saying that men's greater effort underlies their superior performance." Ibid.,172–73.

114. Ibid., 239.

115. Another example is the argument against moving "beyond marriage" to recognize alterative legal forms and to deemphasize the conjugal marriage model.

116. The Institute for American Values, founded by David Blankenhorn, is a central organization in the marriage movement.

117. Don S. Browning, "Linda McClain's *The Place of Families* and Contemporary Family Law: A Critique from Critical Familism," *Emory Law Journal* 56 (2007): 1383–1405.

118. McClain, *The Place of Families*, 135–36.

119. Don S. Browning et al., *From Culture Wars to Common Ground*, 2d ed. (Louisville, KY: Westminster John Knox Press, 2000); McClain, *The Place of Families*, 135–36.

120. David Blankenhorn, *The Future of Marriage* (New York: Encounter Books, 2007).

121. Coalition for Marriage et al., "The Marriage Movement: A Statement of Principles," 2000, 9, http://www.americanvalues.org/pdfs/marriagemovement.pdf.

122. David Popenoe, "Testimony of David Popenoe," Hearing on Welfare and Marriage, House Ways and Means Committee (May 22, 2001).

123. Linda C. McClain, "Love, Marriage, and the Baby Carriage: Revisiting the Channelling Function of Family Law," *Cardozo Law Review* 28

(2007): 2133–83; Carl Schneider, "The Channelling Function of Family Law," *Hofstra Law Review* 20 (1992): 495–532.

124. *Goodridge v. Department of Public Health*, 798 N.E.2d 941, 983–1005 (Mass. 2003).

125. Ibid., 961.

126. Ibid., 961–62.

127. Ibid., 995.

128. Ibid.

129. Ibid., 996.

130. Institute for American Values et al., *Marriage and the Law: A Statement of Principles* (New York: Institute for American Values, 2006), 15.

131. *Hernandez v. Robles*, 855 N.E.2d 1 (N.Y. 2006).

132. Ibid., 7.

133. Ibid.

134. Kenji Yoshino, "Too Good for Marriage," *New York Times*, July 14, 2006, A19.

135. *Lewis v. Harris*, 875 A.2d 259 (N.J. App. Div. 2005). The New Jersey Supreme Court overturned the appellate court, *Lewis v. Harris*, 908 A.2d 196 (N.J. 2006), and the legislature enacted a civil union law in response to that ruling.

136. *Lewis*, 875 A.2d at 276–78 (Parrillo, J., concurring).

137. Ibid. at 276 (quoting Daniel Cere, "The Conjugal Tradition in Post Modernity and the Closure of Public Discourse" (unpublished manuscript, 2003).

138. Ibid.

139. McClain, "Love, Marriage, and the Baby Carriage," 2155–83.

140. *Hernandez*, 855 N.E.2d at 32.

141. Ibid.

142. Marriage Equality Act, A08354 Memo, June 29, 2011, http://www.assembly.state.ny.us/leg/?default_fid= (accessed October 27, 2011).

143. *Kerrigan v. Commissioner of Public Health*, 957 A.2d 407 (Connecticut 2008).

144. Ibid., 424.

145. Ibid.

146. Ibid., 424 n.19.

147. Ibid., 477 n.79.

148. Ibid., 474.

149. Ibid., 515–16.

150. Katharine T. Bartlett, "Feminist Legal Methods," *Harvard Law Review* 103 (1990): 829–88.

151. Adrienne Zihlman, "The Paleolithic Glass Ceiling: Women in Hu-

man Evolution," in *Women in Human Evolution,* ed. Lori D. Hager (New York: Routledge, 1997), 91.

152. Hager, *Women in Human Evolution,* ix.

153. Ibid.

154. Zihlman, "The Paleolithic Glass Ceiling," 99.

155. Ibid., 102.

156. Dean Falk, "Brain Evolution in Females: An Answer to Mr. Lovejoy," in Hager, ed., *Women in Human Evolution,* 115.

157. Zihlman, "The Paleolithic Glass Ceiling."

158. Linda Marie Fedigan, "Is Primatology a Feminist Science?," in Hager, ed., *Women in Human Evolution,* 65.

159. Ibid.

160. Ibid., 68.

161. Ibid.

162. Sarah Blaffer Hrdy, *Mothers and Others: The Evolutionary Origins of Mutual Understanding* (Cambridge, MA: Belknap Press of Harvard University, 2009), 22.

163. Ibid.

164. Ibid., 159.

165. Ibid., 162.

166. Ibid., 166.

167. Ibid., 167–68.

168. Ibid., 166.

169. Ibid., 288–90.

170. Ibid., 290–94.

171. Ibid., 239–40.

172. Ibid., 258.

173. Ibid., 255.

174. Ibid., 241–43.

175. Ibid., 245.

176. Ibid., 253, 261.

177. Ibid., 261–64.

178. Ibid., 271.

179. Ibid., 264–65.

180. Ibid., 265.

181. Martha Albertson Fineman, *The Neutered Mother, the Sexual Family, and Other Twentieth Century Tragedies* (New York: Routledge, 1995); Martha Albertson Fineman, *The Autonomy Myth: A Theory of Dependency* (New York: New Press, 2004).

182. Rachel L. Swarns, "An In-Law Is Finding Washington to Her Liking," *New York Times,* May 4, 2009, A11.

183. Annie Murphy Paul, "The Real Marriage Penalty," *New York Times,*

November 19, 2006, Magazine, Section 6, 22; Christine R. Schwartz and Robert D. Mare, "Trends in Educational Assortative Marriage From 1940 to 2003," *Demography* 42 (2005): 621.

184. Cynthia Grant Bowman, *Unmarried Couples, Law, and Public Policy* (New York: Oxford University Press, 2010), 106–11.

185. Pepper Schwartz, *Love between Equals: How Peer Marriage Really Works* (New York: Free Press, 1994).

186. McClain, *The Place of Families*, 134–35, 141–47.

187. E. Mavis Hetherington and John Kelly, *For Better or for Worse: Divorce Reconsidered* (New York: Norton, 2002), 30–31.

188. Margaret Brinig and Steven Nock, "Weak Men and Disorderly Women: Divorce and the Division of Labor," in *The Law and Economics of Marriage and Divorce*, ed. Antony W. Dnes and Robert Rowthorn (New York: Cambridge University Press, 2002), 171, 188.

189. Lindsey McCormack et al., "Power Couples: See What Happens When Harvard Meets Harvard," *02138* (Winter 2007): 62–78.

190. Jenice Armstrong, "The Sleaze-fest Continues," *Philadelphia Daily News*, March 20, 2008, 35. Readers may view the show at http://www .msnbc.msn.com/id./235752221/.

191. Dr. Laura C. Schlessinger, *The Proper Care and Feeding of Husbands* (New York: HarperCollins, 2004), 3.

192. Harvey C. Mansfield, *Manliness* (New Haven: Yale University Press, 2006), 18.

193. Eduardo Porter, "Tales of Republicans, Bonobos and Adultery," *New York Times*, July 3, 2009, A20.

194. Leslie Kaufman, "Political Wife's Hard Line Strikes Chord," *New York Times*, June 27, 2009, A12.

195. "9 Reasons Why Men Cheat," lifescript: healthy living for women, February 11, 2011, http://www.lifescript.com/Life/Relationships/ Wreckage/6_Reas.

196. Alan Greenblatt, "Are Politicians Especially Prone to Affairs?," National Public Radio, May 17, 2011, http://www.npr.org/2011/05/17/ 136395606/are-politicians-especially-prone-to-affairs.

197. "Why Politicians Cheat on Their Wives," *LiveScience*, June 25, 2009, http://www.livescience.com/9686-politiicians-cheat-wives.html.

198. "9 Reasons Why Men Cheat."

199. Ibid.

200. Mark Egan, "Tiger, Jesse Are Exceptions, Not Rule; Looking at Other Women Not a Sign That a Man Will Stray, Author Says," *Times Colonist* (Victoria, British Columbia), April 15, 2010.

201. Ibid.

202. "Why Powerful Men (Like Arnold) Cheat," *FoxNews*, May 17,

2011, http://www.foxnews.com/health/2011/05/17/powerful-men-like
-arnold-cheat/print (linking to Robin Nixon, "10 Things Every Woman
Should Know about a Man's Brain," April 9, 2010, http://www.livescience
.com/6327-10-woman-man-brain.html).

203. Belinda Luscombe, "Marriage: What's It Good For?," *Time*, November 29, 2010, 48–56 (featuring magazine cover, "Who Needs Marriage?").

204. Ibid.

205. United Nations Department of Economic and Social Affairs, *Men in Families and Family Policy in a Changing World* (New York: United Nations, 2011), 11; see also Jennifer L. Hook, "Care in Context: Men's Unpaid Work in 20 Countries, 1965–2003," *American Sociological Review* 71 (2006): 439 (literature review).

206. *Men in Families*, 11 ("[r]ecent multi-country study including lower, middle, and higher-income countries found that mean time spent on unpaid care work by women is from 2 to 10 times greater than that spent by men").

207. Stephanie Coontz, "British Monarchy Catches Up with Modern Marriage Trends," April 26, 2011, http://www.stephaniecoontz.com/articles/article64.htm.

208. Pew Research Center, *The Decline of Marriage and Rise of New Families* (November 18, 2010), ii, 26.

209. Ibid., 30–31. There are, however, some "significant differences by race."

210. Jerry A. Jacobs and Kathleen Gerson, *The Time Divide: Work, Family, and Gender Inequality* (Cambridge, MA: Harvard University Press, 2004).

211. Nancy Hirschmann, "Wed to the Problem? The Place of Men and State in Families," *The Good Society* 17 (2008): 52–55.

212. Mary Anne Case, "How High the Apple Pie? A Few Troubling Questions about Where, Why, and How the Burden of Care for Children Should be Shifted," *Chicago-Kent Law Review* 76 (2001): 1753–86.

213. Hirschmann, "Wed to the Problem?," 52–55.

214. Joshua Coleman, *The Lazy Husband: How To Get Men to Do More Parenting and Housework* (New York: St. Martin's Press, 2005).

215. Mansfield, *Manliness*, 9, 13.

216. David Popenoe and Barbara Dafoe Whitehead, "The State of Our Unions," 1999, http://www.marriage.rutgers.edu.

217. McClain, *The Place of Families*, 142–51.

218. Linda Hirshman, "Homeward Bound," *American Prospect* 16 (December 2005): 20–26; Linda R. Hirshman, *Get to Work: A Manifesto for Women of the World* (New York: Viking, 2006).

219. I must leave that task to another day. However, a helpful approach to learning about how evolutionary theory could guide thinking about law

and policy making is found in Owen Jones, "Time-Shifted Rationality and the Law of Law's Leverage: Behavioral Economics Meets Behavioral Biology," *Northwestern University Law Review* 96 (2001): 1141–1205. Jones contends that, once we appreciate that our current brains have a "tool box" that was "ecologically rational" in "ancestral times" but that may not be as adaptive as times change, then we can better understand what seems to be sometimes irrational behavior. Notably, Jones does not espouse the view that social engineering is doomed because it comes up against hardwired constraints on the brain. Rather, he suggests that "we can usefully consider law to be a lever for moving human behavior in directions it would not go on its own." Ibid., 1187. He identifies the dilemma that the human brain "tends to process information in ways" that tend to yield an adaptive solution to a problem "encountered in the environment of evolutionary adaptation," and this may account for seeming irrationality today. Explanation, he stresses, is not justification, but it can help us to appreciate the evolutionary "underpinning" to certain areas of behavior, including those discussed in this essay.

220. The September 27, 2010, *Newsweek* cover depicted a man holding a child, with the headline "Man Up! The Traditional Male Is an Endangered Species. It's Time to Rethink Masculinity." For the accompanying story, see Andrew Romano and Tony Dokoupil, "Men's Lib," *Newsweek*, September 27, 2010, 43.

221. Ibid., 45–46.

222. Ibid., 46.

223. See Katrin Bennhold, "Flexible Workweek Alters the Rhythm of Dutch Life," *New York Times*, December 30, 2010, A10 (reporting on success of the "daddy day" in shifting men toward part-time work).

224. *Men in Families*, 1, 11–12.

INDEX

Adams, John, 240–41
Age, and nature, 309–13
Altruism: behavioral, 7, 10; biological, 7; failure, 9–11, 19–23, 28–29; profile, 8; psychological, 7–9, 19, 21
Arden, Elizabeth, 309–10
Aristotle: and approach depending upon nature of the subject, 280; and biopolitical science, 221, 223, 238; and breaches of moral code, 83–84; and comparisons, 274; and humans as political animals, 235, 278; and prudence, 246, 248–49; regime analysis of, 236; and slavery, 233
Arnhart, Larry, 267–75, 277–84, 288–89
Atkins v. Virginia, 150

Balaban, Evan, 362
Balog, Kari, 318
Baron-Cohen, Simon, 364
Behavioral genetics: assumptions of, 100–101; behavioral morality and, 120–24; gene-environment interactions and, 106–7; "hidden environment" in, 107, 110; and Human Genome Project, 101, 109; "inflated" heritabilities in, 106–7; "missing heritability" in, 102, 110–11; shift in role of environment in, 107–10
Behavioral morality: and agency, 131–32; and blameworthiness, 116–17, 132–36, 138–39; and call to rethink "reasonableness," 166–68, 177–78; and call to rethink "unreasonableness," 167–69, 178–89; and capacity, 136–37; and challenges to criminal responsibility, 130–37, 139–41; claims about causation and responsibility in, 175–77; and criticisms of the criminal justice system, 115, 130–31, 138–41; defined, expanded, and mapped, 169–74; and discomfort with criminal stigma, 147, 150–52; distinguished from evolutionary morality, 172; distinguished from law and evolutionary biology, 127–29; and evolutionary causes of criminal behavior, 118–20; as a form of moral philosophy, 115–18; and free will, 130; and genetic causes of criminal behavior, 120–24; and naturalistic fallacy, 129; and neurobiological causes of criminal behavior, 124–27; and proximate versus ultimate causes of deviant behavior, 127–29; as rebutting culpability, 147–50; as undermining retributivism, 117. *See also* Causal explanations of criminal behavior; Reasonableness; Stigma
Benedict, Ruth, 286
Berlin, Isaiah, 246
Biopolitical science: advantages of, 279–81, 288–89; alternative approaches to, 284–89; approach of, is both Aristotelian and Darwinian, 221, 278–79; challenges for, 281–84; and deep history, 236–38; and deficiencies of contemporary political science, 222–25, 254–55;

Biopolitical science (*continued*)
disadvantages of, 279; framework
for, 225; method of is pluralistic and
empirical, 278; need for, 267–68,
272, 275; objections to, 249–54; and
political cultures, 234–45; and political judgments, 245–49; and political
universals, 225–34; superior to *a
priori* approaches to explaining human behavior, 287–88; superior to
views that claim human exemption
from laws of nature, 285–87. *See also*
Lincoln, Abraham, and Emancipation Proclamation
Bouchard, Thomas, 107
Boyd, Richard, 33
Bradley, Joseph P. (Justice), 360–61
Bradwell, Myra, 360
Bradwell v. Illinois, 360
Brain: alleged differences between
male and female brains as explaining sex differences and sex inequality, 349–59; brain differences and
culpability, 179–84; interplay of
physical, social, and cultural environ-
ments in altering, 365–66. *See also*
Neurosexism
Brennan, William (Justice), 319
Brink, David, 33
Brizendine, Louann, 349, 350–59, 362–
65. *See also* Brain; Neurosexism
Brooks, David, 350
Buss, David, 349, 352, 376–77

Cartesian, 118, 287. *See also* Descartes,
Rene
Casebeer, William D., 171–72
Case, Mary Anne, 379
Caspi, Avshalom, 108, 121
Causal explanations of criminal behavior: claim that all physical causes of
criminal behavior are exculpatory,
173, 175–76; claim that only aberrant
physical causes of criminal behavior
are exculpatory, 173, 175–76, 178–
84, 188–89; and criminal culpability,

169; and criminal responsibility, 194–
95, 198–205; objections to including
causation in a theory of criminal
responsibility, 205–9; relationship
to legal consequences, 168; and
stigma, 168, 173, 184, 187, 206–08.
See also Behavioral morality; Criminal
responsibility
Cere, Daniel, 368
Chaisson, Eric, 237
Chambers, Robert, 237
Christian, David, 236–37
Churchill, Winston, 245
Churchland, Patricia S., 171–72
City of Cleburne v. Cleburne Living Center,
321–22
*Cline, General Dynamics Land Systems,
Inc. v.,* 320
Cohen, Jonathan, 117, 130, 138, 151,
175
Coleman, Joshua, 379
Constructivism: and progressive arguments that identity categories are
socially constructed, 293; and progressive embrace of constructivist
rather than essentialist view of gender differences, 300, and semantics
for "wrong," 16–17
Coontz, Stephanie, 377
Cordy, Robert (Justice), 367
Criminal responsibility: agency and,
131–32; blameworthiness and, 132–
36; and diminished capacity, 135–37;
external versus internal tests of, 138–
39; insanity and, 136–37, 203; involuntariness of conduct and, 131–32;
mens rea and, 132–36; standard view
of, 198–99, and criticisms of standard view of, 199–205. *See also* Causal
explanations of criminal behavior;
Culpability
Crook v. State, 149
Culpability: behavioral moralist claims
to rebut, 147–50; biologically rooted
moral deviance and, 167; brain difference and, 179–84; and the death

penalty, 147–50; resistance to differentiated culpability, 184–88. *See also* Causal explanations of criminal behavior

Culture: cultural evolution and history of regimes, 238–42; influence on moral views, 61; moral pluralism and, 62; political culture, 234–45

Dana, Dr. Charles, 360

Darwin, Charles: and biopolitical science, 221, 223–24, 255, 278–79; Darwinian understanding of human nature, 269–73; and "deep history" of politics, 236–38; *The Descent of Man*, 233, 278; and evolutionary explanation of moral sentiments, 31; and group-selected morality, 227–29, 245; and "hostile forces," 19; and moral progress, 235; and multiple forms of selection, 280; *The Origin*, 5, 278; and other-regarding moral concerns, 253; and pragmatic naturalism, 5. *See also* Natural selection

Davenport, Charles, 101

de Waal, Frans, 73, 247, 286

Debunking (evolutionary explanation) of moral judgment: competitive nature of morality and, 72–76; domination and exclusion and, 75; explained and distinguished from vindicating explanation, 31–35; limitations of, 52–53, 76; in relation to cognitive judgments, 39–53; and two faces of morality, 32, 76–77. *See also* Moral judgment; Vindicating (evolutionary explanation) of moral judgment

Deep history, 236–40, 272–75

Dennett, Daniel, 195

Descartes, Rene, 267–68, 285. *See also* Cartesian

Dewey, John, 5–7, 21, 27–28

Diamond, Larry, 233

Disability: and nature, 300–305; medical model of, 293, 301–02; social model of, 293, 300–305

Eisley, Loren, 286

Else-Quest, Nicole, 362

Ely, John Hart, 320–22

Ethical project, 5, 9–12, 17–19, 20–22, 25–29

Ethics: authority of, 23–24, 27, 29; ethical change, 6, 13; ethical pluralism, 22, 29; ethical progress, 12–13, 17–18, 21–22, 24, 29; ethical truth, 12, 17–18, 22–24; function of to remedy altruism failures, 19–21, 23, 29; and functional conflict, 21; naturalistic, 4; and normative guidance, 9–11; as a social technology, 18, 23, 25, 28. *See also* Ethical project

Ex Parte Jennings, 135

Ex Parte John Wayne Rice, 131

Faces of morality: Kantian, 76–77; Nietzschean, 76–77. *See also* Debunking (evolutionary explanation) of moral judgment; Vindicating (evolutionary explanation) of moral judgment

Farahany, Nita, 166–79, 184–89, 194–95, 198, 204, 206–9, 212–16

Fausto-Sterling, Anna, 365

Fine, Cordelia, 348, 359–62, 364–66

Finer, S. E., 236, 240

Flagg, Barbara, 314

Flynn, James, 107–8

Frankfurt, Harry, 204

Friedan, Betty, 380

Frontiero v. Richardson, 319, 321

Galileo, 314

Galton, Francis, 101

Gazzaniga, Michael, 175

Gender. *See* Sex, and nature; Sex differences; Sex equality

Gibbard, Allan, 62

Gibbon, Edward, 274

Gilligan, Carol, 351

Ginsburg, Ruth Bader (Justice), 361

Goldberg, Suzanne, 323

Goodall, Jane, 235, 247

Goodman, Nelson, 4
Goodridge v. Department of Public Health, 367
Graham v. Florida, 150
Grant, Ulysses S., 245
Greely, Henry T., 124
Greene, Joshua, 117, 130, 138, 151, 175
Griffin, John Howard, 316

Hahn, Harlan, 304
Hamer, Dean, 306
Hamilton, Alexander, 240
Hammonds, Evelynn M., 313
Hart, H. L. A., 60, 87–89, 138
Heidegger, Martin, 215
Heritability: cultural and educational changes as distorting heritability statistics, 107–8; environment influences on, 106–11; and Equal Environment Assumption, 104–6; "missing" heritability, 102, 110–11; misunderstanding and misuses of, 102–3; twin studies and, 102–6, 110. *See also* Behavioral genetics
Hernandez v. Robles, 368–69
Herndon, William, 237
Hines, Melissa, 362, 365
Hirschmann, Nancy, 379, 380
Holmes, Oliver Wendell, Jr. (Justice), 138, 142–43
Hoskins v. State, 148
Hrdy, Sarah Blaffer, 372–74
Hubbard, Ruth, 318
Hume, David, "sensible knave" of, 25–26

Immutability: age and, 320–21; assumption of immutable nature, 294, 295; disability and, 321–22, 323–24; law in relation to, 318–24; and legal requirement to alter nature, 323–24; race and, 319; sex and, 319–20; sexual orientation and, 322–23. *See also* Nature
Insanity defenses, 203

James, William, 18
Jones, Owen, 128
Jordan-Young, Rebecca, 363. *See also* Young, Rebecca

Kant, 76–77, 286. *See also* Kantian
Kantian, 10, 26, 76–77. *See also* Kant
Katznelson, Ira, 318
Kaye, Judith (Chief Judge), 369
Kerrigan v. Commissioner of Public Health, 369–70
Kitcher, Philip, 36, 65, 100
Korsgaard, Christine, 285–87

Legal obligation: and moral obligation, 85–92; and "moral semantic foundationalism," 87–88; as sometimes overriding morality, 33, 78, 91; and view of "legal parallelism," 89–92
Leroi, Armand Marie, 314
LeVay, Simon, 305–06
Lewis v. Harris, 368
Lewontin, Richard, 214–15
Liberman, Mark, 362
Lincoln, Abraham: and Emancipation Proclamation, 221–25, 231–34, 242–45, 248–50, 254, 268–72, 277, 282; and understanding of "deep history," 237–38
Linton, Simi, 301

Machiavelli, Niccolo, 230, 267
Madison, James, 240–42
Mansfield, Harvey, 376, 379
Mantilla, Karla, 305
Marriage: channeling function of, 366–67; criticisms of ignoring sex differences in, 366–67; egalitarian marriage and cultural limits concerning it, 374–80; evolutionary psychology and, 366–67; as a form of social engineering, 366–70; marriage movement as promoting, 366–67, 370; power and infidelity in, 375–77; work/family conflict and, 378–80. *See also* Same-sex marriage

Mealey, Linda, 119
Middleton, Catharine, 377
Mill, John Stuart, 11
"Missing" heritability. *See* Heritability
Moore, Michael, 33, 175, 194, 209
Moral facts, 32, 60, 65–66, 70–71, 80
Moral illusions: breach of moral code
and, 82–85; competitive versus cooperative functions of moral judgment
and, 78; connection between legal
and moral obligation and, 86–88, 92;
and false moral judgments, 32–33,
77–87; pluralism and, 80–82; universal truth and, 80–82
Moral judgment: contractualism and
utilitarianism as standards of, 65–71;
evolutionary explanation of capacities for, 31; and moral discussion and
disagreement, 63, 79; and moral
skepticism, 71–72; and "narrow reflective equilibrium," 67–68; objectivity of, 33–34, 60–65; special practical
authority of, 33–34, 66–72; two faces
of, 32, 53, 76–77; and "wide reflective
equilibrium," 69. *See also* Debunking
(evolutionary explanation) of moral
judgment; Vindicating (evolutionary
explanation) of moral judgment
Moral obligation: "internal point of
view" and, 60, 88; and legal obligation, 85–92; natural function of is to
resolve social contract problems, 53–
60; psychological attitudes underpinning, 59–60. *See also* Legal obligation

Moral pluralism, 62, 80–82
Moral realism, 15–17, 33
Morse, Stephen, 175, 194, 209
Morton, Samuel, 233
*Murgia v. Massachusetts Board of Retire-
ment,* 320

Naturalism, 3–4. *See also* Pragmatic
naturalism
Naturalistic fallacy, 3–4, 65, 129, 208
Natural selection: and competition, 73;

and cultural evolution, 235; and Darwinian pluralistic framework, 279;
and evolution of ethical practice, 12;
and evolutionary explanations, 41–
43; 50–51; and fallibility in science,
281; and legal and moral obligation,
88–90; and men's investment in
children, 372; and multiple forms of
selection, 280; and resolution of social contract problems, 55; and social
dominance hierarchies, 38. *See also*
Darwin, Charles
Nature: appeals to as constraining sex
equality, 347–66; assumptions about,
294–96; constructivist critics of in
favor of views that identity categories
are socially constructed, 293, 307,
309–11; feminist resistance to arguments from nature, 293, 297–300; as
having no constant meaning, 324–
26; and nature-versus-culture debate
concerning identity categories, 293;
and political change, 293, 298–300;
and the politics of prehistory, 370–
74; progressive resistance to "nature
talk," 293, 315. *See also* Age; Disability; Immutability; Race; Sex; Sexual
orientation
Neurobiology: behavioral morality and,
124; and neurobiological causes of
criminal behavior, 124–27
Neurosexism: alleged sex differences as
embodying, 359–66; charges of, 348;
criticisms of Brizendine's work as
embodying, 359–66; distinctions between biology and social causes and,
365–66; problematic experiments as
illustrating, 364. *See also* Brain
Newton, Isaac, 279–80
Nietzche, Friedrich, 26–27, 76–77, 91
Noll, Mark, 245
Nott, Josiah, 233

Oakeshott, Michael, 246
Obama, Michelle, 374
O'Connor, Sandra Day (Justice), 361

Parenting: alloparents and, 372–74;
"cooperative breeding" and compe-
tition, 372–74; the "grandmother
hypothesis" and, 373; male invest-
ment in, 372; parental bonding with
children, 356–57
Parrillo, Anthony (Judge), 368–69
People v. Ledesma, 135
People v. Reinoso, 134
People v. Speights, 133
People v. Urdiales, 137
Plato, 12, 285
Political science. *See* Biopolitical science
Pope, Alexander, 324
Popenoe, David, 367
Pope Urban II, 269–71
Posner, Richard (Judge), 353
Pragmatic naturalism, 4–6, 10–12, 15,
18, 21–27
Prehistory: and females as agents of
evolutionary change, 371; and the
Man as Provisioner thesis, 371; poli-
tics of as deemphasizing women's
roles in evolution, 370–71; prima-
tologists putting female-centered
world view at center of evolutionary
study, 371

Race, and nature, 313–18
Railton, Peter, 33, 65
Raine, Adrian, 125
Rawls, John, 80, 82
Raz, Joseph, 117
Reasonableness: behavioral morality's
criticism of objective formulation of,
142; behavioral sciences and, 144–
46; call to rethink reasonableness,
142–46; call to rethink "unreasonableness," 167–69, 178–89; "fictional
notion" of, 213–14; functions of, 143;
minimum rationality and, 183–84;
questioning the objectivity of, 213–
14; the reasonable person standard
and norms of behavior, 142–43, 213;
supporting an objective standard
of, 143

Reasonable person standard. *See*
Reasonableness
Romanes, George, 360
Roper v. Simmons, 149

Same-sex marriage: criticisms of for
ignoring "conjugal" marriage's
evolutionary significance, 368–69;
criticisms of for ignoring sex differences, 367–70; civil unions as
violating equal protection, 369–70;
criticisms of arguments against, 369–
70; *Goodridge v. Department of Public
Health*, 367; *Hernandez v. Robles*, 368–
69; *Lewis v. Harris*, 368–69. *See also*
Marriage
Sanford, Jenny, 376
Sanford, Mark (Gov.), 376
Satel, Sally, 313–14
Scanlon, T. M., 69
Schlessinger, Dr. Laura, 375–76, 379
Schwarzenegger, Arnold (Gov.),
376–77
Science: criticism of objective characterization of, 214–15; interdependence of with fiction, 214, 216; and
need to find certainty, 215–16; practice of is informed by subjective and
objective norms, 216
Scott-Maxwell, Florida, 309–10
Sedgwick, Eve, 298–99
Sex, and nature, 297–300
Sex differences: alleged differences
between male and female brains as
explaining, 349–59, and criticisms
of, 359–66; evolutionary explanations of, 349–59; gender essentialism
and, 365
Sex equality: appeals to differences
between "male" and "female" brains
to explain, 348–49, 349–60, 362–66;
appeals to nature as a constraint
upon, 347–66; cultural limits to at-
taining, 378–80; and division of labor
in the home, 378–80; as important
to marriage quality, 380; problems

of achieving, 347–49; and sameness-difference debate, 348; social engineering to foster, 347–49, 380–81; and work-family conflict, 378–80. *See also* Neurosexism

Sexual orientation, and nature, 305–9

Shapiro, Scott, 88

Sherman, William Tecumseh, 245

Sinnott-Armstrong, Walter, 126

Skyrms, Brian, 56–57

Slavery, as an example of ethical progress, 13–17. *See also* Lincoln, Abraham, and Emancipation Proclamation

Slobogin, Christopher, 175

Sober, Elliot, 105

Social-contract problems: evolutionary altruism and, 56; natural function of our sense of moral obligation is to resolve, 35, 53–60, 62; natural selection as solving, 55; and responses to breaches of communal norms, 57–58

Social engineering: claim that it ignores natural sex differences, 347–49; to foster sex equality, 347–49, 380–81; marriage promotion as a form of, 366–70. *See also* Sex equality

Social model: of disability, 300–05; distinguished from medical model of disability, 293, 301–2; of group identity, 293. *See also* Nature

Socrates, 25

Spitzer, Eliot (Gov.), 375–76

Spitzer, Silda Wall, 375–76

Stanton-Ife, John, 150

State v. Payne, 134

Stein, Michael, 301

Stigma: behavioral morality's discomfort with, 147, 150–52; normative justification for, 206–8; psychological versus normative conceptions of, 150–52; as a tool for creating new norms of conduct, 152; as a tool for enforcing norms, 152, 207. *See also* Causal explanations of criminal behavior

Stone, Geoffrey, 316

Strauss, Leo, 246

Sturgeon, Nicholas, 33

Summers, Lawrence, 293, 297–300

Tennyson, Alfred, 37

Thrasymachus, 25–26

Thucydides, 245

Trivers, Robert, 352

Tufts, James, 5

U.S. v. Eff, 137

Unreasonableness. *See* Behavioral morality; Reasonableness

Vindicating (evolutionary explanation) of moral judgment: contractualism and utilitarianism and, 66–71; explained and distinguished from debunking explanation, 31–35; limitations of, 46–50, 72; in relation to cognitive judgment, 39–53; and two faces of morality, 32, 76–77. *See also* Debunking (evolutionary explanation) of moral judgment; Moral judgment

Wilson, David Sloan, 228

Wilson, E. O., 100, 225, 249–50

Wolfe, Tom, 195, 204

Woodhall v. Commonwealth, 147

Woolman, John, 14–17, 21–22, 28

Wright, Robert, 349–50

Yoshino, Kenji, 368

Young, Rebecca, 362. *See also* Jordan-Young, Rebecca

Zarella, Peter (Justice), 370